Reappraising Cult Horror Films

Reappraising Cult Horror Films

From Carnival of Souls *to* Last Night in Soho

Edited by
Lee Broughton

BLOOMSBURY ACADEMIC
NEW YORK • LONDON • OXFORD • NEW DELHI • SYDNEY

BLOOMSBURY ACADEMIC

Bloomsbury Publishing Inc, 1359 Broadway, New York, NY 10018, USA
Bloomsbury Publishing Plc, 50 Bedford Square, London, WC1B 3DP, UK
Bloomsbury Publishing Ireland, 29 Earlsfort Terrace, Dublin 2, D02 AY28, Ireland

BLOOMSBURY, BLOOMSBURY ACADEMIC and the Diana logo are trademarks of
Bloomsbury Publishing Plc

First published in the United States of America 2024
Paperback edition published 2026

Volume Editor's Part of the Work © Lee Broughton, 2024

Each chapter © of Contributors

For legal purposes the Acknowledgements on p. viii constitute an extension of this
copyright page.

Cover design: Eleanor Rose
Cover photograph: Candace Hilligoss in *Carnival of Souls*, 1962, dir. Herk Harvey,
Harcourt Productions © Pictorial Press Ltd / Alamy

All rights reserved. No part of this publication may be: i) reproduced or transmitted in any form,
electronic or mechanical, including photocopying, recording or by means of any information
storage or retrieval system without prior permission in writing from the publishers; or ii) used
or reproduced in any way for the training, development or operation of artificial intelligence
(AI) technologies, including generative AI technologies. The rights holders expressly reserve
this publication from the text and data mining exception as per Article 4(3) of the
Digital Single Market Directive (EU) 2019/790.

Bloomsbury Publishing Inc does not have any control over, or responsibility for, any third-
party websites referred to or in this book. All internet addresses given in this book were
correct at the time of going to press. The author and publisher regret any inconvenience
caused if addresses have changed or sites have ceased to exist, but can accept no
responsibility for any such changes.

A catalog record for this book is available from the Library of Congress.

ISBN: HB: 978-1-5013-8758-6
PB: 978-1-5013-8755-5
ePDF: 978-1-5013-8756-2
eBook: 978-1-5013-8757-9

Typeset by Deanta Global Publishing Services, Chennai, India

For product safety related questions contact productsafety@bloomsbury.com.

To find out more about our authors and books visit www.bloomsbury.com and
sign up for our newsletters.

Contents

List of figures   vii
Acknowledgements   viii
About the editor and contributors   ix

Introduction: Cult horror films and cult movies *Lee Broughton*   1

Part I Lone features

1. *Carnival of Souls* as seen by its creators *Bill Shaffer*   19
2. A 'totally emancipated female': Julie Ege, Britain's crises of masculinity and Roy Ward Baker's *The Legend of the 7 Golden Vampires* *Lee Broughton*   35
3. Wandering the labyrinth of space-time and eternity in Stanley Kubrick's *The Shining* *Kamil Kościelski*   55
4. The candy-coloured uncanny: Childish pleasures in *Killer Klowns from Outer Space* *Cynthia J. Miller and Tom Shaker*   72
5. Death is the price: Racial segregation, urban gentrification and the horrors of *Candyman* *Phevos Kallitsis*   89
6. Decide for yourself: Cult, controversy and anti-capitalism in *The Hunt* *Craig Ian Mann*   109

Part II Cult horror directors

7. 'We are going to do something nasty': The cult horror films of Harry Kümel *Mark Goodall*   131
8. (Re)positioning Ken Russell as a cult horror auteur *Matthew Melia*   149

Part III Cycles and clusters

9. *Deliverance* derivations: Counter constructions of white trash in 1970s horror cinema *Xavier Mendik*   169
10. Hybrid horror from Australia *Pete Falconer*   188

11 'I can't believe so many horror fans aren't watching *Inside*':
The cult status of twenty-first-century French horror cinema
Alice Haylett Bryan — 206
12 Vertical violence: Horror cinema's terrible towers *Kev Bickerdike* — 223
13 The Investigative Outsider and the use of *Nemein* as a narrative state change driver in cult horror cinema *James Shelton* — 240

Index — 257

Figures

1.1 *Carnival of Souls*: The cast and crew pictured at the reunion event held in Lawrence, Kansas, on 24 November 1989 30
1.2 *Carnival of Souls*: Herk Harvey in his ghoul make-up menaces the author's son James Shaffer at the reunion event held in Lawrence, Kansas, on 24 November 1989 31
2.1 *The Legend of the 7 Golden Vampires*: Professor Lawrence Van Helsing (Peter Cushing) is left humiliated and emasculated when Chinese academics scoff at his theories about vampires 44
2.2 *The Legend of the 7 Golden Vampires*: The wealthy Scandinavian traveller Vanessa Buren (Julie Ege) is a 'totally emancipated female' whose earrings alone are 'worth a fortune' 48
3.1 *The Shining*: The exact place where the window of Ullman's office should be located 62
4.1 *Killer Klowns from Outer Space*: Evil aliens that look and act like clowns 74
5.1 *Candyman*: Chicago as presented in *Candyman* (1992) 94
5.2 *Candyman*: The sequence of spaces in *Candyman* (1992) juxtaposed to key events and the evolution of the Candyman myth 98
7.1 *Daughters of Darkness*: The countess (Delphine Seyrig) connotes exotic luxury 136
7.2 *Malpertuis*: An incredible and vivid tableau featuring Euryale (Susan Hampshire) and Jan (Mathieu Carriere) 140
9.1 *Scum of the Earth*: Direct to camera depravity and the pseudo-medical gaze 179
10.1 *Turkey Shoot*: The fanged and furry Alph (Steve Rackman) 194
13.1 *The Wicker Man*: Howie (Edward Woodward) comes across as condescending and arrogant 246

Acknowledgements

Thanks go to Katie Gallof, Alyssa Jordan, Stephanie Grace-Petinos and all at Bloomsbury Academic for their help in bringing this volume to print.

Thanks also to Mrs Brewster (my inspirational high school English teacher), Marco Brunello, Ian Christopher, Alex Cox, Anne-Marie Paquet-Deyris, Russell Downing, Glenn Erickson, Christopher Frayling, Kristyn Gorton, Vivienne Griggs, Lindsay Hallam, Jo Garde-Hansen, David Ibitson, Beth Johnson, Harry Kümel, Josie Mills, Tracey Mollet, Madeleine Newman, Shelley O'Brien, Judith Partridge, Alison Peirse, John Power, Vishnu Prasad, Penny Rivlin, Eleanor Rose, Scooby-Doo and the Mystery Incorporated gang, Neil Washbourne, Thomas Wellings and Judy Young. And last, but not least, a big thank you to every one of the fine scholars who contributed a chapter to this collection.

An earlier version of Chapter 3 entitled 'In the labyrinth of time and eternity. On Stanley Kubrick's "The Shining"' appeared in the academic journal *Przestrzenie Teorii (Spaces in Theory)*, no. 22 (2014): 171–87.

About the editor and contributors

Lee Broughton is a lecturer in film and media in the School of Media and Communication at the University of Leeds, UK. He also teaches on the Arts and Humanities programme that is offered by the university's Lifelong Learning Centre. Lee is the author of *The Euro-Western: Reframing Gender, Race and the 'Other' in Film* (2016) and the editor of *Critical Perspectives on the Western: From A Fistful of Dollars to Django Unchained* (2016) and *Reframing Cult Westerns: From The Magnificent Seven to The Hateful Eight* (2020). His research interests include the Western, horror films and cult movies more generally. Lee has contributed chapters and articles to numerous edited collections and academic journals and has worked on the extra features for a number of Blu-ray releases.

* * *

Kev Bickerdike is a PhD candidate at Sheffield Hallam University, UK, where his thesis examines representations of space and place in British horror cinema, and the tensions that arise when space is subject to competing attempts to invest it with meaning.

Alice Haylett Bryan is a lecturer in film history at Queen Mary University of London, UK. Her recent publications include: 'Inhospitable landscapes: contemporary French horror cinema, immigration and identity' in *French Screen Studies* (2021), and 'The weird sex scenes of Yorgos Lanthimos' in *The Cinema of Yorgos Lanthimos*, edited by Eddie Falvey (2022). She is a co-editor of the *21st Century Horror* series.

Pete Falconer is a senior lecturer in film and television at the University of Bristol, UK. He is interested in the forms and genres of popular cinema and the critical challenges that these can present. His current work focuses on horror movies and aesthetic evaluation. His first monograph, *The Afterlife of the Hollywood Western*, was published in 2020.

Mark Goodall is an associate professor in film and media at the University of Bradford, UK. He is the author of *Sweet and Savage* (2006), a book about mondo films, the co-editor of *New Media Archaeologies* (2019) and a series of books called *Gathering of the Tribe* (2012–ongoing), about music and the occult. He co-produced and directed the film *Holy Terrors* (2017), based on the stories of Arthur Machen, and the short film *The Beckoning Fair One* (2021), based on a story by Oliver Onions that inspired 'The Shining'. He is also singer/guitarist with the group Rudolf Rocker.

Phevos Kallitsis is an architect and senior lecturer in the School of Architecture, University of Portsmouth, UK. He has worked as an architect in collaboration with different architectural offices. He has also worked as a cinema critic and a set and exhibition designer. His research focuses on the interconnectedness of cinema with urban and architectural spaces with a particular interest in horror, urban fear and safety and urban regeneration. He also works on queer studies, sexuality and urban space. He is teaching architectural design, interior design and queer theories on urban and architectural space in the UK and in Greece.

Kamil Kościelski holds a PhD in film studies from the Adam Mickiewicz University in Poznań, Poland. He is the author of the scientific monograph *What an Excellent Day for an Exorcism . . . American Horror Films of the 60s and 70s* (2014), which discusses the relationship between horror movies and the public mood of the said decades. He has also published articles in the *Journal of Scandinavian Cinema*, *Kwartalnik Filmowy* (*Film Quarterly*) and *Przestrzenie Teorii* (*Spaces in Theory*). His PhD thesis ('In the labyrinth of Stanley Kubrick. Multilevel and multifaceted analysis of *The Shining*') is a thorough analysis of Stanley Kubrick's *The Shining*.

Craig Ian Mann is a lecturer in film and media at Sheffield Hallam University, UK, where he researches the politics of popular genre cinema. He is the author of *Phases of the Moon: A Cultural History of the Werewolf Film* (2020) and is currently writing his second book, *Bleeding Us Dry: Independent American Horror and Anti-Capitalism*. He is the principal organizer of the Fear 2000 conference series and booklet editor for Eureka Entertainment.

Matthew Melia is a senior lecturer in English literature, film and media at Kingston University, UK. He is co-editor of *The Jaws Book* (2020), *Anthony*

Burgess, *Stanley Kubrick and A Clockwork Orange* (2022), *The Jurassic Park Book* (2023) and the editor of *The Films of Ken Russell* (2023). He is currently writing a monograph about Ken Russell's *Gothic* and editing a special edition of *Cinergie Il Cine e le Altre Arti* entitled 'Franchising *Jurassic Park*'. Matt's other publications include contributions to *Shadow Cinema: The Historical and Production Contexts of Unmade Films* (2021), *The Bloomsbury Companion to Stanley Kubrick* (2021) and *Reframing Cult Westerns* (2020).

Xavier Mendik is a professor of cult cinema studies at Birmingham City University, UK, from where he runs the *Cine-Excess* International Film Festival. He is the author, editor and co-editor of nine volumes that explore cult and horror film traditions. Some of his publications in this area include *Shocking Cinema of the 70s* (co-edited with Julian Petley, 2022), *Bodies of Desire and Bodies in Distress: The Golden Age of Italian Cult Cinema* (2015), *Peep Shows: Cult Film and the Cine-Erotic* (2012) and *The Cult Film Reader* (co-edited with Ernest Mathijs, 2008). Xavier has also completed a number of documentaries on cult and horror film traditions, most recently *The Quiet Revolution: State, Society and the Canadian Horror Film* (2020).

Cynthia J. Miller is a cultural anthropologist specializing in visual media. She teaches in the Marlboro Institute for Liberal Arts at Emerson College, USA, and is the editor or co-editor of twenty scholarly volumes, including *Dark Forces at Work: Essays on Social Dynamics and Cinematic Horrors* (2019) and *Journeys into Terror: Essays from the Cinematic Intersection of Travel and Horror* (2023). She is the recipient of the Peter C. Rollins prize for a book-length work in popular culture and the James Welsh prize for lifetime achievement in adaptation studies, and serves on the editorial boards of *The Journal of Popular Culture* and *The Journal of Popular Television*.

Bill Shaffer is a former public television producer/director whose involvement with *Carnival of Souls* (1962) began in 1988 when he taped a story about the origin of the film with its writer and director. Shaffer continued to follow the story of the film's afterlife as it picked up speed with a theatrical re-release in 1989. He also created a TV special about the film which also became part of a Criterion Collection Special Edition DVD (for which Shaffer was credited as Associate Producer). Shaffer's master's thesis was on the films of Sergio Leone and he has presented talks about Leone's work.

Tom Shaker is an independent scholar and has spent over thirty years as a college professor, teaching and directing the Communications Program at Dean College, USA. He has also taught at Northeastern University, UMass and Worcester Polytechnic Institute. He is the co-author of *A Treasury of Rhode Island Jazz & Swing Musicians* (2016) and *In Harmony: Early Vocal Groups: Remembered & Celebrated* (2020). He co-produced the award-winning documentary film *Do It Man: The Story of the Celebrity Club* (2018). He is a podcast contributor to Rhody Radio and hosts *The Soul Serenade*, a classic soul and funk show on NPR affiliate WICN in Worcester, MA.

James Shelton is an independent scholar with a research interest in the function of retributive justice and *nemein* in relation to narrative mechanics. This research has expanded over time to include analyses of political and genre concerns. In his day job James works as the senior research administrator at Buckinghamshire New University, UK.

Introduction

Cult horror films and cult movies

Lee Broughton

The horror film today: A cult genre?

The horror film is a genre that has been part of the cinematic landscape since the early days of cinema. It is also a genre that no one country can claim absolute ownership of since its key ingredients – the supernatural and/or the monstrous antagonist, oppressive locations and people in peril – are elements that are able to become manifest in any corner of the world. Indeed, the history of horror cinema is very much the history of a genre that has always been present in some shape or form at some time, *somewhere*. For example, a number of countries produced short horror films during the early days of silent cinema, with key titles being the likes of Georges Méliès's French film *The Haunted Castle* (*Le chateau haunte*, 1897) and Walter R. Booth's British film *The Haunted Curiosity Shop* (1901).

From there the horror film has often been associated with different centres of production during different time periods. We might look to the wonders of the silent feature-length expressionist films from Germany that were made during the 1920s, the Universal and RKO films that were produced in Hollywood during the 1930s and 1940s, the Hammer, Amicus and Tigon films produced in Britain during the late 1950s, the 1960s and the early 1970s, the varied horror films coming out of Italy during the 1980s, J-Horror films produced in Japan during the late 1990s and the early 2000s, the extreme French horror films of the 2000s and so on. The aforementioned regional peaks in horror film making might serve as 'horror headlines' but in terms of charting the production of horror films worldwide, they are woefully insufficient reference points. No mention of Spanish horror, Hong Kong horror, Indonesian horror, Indian horror, Australian horror, South Korean horror, Mexican horror, Brazilian horror or Turkish horror to name just a handful of countries that have been interesting and important centres of horror film production at one time or another.

In terms of its general acceptance by the public, the horror film has always been something of a contradictory genre, simultaneously very popular but also still something of a niche genre or an acquired taste. At this moment in time, the genre is perhaps more popular – or should that be more voluminous – than ever. M. J. Simpson illustrates this when he notes that

> 80% of all British horror films have been made in the past 20 years. . . . British horror feature films produced and released during the 20th century (basically 77 years from 1933 to 1999) = 250(-ish) . . . British horror feature films produced and released during the first two decades of the 21st century = 1,050 (-ish). (2020: 6)

Obviously the relatively inexpensive nature of filmmaking these days (reasonably priced but effective digital cameras abound while desktop editing suites are often supplied with new computers free of charge) and new distribution channels (which might not even involve the consideration of a cinema release) have all had an impact here. However, the number of new horror films that get listed as DVD or Blu-ray releases on Amazon or as recommendations on your favourite streaming service suggest that a similar pattern is being played out in a number of countries around the world. And yet it is still a common occurrence to meet people who will tell you, 'I don't and won't watch horror films under any circumstances and cannot understand why anybody would choose to do so.' The content of horror films is generally marketed as – and accepted to be – transgressive and/or excessive at some level, so in one sense it might be argued that within the wider cinematic landscape the horror genre is actually a cult genre. Or that every horror film inherently possesses some of the qualities that are needed for a film to become a cult movie. Either way, it is clear that there are horror films – obscure and popular examples, well-made and poorly made examples, and all manner of efforts in between – that have acquired cult movie status.

There will be no attempt to offer a precise definition of what might make a film a cult film given here though interested parties are pointed towards the introductory section of *Reframing Cult Westerns: From The Magnificent Seven to The Hateful Eight* (Broughton 2020) which includes a wide-ranging review of academic literature relating to cult films more generally. There are two conclusions from that literature review (Broughton 2020) that are worth repeating here. Firstly, cult films can theoretically belong to any genre, be popular or art-house productions and be judged to be trash or high art and all things in between, which means that providing a workable definition or a set of common properties is difficult. Indeed, Mark Jancovich, et al, contend that 'the term "cult movies" covers a multitude of sins' while acknowledging that such films cannot be 'defined according to some single, unifying feature shared by all cult movies' (2003: 1). Secondly, deeper consideration is always possible and Ernest Mathijs and Xavier Mendik (2008) have provided the basis for a more nuanced approach to defining cult movies. Mathijs and Mendik suggest that

> it is essential to carve out the elements that surround cult cinema. Typically, a cult film is defined through a variety of combinations that include four major elements:
>
> 1. *Anatomy*: the film itself – its features; content, style, format and generic modes.
> 2. *Consumption*: the ways in which it is received – the audience reactions, fan celebrations and critical reactions.
> 3. *Political economy*: the financial and physical conditions of presence of the film – its ownerships, intentions, promotions, channels of presentation, and the spaces and times of its exhibition.
> 4. *Cultural status*: the way in which a cult film fits a time or region – how it comments on its surroundings, by complying, exploiting, critiquing or offending. (2008: 1)

Mathijs and Mendik duly advise that not 'all of these elements need to be fulfilled together in order to speak of a film as a cult film. But . . . each of them is of high significance in what *makes* a film cult' (2008: 1).

Some of the films included in *Reappraising Cult Horror Films* might surprise some older readers. Certainly, when this book was first conceived several years ago my – and the wider world of horror fans' – concept of what a cult horror film might be was much more rigid and an obvious and limiting canon was very much apparent. But, as I. Q. Hunter has noted, 'no one is quite sure what cult means any more' (2016: xii). Hunter argues that cult 'has merged with popular media fandom' (2016: xii) and one consequence of this is that 'the definition of cult films has unquestionably become rather vague and contested' (2016: 17). I would argue that cult horror fans instinctively judge whether a film that they have chanced upon holds the potential to be classified as a cult movie by assessing its formal properties and measuring them against those of established cult films. So *mise-en-scene*, narrative, acting and so on all still have an important part to play here.

But, to my mind, the way that a film makes the viewer *feel* is an equally important consideration when we are talking about cult horror films. So many of the films included in this volume upset classical narrative conventions in ways which leave me with a strange indefinable feeling that I have come to associate with my personal take on the cult horror film experience. And, remarkably, I find that the same strange indefinable feeling is able to present itself during the countless repeat viewings that such films necessarily demand. It is a feeling that familiarity cannot diminish.

In terms of the communal cult film experience once enjoyed by the patrons of midnight movie screenings, Hunter suggests that 'blogs, tweets, Instagram and chatrooms are the new rep theatres' (2016: xiii). This is undoubtedly true in part for cult horror communities, who now gather virtually around tweets that are governed by exclusive group hashtags and partake in group tweet-alongs to live television broadcasts of cult horror films. An imagined sense of community might also be generated for some fans of cult horror films via their unwavering and partisan support for the specialist products issued by particular boutique Blu-ray labels. But cult horror film fans are still able to gather in person thanks to the presence of an ever-growing number of annual horror film festivals. These festivals offer an experience that can sometimes be akin to that of an old midnight movie screening albeit only for a limited number of nights per year.

I would argue that all of the horror films included in the present collection could be considered to be cult films if their 'cult movie credentials' were to be tested and assessed using the criteria mapped out by Mathijs and Mendik (2008) and others. But that is not the purpose of this book (indeed, a good number of its chapters successfully function without referring to cult film theory at all). Similarly, this book does not purport to be a history of cult horror cinema – such a task would be impossible given the size of the book and the number of chapters it contains. Rather, the present collection represents an opportunity to reappraise a selection of notable cult horror films by critically exploring them from new theoretical and analytical angles or aligning them with similarly themed films (or films by the same director in the case of two chapters) in order to tease out new meanings and insights or previously overlooked aspects that might go some way towards identifying just why these particular films continue to capture the imaginations of those genre fans who have taken them to their hearts and accredited them with cult film status.

Selected writings on cult horror films

Horror film fans have never really been short of reading matter. The 'monster kid' phenomena that followed in the wake of classic horror films being licensed to American TV in the late 1950s spawned Forrest J. Ackerman's *Famous Monsters of Filmland* magazine (1958–83) and a sizeable number of similarly themed publications. A corresponding phenomenon occurred in the UK during the 1970s when classic and more recent horror films flooded that nation's TV screens and magazines such as Roger Cook, Jan Cook and Dez Skinn's *Monster Mag* (1973–6) and Skinn's *House of Hammer* (1976–8) – along with other similarly themed British magazines and imported overstocks of earlier American periodicals – duly met the reading needs of young British horror film fans. When those kids progressed onto books, the likes of Denis Gifford's *A Pictorial History of Horror Movies* (1973) and *Monsters of the Movies* (1977), alongside Alan G. Frank's *Horror Movies: Tales of Terror in the Cinema* (1974) and *Monsters and Vampires* (1976), were the usual tomes of choice. All of these publications featured writings on films that are now acknowledged to be cult horror movies but, perhaps more importantly, for many of their young readers these image-laden magazines and books set the horror film itself up as a cult text that was eminently worthy of their attention and devotion.[1]

The present volume might be the first book dedicated solely to the critical analysis of cult horror films. But, as the previous paragraph suggests, any publication about horror films will invariably feature some writing about a horror film that could be classified as a cult movie. Indeed, this section will act as a select and necessarily brief review of a number of books that have included a focus on some cult horror films as part of their wider remit of covering the horror genre in some other capacity. These books tend to set out to examine their selected horror films as national or regional phenomena. In terms of American films, Stephen Thrower's large format monograph *Nightmare USA: The Untold Story of the Exploitation Independents* (2008) focuses firmly on horror and exploitation films made by independent film producers in the United States between 1970 and 1985. This is a very comprehensive book that breaks its content down into regional case studies. Thrower mostly employs a historical

---

[1] For further reading on the 1970s monster kids' cultural engagement with the horror genre more generally see *70s Monster Memories* (2015) edited by Eric McNaughton. Also of interest is Michael Galley's *Dracula, Frankenstein and Friends* (2021), which takes the films presented in the 1977 iteration of BBC Two's annual season of late-night horror double bills (which ran in the UK from 1975 to 1981) as its jumping-off point.

and industrial case study approach, which also includes interviews with some of the films' directors and short film reviews. Also worthy of mention here in terms of American cinema is V. Vale and Andrea Juno's large format edited collection *Incredibly Strange Films* (1986). While this collection focuses on cult movies more generally, cult horror films and their directors are well represented and the book features essential interviews with key directors that are accompanied by mini essays that offer comment on some of their films.

In terms of European cinema, Patricia Allmer, Emily Brick and David Huxley's edited collection *European Nightmares: Horror Cinema in Europe Since 1945* (2012) covers a variety of continental horror films, some of which could be classified as cult horror films. There is a quite heavy emphasis on the use of academic theory in *European Nightmares* (ranging from psychoanalysis and Deleuzean film theory to reception studies) though some chapters use a more straightforward historical and industrial case study approach. It is also worth mentioning Steven Jay Schneider's edited collection *100 European Horror Films* (2007) here. This thoroughly accessible but digest-sized book features capsule reviews of 100 European horror films, including a number that could quite readily be classified as cult movies. Similarly worthy of mention is Pete Tombs and Cathal Tohill's equally accessible large format monograph *Immoral Tales: Sex and Horror Cinema in Europe, 1956–1984* (1995). This well-written book focuses on a wide range of European films of a cultish nature that tend to be horror/sex/erotica hybrids. Coverage of these films – of which some could be classified as cult horror films – and their directors tends to be presented as industrial or historical case studies.

In terms of a worldwide approach to horror films, Steven Jay Schneider and Tony Williams' edited collection *Horror International* (2005) focuses on genre films from around the world. Some chapters take the form of industrial or historical case studies while others make good use of a range of cultural studies theories in order to interrogate and contextualize their chosen films. This collection features work on a number of genre entries that could be classified as cult movies. The same can be said of Steven J. Schneider's edited collection *Fear Without Frontiers: Horror Cinemas across the Globe* (2002), which reads like a more accessible and populist precursor to *Horror International*. This collection is more wide-ranging than *Horror International* and features many more chapters. However, these chapters are shorter in length than the chapters that are generally found in academic edited collections and the majority of the book's chapters take the form of industrial or historical case studies or critical reviews rather than theoretical interrogations of the films in question. Another even more wide-ranging book that is worthy of mention here is Pete Tombs' large format monograph *Mondo Macabro: Weird and Wonderful Cinema around the World* (1997). Tombs' book focuses primarily on strange and cultish films from Asia, Africa and the Far East and, while not all of these films are horror films, a good number of horror films (and some that could be described as cult horror films) are covered. Again, the coverage here is presented mainly as industrial or historical case studies.

Building upon the earlier works of Carol Clover (1992) and Barbara Creed (1993), there has been a relatively recent move to consider the role of gender in horror films at both a narrative and a production level. Kier-La Janisse led the way with the monograph *House of Psychotic Women: An Autobiographical Topography of Female Neurosis in Horror and Exploitation Films* (2012). As its subtitle suggests this book is a fusion of autobiographical writing and film criticism and analysis in which Janisse uses the content of her selected films to reflect upon key episodes in her own life. In doing so Janisse discusses a number of cult horror films. More recently Alison Peirse's edited collection *Women Make Horror: Filmmaking, Feminism, Genre* (2020) was the first volume to feature a roll call of contributors who were all female and the first volume entirely devoted to female horror film makers. Historical case studies and interesting theoretical angles are employed throughout in order to examine the roles that women have played in the production of selected horror films. Some of these films could be classified as cult horror movies.

Reappraising cult horror films

The present collection opens with a part entitled 'Lone features', which includes chapters that examine individual cult horror films. In Chapter 1, Bill Shaffer focuses on one of the most popular and enduring cult horror films, Herk Harvey's *Carnival of Souls* (1962). An original and idiosyncratic exercise in independent regional film making, *Carnival of Souls* is an atmospheric chiller that did good business on the drive-in circuit before becoming a regular fixture on late-night television in the United States. So far so good, except that Harvey and his writer John Clifford did not receive their share of the film's box office receipts. The story of the film's making, afterlife and rediscovery – and Harvey and Clifford's eventual reconnection with their creation – is as compelling as the film's own quite startling narrative. That story is told here via Shaffer's exclusive interviews with both men.

In Chapter 2, Lee Broughton offers a gendered reading of Roy Ward Baker's Hammer film, *The Legend of the 7 Golden Vampires* (1974). Made at a time when the venerable British horror film company was going into decline, the film is actually a co-production with Hong Kong's legendary Shaw Brothers studio. As such it is a hybrid genre film that successfully fuses kung fu action with gothic horror chills. Broughton's chapter argues that the production context and the content of *The Legend of the 7 Golden Vampires* mirror the crises of masculinity and the economic woes that the British nation state was suffering at the time of the film's release. While *The Legend of the 7 Golden Vampires* stars a number of male cult film stars, including Peter Cushing and David Chiang, the chapter features a section that serves as an initial exploration of the career arc that led to the cultification of the film's female lead, Julie Ege.

In Chapter 3, Kamil Kościelski offers critical insight into some of the many enigmas that have resulted in Stanley Kubrick's *The Shining* (1980) becoming a cult horror film. Film fans and scholars alike have poured over Kubrick's film innumerable times in an effort to explain why he seemingly chose to load *The Shining* with a variety of what appear to be obvious inconsistencies at both a narrative and a formal level.[2] Using Kubrick's admiration for the Argentinian writer Jorge Luis Borges as his starting point, Kościelski finds an abstract but working concept of time within Borges's work that can also be successfully applied to events depicted in *The Shining*. Indeed, Kościelski uses Borges's work – and Kubrick's own papers and notes relating to the film's development and production – to offer an original and compelling interrogation and explanation of the spatial and temporal anomalies found within *The Shining*.

In Chapter 4, Cynthia J. Miller and Tom Shaker focus on another much loved cult horror film, Stephen Chiodo's *Killer Klowns from Outer Space* (1988). Here Miller and Shaker tease out the generic tropes that the film shares with science fiction movies from the late 1950s and teen comedies from the 1980s while arguing that the film is much more than just an exercise in playing with genre conventions. *Killer Klowns from Outer Space*'s use of clowns not just as villains but as social and psychological touchstones that we all recognize is argued to be a distinguishing factor that serves to invert the audience's expectations with regard to how clowns might typically be presented and perceived in horror films.

---

[2] See Ian Christopher's *The Games Room: A Novel Interpretation of Stanley Kubrick's Film* The Shining (2020) for a fascinating and highly original exercise in this regard.

Thus, Miller and Shaker reveal that the real threat of the alien clowns lies in the fact that the film's innocent small-town characters do not run from them in terror but towards them with unfeigned delight.

In Chapter 5, Phevos Kallitsis investigates Bernard Rose's Chicago-set urban cult horror film *Candyman* (1992) by critically evaluating the meanings that can be drawn by matching the diegetic locations of the film's key sites of activity to their real-world equivalents. Although the notorious Cabrini Green projects seen in the film have long since been gentrified out of existence, Kallitsis argues that *Candyman*'s depiction of Cabrini Green remains a diachronic representation of the fundamental emotions that were linked to the actual Cabrini Green and thus functions to express and provoke universal fears and anxieties that are associated with dangerous urban spaces. Kallitsis duly tracks two fear-inducing and intertwined narrative strands found within the film: fear of the scary city and fear of the supernatural. In doing so he also successfully maps a cityscape in which social, gendered and racial spaces and contexts are aligned with particular narrative developments.

Part I ends with Chapter 6 and Craig Ian Mann's critical assessment of the heated political discussions that have surrounded Craig Zobel's controversial 'human hunting' film, *The Hunt* (2020). The film features Trumpian 'deplorables' (Republicans) who are hunted by wealthy 'liberals' (Democrats) for sport and has thus been accused of being either too liberal or too conservative in its outlook depending upon the politics of the viewer. Mann's chapter investigates the film's claim to cult status while also exploring the controversy surrounding its content and critiquing the wider critical tendency to interpret *The Hunt* using a rigid ideological spectrum. Indeed, Mann's close political and socio-economic reading of the film concludes that *The Hunt* is perhaps best understood not as a 'conservative', 'liberal' or even 'centrist' film but as an anti-capitalist film.

Part II, entitled 'Cult horror directors', opens with Chapter 7, in which Mark Goodall critically assesses the filmography of the cult Belgian director Harry Kümel. Goodall argues that in the productions under review – *Daughters of Darkness* (1971), *Malpertuis* (1972) and *The Coming of Joachim Stiller* (*De Komst van Joachim Stiller*, 1976) – Kümel blends the well-loved generic tropes of the decadent horror film with elements from the Belgian tradition of the fantastic and the surreal in order to create a new stylistic mode that possesses a quite unique nature. Here Kümel takes generic horror film subject matter and narratives and reworks them from entirely new and highly original perspectives, often combining the practice of the auteur and the experimentation of the avant-garde with those of the film showman and the TV entertainer. As such, Goodall argues that Kümel's remarkable films exist in a critical space where a collision between art and trash produces truly wondrous results.

The part closes with Chapter 8, in which Matthew Melia examines the latter stages of Ken Russell's career and argues that the director was able to become the custodian of his own legacy in the final years of his life. To this end the chapter explores both Russell's film work – including *The Lair of the White Worm* (1988) and *The Fall of the Louse of Usher* (2002) – and his self-reflexive appearance in Keith Fulton and Louis Pepe's punk body-horror 'mockumentary' *Brothers of the Head* (2006). By teasing out the themes and features that they share with Russell's earlier – less obviously horror but equally unsettling – works, Melia argues that all three of these films are actually indicative of Russell's long rooted embeddedness in the horror genre and his desire to continually interrogate his own relationship to it. The chapter thus contextualizes the ways in which Russell was culturally repositioned as, not just a director of horror cinema, but as a cult director too.

The book's third and final part is entitled 'Cycles and clusters' and its chapters deal with the examination of specific groups of cult horror films. The part opens with Chapter 9, in which Xavier Mendik maps out and interrogates the cultural significance of a cycle of American films that he dubs '*Deliverance* derivations' since they are American genre films that took influence from – and sought to capitalize on the popularity of – John Boorman's backwoods' shocker *Deliverance* (1972). American cinema has developed an established set of themes and visual tropes to represent its rural poor across a variety of genres and historical timeframes but its most prolific era in terms of pointedly producing films featuring 'white trash' characters remains the 1970s, when images of debased rurality circulated most prominently within the horror genre. As such, Mendik argues that 1970s horror cinema popularized the American South as a foreboding terrain whose dwellers were prone to exact retribution for their social and political marginality against unwitting urban outsiders. The films that Mendik critically analyses include S. F. Brownrigg's *Scum of the Earth* (1974), William Grefé's *Whisky Mountain* (1977), Michael Miller's *Jackson County Jail* (1976) and John Llewellyn Moxey's *Nightmare in Badham County* (1976).

In Chapter 10, Pete Falconer focuses on a variety of films that were produced in Australia during 1970s and 1980s. Australian popular cinema's more outré efforts from this period are often grouped together under the catch-all banner of 'Ozploitation', a label that has come to denote a mode of exploitation cinema that was characterized by opportunistic sensationalism. As Falconer notes, the practices of exploitation filmmaking, in Australia and elsewhere, often foster generic hybridity since combining genres can be a source of marketable novelty while also helping filmmakers to make the most of limited budgets and resources. More importantly, Falconer argues that hybrid genre films that involved a strong element of horror became a regular feature of Australian popular filmmaking at this time. His chapter thus sets out to map and make sense of the many different forms of hybridity found in Australian horror films that were produced during the Ozploitation period. The films that Falconer critically analyses include Terry Bourke's *Inn of the Damned* (1975), Richard Franklin's *Roadgames* (1981), Brian Trenchard-Smith's *Turkey Shoot* (1982) and Philippe Mora's *Howling III: The Marsupials* (1987).

In Chapter 11, Alice Haylett Bryan critically evaluates the cult status of twenty-first-century French horror cinema. Locating cult status in fan practices rather than in the films themselves, this chapter seeks to evaluate the extent to which the 'Frenchness' of the films impacts upon the way they are discussed by critics and fans alike. Indeed, Haylett Bryan proposes that for an Anglophone audience it is this specific cultural context (the films' connections to the New French Extremity style of the late 1990s/early 2000s and the ongoing debates around auteurism and genre cinema that obsess the French film industry), as well as the films' willingness to depict extreme violence, that encourages certain gatekeeping and knowledge sharing behaviours that are akin to wider conceptions of cult film fan practice. The films that Haylett Bryan discusses include Alexandre Bustillo and Julien Maury's *Inside* (*À l'intérieur*, 2007) and Pascal Laugier's *Martyrs* (2008).

In Chapter 12, Kev Bickerdike tackles cult horror films that feature a tower block as a key location. Tower blocks are a natural feature of the landscape within numerous films and more often than not their presence is simply an element of a wider urban topography. However, there are instances where their spatial particularities (the peculiar experience of insularity and seclusion experienced once inside their corridors and their domineering visual aspects) lend themselves to a variety of effective narrative tensions. Bickerdike argues that tower blocks' propensity for generating spatial tension (both internally and in their external contrast to the other elements within a city) mean that they are particularly well suited to horror genre narratives. In arguing this point he employs spatial and social perspectives to critically read and assess the narratives of Jaume Balagueró and Paco Plaza's *[Rec]* (2007), David Cronenberg's *Shivers* (1975) and James Nunn and Ronnie Thompson's *Tower Block* (2012).

The part and the book ends with Chapter 13, in which James Shelton examines the narrative mechanics of key cult horror films by analysing the manner in which transitions between narrative states occur within their wider story arcs. The impact of retribution and *nemein* on the change between narrative states is an important consideration for Shelton since classical narratives propagate the idea that antagonists should receive the punishment they are due before their film ends. Within the films selected – *The Wicker Man* (Robin Hardy, 1973), *Apostle* (Gareth Evans, 2018), *The Guest* (Adam Wingard, 2014) and *Last Night in Soho* (Edgar Wright, 2021) – Shelton's analysis specifically hinges on the concept of the Investigative Outsider – a character who, in three of the four highlighted case studies, believes that they have a moral duty to bring about a change of narrative state by taking action that will re-establish a form of order to their film's disrupted narrative. In the horror genre, however, this belief – as Shelton's analysis reveals – is often mistaken, resulting in narrative twists that leave a lasting impression.

Bibliography

Ackerman, Forrest J. (ed.). *Famous Monsters of Filmland Magazine.* New York: Warren Publishing, 1958–1983.

Allmer, Patricia, Emily Brick, and David Huxley (eds). *European Nightmares: Horror Cinema in Europe Since 1945.* New York: Wallflower Press, 2012.

Broughton, Lee. *Reframing Cult Westerns: From The Magnificent Seven to The Hateful Eight.* New York: Bloomsbury Academic, 2020.

Christopher, Ian. *The Games Room: A Novel Interpretation of Stanley Kubrick's Film The Shining.* London: de Valion, 2020.

Clover, Carol. *Men, Women, and Chainsaws: Gender in the Modern Horror Film.* Princeton: Princeton University Press, 1992.

Cook, Roger, Jan Cook, and Dez Skinn (eds). *Monster Mag Magazine.* London: Top Sellers Limited, 1973–1976.

Creed, Barbara. *The Monstrous-Feminine: Film, Feminism and Psychoanalysis.* Abingdon: Routledge, 1993.

Frank, Alan G. *Horror Movies: Tales of Terror in the Cinema.* London: Octopus Books Limited, 1974.

Frank, Alan G. *Monsters and Vampires.* London: Octopus Books Limited, 1976.

Galley, Michael. *Dracula, Frankenstein and Friends.* Norwich: Independently published, 2021.

Gifford, Denis. *A Pictorial History of Horror Movies*. London: Hamlyn, 1973.

Gifford, Denis. *Monsters of the Movies*. London: Carousel Books, 1977.

Hunter, I. Q. *Cult Film as a Guide to Life: Fandom, Adaptation and Identity*. New York: Bloomsbury Academic, 2016.

Jancovich, Mark, et al. 'Introduction'. In *Defining Cult Movies: The Cultural Politics of Oppositional Taste*, edited by Mark Jancovich, Antonio Lazaro Reboll, Julian Stringer, and Andy Willis, 1–13. Manchester: Manchester University Press, 2003.

Janisse, Kier-La. *House of Psychotic Women: An Autobiographical Topography of Female Neurosis in Horror and Exploitation Films*. Godalming: Fab Press, 2012.

Mathijs, Ernest and Xavier Mendik. 'Editorial Introduction: What is Cult Film?'. In *The Cult Film Reader*, edited by Ernest Mathijs and Xavier Mendik, 1–11. Maidenhead: Open University Press, 2008.

McNaughton, Eric (ed.). *70s Monster Memories*. Brighton: Buzzy Krotik Productions, 2015.

Peirse, Alison (ed.). *Women Make Horror: Filmmaking, Feminism, Genre*. New Brunswick: Rutgers University Press, 2020.

Schneider, Steven J. (ed.). *Fear Without Frontiers: Horror Cinemas across the Globe*. Godalming: FAB Press, 2002.

Schneider, Steven J. (ed.). *100 European Horror Films*. London: BFI, 2007.

Schneider, Steven J. and Tony Williams (eds). *Horror International*. Detroit: Wayne State University Press, 2005.

Simpson, M. J. *21st Century British Horror Films, Volume 1: Dog Soldiers and Doghouses (2000–2011)*. Leicester: self-published, 2020.

Skinn, Dez (ed.). *House of Hammer Magazine*. London: Top Sellers Limited, 1976–1978.

Thrower, Stephen. *Nightmare USA: The Untold Story of the Exploitation Independents*. Godalming: FAB Press, 2008.

Tombs, Pete. *Mondo Macabro: Weird and Wonderful Cinema around the World*. London: Titan Books, 1997.

Tombs, Pete and Cathal Tohill. *Immoral Tales: Sex and Horror Cinema in Europe, 1956–1984*. London: Titan Books, 1995.

Vale, V. and Andrea Juno (eds). *Incredibly Strange Films*. London: Plexus Publishing Limited, 1986.

Filmography

Apostle (2018), [Film] Dir. Gareth Evans, USA: Netflix.

Brothers of the Head (2006), [Film] Dir. Keith Fulton and Louis Pepe, UK: Potboiler Productions.

Candyman (1992), [Film] Dir. Bernard Rose, USA / UK: PolyGram Filmed Entertainment / Propaganda Films / Candyman Films.
Carnival of Souls (1962), [Film] Dir. Herk Harvey, USA: Harcourt Productions / Centron Corporation.
The Coming of Joachim Stiller (De Komst van Joachim Stiller, 1976), [TV series and Film] Dir. Harry Kümel, Belgium: Algemene Vereniging Radio Omroep (AVRO) / Belgische Radio en Televisie (BRT).
Daughters of Darkness (1971), [Film] Dir. Harry Kümel, Belgium / France / West Germany / USA: Showking Films / Maya Films / Roxy Film / Ciné Vog Films / Gemini Pictures International / Cinépix.
Deliverance (1972), [Film] Dir. John Boorman, USA: Warner Bros. / Elmer Enterprises.
The Fall of the Louse of Usher (2002), [Film] Dir. Ken Russell, UK: Gorsewood Productions.
The Guest (2014), [Film] Dir. Adam Wingard, USA: Picturehouse.
The Haunted Castle (Le Chateau haunte, 1897), [Film] Dir. Georges Méliès, France: Star-Film.
The Haunted Curiosity Shop (1901), [Film] Dir. Walter R. Booth, UK: Robert W. Paul.
Howling III: The Marsupials (1987), [Film] Dir. Philippe Mora, Australia: Bancannia Holdings Pty. Ltd.
The Hunt (2020), [Film] Dir. Craig Zobel, USA: Universal Pictures.
Inn of the Damned (1975), [Film] Dir. Terry Bourke, Australia: Terryrod.
Inside / À l'intérieur (2007), [Film] Dir. Alexandre Bustillo and Julien Maury, France: BR Films / La Fabrique de films.
Jackson County Jail (1976), [Film] Dir. Michael Miller, USA: New World Pictures.
Killer Klowns From Outer Space (1988), [Film] Dir. Stephen Chiodo, USA: Chiodo Bros.
Lair of the White Worm (1988), [Film] Dir. Ken Russell, UK: White Lair.
Last Night in Soho (2021), [Film] Dir. Edgar Wright, UK: Focus Features / Universal Pictures.
The Legend of the Seven Golden Vampires (1974), [Film] Dir. Roy Ward Baker, UK / Hong Kong: Hammer Films / Shaw Brothers.
Malpertuis (1973), [Film] Dir. Harry Kümel, Belgium / France / West Germany: Artemis Film / Les Productions Artistes Associés / SOFLDOC / Société d'Expansion du Spectacle.
Martyrs (2008), [Film] Dir. Pascal Laugier, France: Eskwad / Wild Bunch / TCB Film.
Nightmare in Badham County (1976), [Film] Dir. John Llewellyn Moxey, USA: ABC Circle Films / Ambroad.
[Rec] (2007), [Film] Dir. Jaume Balagueró and Paco Plaza. Spain: Casteleo.
Roadgames (1981), [Film] Dir. Richard Franklin, Australia: Essaness Pictures.
Scum of the Earth (AKA Poor White Trash Part II, 1974), [Film] Dir. S. F. Brownrigg, USA: Zison Enterprises.
The Shining (1980), [Film] Dir. Stanley Kubrick, UK / USA: Warner Bros.

Shivers (1975), [Film] Dir. David Cronenberg, Canada: Cinépix Film Properties.

Tower Block (2012), [Film] Dir. James Nunn and Ronnie Thompson. UK: Earth Star Entertainment.

Turkey Shoot (1982), [Film] Dir. Brian Trenchard-Smith, Australia / UK: Hemdale / FGH /Filmco.

Whisky Mountain (1977), [Film], Dir William Grefé, USA: Whiskey Mountain Production Company.

The Wicker Man (1973), [Film] Dir. Robin Hardy, UK: British Lion Films.

Part I

Lone features

Carnival of Souls as seen by its creators

Bill Shaffer

Introduction

Herk Harvey was a film director who planted his own visions and ideas into short industrial film subjects for the Centron Corporation – a producer of such films based in Lawrence, Kansas. Working in a small staff environment, Harvey often found himself drafted in as an actor, vocal talent or effects coordinator on other people's projects. These projects sometimes included larger budget 'specials' created as entertainment for big corporations to be shown at staff gatherings or special events. John Clifford was a Lawrence, Kansas writer of industrial short films, comedy sketches and a Western novel. John would later say he had to use everything he knew about writing to make the subjects of these short films interesting. Clifford proved himself adept at covering all sorts of short film subjects from grammatical problems, farming implements and plant and home safety to social situations like the proper approach to dating.

The two would come together to make their one and only feature film, the enduring cult classic *Carnival of Souls* in 1962. It started on a day when Harvey was returning from a Los Angeles vacation and caught sight of a deserted and eerie-looking amusement park while travelling through Utah by car. He discovered the place had once been a thriving business called Saltair – a swimming and dancing pavilion with rides and freshwater slides that operated successfully from the mid-1890s up to the late 1950s. As with similar amusement parks like Steeplechase and Coney Island, it had burned down a few times during its half-century of operation and had been duly rebuilt. As the lake receded and the crowds stayed away, the park faded until it was closed in 1959. For Harvey, this became the perfect set for a stylish, spooky horror movie, something he knew he could urge Clifford to write and that he could direct. What came out of this collaboration was a minimalist horror film that would strike a nerve in movie fans for far more years than either of its creators had ever imagined or intended.

The film's novel narrative begins with a simple drag race between a car filled with three girls and another with two young men. However, the drag race leads to tragedy as the car carrying the girls plunges off a bridge into a river below. Hours later, as the police attempt to snare the submerged car, a sole survivor, Mary Henry (Candace Hilligoss) rises from the muddy waters before embarking on a strange and disturbing journey of her own. Something seems to be wrong with Mary's perception of reality from the very beginning. She travels to Salt Lake City to take up residence in an apartment and assume a job as the organist at a local church. On the way there, she encounters the Man (Herk Harvey), a silent zombie-ghoul-ghost who appears infrequently in seemingly impossible places – outside of her car window while she's driving at full speed, in the waters of the great Salt Lake and in the back of the church in which she plays the organ. While in the city, she becomes disconnected from herself and others: it seems that people cannot see or hear her. She also is attracted to an old, deserted carnival area by the lake where she duly walks among the spooky interiors. She is finally drawn to it at twilight to meet the Man and her fate.

Despite its novel narrative and at times striking visuals, *Carnival of Souls* failed financially during its initial release due to a crooked distributor, who absconded with what little money it made in drive-in theatres and then sold the rights to show it on commercial television stations in perpetuity. That TV exposure is where *Carnival of Souls* found its audience as a late-night chiller which frequently surprised and impressed its viewers (whether they be teenagers or adults). Over the years the film's ability to attract and delight new viewers has resulted in *Carnival of Souls* developing its reputation as a bona-fide cult movie. By drawing upon this author's own extensive and exclusive interviews with both Herk Harvey and John Clifford, this chapter will offer fresh insight into the production processes that resulted in *Carnival of Souls* becoming one of the most iconic cult horror films of all time as well as detailing Harvey and Clifford's reactions and responses to the film's remarkable afterlife.

Pre-production and the film's atypical protagonist

Prior to 1962, there had not been a movie (horror film or otherwise) quite like *Carnival of Souls*. Although things have changed over sixty years after its release, it is probably safe to say there also has not been one like it since. Its director, Herk Harvey, was a Lawrence, Kansas-based producer/director/actor who worked for an industrial film company called Centron Productions for almost a decade before the idea for this feature film came along. Harvey recalled:

> I went on a vacation and, coming back from Los Angeles, I saw this place (called) Saltair, which was located just outside of Salt Lake. It's very Russian arabesque in architecture and I saw it at sunset and it was the weirdest looking thing I'd ever seen so I stopped the car and walked about a half mile to take a look at it, noticed it was deserted. It was quite a ways from the lake because Salt Lake had gone down.... So I came back (to Lawrence) and talked to John [Clifford, a writer at Centron Productions], showed him a couple of the pictures that I took when I was there and said, 'you know, that's a great location. We ought to figure out something to do with that'.... So John in his usual way of being inventive comes up with (the script for) *Carnival of Souls* which I thought was a great idea. (Author interview, 1988)

Clifford confides that it took only two weeks to complete the script, primarily to coincide with Harvey's additional two weeks of vacation time which would allow time for shooting to take place.

Clifford's script work for *Carnival of Souls* resulted in an eerie and seemingly gender conscious narrative that has fascinated viewers and academics alike. In more recent years the use of feminist film theory has enabled film scholars to voice some intriguing ideas about the significance of Mary Henry, the film's main character. Chris Olson (2013) describes Mary as being 'a strong-willed, independent, sexually liberated young woman who is being pursued and persecuted by a character known simply as The Man'. As such, Olson (2013) argues that 'the overarching theme of *Carnival of Souls* seems to be one of feminism emerging in the face of patriarchal power, and this becomes significant when taking into account the fact that the film was released in 1962, which is widely considered to be the beginning of the sexual revolution'. Olson (2013) deftly brings together the work of Laura Mulvey (1975) on the male gaze, Mikhail Baktin on the empowering properties of the carnival (1984) and Barbara Creed (1993) on the notion of the monstrous-feminine when analysing the film.

For Olson (2013), Mary is 'positioned as a representation of emergent feminism in two distinct ways. First, Mary is positioned as a victim of patriarchal repression, particularly in the way she is situated as an object in relation to the male gaze'. Here Olson is referring to Mulvey's idea (1975) regarding the objectifying power of the male gaze in films and it is true that Mary is indeed surveyed and objectified in different ways by a succession of quite diverse male characters: the Minister (Art Ellison), for whom she is to play the church organ; the psychiatrist Dr Samuels (Stan Levitt), who seeks to treat her; her lustful neighbour John Linden (Sidney Berger); and the Man (Herk Harvey), the fearsome zombie-ghoul-ghost who stalks her throughout the film. However, Olson (2013) argues that Mary duly 'subverts this oppression and becomes a manifestation of female empowerment through her embrace of the carnival and the carnivalesque, which in this film represents a site of emergent feminism that challenges the dominance of the patriarchy'. Here Olson invokes Bakhtin's (1984) idea that the carnival was the great leveller, a site and brief period of time in which all were temporarily equal. Moving on to the second distinct way in which Mary functions as a representation of emergent feminism, Olson (2013) cites Barbara Creed (1993) and adds, 'Mary becomes a manifestation of the monstrous-feminine, particularly because she is a representation of the abject or the uncanny. Thus she represents a threat to patriarchal power because she exerts control over her own sense of sexual agency, and therefore must be repressed'. Much like the mainstream Hollywood films that were being produced at the time, *Carnival of Souls* features a narrative in which the transgressive female has to be tamed or punished in some way at the film's end in order to uphold the norms of contemporary patriarchal society.

Pursuing a similar agenda to Olson (2013), Christine Sellin (2012) makes the interesting assertion that:

> The true horror in this movie is *not* a result of scary souls trying to kidnap and imprison a dead woman in denial of her ceased existence, but rather the figurative concept of an attempted imprisonment of a feminist woman who *only* wants to live as *she* chooses to – not based on religious, social, or sexual societal norms – by various *men*. The dominance and power that men in her society hold over women make them *more* horrific than the souls of the carnival plaguing her imagination – with the one specific, spectral male that consistently haunts her imagination symbolic of all the men that have tormented her spiritually, psychologically, and sexually.

While it might well be argued that the film's take on gender representation unwittingly captured the zeitgeist of America *c.* 1962, Sellin (2012) is moved to ask, 'Does this film *really* provide intelligent commentary on societal issues (particularly feminine) of the 1960s, or is it less than what we make it out to be?'

The answer might lay in the background information that Clifford has offered regarding how the character of Mary came to be: 'Herk had some ideas about (the script). As I remember, he wanted a man chased around various places and I think he told me that he wanted people coming out of that lake (to participate in) some kind of a dance of death in this place'. However, Clifford explained that he 'switched it to a female (main character) because there seemed to be a little more vulnerability there' (Author interview, 1988). So while the vulnerability that Clifford refers to can indeed be found in Mary, it might also be suggested that the sense of narrative agency that was usually afforded exclusively to male characters in Hollywood films of the time is also found in Mary as a consequence of Harvey's original plans to have a male protagonist. Clifford continued, 'The nice thing about working with Herk is that, over the years (when I'd) come up with something difficult, he'd always say, "You write it the way you think it ought to be and . . . I'll get it shot." . . . Writers appreciate that. He lets me do the writing . . . and I stay out of his directing' (Author interview, 1988).

With the script in place, Harvey offered insights into the trials and tribulations of financing an independent horror film like *Carnival of Souls*:

> I talked to a couple of local investors who then talked to other people and the sum of $13,000 was raised over a weekend, which I thought was really pretty amazing . . . because in those days, that was a pretty good sum, although the idea of doing a 35mm feature film for $13,000 cash was a little staggering, even then. I don't think the investors invested in the project . . . they invested in John and me, simply because they had worked with us in some cases there at Centron and they just kind of knew we were inventive and wanted to do things. (Author interview, 1988)

With the budget in place, the casting of *Carnival of Souls* could begin.

Candace Hilligoss and the casting of *Carnival of Souls*

The main character in *Carnival of Souls*, the haunting/haunted Mary Henry, was played by New York actress Candace Hilligoss, who has another cult horror movie to her credit – Del Tenney's *The Curse of the Living Corpse* (1964). According to Hilligoss, her first meeting with Harvey provided the director with a major – albeit only temporary – problem. Hilligoss recalled in her autobiography that

> years later, Harvey confessed that the night my plane finally landed in Kansas City he was so disappointed when he saw me for the first time. I didn't look like what a Candace Hilligoss, the actress, should look like to him. I appeared dowdy, disheveled and hippie, too plain-looking. It was important to him that the girl be

> pretty. He spent a sleepless night thinking how he would tell me to go home.... The next morning ... as I stepped out of the hotel's elevator, he went into shock at what he called an amazing transformation. I showed up with makeup and my hair curled softly around my face. According to him, my appearance changed like a butterfly emerging from a cocoon. Now I looked like exactly what he wanted. This was the first time I saw Herk smile. (Hilligoss 2016: 190)

Harvey now had his character as originally envisioned.

However, Hilligoss's liking for method acting was something that the director had not counted on. Harvey recalled that Hilligoss

> was the only member of the cast who was not local or from Salt Lake. The only thing was she was a method actress so she always wanted to know 'why is my character doing this, and many times,' like walking across the street in traffic in Salt Lake. The only thing I'd say is 'go across (or) you're going to get killed'. (Author interview, 1988)

For other scenes in the film, 'mood' was the primary motivation. For example, many scenes at the Saltair pavilion required Hilligoss to move as if in a trance. Hilligoss remembered:

> I ask Herk for the reasons why my character would roam through a deserted amusement park then end up wandering inside the pavilion? ... 'All you need to know is Mary Henry's body dies in a car crash. Her soul strives to hang onto life. Having not recognized life's potential, she cannot accept death. The drowned souls attract you to Saltair. They're gonna capture you here. Take you back to the murky salt water – a metaphor for death. That's all there is to it' [was his reply]. (2016: 195)

The apparent clash in preferred methods of acting and directing did not sour Harvey and Hilligoss's relationship but it did work to produce a moving and ethereal performance by the actress.

The shoot

Harvey recalled that shooting on the film started:

> in the fall of 1962, because I remember looking at the Kansas River ... the last scene of the show, Mary Henry comes out in the car with the other two girls and you find out all the girls have been dead all the time and we filmed that down here in late September, early October and the water was cold enough that

I thought I might get arrested (for subjecting the cast to such low temperatures), but we got the shot. Everything worked fine. (Author interview, 1988)

Most of the river shots were filmed in one or two days including an early sequence where the car containing the girls was dropped off of the bridge into the river. Of shooting that sequence, Harvey explained that 'they said you will have to pay for repairing the bridge after we wrecked the car through the bridge railing and all . . . I watched the men repairing it and later I got a bill for twelve dollars for repairing the bridge which would be, of course, a lot different today' (Author interview, 1988). According to Harvey, shooting in Lawrence, Kansas took about nine days while shooting in Salt Lake City and around the Saltair pavilion took about five days.

As with all low-budget filmmaking, shooting on existing locations can save money, but using some of these locations can cause unexpected problems. Harvey recalled that:

> the state of Utah gave us permission to use the pavilion in the film. It was a great location to go to because there was absolutely nobody around most of the time (and) we didn't have enough lights to light the whole (interior of the) pavilion. It was actually the largest dance hall between Chicago and California. We finally managed through a local electrician to hook up from outside and we found out the lights inside the place still worked. (Author interview, 1988)

However, the lighting that was rigged up for this section of the film's shoot did not go unnoticed by people unconnected to the film. Harvey remembered that the pavilion's existing lights:

> plus our own lights allowed us to go ahead and film the big ballroom sequence, but that thing hadn't been lit for years and the people who lived around the lake all of a sudden, started calling the police (asking) 'what's going on at Saltair?' and the police didn't even know so they came out to find out, but it all worked out well. It really is one of the most isolated locations I've ever been on, though. (Author interview, 1988)

Of this incident, Candace Hilligoss recalled 'Herk in his nightmarish, ghoul makeup and black frock coat descended the staircase in a hurry as the cops drew their guns. Forty dancing ghouls appeared on the balcony. Their white faces with blacked-out eyes peered down . . . [and before long] . . . there was some good-natured chuckling from Salt Lake City's law enforcement' (2016: 197).

The 'forty dancing ghouls' referred to here represent an interesting bit of casting. The ghostly zombie dancers who appear in the film's Saltair sequence were actually played by twenty boys and twenty girls who were members of the Mormon School of Dance in Salt Lake City, Utah. Hilligoss recalled that she 'asked Herk how he managed to pull this one out of his hat' and he replied that the dance school had accepted a donation from him (2016: 196). Hilligoss added that the school's dancers 'were more than willing to come; they were quite thrilled to be portraying ghouls in a movie. This had never happened to them before. They (provided) their own costumes of black leotards and skirts; also they are excited to paint their faces phantom-like. Copying Herk, they smeared black greasepaint around their eyes' (2016: 196). This kind of fun detail offers further interesting insights into the world of regional low-budget filmmaking during the 1960s.

The Mormon School of Dance members were also involved in the shooting of what turned out to be the most heart-breaking omission from *Carnival of Souls*. At some point a reel of film (about ten minutes long) was shot with the further participation of the dancers as in the script they were meant to be seen entering the pavilion from various locations outside and within Salt Lake. Harvey describes how:

> we lost a roll of film that I think was very critical. We had this long shot. It was a great evening at Salt Lake and they have all these pilings out in the water, just lone pilings . . . and I had people in dark costumes behind the pilings and then, on cue, it's as though the pilings start to move, but it's really all these people who start to move toward the pavilion. And then we had some scenes of hands coming up on the pavilion and then faces and this is the first time you see these people (the ghouls) . . . before the dance of death sequence. (Author interview, 1988)

These additional location shots of the ghouls would have added further horror elements and atmosphere to *Carnival of Souls* but, as Harvey added: 'the lab screwed it up. In the processing, they simply over-exposed it and ruined it (and) that was about eight minutes of film, but still it's one of those things we would like to have had' (Author interview, 1988). Instead, Harvey had to use an entirely different location for the filming of these scenes after he returned from Salt Lake City. Harvey confirmed that 'we shot those in a swimming pool at an apartment (building) where I lived in Lawrence . . . with totally different actors in close-ups' (Author interview, 1988).

The aftermath

The first of many disappointments relating to *Carnival of Souls* occurred when the film had its premiere in Lawrence in the fall of 1962. The audience was hushed throughout and quietly left without comment or applause. The audience certainly knew that it was a horror movie but they appeared to be confused as to precisely what kind of horror movie *Carnival of Souls* might be. Where was the blood and gore? Herk Harvey was convinced that it was simply an off the wall movie that stood little chance of fully impressing his local audience. Candace Hilligoss recalled that on the night of the premiere one of Harvey's 'investors approached him and said, "Interesting, Herk. Like a Cocteau or a Bergman movie, you said. My, my, very interesting. Well, good luck, anyhow"' (2016: 201).

To compound matters, Harvey encountered difficulties when he tried to show the film to executives at the Hollywood studios. He found few that would even look at *Carnival of Souls* once they were made aware of the film's miniscule budget. In New York, Harvey was able to screen the film at United Artists, but the executives there were 'neutral' about it. Candace Hilligoss attended one of the screenings with her agent and she recalls that his immediate response was 'You're too weird [meaning Candace herself, *not* the character she was portraying]. I can't represent you anymore. I have a reputation to protect' before dropping her and walking out of her life (2016: 201).

Harvey finally signed a seven-year contract with a small, newly formed, independent distributor called Herts-Lion towards the end of 1962. Kenneth Herts, the company president, wanted to pair *Carnival of Souls* with another horror film that he had picked up, Herbert L. Strock's *The Devil's Messenger* (1962). Strock's film was a portmanteau horror show that featured three episodes that had been lifted from a television series, *13 Demon Street* (1959). These three episodes were held together by newly shot linking scenes featuring the horror film icon Lon Chaney Jr (who had also hosted the television series that they had been lifted from). The company shortened both films to eighty minutes or less resulting in fewer 35mm reels to ship out and return. Herts-Lion was not interested in showing the film in art house cinemas but ventured into the drive-in theatre market instead. Harvey recalled that:

> we got glowing reviews to start with. I went to South America on another film (for Centron), and when I came back, it was obvious they owed us considerable money, but they hadn't paid us a cent. When I started investigating, I got a check that

bounced, then no replies and the next thing I knew, the president of the company had gone to Europe . . . and the funds had gone with him. (Author interview, 1988)

One of the other things the Herts-Lion company had done (without Harvey's permission) was to sell the television rights to *Carnival of Souls* for an unspecified amount of time. Not only were multiple film prints literally left in the drive-ins at which they were shown but multiple TV prints were also allowed to play at TV stations in perpetuity. But here may have laid the silver-lining that Harvey, Clifford and Hilligoss had never expected because this state of affairs meant that *Carnival of Souls* was a film that never went away.

Revival

In the years following its release, *Carnival of Souls* garnered an audience of fervent fans in a variety of age groups who have embraced the film as either part of their lives or an important turning point in their lives. It is a bona-fide cult movie. Screenplay writer John Clifford explains:

> I think the film appeals to teenagers because it's about a young woman who's out in the world and she doesn't know what's happening to her, she doesn't know what's going on. Everything is very uncertain . . . and I have a feeling that subconsciously, teenagers who are about to enter the world have these (same) feelings. They don't know what's ahead and they don't understand everything out there, although they might not admit it. Somehow the film taps some of that feeling in kids because for some reason, teenagers have always liked it, right from the beginning. Originally, we got letters from people in Hollywood and various places, praising the film as the best, little, low-budget, independent film they'd ever seen . . . but a certain number of teenagers (who were seeing it on late-night television) seem to be fascinated by it. (Author interview, 1988)

But as well as appealing to teenagers, *Carnival of Souls* also appeals to aficionados of art house films. Clifford recalled that

> Herk had some friends come back from Sweden and they said it was playing in downtown art houses there and (these) people would go to the coffee shops afterwards, sit around and discuss it. That was probably the first indication we had that maybe the film was a little bit 'arty' (laughs). I mean we were just trying to make a good film. I don't think we ever started out to do art. (Author interview, 1988)

Harvey had wanted *Carnival of Souls* to have the 'look of an Ingmar Bergman and the feel of a Jean Cocteau' (Author interview, 1988), which suggests that he would have been thrilled to hear that the film was playing in art house theatres, but he also observed:

> This (resurgence of) interest in *Carnival of Souls* has kind of built up through a period of time. Actually, it's kind of flattering in a sense. A number of people start asking questions like 'Did you really intend to do this and this?' which as John said we intended just to make a good horror film . . . and one that had some pizazz to it. A lot of these things (people read into the film) we really didn't consider, but it's nice to have them consider it now because the film seems to have much more depth than we ever gave it, probably. (Author interview, 1988)

Clifford added, 'they're asking us what we were thinking about years and years ago . . . and they're talking to a couple of guys who can hardly remember what they were doing last week (both laughed)' (Author interview, 1988).

Near the summer of 1988, the author of this chapter contacted both Harvey and Clifford about doing a public television interview for a series on Kansas places, people and events. Both men graciously agreed to it. I asked John Clifford if there was any way I could screen the film and he invited me over to his apartment in Lawrence where we saw it in a very common format for the time – on VHS tape. Since the film had not been properly copyrighted, multiple copies from diverse distributors surfaced during the VHS era. It was fascinating to watch the film with Clifford nearby offering a running commentary. Both Clifford and Harvey met for the interview near the Kansas River. Recollected stories (now used as the basis for this chapter) flowed out of each individual, but overall, they felt this would be their final interview regarding this movie. Shortly after we parted, Harvey got a call from a small film company – Panorama Entertainment – that wanted to re-release the film in theatres across the country. Harvey had found the original negative and re-inserted missing footage removed by Herts-Lion, therefore a finished 'Director's Cut' was now available. The re-release was a modest success, but (as Herk and John later pointed out) it was just great to see *Carnival of Souls* getting shown again and almost all of the critical reviews that these screenings garnered were strikingly positive. Be it kitsch or art, 'Carnival' is at least viable, so far earning $1.2 million in forty-seven cities according to Tim Allis and Grant Ellis (1990: 94–5).

The climax of this revival of *Carnival of Souls* for me took place on a sunny day in 1989 when the cast was reunited for a screening of the film at Liberty

Figure 1.1 *Carnival of Souls*: The cast and crew pictured at the reunion event held in Lawrence, Kansas, on 24 November 1989. Left to right: Larry Sneegas (car driver / production manager), Sidney Berger (John Linden), John Clifford (writer), Candace Hilligoss (Mary Henry), Stan Levitt (the Doctor), Art Ellison (the Preacher) and Herk Harvey (the Man / producer and director). Image © 1989 Bill Shaffer.

Hall, an art-house theatre in downtown Lawrence, Kansas (see Figures 1.1 and 1.2). The theatre was sold out and I felt honoured to be invited for the whole day. Earlier in the afternoon, the cast was interviewed at the nearby Eldridge Hotel and director/actor Herk Harvey appeared in his ghoul make-up and black suit once again. He wore the suit and make-up all day and evening. I met and interviewed many members of the cast including Candace Hilligoss during that time. As the film began in the theatre, I looked around and asked John Clifford where Herk was seated. He responded that Herk was outside somewhere, too nervous to stay inside, adding, 'He hates to be inside with a crowd when they're watching his movie. It just tears him up'. I ventured outside after that to observe Herk out on the sidewalk, sweating and smoking a cigarette, still looking as ghoulish as ever in full make-up. I could not say anything to him – it was just too bizarre a scenario – but I later wished that I had taken a picture.

A few months afterwards, the film received an official release on VHS tape and Laserdisc (through Vid-America) with a new introduction featuring Herk Harvey

Figure 1.2 *Carnival of Souls*: Herk Harvey in his ghoul make-up menaces the author's son James Shaffer at the reunion event held in Lawrence, Kansas, on 24 November 1989. Image © 1989 Bill Shaffer.

which was shot in the studio at KTWU (the public television affiliate where I worked). A few years later, the Criterion Collection called me about using the footage I had shot for a full-scale DVD release of the film which would include both the Herts-Lion shortened release and the new 'Director's Cut'. During the time between the VHS release (through Panorama Entertainment) and this Criterion DVD Special Edition in 2000, I had combined the earlier interview with Herk and John with footage from the re-premiere for a free-standing half-hour special entitled, *The Movie That Wouldn't Die!* (1990). I volunteered as much material as I could find including this special for the Criterion release in 2000 and I was rewarded by being credited as the Associate Producer of this two-disc set. The producer of the Criterion set, Susan Arosteguy, had first seen *Carnival of Souls* while working part-time at a video store during her days as a student at the University of Colorado and she recalled, 'It was just one of those B-movies that was sort of infamous. I just thought it was a really sort of amazing example of a B-movie that's still very artful and affecting. I just loved it, always' (Bierman 2019).

Finally, in 2016, a Blu-ray edition was assembled and released (with most of the supplemental features carried over from the DVD) through Criterion again. In a unique sort of irony not even Herk Harvey could have foreseen, *Carnival of Souls* as a Criterion Collection title now shares shelf space with Jean Cocteau's *Beauty and the Beast* (*La belle et la bete*, 1946) and *Orpheus* (*Orphee*, 1950) as well as Ingmar Bergman's *The Seventh Seal* (*Det sjunde inseglet*, 1957) and *Wild Strawberries* (*Smultronstallet*, 1957). For a film in which Harvey desired the look of a Bergman and the feel of a Cocteau (Author interview, 1988), proof of his achievements may get no better than this. Herk Harvey died in 1996 and John Clifford died in 2010. Their final thoughts on their experiences? Harvey observed, 'all I can say about *Carnival of Souls* is . . . it's a heck of a note when a film that has failed financially is your total breadth of success in the feature film market . . . just one of those things' (Author interview, 1988) while Clifford recalled 'I got through *Carnival of Souls* with nothing more than a mild case of the willies. Actually, it left me thinking (years later) how pleasant it must be for these two silver-haired gents to have their work confirmed and exalted after all these years' (Gurley Jr. 1989: B-1).

Conclusion: The relevance of *Carnival of Souls* today

Reviewers have continued to find much to admire in *Carnival of Souls*. Anne Billson (2016) was struck by the film's unique locations, commenting that 'it's like a case study in low-budget filmmaking – how to get a lot out of very few resources, found locations, not studio sets. The whole pavilion, but also the landscape (was) a flat, rather sinister landscape'. Terence Rafferty of *The New Yorker* observes, 'It's a real hour-of-the-wolf movie: it wakes you up and keeps you up . . . Harvey achieves some terrifying and original scenes, even the movie's cheapness is expressive . . . somehow it all works. Harvey pulls us through the movie by alternating scenes of everyday life with visions of death . . . we're never entirely sure where we are' (1989: 88). Rafferty's (1989) review directly references Ingmar Bergman's *Hour of the Wolf* (*Vargtimmen*, 1968) and I know Herk would have been doing somersaults of delight after reading that one. Peter Travers of *Rolling Stone* enthuses 'Back in 1962, Herk Harvey's $30,000 black-and-white Hell-raiser was dumped on the drive-in circuit and forgotten. Now, gloriously undead, this eerily atmospheric chiller about a church organist who escapes a car wreck not quite alive – returns to claim its place as a horror classic' (1989: page number not known). Stephen Holden thoughtfully observes that 'despite its flaws, *Carnival of Souls* is more than just a mere curiosity. Its portrait of a lonely, intrepid rationalist besieged by spirits carries an eerie chill' (1989: 2D). More recently, Christine Sellin (2012) opines that 'although the film may have provided corny scares (literally – it was a low-budget Midwestern cornfield flick) to unsuspecting audiences, I have found that it is much more intelligent than what may have been intended in its creation'. *Carnival of Souls* is clearly a film that can engage and intrigue an audience on a number of different levels.

So is *Carnival of Souls* still relevant in a new century? I certainly think so, but part of its success is being just what it is – a simple well-made little movie that still succeeds in spite of its very limited budget, the straightforward intelligence of its story and the persistence of its director and writer. Does it still haunt the viewer? I would say yes. It has that kind of 'eerie staying power' in its images and in its musical score. The moments of silence and reflection have more power than the film's often loopy dialogue and narrative situations. Why does the film still maintain this power? Because people are still discovering it and its backstory. It still weaves a spell over sixty years after it was made. And that is why it remains one of the best known cult horror films of all time.

Bibliography

Allis, Tim and Grant Ellis. 'Decades After its First Incarnation, *Carnival of Souls* Has a Spooky, Cult Rebirth'. *People Magazine* 33, no. 2 (15 January 1990): 94–5.

Author interview. Herk Harvey and John Clifford were Interviewed by Bill Shaffer at the Kansas River Near Lawrence, Kansas in the Summer of 1988.

Bakhtin, Mikhail. *Rabelais and His World*, translated by Helene Iswolsky. Bloomington: Indiana University Press, 1984.

Barnes, Brian. 'Rising from its Grave'. *Kansas City Star*, 29 January 1990, 3-D.

Bierman, Courtney. 'This 1962 Cult Classic Filmed in Lawrence Is "The Scariest Movie Ever"'. *KCUR*, 27 October 2019. Available online at: https://www.kcur.org/arts-life/2019-10-27/this-1962-cult-classic-filmed-in-lawrence-is-the-scariest-movie-ever# (accessed 4 November 2021).

Billson, Anne. Quoted in the Video Essay 'Regards from Nowhere' by David Cairns on the Criterion Collection Blu-ray Release of *Carnival of Souls*, 2016.

Creed, Barbara. *The Monstrous-Feminine: Film, Feminism, Psychoanalysis*. London: Routledge, 1993.

Gurley, George H. Jr. 'Horror Need Not Be Vulgar'. *Kansas City Times*, 31 October 1989, B-1.

Hilligoss, Candace. *The Odyssey and the Idiocy: Marriage to an Actor, a Memoir*. Sarasota: First Edition Design Publishing, 2016.

Holden, Stephen. 'Fatalistic Angst Earned Cult Film Its Status'. *Lawrence Journal-World*, 23 July 1989, 2D.

Mulvey, Laura. 'Visual Pleasure and Narrative Cinema'. *Screen* 16, no. 3 (1975): 6–18.

Olson, Chris. 'Carnival of Souls and Emergent Feminism in the Early Half of the Sexual Revolution'. *Seems Obvious to Me: Adventures in Pop Culture Studies*, 9 December 2013. Available online at: https://seemsobvioustome.wordpress.com/2013/12/09/carnival-of-souls-and-emergent-feminism-in-the-early-half-of-the-sexual-revolution/ (accessed 2 November 2021).

Rafferty, Terence. 'Carnival of Souls – The Current Cinema'. *The New Yorker*, 11 September 1989, 88.

Sellin, Christine. 'Christine's Movie Macabre – Feminprisonment: Defending a Damned Damsel'. *JFR Blog*, 10 October 2012. Available online at: https://lewislitjournal.wordpress.com/2012/10/10/christines-movie-macabre-4/ (accessed 28 October 2021).

Travers, Peter. 'Now Playing'. *Rolling Stone*, 563, 19 October 1989.

Filmography

Beauty and the Beast / La belle et la bete (1946), [Film] Dir. Jean Cocteau, France: Les Films Andre Paulve.

Carnival of Souls (1962), [Film] Dir. Herk Harvey, USA: Harcourt Productions / Herts-Lion Productions.

The Curse of the Living Corpse (1964), [Film] Dir. Del Tenney, USA: Deal Productions / Iselin-Tenney Productions.

The Devil's Messenger (1962), [Film] Dir. Herbert L. Strock and Curt Siodmak, Sweden / USA: Herts-Lion International Corps.

Hour of the Wolf / Vargtimmen (1968), [Film] Dir. Ingmar Bergman, Sweden: Cinematograph AB / Svensk Filmindustri (SF).

The Movie That Wouldn't Die (1990), [TV Special] Dir: Bill Shaffer, USA: KTWU Public Television.

Orpheus / Orphee (1950), [Film] Dir. Jean Cocteau, France: Andre Paulve Film / Films du Palais Royal.

The Seventh Seal / Det sjunde inseglet (1957), [Film] Dir. Ingmar Bergman, Sweden: Svensk Filmindustri (SF).

13 Demon Street (1959), [TV Series], Dir. Various, USA: Herts-Lion Productions.

Wild Strawberries / Smultronstallet (1957), [Film] Dir. Ingmar Bergman, Sweden: Svensk Filmindustri (SF).

2

A 'totally emancipated female'

Julie Ege, Britain's crises of masculinity and Roy Ward Baker's *The Legend of the 7 Golden Vampires*

Lee Broughton

Introduction

There is a lot to like about Roy Ward Baker's East-meets-West cult horror film *The Legend of the 7 Golden Vampires* (1974) [*7 Golden Vampires* hereafter]. Peter Cushing's fine performance, the liberated nature of Julie Ege's character, the well-choreographed kung fu action, the martial nature of the horse-riding Golden Vampires and their hordes of cowled and skull-faced minions who bring to mind the undead Knights Templar encountered in Amando de Ossorio's 'Blind Dead' films, the striking lighting employed in Dracula's castle and in the Golden Vampires' temple, the cool special effects that are deployed when the vampires die and so on.

But the film is also a fascinating time capsule that appears to have much to say about the state of Britain at the time of its production. The British nation state had experienced a series of ever-deepening crises of masculinity in the decades leading up to the early 1970s. The appeasement of Adolf Hitler during the 1930s, the loss of empire territories following the Second World War and the Suez Crisis of 1956 had seen Britain lose its standing as an international superpower while the rise of the consumer society during the 1960s and the emergence of second wave feminism during the early 1970s had in turn led to public debates about the changing nature of gender roles and gendered power relations within the UK's society at large (Broughton 2016). Britain's contemporaneous status as the 'sick man of Europe' in economic terms only added further to the nation state's sense of emasculation.

Whether by accident or design, *7 Golden Vampires* seems to have captured the zeitgeist of early 1970s Britain and scenarios that appear to allegorically reflect the UK's contemporaneous mood and circumstances are present at various points throughout the film before an element of meaningful wish fulfilment – which results in a symbol of British patriarchal values winning the day – is introduced for the film's finale. As such, this chapter offers a gendered reading of *7 Golden Vampires* that considers the extent to which the film's narrative might make reference to the crises of masculinity and the economic turmoil that were being suffered by the British nation state at the time of its production.

Critical contexts

Public discourse and debates about gender and sexual equality were commonplace in the UK when *7 Golden Vampires* was being produced. 'Females only' industrial action and demonstrations based on the issues of work and pay during the late 1960s had led to the introduction of the Equal Pay Act of 1970 (Sandbrook 2012). The further growth of the Women's Liberation Movement during the early 1970s resulted in groups of British women organizing 'themselves into petitioning, activist groups, at times radical and revolutionary, to lobby and gain publicity and support for equal rights and status for women' (Forster and Harper 2010: 4). Their bold actions eventually led to the introduction of the Sex Discrimination Act of 1975.

Britain's economy and its place in the world was also in flux at this time. Trade with the British Commonwealth of Nations was stagnating and becoming a member of the European Economic Community (EEC hereafter) was regarded to be a much-needed alternative. Indeed, Richard Weight observes that during the early 1970s 'the standard of living of the Six [existing EEC member states] was nearly three times higher than Britain's . . . [and] . . . the promise of a share in the Continent's wealth was making membership more attractive to the British' (2002: 478). Applications to join the EEC during the 1960s had led to Britain suffering two humiliating and emasculating refusals but the country finally became a member state on 1 January 1973 (Ahmed 2018: 14). That same year, the effects of the oil crisis, inefficiencies in her manufacturing and production sector and spiralling inflation would see Britain's economy slipping into recession. However, concerns about the wider impact that membership of the EEC might have on British sovereignty and trading options elsewhere led to much debate and a public referendum on continued membership. The referendum took place on 5 June 1975 and 'remainers' won with a vote share of 67.23 per cent (Ahmed 2018: 15).

Much like the rest of Britain's film industry, Hammer Films – the country's foremost producer of horror films – was also suffering a change of fortunes and falling box office receipts led to the company trying to put new spins on old formulas. While the resulting efforts ultimately did not save Hammer, they do represent an interesting body of films whose content often appears to speak to contemporaneous preoccupations and debates about feminism, gender, emasculation and sexual equality. Indeed, the same pointed narrative plays out – in one way or another – with regularity across a multitude of films produced in Britain at this time: an unruly and uncommonly strong female character exhibits behaviour that upsets the weakened patriarchal order until she is tamed or punished in some way, usually by men. Interestingly, since in the Western genre the protagonist has to win, the British wound up producing a cycle of Westerns during the early 1970s in which the gendered rules of the genre were completely upended. These unusual Westerns chime with the times by featuring strong and unruly female protagonists but they are further distinguished by the fact that their atypical women are allowed to survive their films triumphant and without suffering narrative punishment of any kind (Broughton 2016).

Of the Hammer films produced at this time, *7 Golden Vampires* remains particularly interesting. It appears to have much to say about gender norms and the contemporaneous 'battle of the sexes' that was being fought within British society. But the film's narrative – and its production history – also seem to speak to Britain's failing economy and her reduced standing on the world stage. With Hammer's traditional sources of funding all but dried up and proposed co-production deals with Australian financiers failing to materialize, Denis Meikle reports that the Chinese wife of writer-producer Don Houghton arranged a meeting between Hammer's owner Michael Carreras and Run Run Shaw, the 'oriental movie mogul extraordinaire and co-owner of Shaw Studios, the biggest film factory in Southeast Asia' (2009: 211). The result of their meeting would be a novel co-production – *7 Golden Vampires* – that would aim to merge two popular genres: the horror film and the martial arts movie. Set in China in 1904, the film has a Scandinavian woman, Vanessa Buren (Julie Ege), financing a mission to the remote village of Ping Kwei so that Professor Lawrence Van Helsing (Peter Cushing) and Hsi Ching (David Chiang) can vanquish the legendary Golden Vampires who continue to prey on the village's inhabitants.

Cult actors

Peter Cushing and David Chiang are both regarded as cult actors in horror and martial arts circles respectively. However, this section will focus upon the cultification of their co-star in *7 Golden Vampires*, Julie Ege, since there has been relatively little written about her in this regard. Defining the qualities that result in an actor being classified as a cult film star is just as difficult as defining the qualities that result in a film being classified as a cult movie. At the turn of the 1980s home video releases and TV screenings brought Ege's films to a new generation of fans as well as prompting a number of questions that served to surround her with an air of mystery that undoubtedly played a part in her ongoing cultification. Biographical information about Ege was scarce during the 1980s but it was clear that she had enjoyed a massive public profile in the UK during the early 1970s. So why had she not made more films and enjoyed a longer film career? Given that Ege's filmography was relatively small, how and why could such a high proportion of her films be so offbeat and obscure enough to already be classified as cult movies? And, perhaps more pressingly, why had Ege herself suddenly vanished into obscurity around 1976? None of these questions were answered when Ege was granted an entry in Danny Peary's book *Cult Movie Stars* (1991: 173) but that entry did serve to validate her status as a cult film star.

While the present chapter does not allow space for an in-depth investigation into the cultification of Julie Ege it will offer some insight into the circumstances that governed the unusual career path that led to her becoming a cult film star. As will be discussed, Ege's lived experiences would often lend a kind of 'art-imitating-life' dimension to her film work that seemed to feed into her star persona and contribute to her status as a cult icon. A model, a TV commercial actress and a former Miss Norway, Ege moved to the UK in the 1960s to work as an *au pair* and to study at a language school with the hope of improving her English language skills (Solberg 1997). Modelling assignments in the UK duly provided Ege with a calling card that allowed her to get a foothold in the British film industry, which led to small parts in Peter Yates's *Robbery* (1967) and Peter R. Hunt's *On Her Majesty's Secret Service* (1969). In 1970 she attained an 'introducing' credit for her perfectly pitched and delivered role as Inga – a beleaguered advertising executive's (Marty Feldman) Scandinavian *au pair* – in Jim Clark's *Every Home Should Have One* (1970). In that film, the fortuitous way that Inga wins a beauty-based talent contest when her photograph is submitted by a third party, the role in a TV commercial that it leads to and her job as an *au pair* mirror the circumstances that led to Ege becoming Miss Norway, her early career in Norwegian TV ads and her first job in the UK.

The success of the film saw Ege do 'a spate of newspaper and magazine articles, pictures, radio and television interviews, promotional tours . . . [and receive] . . . the star treatment generally' (Firth 1970: 23), which resulted in her becoming popular with the readers of Britain's daily newspapers and glossy tabloid magazines. Indeed, *The Money Programme* (1970) reported that 'in two years the amount of press coverage given to Julie Ege has risen to more than 2,000 column inches, 166 feet or 55 yards . . . the press has been her best friend'. 'Ubiquitous' was a term that was often used in conjunction with Ege at this time and it seems clear that promotion and publicity – and the attendant hard work – played a key role in her initial cultification. At this time the British press were keen to push Ege's Scandinavian heritage and fun personality while also making mention of her role as Inga the *au pair* and, in some ways, their approach spoke to and exploited contemporaneous British male fantasies about sexual stereotypes and the perceived exotic nature of young women from overseas, as exemplified by the content of Val Guest's British sex comedy *Au Pair Girls* (1972).

Kate Egan and Sarah Thomas observe that

> Stardom is conventionally drawn as a signifier of mainstream appeal, an ultimate marker of commodification within capitalistic consumer culture, reliant on a mass media circulation of images . . . based around marketing rhetoric, artifice and the manufacture of star personae. (2013: 2)

Before long Ege was a highly recognizable and popular celebrity-cum-media personality whose star persona – as mediated and promoted by the British press and glossy tabloid magazines – clearly appealed to the British public and, as *The Money Programme* (1970) reported, a pointed decision was made to exploit her popularity and turn her into a full-blown film star of the 'sex symbol' variety. However, when *The Money Programme* (1970) asked Ege, 'Do you want to be a big star?' her response was 'I can't think like that . . . I've been very lucky . . . it's been mostly luck . . . I have done my best . . . [maybe] if I have the talent . . . I must say "if" because I don't know, you know'. Ege's continued modesty and the increasingly self-deprecating and humorous way that she chose to talk about and assess her work is something that differentiated her from most aspiring actors of the time and – in addition to endearing her to the British public – I would argue that it was a key personality trait that played a part in her ongoing cultification.

Talks were underway for Ege to appear in Roy Boulting's Peter Sellars vehicle *There's a Girl in My Soup* (1970) when the narrative of the talent contest entered her life once again and in June 1970 she was unveiled as the much publicized 'winner of a world-wide talent search conducted by Columbia Pictures and Sir James Carreras [of Hammer Films] to find the screen's new sex symbol for the seventies' (*Kine Weekly* 1970: 13). As per the stipulations of the contest, Ege's first role for Hammer was as Nala the cave girl in Don Chaffey's prehistoric drama *Creatures the World Forgot* (1971) (*Creatures* hereafter). The film was meant to do for the contest's winner what Chaffey's *One Million Years B.C.* (1966) had done for Raquel Welch but *Creatures* was a very different film. Ege told *The Money Programme* (1970), 'I don't think stone age people were speaking at all so we were grunting, making noises... I think it's going to be very good because it's like a documentary with the right outfits. There was nothing glamorous about it'. Unfortunately, Ege's astute observations go some way to explaining why the film was a box office failure.

Creatures is a brave and mature piece of filmmaking in many regards but its styling and content only served to alienate its intended popular cinema audiences. Watching the film *is* akin to watching a documentary about primitive tribes. But with no documentarian voice-over in place to explain the tribal hierarchies or the significance of the tribes' grunts, rituals and other actions, *Creatures* demands a lot of patience, commitment, concentration and cognitive work from its viewers. In a departure from Hammer's previous prehistoric films, *Creatures* is also historically accurate in as much as it is not enlivened by any dinosaur action. Furthermore, the film features a distinct lack of 'Hammer glamour'. Ege recalled that she was 'deglamourized for a more naturalistic look with mud smeared on my body and an old unflattering fur bikini' (Solberg 1997). Also of note is the fact that Ege does not appear until an hour into the film and when she does she is sporting a dark wig that makes her almost unrecognisable. As such, Ege's star persona – as generated by her appearances in *Every Home Should Have One*, the British press and glossy tabloid magazines – was completely missing from *Creatures*.

Publicity duties for *Creatures* took Ege to the United States but she recalled that her 'refusal to go along with the long line of suggestive proposals from Hollywood producers prevented' her 'from pulling a larger deal with the American film industry' and she decided to stay in England where she 'felt more at home' (Solberg 1997). Since the British film industry was seemingly only interested in producing horror films and sex comedies at this time, this decision would inevitably take Ege deeper into a world of offbeat films that were destined to become classified as cult movies. The publicity for *Creatures* did serve to further enhance Ege's already considerable public profile in the UK, resulting in crossovers to TV where she appeared as a guest on a number of quiz shows, celebrity panel shows and variety shows. And in an article for *Variety* that set out to list and predict which current British actors might become major stars, Jack Pitman was compelled to add 'if measured by press-clippings there's Julie Ege, onetime Miss Norway and easily Britain's current cheesecake champ' (1971: 31). Ege's star persona was a bit more in evidence in Bob Kellett's comedic and saucy Frankie Howerd vehicle *Up Pompeii* (1971) – which was on release in the UK at roughly the same time as *Creatures* – but in this historical romp her voice was dubbed by another actor in a very obvious way. *Up Pompeii* was a box office success but the dubbing issue meant that – just as with *Creatures* – Ege's star persona and performance were not fully mediated to the film's audience.

Ege rounded 1971 out with an appearance in the 'Gluttony' episode of Graham Stark's portmanteau comedy film *The Magnificent 7 Deadly Sins*. With her star persona fully in evidence here, Ege delivers a perfectly pitched performance as Ingrid, the head of a health food company who fails to seduce her advertising executive (Leslie Phillips) because he cannot stop thinking about unhealthy foodstuffs. The same can be said of her turn as Armitage's (Donald Sinden) glamorous and amorous wife Utta in Jim Clark's eccentric espionage spoof *Rentadick* (1972). In some ways Ege carries the film since it is her intermittent but perfectly delivered exposition that enables the viewer to make sense of *Rentadick*'s completely crazed but somehow compelling narrative. *The Money Programme* (1970) had suggested that Ege might possess 'the talent of a sexy comedienne' while her boyfriend for much of her time in England, the Beatles' associate Tony Bramwell, recalled that 'she was very funny and completely got British humour. That made her a natural for those sort of films' (Buckland 2008). Both assertions are ably supported by Ege's comedy film work but she was appearing in offbeat productions that were not attracting huge audiences. However, she did remain famous enough to play herself in a cameo in Bob Kellett's *The Alf Garnett Saga* (1972). The satirical scene in question opens with the arch-bigot and hypocrite Garnett (Warren Mitchell) complaining about the number of Europeans that he perceives to be 'swarming' into the UK and the prospect of Britain joining the EEC. But when Garnett inadvertently ingests illicit drugs, one of his subsequent hallucinations involves him happily making love to Julie Ege, a Norwegian currently residing in London.

One key aspect of Ege's popularity in the UK – and possibly her cultification more generally – was the enthusiastic way that she made inroads into so many areas of British popular culture. Ege recorded a version of John Lennon's 'Love' in 1971 but in her by now familiar self-deprecating manner she told *Photoplay Film Monthly* 'I can't sing at all . . . . I tried it for fun' (1971: 12). When the satirical magazine *Punch* (1971) did a 'Punch goes Playboy' issue Ege was chosen to be the cover model. A cursory examination of Getty Images' (2022) holdings reveals pictures of Ege presenting Jethro Tull with a gold disc on 22 February 1971, helping the British to celebrate 'Decimalisation Day' at some point in the same month, presenting an award to the winner of the European Speedway Championship (Ivan Mauger) at Wembley Stadium on 22 August 1971, compering the Wembley Festival of Music (featuring The Faces, The New York Dolls and The Pink Fairies) on 29 October 1972 and helping the ventriloquist Ray Alan unveil his newly aged Lord Charles dummy on 1 April 1974.

Ege's link up with Ray Alan is indicative of an association that she fostered with Britain's 'old guard' of popular musical hall stars and current variety entertainers. For example, *Television Mail* reports how Ege 'transported a £15,000 cheque' for charity at a NABS 'Celebrity Stag Night' held at the Hilton Ballroom where Tommy Trinder also 'raised thousands of pounds with an auction' (1972: 8). And Ege was on the judging panel and awarded prizes, alongside Arthur Askey, to the winners of the finals of the St. George's Taverns £5,000 Pub Entertainer of the Year Contest, which was held at The Empire Ballroom in Leicester Square (Hepple 1973: 6). The following year *Variety* reported that Ege and Frankie Howerd were 'heading out as a combo to entertain British troops down in Cyprus' (1974: 11). 1974 was a pivotal year for Ege as she appeared in the three cult horror films which genre fans remember her for: *7 Golden Vampires*, Freddie Francis's *Craze* and Jack Cardiff's *The Mutations*. Art imitated life for Ege once again in *The Mutations* when she found herself playing Hedi, a Scandinavian student studying in London.

It turns out that Ege's subsequent 'disappearance' had no great mystery at its centre. Not impressed with the kinds of film scripts that were now being sent her way (Solberg 1997), Ege took to the stage and starred in *The Mating Game* 'at the Windmill, Great Yarmouth, for the summer season' of 1976 (*Stage and Television Today* 1976: 1) before returning to Norway when she was invited to join a regional theatre company there (Solberg 1997). Ege brought the curtain down on her theatre career in 1978 following a run as Columbia in an Oslo production of *The Rocky Horror Show*. A mother of two young daughters, Ege was now looking for a more stable lifestyle and elected to live a quiet life by choice (Solberg 1997). By the mid-1980s she was fulfilling a childhood dream by studying to become a nurse, but a cancer diagnosis led to a struggle with the disease that lasted twenty-two years (Buckland 2008).

Ege continued working as a nurse and the sporadic appearances that she made in the British press over those twenty-two years tended to be feature articles about her illness that she hoped would 'help other women' and prevent them from suffering 'in silence or isolation' (Buckland 2008). In 1997 a contented Ege told Niels Solberg 'I love my new life and career . . . Norway offers a pace of life that suits me perfectly. As for my film career, I had fun while it lasted and met some wonderful people' (Solberg 1997). Sadly, Ege became the focus of attention for the British press for one last time when they published obituaries following the announcement of her untimely death on 29 April 2008. Her daughter Joanna's own tribute read 'She was a nurse and loved the job. You would never have known she had this rich, glamorous past if you'd met her. You would have just been struck by her energy, her smile and her determination to help people' (Buckland 2008).

An analysis of *The Legend of the 7 Golden Vampires*

Although Van Helsing is a 'foreign physician from the Netherlands' in Bram Stoker's source novel, Joseph Chang observes that the Van Helsing played by Peter Cushing in Hammer's *Dracula* (Terence Fisher, 1958) 'is without a shadow of a doubt a quintessential British gentleman – whether in speech, appearance, or thoughts – with all traces of foreignness eradicated (perhaps except the name itself)' (2022: 84). And the same can undoubtedly be said of Cushing's Van Helsing in the subsequent Hammer films that the character appeared in. As such, Professor Lawrence Van Helsing can be read as symbol that readily represents Britain in *7 Golden Vampires*.

Britain's reduced standing on the world stage during the early 1970s is inferred during Van Helsing's introductory scene, where he is shown giving a lecture on vampirism at the University of Chungking. Rather than being an all-knowing and all resourceful great white saviour figure, Lawrence is presented as a man who is out of his depth and in need of local assistance and regional expertise. He admits that he needs the Faculty of Chinese History's 'help', their 'knowledge', their 'facilities' and access to their 'documents' and he expresses a willingness to

Figure 2.1 *The Legend of the 7 Golden Vampires*: Professor Lawrence Van Helsing (Peter Cushing) is left humiliated and emasculated when Chinese academics scoff at his theories about vampires.

work alongside them as an equal. But rather than being flattered by the esteemed Westerner's interest in their culture and his admission that he needs their help, the Chinese academics rudely dismiss Lawrence's theories as fairy tales and he is left humiliated when they walk out of his lecture en masse (see Figure 2.1). As they leave an emasculated Lawrence is reduced to begging them to take him seriously but his pleas are simply ignored.

A similar theme can be detected in the film's next scene wherein the British trade consul (Robert Hanna) tells Van Helsing's son Leyland (Robin Stewart), 'These are difficult times. As the British trade consul in Chungking, I have to warn compatriots to tread carefully. I'm only allowed to remain here by the grace of the local authorities. Any embarrassment could destroy all the goodwill I've built up'. And in reference to the villainous tong leader Leung Hon's (Han Chen Wang) presence at his gathering, the trade consul explains, 'Unfortunately I cannot pick and choose my guests these days'. These two scenes are suggestive of the post-colonial world of the early 1970s; a world in which Britain and her representatives were no longer automatically respected and revered in overseas territories; a world in which the UK's trade relations with other countries were particularly precarious and seemingly of more importance to Britain than her trading partners; and a world in which Britain was being forced to accept that she was no longer an international superpower.

Interestingly, Leyland shares a name with the then failing car manufacturer British Leyland. Created through the merger of British Motor Holdings and Leyland Motors in 1968, the British Leyland Motor Corporation was a flagship motor industry giant that soon became synonymous with the UK's economic woes and trade problems during the early 1970s due to numerous clashes between the company's management and its workers with regard to how a number of its divisions should best be run (Shropshire Star 2018). The fiscal embarrassments and management-level incompetency associated with Britain's manufacturing sector and wider economy during the early 1970s are also encoded within Lawrence. When Hsi Ching asks Lawrence to travel to the remote village of Ping Kwei in order to assist in vanquishing the Golden Vampires, the Professor tells him, 'An expedition into the hinterland would require a small army of bearers and guards. And quite a lot of money, for equipment and so forth. I have very little [money] I'm afraid'. But the vampire hunter is not only impoverished financially, his project management skills are found to be lacking too. The guards that he mentioned are not actually needed thanks to the martial arts skills that Hsi Ching and his siblings possess and the 'small army of bearers' that Lawrence factored into his hypothetical plans amounts to just two men in reality.

Vanessa Buren is another character who appears to be loaded with interesting symbolic meaning. I. Q. Hunter observes that Vanessa's Scandinavian heritage is 'a coded reference' that would chime with the idea that 'Scandinavia meant unbridled sexuality' in the minds of contemporaneous British cinemagoers (2002: 142). But while Vanessa is an attractive woman, and has a liberated outlook, she does not really do anything that would support this stereotypical reading of her character. Vanessa has to be Scandinavian in order for the film to accommodate Ege's Norwegian accent but as a character she is represented with dignity. Vanessa's period clothing is not designed to titillate the viewer and she remains clothed throughout (which is of significance when it is considered that Ege had been saddled with nude bathtub scenes in the same year's *The Mutations* and the previous year's *Not Now Darling* [Ray Cooney and David Croft 1973]).

However, given the nature of the public debates about the pros and cons of Britain's recent membership of the EEC, which were still raging in the UK at the time of the film's release, Vanessa, her accent, her confidence and boldness, the wealth that she controls and her ability to get things done might represent a vaguely sketched image of contemporaneous 'Europeanness'. Indeed, if Lawrence symbolizes an emasculated, financially impoverished and poorly managed Britain, it should follow that the liberated Vanessa could be a symbolic stand in for Europe. Certainly, the sense of economic affluence and stability, fiscal efficiency and market savvy know-how that pro-EEC Britons hoped to benefit from when Britain joined the trading block in 1973 can be detected in Vanessa.

Conversely, her cocksure and pushy attitude and liberated outlook could equally play to the fears of those Britons who were concerned that Britain's continued membership of the EEC would lead to a loss of sovereignty and moral decline.

While speculation of this nature remains interesting, it must be stressed that Vanessa should be read first and foremost as being a representative of the emergent strong and independent women whose demands for equality were posing a threat to the norms of patriarchal society in Britain at the time of the film's production. Indeed, the foreign policy and economics-related crises of masculinity that were crippling the British nation state during the early 1970s had been further exacerbated by the activities of the Women's Liberation Movement, the emergence of second wave feminism and public debates about sexual equality (Forster and Harper 2010). Furthermore, it can be argued that – whether by accident or design – a variety of British films from the early 1970s captured the zeitgeist in this regard. Peter Hutchings points to the reactionary appearance of a new type of female antagonist in Roy Ward Baker's 1970 Hammer film, *The Vampire Lovers* (1993: 160). Here a sexually aggressive lesbian vampire, Carmilla (Ingrid Pitt), is presented as 'a sexual liberator of females trapped within patriarchal households and definitions of the feminine' who also possesses the normally masculine attribute of free movement (Hutchings 1993: 160–1). Hutchings detects 'the wider rejection and casting out' of male authority figures in Hammer's early 1970s films more generally (1993: 159) while specifically noting a recurrent narrative-editing pattern in *The Vampire Lovers* that presents shots of a male character looking at a female character, followed by images of the male character in a state of powerlessness or inadequacy (1993: 163).

Hutchings's (1993) observations can be readily applied to a range of other British films from this period and examples would include Roy Ward Baker's *Dr Jekyll & Sister Hyde* (1971) and Robert Fuest's *The Final Programme* (1973). These films – in common with *The Vampire Lovers* – all feature strong and active female characters who upset patriarchal order before being demonized and then tamed or punished in some way at their film's end. As such, their narratives play like exercises in wish fulfilment that are designed to soothe the fears and anxieties of an emasculated patriarchal society. And Vanessa's story arc in *7 Golden Vampires* very much follows this pointed agenda. Film scholars are familiar with Laura Mulvey's (1975) work on classical Hollywood cinema and her observations regarding the patterns of taming and punishment that are visited upon the active and unruly female characters found in American films from cinema's golden age. However, as I have discussed elsewhere (Broughton

2016), these narrative patterns had also been a long-standing feature of gothic literature, where they were found in two distinct variants that would subsequently appeal to the ideological needs of male horror film makers.

The first variant features active heroines who are allowed to act like protagonists and pursue adventures in which their experiences are central to – and indeed serve to drive – the unfolding narrative. However, this variant usually features a conservative ending in which traditional gender boundaries are restored when the heroine acquires a new purpose in life through marriage (Punter and Byron 2004: 279). In essence, these unruly females are being tamed when the bonds of matrimony result in them being coded as the weaker partner while societal norms ensure that they lose whatever sense of agency and independence they might have once possessed. The second variant occurs when there is an agenda to demonize and punish female characters in a more obvious and heavy-handed way. Here female characters are presented as monstrous antagonists. And in the instances where a female monster is allowed to enjoy narrative focus and agency, traditional gender boundaries are eventually restored by the complete destruction of the monster (Hutchings 1993: 163).

As will be discussed, Vanessa is eventually caught in the double bind of being an active and independent woman and a monstrous female. As if this was not enough to seal her fate, she also initiates an interracial romance with Hsi Ching along the way. In terms of classical Hollywood cinema and popular cinema more generally, until relatively recently interracial love affairs were deemed to be problematic and narrative punishment of some description would typically be visited upon one or both of the participants. For example, Edward Buscombe notes that while love affairs between white males and Native American females could be portrayed with some degree of sympathy in American Westerns, Hollywood filmmakers found love affairs between Native American men and white women 'altogether more difficult' to sanction (2006: 127). Interestingly, direct parallels can be drawn between Buscombe's (2006) observations concerning the representation of romance, race and gender seen in American Westerns and the equivalent representations found in *7 Golden Vampires*. Indeed, Hsi Ching's relationship with Vanessa is doomed, while Leyland's relationship with Hsi Ching's sister, Mei Kwei (Shih Szu), is allowed to develop.

Hunter argues that Vanessa is not 'demonised for her independence and sexuality' (2002: 142) but much negative and sexist comment is made about her independence by the film's white British male protagonists. For example, the

British trade consul tells a clearly enamoured Leyland that the recently widowed and well-provided for Vanessa is 'on a world tour. Actually travelling alone. Can't say I approve. Dash it all, they'll want the vote next'. And when Vanessa offers to finance the trip to Ping Kwei on the condition that she goes along too, an outraged Lawrence responds, 'It is quite out of the question. A woman couldn't possibly make such a hazardous trip . . . I really must protest'. Leyland, who had exasperatedly referred to Vanessa as a 'totally emancipated female' earlier in the evening, now resignedly calms his father's protests with the words, 'It won't do the slightest bit of good . . . the lady has a will of her own' (see Figure 2.2).

The narrative-editing pattern that Hutchings found in *The Vampire Lovers*, wherein shots of a male character looking at a female character are followed by images of the male character in a state of powerlessness or inadequacy (1993: 163) can also be found in *7 Golden Vampires*. By mapping Hutchings's (1993) observations onto the scene where Vanessa insists on financing – and being a member of – the expedition to Ping Kwei, we can detect instances where she leaves both Lawrence and Leyland in a state of inadequacy. This ability to make the representatives of white British patriarchal order feel inadequate is an early indication that Vanessa will be punished before the film's end. However, more crucial than this is Vanessa's function as a character who is responsible for revealing – and providing reminders of – Leyland's emasculated nature. When Leung Hon offers to escort Vanessa home from the British trade consul's gathering, Leyland intervenes in a chivalrous manner and indicates that he has already offered to escort her home. When Leyland is informed that he has

Figure 2.2 *The Legend of the 7 Golden Vampires*: The wealthy Scandinavian traveller Vanessa Buren (Julie Ege) is a 'totally emancipated female' whose earrings alone are 'worth a fortune'.

caused a now angry Hon to lose face he is forced into the embarrassing and emasculating position of having to ask the trade consul to provide a further escort to protect both himself and Vanessa.

Leyland's sense of embarrassment and emasculation plumbs new depths on the journey home. In the first instance his interest in the exotic Scandinavian appears to be rebuffed when a frank talking Vanessa tells him, 'I'm not a retiring English rose.... I don't take to blushing and I certainly don't faint away at the first improper suggestion.... I think you might like your women more fragile, perhaps. Oh, dear, I am embarrassing you. Let's change the subject'. In the second instance, when Hon's thugs attack and kill the men who make up their escort, Leyland is initially powerless to act in the couple's defence. When Hsi Ching's brothers Kwei and Ta subsequently intervene on their behalf, Leyland merely stands and watches in awe. When he is eventually drawn into the fighting his first instinct is to ungracefully rugby tackle one of the assailants to the ground. However, his subsequent and unconvincing adoption of a Marquis of Queensbury British boxing stance proves to be completely ineffectual against his assailant's Chinese kung fu moves and he has to be rescued from impending doom by Kwei. Here the white British patriarchal order that Leyland represents is being further emasculated by the actions of both good and bad oriental men. And, in a reversal of usual gender roles, when the fighting is over it is Vanessa who runs to Leyland and comforts him while asking, 'Are you all right?'

Leyland is also left wanting when the expedition to Ping Kwei gets underway. When Hon's army of tongs attack he again watches from the side lines while Hsi Ching and his six brothers engage the villains in combat. He is further emasculated when Mei Kwei throws herself into the violent melee and employs her impressive martial arts skills to despatch numerous tongs. When Leyland does eventually act he uses his pistol to shoot an approaching tong but this action has the disastrous effect of making two of the expedition's horses bolt for freedom. Having been spurned by Vanessa, Leyland soon turns his romantic attentions towards Mei Kwei. Interestingly, the scene in which Leyland makes his feelings about Mei Kwei known is a scene in which she has been returned to her normative gender position: she is washing the expedition's dishes after dinner as opposed to killing villainous tongs.

Here the oriental Mei Kwei is captured in a shot that represents both Leyland and Vanessa's point of view, a scenario that necessarily evokes the colonial gaze of the West upon the East. This scenario also confirms that Vanessa possesses the power of the gaze more generally, a power that Mulvey (1975) indicates is normally considered to be a masculine attribute. At Vanessa's suggestion, Leyland moves to assist Mei Kwei with washing the dishes and thus – by dint of being directed by a woman and doing what was then seen as 'women's work' – he is emasculated yet again. At this point, Vanessa changes position and Hsi Ching becomes the erotic object of her gaze. By looking at him in this way, Vanessa has again adopted the kind of masculine viewing position that Mulvey's (1975) work details and her subsequent act of physically moving to join him with romantic intentions (instead of waiting for him to act upon her) is a masculine action too. Vanessa is transgressing traditional gender boundaries to such an extent that taming or punishment of some kind can be the only logical outcome for her.

It has already been established that Leyland is too emasculated to tame Vanessa by drawing her into a normative heterosexual relationship. It simply would not be believable for Vanessa to be presented as the weaker partner in a relationship with Leyland. By contrast, the brave and masculine martial artist Hsi Ching has the makings of a much more plausible suitor for Vanessa. He could surely tame her through marriage and he would be believable when presented as the stronger partner in their relationship. Unfortunately for Vanessa, we have seen that popular filmmakers at this time were unlikely to bless an interracial relationship involving a white woman with a positive outcome. Indeed, Hunter observes that *7 Golden Vampires* chooses to back away from 'depicting sexual relations between a Chinese man and a white western woman, implying that such transgressive liaisons lead to tragedy' (2002: 143). As such there are no avenues by which Vanessa can be tamed via a normative romance and marriage.

Thus, there is only one way that Vanessa's story can end. In the cruellest narrative contrivance of any Hammer film, Vanessa is bitten by one of the Golden Vampires at the height of the film's final battle and she is transformed into a monstrous female, the type of strong and unruly female that cannot be tamed, only destroyed. When Hsi Ching comes to her aid, she bites him and he is compelled to destroy her. In the act of doing so he forces her backwards onto a protruding wooden spike and so an act of penetration occurs between the two. This symbolic consummation of their love – and the fact that he will soon transform into a vampire too – necessarily means that Hsi Ching must be punished too. When he bravely pulls himself onto the wooden spike that is protruding from Vanessa's chest the fact that he is penetrated by a phallic symbol that is appended to a woman serves to emasculate him in death. With the threat of the strong white woman now erased, the formerly emasculated duo of Lawrence and Leyland Van Helsing find that their sense of masculinity has become somewhat invigorated. And it becomes invigorated further when more of the film's true markers of traditional notions of masculinity – Hsi Ching's brave band of oriental brothers – are killed in combat with the Golden Vampires and their undead minions.

Indeed, the stage is soon set for the film's chief symbol of white British patriarchy to save the day. Mei Kwei is kidnapped by the final Golden Vampire and Leyland attempts to rescue her from the vampires' temple. Leyland himself soon needs rescuing too and his father duly arrives, flanked by Hsi Ching's two remaining brothers. Driven by the patriarchal instinct to protect his offspring, Lawrence grabs a spear from one of the brothers and despatches the vampire that is threatening his son's life while the now emasculated brothers simply look on in awe. Hunter notes that the film ends with Mei Kwei 'presumably in some relationship with Leyland' (2002: 143). Since we have already seen the pair kissing and making romantic overtures towards each other, that relationship can only be a normative heterosexual relationship in which Mei Kwei is necessarily tamed and presented as the weaker partner. To this end, when Leyland departs, he has been fully masculinized: his right arm is protectively wrapped around a now weakened Mei Kwei and her two brothers follow on behind the pair in a deferential manner. As such the scene in the vampires' temple effectively shows the film's symbols of white British masculinity finally outperforming, dominating and taming the film's symbolic representations of a strong and unruly Orient. Here the symbols of Britain abroad suggest that the country has the qualities needed to be a mighty imperial power once more.

Lawrence is left in the temple alone and he soon has to deal with Dracula (John Forbes-Robertson), who has taken on the form of the Golden Vampires' High Priest, Kah (Shen Chan). When he allows himself to be goaded into transforming back into his true form, Dracula says the following words: 'Right, Van Helsing. You will once more see my face. . . . Behold, Van Helsing. Look on me now'. As previously noted, Mulvey (1975) deems the gaze to be a masculine attribute and the act of looking to be a masculine action. When Dracula demands that Lawrence looks at him, he becomes the object of Lawrence's masculine gaze and thus takes on a feminine position that has an emasculating effect. As if to emphasize this, Dracula's face actually sports what looks like feminizing make-up. Indeed, Hunter describes this Dracula as being 'a lurid caricature of "decadence" – a rouged and lipsticked old queen' (2002: 144). Thus we are not too surprised when Lawrence subsequently despatches his arch-enemy with relative ease.

And so the film ends with its representatives of white British patriarchal order fully masculinized and in completely dominant positions. Vanessa, the confident and wealthy symbol of Europeanness, and Dracula, the aberrant and immoral symbol of a darker threat (perhaps a Cold War inflected threat given his East European origins and his alliance with China's dark forces), have been destroyed and erased. Strong women (as represented by Vanessa and Mei Kwei) have been punished and tamed. And the power of oriental masculinity (as represented by Hsi Ching and his brothers) has been severely diminished.

Conclusion

It is possible to read the narrative of *7 Golden Vampires* as an exercise in wish fulfilment. In the first instance, the film allegorically acknowledges many of the real-world circumstances – Britain's loss of superpower status on the world stage, her economic woes, her uneasy relationship with and mixed attitudes towards Europe and the EEC and the rise of second wave feminism and strong women – that had led to the British nation state suffering a series of severe crises of masculinity during the years leading up to the early 1970s. However, Don Houghton's pointed screenplay subsequently works hard to ensure that any fears and anxieties prompted by these real-world circumstances are negated and banished from the contemporaneous viewer's mind by allowing *7 Golden Vampires*' fictitious representatives of white British patriarchal order to confront head on – and tame or destroy – any cultural or gender specific entity that might serve to question their innate sense of superiority and worth. When the Van Helsings take the packet boat back to England, Britannia will be ruling the waves once more and all will be well with the world.

Bibliography

Ahmed, Ahmed L. M. 'The Social Background of Brexit'. *Copernican Journal of Finance and Accounting* 7, no. 4 (2018): 9–29.

Broughton, Lee. *The Euro-Western: Reframing Gender, Race and the 'Other' in Film.* London: Bloomsbury Academic, 2016.

Buckland, Danny. 'From sex Symbol to Angel of the Wards'. *Sunday Express*, 11 May 2008. Available online at: https://www.express.co.uk/expressyourself/44120/From-sex-symbol-to-angel-of-the-wards (accessed 12 June 2022).

Buscombe, Edward. *'Injuns!': Native Americans in the Movies*. London; Reaktion Books, 2006.

Chang, Joseph. 'Reviving the Undead: The Resurrection of the British Empire in *Dracula* (1958)'. *Horror Homeroom: Classic Horror*, Special Issue 6, Summer 2022. Available online at: https://www.horrorhomeroom.com/special-issue-6/ (accessed 20 December 2022).

Egan, Kate and Sarah Thomas. 'Introduction: Star-Making, Cult-Making and Forms of Authenticity'. In *Cult Film Stardom: Offbeat Attractions and Processes of Cultification*, edited by Kate Egan and Sarah Thomas, 1–17. Basingstoke: Palgrave Macmillan, 2013.

Firth, Vincent. 'Every Home Should have this One', *Monthly Film Review* 20, no. 7 (July, 1970): 23–5.

Forster, Laurel and Sue Harper. 'Introduction'. In *British Culture and Society in the 1970s: The Lost Decade*, edited by Laurel Forster and Sue Harper, 1–12. Newcastle upon Tyne: Cambridge Scholars Publishing, 2010.

Getty Images. 'Julie Ege'. 2022. Available online at: https://www.gettyimages.co.uk/photos/julie-ege (accessed 2 December 2022).

Hepple, Peter. 'St. George's Night in Leicester Square'. *The Stage and Television Today* 4811 (28 June 1973): 6.

Hunter, I. Q. 'Hammer Goes East: A Second Glance at *The Legend of the 7 Golden Vampires*'. In *Shocking Cinema of the Seventies*, edited by Xavier Mendik, 138–46. Hereford: Noir Publishing, 2002.

Hutchings, Peter. *Hammer and Beyond: The British Horror Film*. Manchester: Manchester University Press, 1993.

Kine Weekly. 'Columbia, Hammer Unveil a New Star', *Kine Weekly* 633, no. 3272 (27 June 1970): 13.

Meikle, Denis. *A History of Horrors: The Rise and Fall of the House of Hammer*, Revised edn. Lanham: Scarecrow Press, 2009.

The Money Programme. Series 6, Episode 3. BBC 2, 15 October 1970.

Mulvey, Laura. 'Visual Pleasure and Narrative Cinema'. *Screen* 16, no. 3 (Autumn 1975): 6–18.

Peary, Danny. *Cult Movie Stars*. London: Simon & Schuster, 1991.

Photoplay Film Monthly. 'Julie Cuts a Record'. *Photoplay Film Monthly*, April 1971: 12.

Pitman, Jack. 'Whose for Stardom in '71? Only Glenda Made It Last Year'. *Variety* 263, no. 1 (19 May 1971): 31.

Punch. 10–16 November 1971: cover.

Punter, David and Glennis Byron. *The Gothic*. Oxford: Blackwell Publishing, 2004.

Sandbrook, Dominic. *The 70s*. BBC 2, 16 April–14 May 2012.

Shropshire Star. 'Merger that Killed Our Car Industry'. *Shropshire Star*, 17 January 2018. Available online at: https://www.shropshirestar.com/news/business/2018/01/17/merger-that-killed-our-car-industry/# (accessed 12 April 2022).

Solberg, Niels. 'Julie Ege: The Last of the Glamour Queens'. *Psychotronic Video* 24 (1997): 60–4. Available from: https://archive.org/stream/Psychotronic_Video_24/Psychotronic_Video_24_djvu.txt (accessed 20 August 2022).

The Stage and Television Today, 'David Gordon Produces the Good'. *The Stage and Television Today* 4968 (1 July 1976): 1.

Television Mail, 'NABS Boxing Benefit Makes £15,000'. *Television Mail* 681 (27 October 1972): 8.

Variety. 'Chatter: London'. *Variety* 276, no. 5 (11 September 1974): 77.

Weight, Richard. *Patriots: National Identity in Britain 1940–2000.* London: Macmillan, 2002.

Filmography

The Alf Garnett Saga (1972), [Film] Dir. Bob Kellett, UK: Columbia Pictures Corporation / Associated London Films.

Au Pair Girls (1972), [Film] Dir. Val Guest, UK: Kenneth Shipman Productions / Tigon Pictures.

Craze (1974), [Film] Dir. Freddie Francis, UK: Harbour Productions Limited.

Creatures the World Forgot (1971), [Film] Dir. Don Chaffey, UK: Hammer Films.

Dr. Jekyll & Sister Hyde (1971), [Film] Dir. Roy Ward Baker, UK: Hammer Films.

Dracula (1958), [Film] Dir. Terence Fisher, UK: Hammer Films.

Every Home Should Have One (1970), [Film] Dir. Jim Clark, UK: British Lion Films.

The Final Programme (1973), [Film] Dir. Robert Fuest, UK: Anglo-EMI Film Distributors / Goodtimes Enterprises / Gladiole.

The Legend of the 7 Golden Vampires (1974), [Film] Dir. Roy Ward Baker, UK / Hong Kong: Hammer Films / Shaw Brothers.

The Magnificent Seven Deadly Sins (1971), [Film] Dir. Graham Stark, UK: Tigon Pictures.

The Mutations (1974), [Film] Dir. Jack Cardiff, UK: Cyclone / Getty Pictures Corp.

Not Now Darling (1973), [Film] Dir. Ray Cooney and David Croft, UK: LMG Film Productions Limited / Sedgemoor Productions Ltd / Not Now Films.

One Million Years B.C. (1966), [Film] Dir. Don Chaffey, UK: Associated British Pathe / Hammer Films / Seven Arts Productions.

On Her Majesty's Secret Service (1969), [Film] Dir. Peter R. Hunt, UK: Eon Productions.

Rentadick (1972), [Film] Dir. Jim Clark, UK: David Paradine Productions / The Rank Organisation / Virgin Film Productions Limited.

Robbery (1967), [Film] Dir. Peter Yates, UK: Joseph E. Levine / Oakhurst Productions.

There's a Girl in My Soup (1970), [Film] Dir. Roy Boulting, UK: Columbia Pictures / Frankovich Productions / Ascot Productions.

Up Pompeii (1971), [Film] Dir. Bob Kellett, UK: Anglo-EMI / Associated London Films.

The Vampire Lovers (1970), [Film] Dir. Roy Ward Baker, UK: Hammer Films / Fantale Films.

3

Wandering the labyrinth of space-time and eternity in Stanley Kubrick's *The Shining*

Kamil Kościelski

Introduction

Stanley Kubrick was an artist who strove to develop the meaning of his movies on several different levels and who incorporated a range of cultural contexts in his work. His filmography is testimony to his erudition. It contains multiple references to literature, art and music. For example, numerous allusions to eighteenth-century art have been noted in *Barry Lyndon* (Stanley Kubrick, 1975) such as the comparison between Lady Lyndon (Marisa Berenson) and Miss Robinson as depicted by the painter Thomas Gainsborough (Jansen 1984: 162). Also well known is the reference to Jonathan Swift's *Gulliver's Travels* (1726) found in *Dr Strangelove* (Stanley Kubrick, 1964) (Calabrese 1985: 43). In Swift's piece 'Laputa' is the name of a flying island populated by scientists, while in Kubrick's movie it is a soviet military rocket base.

These examples illustrate a distinctive feature of Kubrick's signature artistic strategy. He allows his movies to be interpreted from conceptual points of view which often differ from the prima-facie story of the plot. As is usual within Kubrick films, he provides no explicit clues either about his own intentions or the connections he makes to other branches of the arts. He is a director who avoids literal interpretation of his movies. Kubrick himself claimed that

> for a movie or a play to say anything really truthful about life, it has to do so very obliquely, so as to avoid all pat conclusions and neatly tied-up ideas. The point of view it is conveying has to be completely entwined with a sense of life as it is, and has to be got across through a subtle injection into the audience's consciousness. Ideas which are valid and truthful are so multi-faceted that they don't yield themselves to frontal assault. The ideas have to be discovered by the

audience, and their thrill in making the discovery makes those ideas all the more powerful. (1960/1961: 14)

The Shining (Stanley Kubrick, 1980) begins with Jack Torrance (Jack Nicholson) taking the job of Winter caretaker at the remote Overlook Hotel. Isolated and inaccessible to tourists, Jack, his wife Wendy (Shelley Duvall) and their son Danny (Danny Lloyd) will be the only people living there and Jack hopes that the solitude will enable him to write a book. However, Jack soon starts receiving visits from the hotel's long-dead former employees. This chapter will argue that certain literary references found in *The Shining* can be used to make sense of the concept of time that the director chose to imbue the film with. Resolving Kubrick's uncanny treatment of the fourth dimension in *The Shining* may best be approached by a closer examination of the writings of Jorge Luis Borges, whom Kubrick mentioned in an interview about the film:

> In order to make people believe the story it's very important to place it in something that looks totally real, and to light it as if it were virtually a documentary film, with natural light coming from the light sources, rather than dramatic, phony lighting, which one normally sees in a horror film. I compare that with the way Kafka or Borges writes, you know, in a simple, non-baroque style, so that the fantastic is treated in a very everyday, ordinary way. (Foix 2013: 463)

Borges was an internationally acclaimed Argentine writer, poet and essayist whose works feature a multitude of personal philosophical reflections. The world as represented in Borges's writings appears suspended between dream and reality; a fantastical quality which led to his work having a great impact on the magic realism movement. Kubrick has clearly indicated that he was familiar with Borges's prose by comparing his own way of depicting reality with Borges's literary style. Furthermore, it should be noted that the motif of the labyrinth is an important theme in the Argentinian writer's works (Głowiński 1994: 154) as well as in Kubrick's film. Significantly, the motif of the labyrinth is not present in Stephen King's source novel, *The Shining* (2019).

Głowiński (1994) draws our attention to the labyrinthine nature of time in Borges's work; a significant theme which is possibly best exemplified by its prominent role in 'The Garden of Forking Paths' (Borges 2000a: 44–54). Głowiński's (1994) argumentation is crucial to understanding how *The Shining* and Borges's prose interrelate. Consequently, it is the most appropriate starting point for studying the conceptual coexistence of parallel worlds which begin to coalesce and intersect with each other as *The Shining*'s plot develops. Such an idea of time in Borges's works is excellently demonstrated in the following excerpt from 'The Garden of Forking Paths':

> Ts'ui Pen ... abandoned ... all in order to compose a book and a labyrinth.... the garden of forking paths was the chaotic novel.... *The Garden of Forking Paths* is an incomplete, but not false, image of the universe as conceived by Ts'ui Pen. Unlike Newton and Schopenhauer, your ancestor did not believe in a uniform and absolute time; he believed in an infinite series of times, a growing, dizzying web of divergent, convergent, and parallel times. That fabric of times that approach one another, fork, are snipped off, or are simply unknown for centuries, contains all possibilities. (Borges 2000a: 49–53)

In one of his essays 'A New Refutation of Time' Borges revealed his rejection of the notion of there being only one time; a time in which all facts would converge (2000b: 317–32). Borges's thoughts were based on Berkeley's and Hume's observations about the perception of reality (2000b: 317–32). They suggest that the world is first filtered by our senses and only then by our mind and so becomes a unique projection for every single one of us. So how – as these philosophers ask – can we attempt to speak about the existence of an absolute space; one which would not be based on a purely subjective perception of reality? Borges, guided by similar logic, asks, 'if time is a mental process, how can it be shared by countless, or even two different men?' (2000b: 322). This notion is given further credence within the world of physics by the observation that the 'theory of relativity put an end to the idea of absolute time' (Hawking 1988: 21). Borges also states that the idea of the refutation of time is present in many of his works (2000b: 318). According to Michal Głowiński, in Borges's work, a labyrinth 'is not ... only a spatial category, it refers also ... to time' which means that 'time can no longer be linear in nature, but becomes like space shaped by the pattern of a labyrinth' (1994: 205–6, author's translation).

The Shining is not the only Kubrick film that shows his interest in the idea that several time streams can co-exist and converge. For example, the closing 'Star Gate' scene of *2001: A Space Odyssey* (Stanley Kubrick, 1968) – which shows Bowman (Keir Dullea) travelling outside of time and space and the subsequent birth of a new kind of man (the so-called 'Star Child') – indicates that Kubrick did indeed share that way of perceiving time (Kuberski 2012: 47). Hence, this chapter will draw parallels between the contents of Borges's literary works and the perplexing events that unfold in *The Shining*, in order to offer a new understanding of Kubrick's representation of time in that film. Furthermore, the apparent coexistence of different time streams in *The Shining*, in turn, chimes with the theological idea of eternity. The chapter will argue that this concept informs aspects of *The Shining*'s main character's nature – especially his desires, aspirations and anxieties.

The labyrinthine nature of space-time

The encounter between Jack and Lloyd the bartender (Joe Turkel) in the hotel's Gold Room is a perplexing one. The scene may evoke the feeling that Jack is gradually going mad. This impression is reinforced when the barman mysteriously disappears (along with all the alcohol that was present) when Wendy enters the scene. The next indication of Jack's insanity may be the sequence in which Wendy discovers the continuous repetition of a single sentence ('All work and no play makes Jack a dull boy') in her husband's book manuscript. At this point in the film it seems logical to conclude that the mysterious and uncanny characters who keep appearing in the hotel are figments of Jack's deranged mind.

However, the conversation between Jack and Grady (Philip Stone) – the hotel's former caretaker – in the Gold Room's washroom is one of several elements which seemingly contradict the assumption that the Overlook's ghosts are merely products of Jack's imagination. Grady informs Jack that Danny has contacted Hallorann (Scatman Crothers) – the hotel's resting head chef – for help. But earlier events depicted onscreen suggest that it would be impossible for Jack to possess any knowledge of the actions taken by his son. Danny and Hallorann make telepathic contact when Jack is in room 237. On returning to the family quarters, Jack is informed by Wendy that Danny is still asleep. Then, during the conversation with his wife, Jack goes into a rage, leaves the room and after a while finds himself in the Gold Room, where he has his first encounter with Grady. Nothing in that sequence of events indicates that Jack could, at any time, have had any knowledge of any of the steps taken by Danny. Furthermore, he even poses the question to Grady about how Danny could have contacted Hallorann. There is no indication in the film that Jack and Wendy are aware of Danny's paranormal abilities. This all suggests that Grady exists outside of Jack's mind. Indeed, in a later scene where Jack is locked in a pantry, it is implied that Grady is the person who releases him. Thus the consequences of the actions of the Overlook's ghosts are too tangible to allow all of the strange events experienced there to be blamed on the alleged delusions of Jack.

It is worth mentioning that in the scene featuring Lloyd the barman, there is not even one single take from Jack's point of view. On the contrary, this subjective camera angle is something Kubrick deliberately seems to avoid. In the Gold Room Jack seems to be depicted in the direct line of sight of the barman who has suddenly appeared. When Lloyd is seen in the next shot, the camera noticeably moves behind Jack's back, but is still not aligned with his point of view. This refutes any hypothesis that the viewer sees the events in the Gold Room from Jack's perspective. When discussing this bar scene, Omar Calabrese makes allusions to separate 'possible worlds' which co-exist and intersect (1985: 38). To add to the complexity Jack also makes a comment about Lloyd being the 'Best goddamned bartender from Timbuktu to Portland, Maine. Or Portland, Oregon, for that matter'. This is uncanny and unsettling as it implies that the two men have actually met before.

Equally peculiar is the sudden appearance of Grady, who – according to Jack – is the ex-caretaker of the Overlook. The two characters encounter each other at the 1920s ball held in the Gold Room. A crucial point here is the change in Grady's first name. When Jack is interviewed by Ullman (Barry Nelson) – the general manager of the Overlook – at the beginning of the film, Grady is referred to as Charles and it is explained that Grady went mad during the Winter of 1970 and murdered his entire family before committing suicide. Later on, Jack recognizes Grady to be his predecessor and, surprisingly, calls him Delbert. In Stephen King's book there is no such plot point. A similarly strange detail is present in the film in relation to Grady's daughters. Ullman states that at the time of the tragedy they were aged eight and ten years old. Later on, however, they are presented as twins. According to the materials found in the Kubrick Archives, Grady's daughters are about twelve and are called Rose and Molly. The archival materials contain an excerpt from a fabricated newspaper article describing the tragedy in the Grady family which was probably prepared for use in the scrapbook, which Jack finds in both the book by King and in the movie by Kubrick (SK/15/2/2/1/4/5).

It would seem that Kubrick consciously decided to give these particular characters multiple identities. This idea, however, becomes less mysterious when we consider the concept of time described by one of the characters in Borges's 'The Garden of Forking Paths':

> In all fictional works, each time a man is confronted with several alternatives, he chooses one and eliminates the others; in the fiction of the almost inextricable

Ts'ui Pèn, he chooses – simultaneously – all of them. He creates, in this way, diverse futures, diverse times which themselves also proliferate and fork. Here, then, is the explanation of the novel's contradictions. . . . In the work of Ts'ui Pèn all possible outcomes occur. . . . This network of times which approached one another, forked, broke off, or were unaware of one another for centuries, embraces all possibilities of time. We do not exist in the majority of these times; in some you exist, and not I; in others I, and not you; in others both of us. In the present one, which a favourable fate has granted me, you have arrived at my house; in another, while crossing the garden, you found me dead; in still another, I utter these same words, but I am a mistake, a ghost. (2000a: 51–3)

Borges's piece assumes the existence of separate and varied identities for the same person depending upon the particular time stream that they find themselves in. Knowing this short story, it becomes easier to justify Grady's uncanny name change. It also makes it less problematic to explain how Grady appears at the ball in the 1920s as a waiter and why Jack recognizes him to be the caretaker of the Overlook who died in 1970. Nor is it problematic any more to answer the question why, according to his supposed predecessor, it had always been Jack who was the caretaker of the hotel. Grady initially contradicts the fact that he had murdered his own family. As the conversation progresses, however, he makes a rather euphemistic comment about how he had to 'correct' his daughters because one of them had almost burnt down the hotel. He also mentions that his wife tried to stop him, which was the reason why she too needed to be 'corrected'. These seemingly minor instances of ambiguity present in the conversation refer to the actual dramatic events that took place at the Overlook. At first glance, it is hard to explain where the contradictions in Grady's utterances are rooted. An alternative identity for Grady may be interpreted as being analogous to a forking path in 'The Garden of Forking Paths'. Indeed, this notion of the labyrinthine nature of time clarifies the way in which the different lives of Jack Torrance, Grady and the people at the ball in the 1920s intersect.

The uncanny nature of time is at its most distinctive at the end of *The Shining*. The final scene reveals a photograph from 1921 that hangs in the hotel's lobby. It depicts Jack standing among other people. As the camera approaches the photograph, a piece of music called *Midnight, The Stars and You* (Woods, Campbell, Connelly 1934) gradually becomes louder and clearer making it seem as if the music is diegetic and is actually emanating from within the photograph. This very same song can also be heard in the scene of the ball in the Gold Room. Both uses of this song are surprising as, anachronistically, it was actually recorded in the 1930s (Gengaro 2014: 211). In the closing sequence of the movie the furniture in the hall is now covered with white canvas. Also the red sofa previously positioned under the pictures on the wall, has disappeared. Moreover, the photograph itself is different to the one that was hanging there in the earlier scenes of the film (as becomes apparent upon examining the scene when Hallorann returns to the Overlook). All of these alterations prevent us from establishing exactly when the closing scene actually took place. It is also difficult to determine which room of the Overlook the photograph was taken in. Logic might suggest the Gold Room where Jack attended the ball set in the 1920s. However, the layout of the interior in the picture does not support this conjecture. Moreover, Kubrick did not even take this picture, but with the use of photomontage, he substituted the original figure at its centre with an image of Jack Nicholson. This plot point does not feature in King's book and was entirely Kubrick's own idea which makes it even more curious. It reinforces the contention that the mysterious nature of space-time as depicted in the closing scene was fully intended by the director. Furthermore, the element of mystery regarding the fourth dimension confronts the viewer right from the start of the film. When Jack first arrives at the hotel, next to the board advertising the Gold Room there is a closed door behind which there is an oddly dressed couple wearing ball gowns and clothing from the 1920s. And the dresses worn by the ghostly twins seem to date from the same period even though we are told that they were murdered in 1970.

The labyrinths in *The Shining* and in Borges's prose both concern time and space. The obvious example of this is the inconsistent interior design found within the Overlook's rooms. There is a definite lack of co-ordination between the decor of Room 237, the apartment of the Torrance family, the Gold Room and the washroom where Jack talks to Grady. This variation of interior design is not coincidental. Indeed, it is also the case that some of the structural features of the hotel's rooms represent physical impossibilities, which suggests that they should not be able to exist side by side. This becomes evident when segments from the film are scrutinized and contrasted with each other.

In the initial part of the film Ullman gives Wendy and Jack a tour around the hotel. He also shows them the apartment they will live in. Before entering, Jack turns around to watch two young women leaving the hotel. On the one hand, his behaviour gives the viewer a sense of his personality; on the other hand, it draws our attention to the elements in the background. At the far end an EXIT sign indicating a fire escape is noticeable. However, as is demonstrated by different plot sequences later on, an exit in this location would not be plausible. If the EXIT is in the location that this early scene suggests, the stairs leading down from the fire escape would be situated right outside the window of the Torrance family's bathroom. When Danny uses the bathroom window to escape from the hotel there are no stairs present. Various inconsistencies in the set design were deliberately planned even during initial pre-production on *The Shining*. One of these was the Torrance family bathroom window, which, contrary to all logic, does face the fire escape (SK/15/2/3/3). The floor plan of the apartment occupied by the family also raises questions. The positioning of the windows suggests that at least on one side the Torrance family quarters do not adjoin any other room. However, based on the exterior shots of Danny escaping through the bathroom window, one can conclude the opposite. This sequence suggests that there are other hotel premises adjoining the suite. There are many more such inconsistencies to be found in the film. A meticulous analysis of the scene where Wendy finds the corpse of the murdered Hallorann leads to the conclusion that the existence of the window seen in Ullman's office is not physically possible (SK/15/2/3/3) (see Figure 3.1).

Another intriguing moment that is indicative of the coalescing of parallel worlds is when Hallorann shows Wendy and Danny around the kitchen. During the tour he leads them towards a walk-in freezer and grabs the handle intending to open the door, at which point a cut occurs. The following shot depicts the scene from inside the freezer. Here we see the door opening to the left, even

Figure 3.1 *The Shining*: The exact place where the window of Ullman's office should be located.

though in the previous shot it was clearly indicated that the door opened to the right. Hallorann then tells the pair about the contents of the freezer after which they make to leave it. The next cut takes us back to the corridor, and this time the door handle is consistent with the previous shot that depicted the inside of the freezer. And yet, in this new corridor shot, the mise-en-scene behind the characters differs from the mise-en-scene that was present before the camera cut to the inside of the walk-in-freezer. In this new shot, the camera is backing away, the characters follow it and suddenly, on the right, a table with various dishes on it comes into view. It is the same table that was previously located right by the door that Hallorann opened at the beginning of the scene.

The situation can be summarized quite simply – the chef wants to show the Torrance family the walk-in-freezer, grabs the door handle and suddenly the action is moved to a room across the corridor. The clear implication that it is engagement with such doors that enables passage between 'parallel worlds' is demonstrated by the following further scenarios in *The Shining*. Danny's attempt to turn the knob on the door of room 237 seems to prompt the spectral appearance of the twins who haunt him. Jack meets the mysterious barman Lloyd only after Danny enters the room. The situation grows even more uncanny after Jack himself walks into room 237. This is the crucial moment, when all 'paths' start to converge, which is proved during the scene of the ball in the Gold Room when the lives of people from different decades intersect. All of these space-time anomalies lead to the conclusion that the story is constructed in such a way as to give the impression that many possible worlds are coexisting simultaneously.

The labyrinth and eternity

The labyrinthine nature of time in *The Shining* echoes Borges's writings. The Argentinian author discusses the notion of the fourth dimension in his work in the context of the theological idea of eternity. Borges mentioned in an interview that his short story 'The Aleph' refers to this concept which, according to him can be described as the 'audacious hypothesis that there is an instant and in that instant converges the past . . . the present and the future' (Borges and Ferrari 2014: 18). The writer also shares the conviction that the ability to experience all times at once is 'a divine attribute' (Borges and Ferrari 2014: 18).

Borges's perception of time corresponds with Saint Augustine's (2006) concept of eternity in the eleventh book of *Confessions*. The philosopher contrasts the

Absolute with the insignificance of a man who is able to experience time only in a linear way (i.e. on a continuum of past, present and future). According to Saint Augustine (2006) the existence of God in his almightiness cannot be restricted to one certain point on a timeline since the greatness and prominence of the Maker cannot be limited temporally or spatially. The magnitude of God is defined by the Absolute being present at any given time, which means that He is eternal (Augustine 2006: 233–60). Therefore if, after dying, a man meets God in eternity, his soul is no longer bound by constraints of time. This is the reason why in many mythologies and beliefs the world of the dead is referred to as the realm of eternity.

The coexistence of different spaces and times in *The Shining* is an excellent illustration of the idea of eternity which took the form of a labyrinth in both Borges's and Kubrick's works. The concept of eternity was a principal interest of Kubrick ever since the early stages of the project. In a phone call to Stephen King he asked if the writer agreed that all ghost stories are in fact very optimistic in their nature since the fact they give hope of life after death, makes them quite uplifting (LoBrutto 1999: 414). This seemingly trivial anecdote illustrates the idea of eternal life which, according to the director, lies at the heart of all stories that contain a supernatural element. Similar conclusions are described in the materials in the Kubrick Archive. In the director's private copy of King's book, he underlined the words '[Jack] wants to be one of them and live forever', and in the margin, he left a note saying 'Immortality basis of horror. V.[ery] important' (SK/15/1/2: 374). The underlined words come from a chapter in which Danny hears the voices of the ghosts inhabiting the hotel. On that same page Kubrick wrote, 'There should be a short poem which we hear many times. Come with me and we will be together forever, and forever or just hear the word ". . . forever"' (SK/15/1/2: 374). His notes clearly indicate that the word 'forever' was firmly connected to the vision of eternity. This initial concept was later reflected in the film. When asked by his son if he likes the hotel, Jack replies that he would like to stay there 'forever'. He repeats it three times, which makes it resemble the words of the twins who haunted Danny in the previous scene. As early as the stage of writing scene outlines, Kubrick wrote in capital letters 'Jack's thoughts about immortality' (SK/15/1/5: 1).

What points us to the idea of eternity in *The Shining* is the coexistence of various time streams – or forking paths – within its narrative. The concept also appears in the previously discussed 'Star Gate' sequence in *2001: A Space Odyssey* and it is no coincidence that that chapter of the film is entitled 'Jupiter and Beyond the Infinite'. This then implies that infinity and eternity may be treated in Kubrick's works as almost synonymous. The idea of the coexistence of various time streams was also found by Kubrick in Stephen King's book. The director underlined the sentence 'Here in the Overlook all times were one' and emphasized it with both a question mark and an exclamation mark (SK/15/1/3: 348). At yet another point, Kubrick highlights the sentence 'All the hotel's eras were together now, All but this current one, the Torrance Era' (SK/15/1/2: 392).

The above-mentioned examples indicate that Kubrick was fascinated by the concept of the interconnecting paths of time that King depicted in his novel and he decided to emphasize this element by introducing the motif of a hedge maze to the film, which in turn tacitly implicates Borges's work. It is no coincidence that when Jack tells Danny that he would like to stay in the hotel 'forever', the featured background music (*Music for Strings, Percussion and Celesta* [Bartók 1951]) is the same that was playing when Jack was previously looking at a model of the maze in the hotel's reception area. It is characteristic of a maze that various paths cross within it, which is also a reflection of the way that time streams meander and cross within the hotel. Furthermore, the Overlook is also compared to a maze by Wendy. In the Argentinian author's prose this symbol relates to his idea of eternity signifying the spiritual and divine world. Knowing that, the sentence underlined by Kubrick in the novel, 'Nobody shines on all the time, except maybe for God up in heaven', (SK/15/1/3: 92) becomes all the more interesting.

Jack's thoughts about immortality

All the ideas and thoughts so far prompt us to wonder what motivates Jack. He grows bitter when his writing stalls for he has doubtlessly been hoping that his novel-to-be is going to be his route to life-altering success. This is why, when Wendy suggests for the first time that they should leave the hotel, Jack snaps at her

> It is so typical of you to create a problem . . . when I finally have a chance to accomplish something! . . . I could really write my own ticket if I went back now, couldn't I? Shovelling out driveways, work in a car wash. . . . I have let you fuck up my life so far, but I am not going to let you fuck this up.

His words reveal his high aspirations and his conviction that he has been born to accomplish greater goals. The preliminary versions of the screenplay emphasize his ambitions and overly high expectations of life equally strongly. In a synopsis of the scene where Jack returns from his interview with Ullman, he ironically observes, 'Writer to be of great American novel . . . Holder of Master's degree in English and former prep school teacher wins job as janitor' (SK/15/1/6: 2). In another bound and annotated script, he bitterly states 'Jack Torrance who was going to write the great American novel – a goddamn high school English teacher' (SK/15/1/24: 99–100).

Behind the main character's aspirations is one more desire. Jack wishes to stay in the hotel 'forever' which, according to Kubrick's notes, is closely related to the concept of eternity. Thus, it can be concluded that all expectations connected to the novel Jack is working on and his eagerness to stay in the hotel 'forever' are two sides of the same coin. Michel Ciment noticed that the titles of the chapters in *The Shining* successively refer to months, days and hours which create the impression that 'in the movie time is gradually reduced'. Therefore, Ciment shares 'the belief that Kubrick's basic problem is his struggle with time' and 'his protagonist must accomplish a goal, but he runs out of time'. Ciment indicates:

> The matter is true for Kubrick himself – his work and private life and his movies alike. Like every other person so deeply experiencing the issue of time, he is fascinated by immortality understood as a result of negating time, in *The Shining* the idea of immortality appears . . . the most basic issue is refutation of death, vanquishing it. Every point that contradicts the time is a battle with death. I believe that Kubrick's work expresses this conflict in a profound way. (1985: 26, author's translation)

Hence Jack's obsession is his perceived limited amount of time on earth. He attempts to overcome his mortality by means of the creative process. He sees his writing as an opportunity to – as the poet said – rise above this earthly vale. Richard Combs draws our attention to the fact that Jack is looking for immortality (1980: 222) and according to Pauline Kael (2022) 'the central character of this movie is time itself, or, rather, timelessness'.

Jack's attitude and creative aspirations are signs of the protagonist's pursuit of eternity, which in turn proves to be a trigger for the events that follow. This crucial theme is metaphorically, but at the same time, clearly conveyed in the opening sequence of *The Shining*. At the beginning we can hear a track called

Dies Irae (Wendy Carlos and Rachel Elkind 1980), which was inspired by the *Symphonie Fantastique: An Episode in the Life of an Artist* (Hector Berlioz 1971) (Gengaro 2014: 211). This reference highlights the fact that Jack is an artist and should be perceived as such. The opening sequence portrays Jack heading towards the Overlook located far up in the mountains. This movement towards 'higher grounds' is further stressed by the road taken by Jack. The actual road where filming took place shares its name with the mountain that it runs alongside: the *Going-to-the-Sun Road* is so-called because, according to a local legend, a god called 'Sour Spirit' descended from the sun in order to teach the Black Feet tribe the basics of hunting. On leaving, the god left its image on top of the mountain, which was meant to inspire the Indians. The legend says that the Sun in the name of the mountain symbolizes the spiritual world (Timber Wolf Resort 2022). In Kubrick's editing remarks there is a note saying '"Road to the Sun" B.P. Plates' (SK/15/9/33), which clearly indicates that Kubrick knew the name of the road and which makes the choice of the location seem thoroughly deliberate.

Considering Jack's literal and metaphorical rise towards 'higher grounds', it seems equally intentional that he consequently finds himself among yellow objects, this being the colour of the Sun (Marschall 2009: 75). Shades of this colour are noticeable in various items and aspects of set design which accompany Jack – a Volkswagen car, a jacket, a tennis ball, liqueur that is spilled by Grady and orange juice brought by Wendy for breakfast. *Going-to-the-Sun Road* leads Jack to the Overlook located high up in the mountains. This upward movement is further accentuated by the opening blue credits moving up the screen. The colour blue is also evident in the scene that demonstrates that Jack is possessed by the idea of eternity (Bienk 2008: 130). Jack, as well as Grady's daughters, while reciting their signature words 'forever and ever and ever', are wearing blue clothes, the colour which is frequently connected with transcendence (Bienk 2008: 130). Jack's desire to stay in the Overlook 'forever' and the character of the opening credits underline the symbolic meaning of the colour blue – especially if one considers the meaning of both scenes and their significance in the narrative.

The symbolic death of Jack in the middle of the hedge maze, where all the 'paths' cross is not without substance. The photograph shown at the end of the movie implies that Jack joined the world where all the paths of time converge. Paolo Cherchi Usai argues that the center of the labyrinth is 'the meeting point of all possible itineraries (of all imaginable times for the Overlook)' (1998: 135). Reaching the heart of the maze is often interpreted as a win over space and time (Hani 1962: 107–8), which can be linked to Jack's pursuit of eternity. In his comprehensive study about the labyrinth, Paolo Santarcangeli explains that the image of the maze

> illustrates a man's journey towards death and rebirth – and as such the image of infinity. A labyrinth assumes . . . two aims. For a wanderer who enters a labyrinth the aim is to reach the central chamber, the vault of mystery, but when he reaches it, he shall leave it and return to the outside world, which translates into being reborn. This is the tenet of all religions which carry the element of mystery and all cults which consider a journey into the labyrinth to be an indispensable process of metamorphosis which results in a completely new person emerging from it. (1967: 173, author's translation)

This implies that in the labyrinth there is a route leading to death and subsequently to an afterlife 'beyond death' (Santarcangeli 1967: 151). Reflecting upon Borges's thoughts on the perception of eternity, and the combined argumentation of the related quotations cited throughout this chapter, ultimately leads to the conclusion that Jack does indeed symbolically overcome space and time. He has transcended the temporal prison which constrained him to a perception of time associated with and limited by his corporeal existence. He has reached eternity and in doing so achieved the divine state according to Saint Augustine.

Conclusion: Demonic transcendence

Borges's works describe a concept of time that can be meaningfully compared to Kubrick's own representation of the fourth dimension within *The Shining*. This concept is closely related to the theological idea of eternity and it is linked with Jack's obsession about his work and achieving immortality. Jack's entire demeanour had been channelled into this objective as was indicated in preliminary versions of the script. The envelope which Grady originally was to hand Jack is another example of this. It contained the following poem card: 'There is no death, / Lifelessness is only a disguise, / Behind which hide, / Unknown forms of life' (SK/15/1/24: 114; SK/15/3/4/8). This message refers to Jack's ambitions while also implying that the Overlook's ghosts can sense his secret desire to be united with them in eternity, which consequently prompts them to tempt him. Thus, it is no coincidence that Lloyd appears in the Gold Room after Jack says, 'I'd give my goddamn soul for just a glass of beer'. Jack's transcendence at the end of the film can be interpreted as an extrapolation of a Faustian pact with the Overlook (Kościelski 2013: 153–70). That is why the ending of *The Shining*, even if perceived as showing Jack's realization of attaining eternity, causes certain anxiety. Transcendence in Kubrick's view can have a demonic nature and Jack's desperate longing for it causes the selfish and ruthless behaviour which instigates his fall from grace. The history of his predecessor(s) Charles and Delbert Grady is repeating itself. The path that Jack follows in the labyrinth was previously wandered by somebody else – no matter where in space, in time or in eternity.

Bibliography

Augustine. *Confessions*, translated by F. J. Sheed. Indianapolis and Cambridge: Hucket Publishing Company, 2006.

Bienk, Alice. *Filmsprache*. Marburg: Schüren Verlag, 2008.

Borges, Jorge Luis. 'The Garden of Forking Paths'. In *Labyrinths*, translated by D. A. Yates, J. E. Irby et al., 44–54. London: Penguin Classics, 2000a.

Borges, Jorge Luis. 'A New Refutation of Time'. In *The Total Library (Non Fiction 1922–1986)*, translated by S. J. Levine and E. Allen, 317–32. London: Penguin Classics, 2000b.

Borges, Jorge Luis and Osvaldo Ferrari. *Conversations*, translated by J. Wilson. London and New York: Seagull Books, 2014.

Calabrese, Omar. 'I "mondi possibili" in Kubrick. Ovvero: La poetica delle porte'. In *Stanley Kubrick: Tempo, spazio, storia e mondi possibili*, edited by Gian Piero Brunetta, 33–44. Parma: Pratiche, 1985.

Ciment, Michel. 'Lo spazio e il tempo nell'opera di Kubrick'. In *Stanley Kubrick: Tempo, spazio, storia e mondi possibili*, edited by Gian Piero Brunetta, 23–8. Parma: Pratiche, 1985.

Combs, Richard. 'Shining, The'. *Monthly Film Bulletin* 47, no. 567 (November 1980): 221–2.

Foix, Vicente Molina. 'An Interview with Stanley Kubrick'. In *The Kubrick Archives*, edited by Alison Castle, 460–3. Köln and London: Taschen, 2013.

Gengaro, Christine Lee. *Listening to Stanley Kubrick: The Music in His Films*. Lanham, Toronto, Plymouth: Rowman & Littlefield, 2014.

Głowiński, Michał. *Mity przebrane*. Kraków: Wydawnictwo Literackie, 1994.

Hani, Jean. *Le Symbolisme du Temple Chrétien*. Agde: Guy Trédaniel: Éditions de la Maisnie, 1962.

Hawking, Stephen. *A Brief History of Time*. London: Bantam Press/Transworld Publishers, 1988.

Jansen, Peter W. 'Kommentierte Filmografie'. In *Stanley Kubrick*, edited by Peter W. Jansen, 7–204. Wolfram Schütte. München, Wien: Hanser, 1984.

Kael, Pauline. 'Excerpts from the New Yorker Review of The Shining'. n.d. Available online at: http://www.visual-memory.co.uk/amk/doc/0050.html (accessed 10 December 2022).

King, Stephen. *The Shining*. London: Hodder and Stoughton, 2019.

Kościelski, Kamil. 'Demonic Transcendence. The Faustian Motif in Stanley Kubrick's *The Shining*'. *Space Theory* 19 (Spring 2013): 153–70.

Kuberski, Philip. *Kubrick's Total Cinema: Philosophical Themes and Formal Qualities*. London and New York: Continuum, 2012.

Kubrick, Stanley. 'Words and Movies'. *Sight & Sound* 30 (Winter 1960/1): 14.

Lacayo, Richard. 'Semper Fi: Kubrick Sticks to His Guns'. *Film Comment* 23, no. 5 (September/October 1987): 11–14.

LoBrutto, Vincent. *Stanley Kubrick*. New York: Da Capo Press, 1999.

Marschall, Susanne. *Farbe im Kino*. Marburg: Schüren Verlag, 2009.

Santarcangeli, Paolo. *Il libro dei labirinti: Storia di un mito e di un simbolo*. Florence: Vallechi, 1967.

Timber Wolf Resort. 'Enjoy Unrivaled Beauty Along Glacier's Going-to-the-Sun Road'. n.d. Available online at: https://www.timberwolfresort.com/going-to-the-sun-road.html (accessed 10 December 2022).

Usai, Paolo Cherchi. 'Kubrick as Architect'. *Cinémas* 9, no. 1 (Autumn 1998): 117–36.

Materials from the Stanley Kubrick Archive

SK/15/1/2 – Incomplete annotated text from Stephen King's novel 'The Shining'.

SK/15/1/3 – Annotated text from Stephen King's novel 'The Shining' (27 February 1977–12 April 1977).

SK/15/1/5 – Scene outlines (20 Jun 1977–6 July 1977).

SK/15/1/6 – Scene synopsis (8 July 1977–12 July 1977).

SK/15/1/24 – Annotated bound script (30 March 1978–2 April 1978).

SK/15/2/2/1/4/5 – Newspaper Article Research and Preparation (1977).

SK/15/2/3/3 – Building Plans (sets) (1977–1978).

SK/15/3/4/8 – Poem Cards.

SK/15/9/33 – Ray Lovejoy (1978–1979).

The online catalogue of the Stanley Kubrick Archive can be found here: https://archives.arts.ac.uk/Calmview/TreeBrowse.aspx?src=CalmView.Catalog&field=RefNo&key=SK (accessed 10 December 2022).

Filmography

Barry Lyndon (1975), [Film] Dir.Stanley Kubrick, UK / USA: Warner Bros.
Dr Strangelove or: How I Learned to Stop Worrying and Love the Bomb (1964), [Film] Dir. Stanley Kubrick, USA / UK: Columbia Pictures.
The Shining (1980), [Film] Dir. Stanley Kubrick, United Kingdom / USA: Warner Bros.
2001: A Space Odyssey (1968), [Film] Dir. Stanley Kubrick, UK / USA: MGM.

Music cited

Bartók, Béla, *Music for Strings, Percussion and Celesta*. Hamburg: Polydor International GmbH, 1951.
Berlioz, Hector. *Symphonie Fantastique: An Episode in the Life of an Artist*. New York City: Columbia Records, 1971.
Carlos, Wendy and Elkind Rachel. *Dies Irae*. Burbank: Warner Bros. Entertainment, Inc., 1980.
Woods, Harry M., Jimmy Campbell, and Reg Connelly. *Midnight, the Stars and You*. London: Cinephonic Music Company, Ltd., 1934.

4

The candy-coloured uncanny
Childish pleasures in *Killer Klowns from Outer Space*

Cynthia J. Miller and Tom Shaker

Introduction

Released in 1988, Stephen Chiodo's *Killer Klowns from Outer Space* [*Killer Klowns* hereafter] takes a familiar science fiction trope – a spacecraft filled with malevolent aliens descending on a small American town – and gives it a surreal twist. The spacecraft that descends on Crescent Cove, trailing a streak of fire across the sky, resembles a circus tent, and the aliens that emerge from it are instantly recognizable as nightmarish versions of clowns: figures with garish costumes, abnormally large heads and grotesquely exaggerated facial features (including bulbous red noses). The weapons they turn on the citizens of the town are equally clownish: pink cotton candy that entraps and embalms, popcorn that mutates into ravenous monsters, lethal custard pies and toy-like ray guns that are anything but toys.

The plot of *Killer Klowns* is built from the same basic elements as *The Blob* (Irvin S. Yeaworth Jr., 1958), *Invasion of the Saucer Men* (Edward L. Cahn, 1957) and other 'teens vs. monsters' B-movies of the late 1950s and early 1960s: a bizarre threat to a small, isolated town; alert, intrepid young people as heroes; and incompetent or scornful adults as secondary, obstructionist villains. Even as they deploy those tropes, however, the filmmakers knowingly remix them with elements that poke fun at 1980s teen comedies and, to a lesser extent, slasher movies. The aliens' abduction of the hero's girlfriend, for example, simultaneously acknowledges and lampoons the use of narratively gratuitous shower scenes as an excuse for inserting nudity into such films.

What ultimately makes *Killer Klowns* more than just an exercise in playing with genre conventions and pushes it firmly into the pantheon of cult films, is its use of clowns not just as villains but as social and psychological touchstones. Circus clowns are among the most iconic – and complex – childhood figures. Comical, festive characters associated with birthday parties, parades, rodeos and circuses, clowns and their images permeated popular culture from the 1950s onwards. However, there has always been a darker side of clowns, a side that suggests that lurking just beneath their jovial greasepaint and costumes is an evil waiting to emerge. That side was given horrifying form in Stephen King's 1986 terror tale *IT* (inspired by real-life killer clown John Wayne Gacy), and our collective relationship with clowns would never be the same.

The grotesque appearance of the invaders evokes the power of clowns to frighten and disturb but, having acknowledged that power, *Killer Klowns* inverts it. The film is saturated with clownish pantomime, magic tricks, shadow puppetry and similar childhood pleasures, and the interior of the clowns' tent-ship has the brilliant colours and skewed geometry of a carnival funhouse. The clowns' assault on the town relies on the townspeople being charmed, and inexorably drawn in, by such lures, with adult caution and better judgement dissolving instantly in their presence. The real threat of the alien clowns, the film suggests, lies in the fact that we do not run from them in terror but towards them, with unfeigned delight. This chapter, then, examines how *Killer Klowns* plays with our affection for formulaic B-movies and our susceptibility to the curiously persistent power of clowns, and the youthful pleasures with which both are indelibly associated.

Just another Friday night

Crescent Cove . . . a cinematic small town like so many others . . . until the clowns came . . .

Killer Klowns begins like many iconic teen films of the 1950s and 1960s. Like a snapshot of mid-century American life, the stage is set: young people out on a Friday night, for burgers and beer and back-seat romance. They are 'good kids' in an era when rebellion reigns, living in a town where families and reputations are known to all. But then, it happens. The night sky brightens as a meteor falls to Earth, and soon, the chaos begins.

While the plot may not be the most essential part of a teen film, this one is reassuringly familiar. Mike Tobacco (Grant Cramer), his girlfriend Debbie Stone (Suzanne Snyder) and their friends are all parked at the town's version of 'make-out point' – with comic relief provided by the hapless Terenzi brothers, Rich and Paul (Michael Siegel, Peter Licassi) and their clown-topped ice cream truck. There is no shortage of laughs as the Terenzis, unable to score romantic dates themselves, interrupt everyone else's amorous pursuits. A bright rendition of 'Pop Goes the Weasel' and off-colour, carnivalesque marketing lines blast from the truck's PA as the film begins its irreverent twist on childhood delights: 'Cool off those hot lips with our tasty, frozen, fruity bars!' and 'We'll give you the stick, you give it a lick!' are met with a wave of empty beer cans, tossed out steamy car windows.

The Terenzis remove any threat of teen sexuality from the scene, making way for a much greater menace. When what appears to be a meteor careens through the darkness, the *true* action of the night begins. Debbie convinces a reluctant Mike to go investigate, as do farmer Gene Green (Royal Dano) and his hound Pooh Bear. Thinking he has witnessed the crash of Haley's Comet, the old man tells the dog 'We're gonna be rich!!' The two, of course, are the clowns' first onscreen victims, when they find what appears to be a circus tent in the middle of the woods: Pooh Bear is caught in a net and farmer Green ends up encased in cotton candy shot from a clown's ray gun. Arriving at the scene slightly later, Mike and Debbie get to explore the interior of the circus tent before escaping and making their way to the Crescent Cove police station, with the clowns following on behind them. It is now clear that these are no ordinary clowns, but rather, evil aliens using some of our richest childhood fantasies to comically annihilate the inhabitants of Crescent Cove (see Figure 4.1).

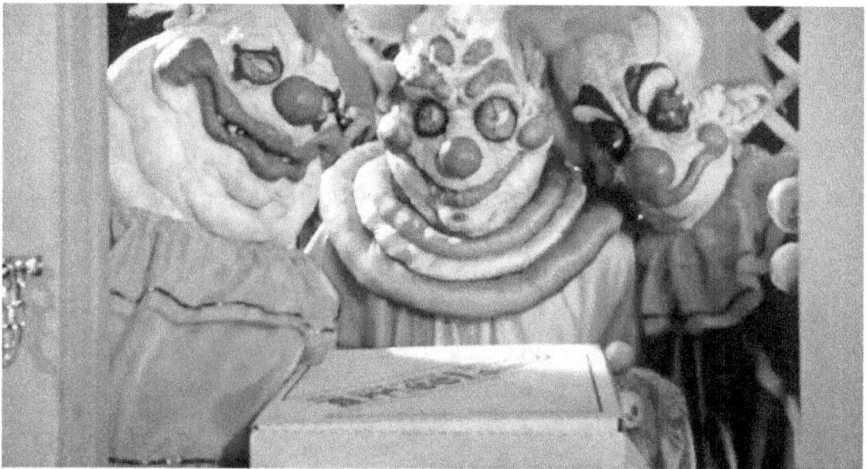

Figure 4.1 *Killer Klowns from Outer Space*: Evil aliens that look and act like clowns.

Killer Klowns' circus big top spaceship and kaleidoscopic decor attracts its victims like . . . children to a circus. Big, bold colours abound, with reds, blues and yellows, bright pinks and florescent greens capturing the audience's eye. Pink cotton candy cocoons, machine guns firing popcorn and balloon dogs that bark all create an illusion of childhood delights that proves deadly for its victims. A far-fetched story, to be sure, especially when coming from a couple of teens who are already despised by the town's veteran police officer, Curtis Moody (John Vernon), and so, the tension builds as Mike and Debbie struggle to convince the authorities that the town is under siege. Only young officer Dave Hanson (John Allen Nelson) is willing to listen to their story – and perhaps only because he is Debby's former boyfriend (a source of tension throughout the film).

As the clowns begin to appear to the locals of Crescent Cove, all seems 'normal' at first. Despite their larger-than-life size, they smile and wave at their 'new friends', delighting them with their unexpected antics. Things go quickly awry as the clowns claim more victims, but for viewers, the horror is muted by laughter. One of the clowns rides his colourful tricycle, childlike, into the midst of a biker gang in a back alley. As they ridicule his tiny bike, the clown pretends to first be hurt and then ready to fight to defend his honour. When one of the bikers jokes, 'What are you gonna do, knock my block off?' the little clown does just that. The head flies, the gang flees, and the audience has little choice but to laugh at the slapstick terror.

The big, colourful, creepy aliens are frighteningly familiar; deadly, yet adorable. Communicating largely in pantomime, they 'speak' to the child in all of us. As John Pannozzi observes, 'Adding to the Klowns' creepiness is their lack of any real spoken dialogue, though the Chiodos' creature designs still give them a *Gremlins*-like perverse charm' (2020: 53). In a scene at the local burger joint (aptly named Big Top Burger), one of the clowns sweetly plays peek-a-boo with a little girl who has been forgotten in her family's dinner conversation. She is fascinated by the big, friendly clown waving at her from outside and leaves the table, unnoticed by her family. Only then do we begin to worry that she will be their next victim.

As the alien clowns rampage through Crescent Cove, no possibility for horrific antics is overlooked. One clown jumps out of a pizza delivery box; another, driving an 'invisible' car forces a teen off the road to certain death; and in one enchantingly horrific scene, a clown entertains people waiting for a bus with a shadow puppet performance. Using his hands (swathed in oversized, clumsy gloves) to cast shapes on the brick wall, the clown's shadows become increasingly elaborate – first a rabbit, then an elephant, then a silhouette of Washington crossing the Delaware. Dave and Mike, coincidentally driving by, pull over to watch as the shadow figure of an exotic dancer morphs into a dinosaur with glowing red eyes. To their horror, the dinosaur suddenly shifts beyond the flat plane of the wall and envelops the crowd of shocked onlookers.

Even in the face of mounting evidence, bitter veteran officer Mooney thinks the clown reports are a big practical joke to get him to retire early. 'I made it through Korea, I can make it through this bullshit', he sputters, but this bravado does not save him from meeting his end at, literally, the hands of the clowns, when a disembodied pair of oversized white gloves appear and choke him to death. In a nod to another childhood comedic icon, Dave enters the station's jail cells in search of Mooney, only to find oversized clown footprints all over the floors, walls and ceiling, directly referencing Daffy Duck's 'Duck Twacy' (a character Daffy Duck performs in *The Great Piggy Bank Robbery* [Robert Clampett, 1946]). The filmmakers then use the recently killed Mooney as a ventriloquist's dummy to terrify the young officer. This scene, featuring a dead Mooney (in partial clown make-up) sitting on the lap of a clown, mouthing 'Don't worry Dave, all we want to do is kill ya' with the clown's bloody arm in his back finally drives the film's horror credentials home.

The film's final scenes compound the comic violence as the clowns kidnap Debby in a giant balloon and attempt to flee into space with Mike, Dave and the Terenzi brothers in pursuit. The clowns are mesmerized when the Terenzis burst through the tent in their clown-topped ice cream truck, commanding over the PA (in a callback to Victor Fleming's *The Wizard of Oz* [1939]), 'I am the great and powerful Jo-Jo! I command you to stop! Do not hurt them! Let them go!' But as the group of teens attempts to flee, 'Klownzilla' (Charles Chiodo) – a giant, menacing clown marionette inspired by King Kong – descends from the big top, destroying everything in its path, starting with the imposter clown 'god', flinging the truck away like a toy. As the truck bursts into flames with the Terenzis still inside, it looks like certain death for Debbie, Mike and Dave. Dave sacrifices himself so that Mike may save Debbie, and the pair watch in horror as the alien big top ascends into the sky. Onboard, Dave defeats Klownzilla by puncturing its nose, causing the monster clown – and the spaceship – to explode into fireworks of otherworldly proportions. Just as it appears that all hope is gone, both Dave and the Terenzi brothers fall to earth in a battered clown car, the Terenzis still comically bickering.

Just as *The Blob* used a large '?' in the sky to signal doubt about what might come next, *Killer Klowns* answers Debbie's question 'Do you think it's over?' with cream pies falling on them out of the darkness to keep viewers guessing about a sequel.

The crisis of clowns

Garish, uncanny and bizarre . . . clowns have always been complex figures in popular culture. Their ambiguity is apparent in a range of characters, from early jesters and tricksters to the sinister and fantastical beings animating contemporary media and art forms. On one hand, clowns' association with circuses, pratfalls and pony parties situates them in the realm of childhood innocence. On the other, their exaggerated features and unpredictable behaviour evoke tension, discomfort and fear, as though madness lurks just below their enormous smiles. Still, as Ezra LeBank and David Bridle – both clowns, themselves – observe:

> [T]he clown's function remains remarkably consistent: to turn established protocols (societal, political, cultural, logical, linguistic, or otherwise) on their heads, and to provoke a new understanding of, and appreciation for, the human condition through a celebration of foible and a mockery of power. (2015: 1)

And indeed, that function can be traced from early performances through to the present day, as clowns have blurred the lines between the sacred and the profane. As LeBank and Bridel (2015) note, tribal clowns and tricksters, Renaissance fools and *commedia* buffoons alike crafted laughter from the midst of ritual and hierarchy, while increasingly exploring human frailties and failings. If we look at late *commedia dell'arte*'s theatrical clowns, for example, with their comedy rooted in class tension and the mockery of convention, we find deeply nuanced characters, such as the mischief-making Harlequin and the innocent, pitiable Pierrot, whose bittersweet commentary often blended laughs with cruelty and tears. These *commedia* figures, condemned by church and state alike as vulgar 'blasphemers' cemented the traditions of theatrical comedy and formalized clowning as a form of popular entertainment for the masses.

As the *commedia* declined and comic 'obscenities' were banned, the contexts of clowning shifted from respectable theatres to circuses, tented one-ring venues where nineteenth-century clowns provided humorous interludes between feats of daring and skill. Slapstick clowns, such as North American Emmett Kelley, grew to be a beloved staple of the circus ring, and moving into the twentieth century, no successful circus lacked their teasing humour and knockabout skits. Silly and playful, these larger-than-life caricatures easily captured the imagination: 'Everything about clowns is exaggerated' Benjamin Radford writes, highlighting not only the clowns' overdrawn smiles and eyes, but also their use of enormous props, such as gigantic shoes and oversized eyeglasses, 'they are creatures of the large and the loud . . . ' (2016: 22). While the practicalities of performing before a large audience may require such exaggeration, clowns' garish appearances and distorted features also serve another purpose, as signs of their exclusion from the conventions of everyday life. Denizens of the circus – a world of spectacle unto itself – clowns simply do not 'fit' comfortably in the worlds inhabited by their audiences. They are, as Freud (1955) suggests, uncanny, disquieting figures that could be us, and of our day-to-day world, but are not.

Clowns are among the most familiar of childhood icons, not only from circuses, but parades and parties, as well. Like a well-worn doll, we instinctively 'know' the clown with its red nose, white greasepaint and exaggerated eyes, and yet, under the right circumstances, the sight of a clown can make our pulses quicken and raise the hair on the backs of our necks. We experience *dread*. Those circumstances? According to Freud (1955), they occur when we encounter the figure of the clown out of its usual context – not in a circus, or a parade, or even in a backyard pony party, but in an office building, on a back road, or in a quiet park. In explaining the way in which an object or individual is made uncanny in literature, Freud writes:

> The situation is altered as soon as the writer pretends to move in the world of common reality. . . . He takes advantage, as it were, of our supposedly surmounted [or overcome] superstitious-ness; he deceives us into thinking that he is giving us the sober truth, and then after all oversteps the bounds of possibility. (1955: 249)

It is here that we begin to understand the disruption caused by the character of the clown when it is removed from the context of the circus. Actor Lon Chaney Sr., known for his macabre portrayals of tortured, grotesque characters, portrayed two of the earliest cinematic evil clowns – in *He Who Gets Slapped* (Victor Sjostrom, 1924) and *Laugh, Clown, Laugh* (Herbert Brenon, 1928) – observed that 'A clown is funny in the circus ring, but what would be the normal reaction to opening a door at midnight and finding the same clown there in the moonlight?' (Barker 1997: 88). Similarly, Anna-Sophie Jürgens writes, 'Malice, deformation and above all violence – these are the characteristics of those circus clowns who become detached from their original context and begin to haunt different media and art forms' (2014: 441).

These unfettered clowns have starred in dozens of films and on television since Chaney's roles, most famously, of course, through Pennywise in adaptations of Stephen King's *IT* (Tommy Lee Wallace, 1990 and Andy Muschietti, 2017) and the Joker in the *Batman* franchise and been referenced in countless others. The 1978 arrest of John Wayne Gacy, who performed as a clown regularly at children's hospitals, cemented the image of the 'Killer Clown' in popular consciousness. The uncanny paradox surrounding the figure of the clown resonated with the Chiodo brothers, as well, leading to the creation of *Killer Klowns*. As Charles Chiodo related:

> I was thinking about what was the most frightening image I could imagine. To me, it was driving down a lonely mountain road all by yourself, and having a car come by, passing you. When you look over, you see a clown with a maniacal smile and he laughs. To me, that was the most horrible image I could think of, what seemed to be an archetypal, primal fear. (*The Making of Killer Klowns*, 2001)

The film exploits the uncanniness of clowns-out-of-context on multiple levels, framing the circus as an entity that is (literally) alien, situating it in the midst of the woods, and then filling the quiet, rural town with a troupe of clowns that, on first glance, amuse and delight with tricks and confections, but are (too late) revealed to be grotesque predators.

Homage to the Bs

Killer Klowns pays homage – with a wink and a smile – to a cycle of mid-twentieth-century teensploitation films aimed at tapping into the youth market at the US box office. With juvenile delinquency viewed as a threat to the moral fabric of the United States equivalent to communism, the 'youth problem' was front and centre in the minds of American institutions. At the same time, newly emerging teenaged consumers of the 1950s and 1960s were becoming the focus for innovation in film, music and other entertainment and rapidly became an attractive target for youth-focused products and marketing. Anxious to attract teen audiences, the motion picture industry released films that catered to the youth market yet reinforced social norms. The framework of these low-budget,

B-grade films was simple: a monster, such as the gelatinous extra-terrestrial ooze in *The Blob*, the sea creature in *The Horror of Party Beach* (Del Tenney, 1964), the prehistoric caveman in *Eegah* (Arch Hall Sr.,1962), the giant spider in *Earth vs. the Spider* (Bert I. Gordon,1958), and others, threatens humanity. Teenagers in the cast, straining at the confines of their small community, are framed as resisting – and misunderstood by – authority, and their attempts to alert the police (or scientists, or other characters representing the 'establishment') are rejected as pranks (Tropiano 2006: 42–4). In each case, however, the monster is only defeated when authority figures and youths join forces and 'adult efforts are infused with teenage bravado and ingenuity' (Miller and Van Riper 2015: 130). In this way, teenagers are depicted as contributing to the welfare of the community and successfully working towards a common purpose with the very adults they seem to oppose in real life, setting aside rebellion in favour of responsibility and the common good.

With social norms reinforced and wayward teens either dead or reconciled with their elders, B-movie studios, such as American International Pictures (AIP), joined major studios like Universal and Columbia Pictures in affirming their roles as guardians of the moral order – all the while capitalizing on the burgeoning teen market. Rebels and 'clean' teens, ne'er-do-wells and monsters, all shared the same cinematic space, clamouring for teen audiences' attention and box office dollars, in films ranging from *Invaders from Mars* (William Cameron Menzies, 1954) to *Teenage Zombies* (Jerry Warren, 1959), where pretty girls, hot-headed boys, make-out sessions and malevolent aliens all shared the screen. The films appropriated and merged the visual lexicons of science fiction, horror, teen romance and small-town comedy to create a familiar, yet novel group of cinematic texts.

Killer Klowns from Outer Space poaches liberally from this good-natured cycle of B-movies in a loving homage to a bygone era in American films. Antagonism between youth and authority is established behind the opening credits, as celebrated punk band The Dickies play the film's title theme. Officer Mooney, a bitter representative of the establishment mutters 'son of a bitch' as a teen carrying grocery bags and drinking from an open can of beer saunters along the crosswalk in front of his patrol car. When the young man reaches the curb and Mooney drives away, the teen turns his head and grumbles, in turn, 'Cops . . .'. To further emphasize the divide, the main teen characters are introduced at a local 'make-out point' where young people are gathered for a night of beer, snacks and fumbling attempts at romance. Mike and Debbie are immediately recognizable as the 'clean teen' heroes – drinking champagne from stemmed glasses while their counterparts guzzle cans of beer and trade innuendos – and clearly more invested in each other than in the forbidden pleasures offered by a secluded location and a car.

Call-backs to familiar mid-century B-movies, as well as later teen-movie fare are scattered throughout the film, most notably, *The Blob*. As John Pannozzi observes in *Laughing to Death: A Look at Horror Comedy*:

> *Killer Klowns*' narrative played like a demented parody of *The Blob*, as a small group of young adults discover one night that clown-like aliens are invading their small town. Attempts to warn the authorities, one of them played by John Vernon, best known as Dean Wormer in *Animal House*, are ridiculed and the clowns murder innocent people with a bizarre, carnival-themed arsenal that includes weapons evoking cotton candy, balloon animals, and other traditionally innocuous imagery. (2020: 53)

Mirroring *The Blob*'s Steve (Steve McQueen) and Jane (Aneta Corsault), the pair sight the supposed 'meteor' and, echoing a similar scene from the film, Mike and Debbie set out on an adventure to find the crash site. Audiences familiar with both films recognize that the homage continues when the aliens' first victim in both cases is an isolated old man; Barney (Olin Howland) is engulfed by the Blob, while farmer Gene Green meets his end encased in a cocoon of bright pink cotton candy.

The character of young officer Dave Hanson, Debbie's ex-boyfriend, becomes the focal point for articulating the traditional B-movie tension between youth and authority as he teams up with Mike and Debbie to thwart the clowns. When awkwardly forced to ride in the police cruiser with Mike (who must ride in the back, like a criminal), Dave attempts to reconcile their relationship, but cannot bridge the divide:

Dave: I'll call the State Police up in Marlboro; maybe somebody up there can tell us what this stuff is. It's not cotton candy, that's for sure.
Mike: Yes! Finally! That's what I've been telling you!
Dave: Look, I'm sorry I was a little tough on you back there. It's been a hard night . . . having Debbie involved just makes it a lot more difficult.
Mike: What can I say? I didn't know sh-
Dave: Hey, it's got nothing to do with you, really, it's me. It's obvious she goes for laughs, not stability.

In good teensploitation fashion, however, the three bond in vanquishing the clowns. After sacrificing himself to save Debbie, Dave narrowly escapes the exploding big top, and all three embrace in joy. In *The Blob*'s parallel reconciliation, high school principal Henry Martin (Elbert Smith) uses a rock to break into his own school (much to the delight of the rebellious teens who have volunteered their help) in order to gather up fire extinguishers to freeze the Blob. The teens, who have continually distressed the townspeople with their drag racing, now use that speed to race back to the diner where Steve and Jane are trapped and save the day. In both cinematic communities, relationships are mended; the moral order, restored.

Textual poaching and interpretive audiences

In 2011 Edward, Stephen and Charles Chiodo reunited on camera to re-examine the making of their 1988 film. The three brothers did not set out to make a cult film, and yet, at the time of this writing, thirty-five years after its release, the film has become a cult classic. Edward Chiodo reminisced, 'It was a labour of love for us, because even before we got into production we'd been thinking of this idea for many years' (*The Making of Killer Klowns*, 2001).

For the Chiodo brothers, the driving force behind the film was the characters; Edward relates: 'Mike Tobacco, the Terenzi brothers, Joe Lombardo; these are people we grew up with. So, the cast of characters really are people that we knew . . .' (*The Making of Killer Klowns*, 2001). His brother Stephen chimes in, 'So, we took those . . . I guess . . . "icons" for us and put them essentially in *The Blob* – in that kind of script – kids trying to communicate to the authorities that there are monsters, with our friends as the main characters' (*The Making of Killer Klowns*, 2001).

But the brothers drew on more than simply personal experience in the crafting of their film, they also drew on their shared knowledge of motion pictures – a knowledge base that they share with audiences of *their* film, creating a second layer of communication referencing classic film images. Phillips and Pinedo have discussed this shared knowledge in relation to what they term cult television programming of the 1950s and 1960s – influential texts that possess a set of 'mutually informing textual features, reception practices, and differentiation from the mainstream' – citing the programmes' parodies and secondary meanings as signalling the beginning of television's cultivation of 'interpretive' audiences that are now more the norm (2018, 21–2). For the Chiodos, however, it was a natural part of the storytelling experience: Edward reveals, 'I guess we threw in all our favourite monster films, and science fiction films, as references. The power chamber [in *Killer Klowns*] is a direct reference to the Krell chamber in *Forbidden Planet* [Fred M. Wilcox, 1956]' (*The Making of Killer Klowns*, 2001). His brother Charles completes the story: 'I believe that's what a lot of filmmakers do. There's certain things that they grew up watching, in motion pictures and television, that stuck with them. I would say it's an homage, bringing it back with just a slight little twist' (*The Making of Killer Klowns*, 2001).

Pop culture scholar Christopher J. Olsen comments on this appropriation of iconic imagery, observing that 'the Chiodo brothers crafted a loving homage to the creature movies of the 1950s and 1960s. The Chiodo's clearly watched a lot of those movies because they deftly send up all the major conventions and characters that routinely pop up in films such as *The Giant Gila Monster* [Ray Kellogg, 1959], *The Creeping Terror* [Vic Savage, 1964] and *It Came from Outer Space* [Jack Arnold, 1953]' (2018: 123). Such 'textual poaching', if you will, is frequently a marker of cult films – drawing on a range of shared points of reference to create a 'community' of viewers who share the same, sometimes idiosyncratic, visual lexicon (Jenkins 1992; Jancovich 2002: 307–8). As Mark Jancovich argues, these films rely heavily on their 'distance from the media' in crafting their cultural identities, yet are, in fact, indebted to them (2002: 309–15). *Killer Klowns*, for example, comes from – and references – a long tradition of low-budget, drive-in, camp, horror, 'date night' movies – many awarded 'cult' status of their own, thus illustrating how central existing cinema culture is to its existence and status. As Jeffrey Sconce illustrates, cult films, or 'paracinema', would include entries from such 'seemingly disparate subgenres as "bad film," splatterpunk, "mondo" films, sword and sandal epics, Elvis flicks, governmental hygiene films, Japanese monster movies, beach party musicals and just about every other historical manifestation of exploitation cinema from juvenile delinquency documentaries to soft core pornography' (1995: 372).

The breadth of genres here is remarkable, but not nearly complete, illustrating how varied the nature of 'cult' films can be, leading Christopher Olson to argue that '[t]he truth is that any movie can inspire devotion among audiences and thereby become a cult film' (2018: xiii). Olson includes *Killer Klowns* in his roster of *100 Greatest Cult Films*, distilling its plotline to the simplest possible elements:

> Two love-struck college students set out to save their sleepy California town from a horde of homicidal clowns that hail from the depths of space. (2018: 122)

Olson's (2018) abbreviated plot summary shines a light on the interchangeability of classic alien invasions teensploitation narratives from the 1950s and 1960s, suggesting that it is also our nostalgia for mid-century 'Americana' that drives the film's appeal. From the local drug store to the police station, to the burger joint, naïve, small-town America is an ideal setting for the arrival of marauding invaders. And regardless of the alien entities – robots, tarantulas, ooze or clowns – the town will be home to a love-struck couple, a sceptical authority figure, a cranky old man and a dim-witted-side kick, all of whom will help save the day. Olson credits the Chiodo brothers with making these iconic, stock characters their own:

> [T]hey play with standard horror movie tropes – like the innocent young lovers who stumble upon the initial invasion (*The Blob*) and the square-jawed authority figure who steps up to the threat – and subvert them in interesting ways . . . Thus, while *Killer Klowns* both spoofs and pays tribute to Cold War-era monster movies and science fiction films, it also deconstructs them in a humorous fashion. (2018: 124)

While not as 'legendary' in the cult realm as, say, Ed Wood's *Plan 9 From Outer Space* (1959), or George Romero's *Night of the Living Dead* (1968), *Killer Klowns* has all the elements of a classic cult film. And, while filmmakers such as Wood and Romero did not necessarily pay as obvious homage to their influences, the Chiodo brothers' approach of exploiting viewers' filmgoing experiences guaranteed that the production had a ready-made audience.

Conclusion

In truth, *Killer Klowns* draws on so much more than *The Blob*, *King Kong* (Merian C. Cooper and Ernest B. Schoedsack, 1933), and other classic films that came before it. The Chiodo brothers draw together cartoons, advertising, childhood innocence, mid-century Americana and, of course, clowns and circus culture, to craft a nostalgic image of small-town life and then turn it on its ear. Stephen Chiodo relates:

> I attempted to expose the danger of blindly trusting popular iconic images by putting a twist on clowns as something other than safe and friendly. Most people consider clowns as something to be trusted, someone you could safely leave your child with to be entertained. I put a spin on that idea and made it fatal to trust a

clown. Like moths to a flame, innocent people are drawn into the playful traps created by the killer klowns. Once they realize the deadly twist, it is too late. Don't trust anyone, especially clowns. (Jürgens 2020: 134)

Killer Klowns confronts these iconic images in ways that look beyond the film text to the wider culture, in ways that engage with the writings of Umberto Eco (1985), Pierre Bourdieu (1984), Kristin Thompson (1977), Jeffrey Sconce (1995) and others who have explored cultural criticism and its complicated relationship with cult film and paracinema. Director Brian Herzlinger (*My Date With Drew*, 2004) agrees, relating, 'What we have here, wrapped up in the body of a B-movie, is a wonderful satire on American culture . . . ' (2013: 135).

But ultimately, it is the film's enduring legacy in popular culture that allows us to think most deeply about its cult status. At the time of its release, *Variety* deemed it a 'klutzy teen scifier that will be better remembered for its title than anything in the picture itself' (*Killer Klowns from Outer Space*, 1988: 31). The passing years have shown otherwise. Twenty-five years after the film's premiere, Herzlinger attests, 'There's not one moment in *Killer Klowns* that you want to fast forward through' (2013: 135).

While coulrophobia, or the fear of clowns, is often discussed as 'near universal', *Killer Klowns* reminds us that it is all just fun and games. The film's iconic props and characters have made forays into the industry's 'mainstream', being featured at Universal Orlando's annual Halloween Horror Nights, as well as at Universal Studios Hollywood, while collectible toys and action figures from the film are in high demand. Trick or Treat Studios has even created a six-foot tall cotton candy cocoon prop that is available to high-end consumers. Its motion picture legacy may be difficult to pin down, due to the now-pervasive nature of the 'evil clown' figure in popular culture, but fans – the lifeblood of any cult film – credit that pervasiveness to the film and see its legacy all around them:

> Despite rarely getting any credit, *Killer Klowns from Outer Space* is believed to have inspired a new generation of horror movies featuring evil clowns such as *All Hallows Eve* [Damien Leone, 2013], *Stitches* [Conor McMahon, 2012], *Zombieland* [Ruben Fleischer, 2009], *Clown* [Jon Watts, 2014], *31* [Rob Zombie, 2016], and *Wrinkles the Clown* [Michael Beach Nichols, 2019]. The 2019 reboot of *Child's Play* [Lars Klevberg] featured a poster of *Killer Klowns from Outer Space* in Andy's bedroom. (*Killer Klowns from Outer Space*, 2022)

Stephen Chiodo attempts to explain the cultural resonance of his film: 'The image of clowns has changed and adapted as time passes. [*Killer Klowns from*

Outer Space] is a pivotal, important step in the ongoing transformation of clown culture. . . . The current reaction to modern clowns as objects to fear, I believe, is a cycle like any other cycle. In time, society's view will change and clowns will change again. But clowns will always be part of our world as they have been for centuries' (Jürgens 2020: 140). And *Killer Klowns from Outer Space* will surely always remain a cherished part of the cult horror film pantheon.

Bibliography

Barker, Clive. *Clive Barker's A-Z of Horror*, Compiled by Stephen Jones. London: BBC Books, 1997.

Bourdieu, Pierre. *Distinction: A Social Critique of the Judgement of Taste*. London: Routledge, 1984.

Eco, Umberto. 'Casablanca: Cult Movies and Intertextual Collage'. *SubStance* 14, no. 2 (1985): 3–12.

Freud, Sigmund. 'The Uncanny'. In *The Complete Psychological Works*, Vol. XVII, 217–56. London: Hogarth Press, 1955 [1919].

Herzlinger, Brian. 'Killer Klowns from Outer Space'. In *The Best Films You've Never Seen*, edited by Robert K. Elder, 135–42. Chicago: Chicago Review Press, 2013.

Jancovich, Mark. 'Cult Fictions, Cult Movies, Subcultural Capital and the Production of Cultural Distinctions'. *Cultural Studies* 16, no. 2 (2002): 309–15.

Jenkins, Henry. *Textual Poachers: Television Fans and Participatory Culture*. New York: Routledge, 1992.

Jürgens, Anna-Sophie. 'Batman's Joker, a Neo-Modern Clown of Violence'. *Journal of Graphic Novels and Comics* 5, no. 4 (2014): 441–54.

Jürgens, Anna-Sophie. '"Greatest Klown on Earth"—and the Killer Klowns from Outer Space'. *Comedy Studies* 11, no. 1 (2020): 133–41.

'Killer Klowns from Outer Space'. Film Reviews, *Variety*, 8 June 1988, 331.

'Killer Klowns from Outer Space'. *Killer Klowns Wiki*, 2022. Available online at: https://killerklowns.fandom.com/wiki/Killer_Klowns_from_Outer_Space (accessed 14 May 2022).

King, Stephen. *IT*. New York: Viking, 1986.

LeBank, Ezra and David Bridel. *Clowns: In Conversation with Modern Masters*. London: Routledge, 2015.

'The Making of Killer Klowns'. Extra Feature on *Killer Klowns from Outer Space* [DVD], USA: Metro-Goldwyn-Mayer, 2001.

Miller, Cynthia J. and A. Bowdoin Van Riper. 'Marketing, Monsters, and Music . . .'. *The Journal of American Culture* 38, no. 2 (June 2015): 130–41.

Olson, Christopher J. *100 Greatest Cult Films*. Lanham, MD: Rowman & Littlefield Publishers, 2018.
Pannozzi, John. *Laughing to Death: A Look at Horror Comedy*. Providence: Think Tank Animate, LLC, 2020.
Phillips, Wyatt D. and Isabel Pinedo. 'Gilligan and Captain Kirk Have More in Common Than You Think: 1960s Camp as an Alternative Genealogy for Camp TV'. *Journal of Popular Television* 6, no. 1 (2018): 19–40.
Radford, Benjamin. *Bad Clowns*. Albuquerque: University of New Mexico Press, 2016.
Sconce, Jeffrey. 'Trashing the Academy: Taste, Excess and an Emerging Politics of Cinematic Style'. *Screen* 36, no. 4 (1995): 371–93.
Thompson, Kristin. 'The Concept of Cinematic Excess'. *CineTracks: A Journal of Film, Communications, Culture, and Politics* 1, no. 2 (Summer 1977): 54–63.
Tropiano, Stephen. *Rebels and Chicks: A History of the Hollywood Teen Movie*. New York: Back Stage Books, 2006.

Filmography

The Blob (1958), [Film] Dir. Irvin S. Yeaworth Jr., USA: Paramount Pictures.
The Creeping Terror (1964), [Film] Dir. Vic Savage, USA: Crown International Pictures.
Earth vs. the Spider (1958), [Film] Dir. Bert I. Gordon, USA: American International Pictures.
Eegah (1962), [Film] Dir. Arch Hall Sr., USA: Fairway International Pictures.
Forbidden Planet (1956), [Film] Dir. Fred M. Wilcox, USA: Metro-Goldwyn-Mayer.
The Giant Gila Monster (1959), [Film] Dir. Ray Kellogg, USA: McLendon-Radio Pictures.
The Great Piggy Bank Robbery (1946), [Film] Dir. Robert Clampett, USA: Warner Bros. Pictures.
He Who Gets Slapped (1924), [Film] Dir. Victor Sjostrom, USA: Metro-Goldwyn-Mayer.
The Horror of Party Beach (1964), [Film] Dir. Del Tenney, USA: Twentieth Century-Fox.
Invaders from Mars (1954), [Film] Dir. William Cameron Menzies, USA: Twentieth Century-Fox.
Invasion of the Saucer Men (1957), [Film] Dir. Edward L. Cahn, USA: American International Pictures.
IT (1990), [TV series] Dir. Tommy Lee Wallace, USA / Canada: Lorimer Television and Dawnfield Entertainment.
IT (2017), [Film] Dir. Andy Muschietti, USA / Canada: New Line Cinema / RatPac-Dune Entertainment / Vertigo Entertainment.
It Came from Outer Space (1953), [Film] Dir. Jack Arnold, USA: Universal International.
Killer Klowns From Outer Space (1988), [Film] Dir. Stephen Chiodo, USA: Chiodo Bros.

King Kong (1933), [Film] Dir. Merian C. Cooper and Ernest B. Schoedsack, USA: RKO Radio Pictures.
Laugh, Clown, Laugh (1928), [Film] Dir. Herbert Brenon, USA: Metro-Goldwyn-Mayer.
Night of the Living Dead (1968), [Film] Dir. George Romero, USA: Image Ten.
Plan 9 From Outer Space (1959), [Film] Dir. Ed Wood, USA: Reynolds Pictures, Inc.
Teenage Zombies (1959), [Film] Dir. Jerry Warren, USA: Governor Films, Inc.
The Wizard of Oz (1939), [Film] Dir. Victor Fleming, USA: Metro-Goldwyn-Mayer.

5

Death is the price

Racial segregation, urban gentrification and the horrors of *Candyman*

Phevos Kallitsis

Introduction

The horror genre consists of an eclectic aggregation of films of different form which are grouped together under the concept of their attempt to shock, scare or horrify the audience (Cherry 2009: 1–51). Among the classic strategies used by the genre to achieve this emotional reaction from its audience has been the foregrounding of feelings of isolation experienced by a given film's characters (Royer and Cooper 2005) within various spatial settings. For this reason, the secluded country house or the quiet suburban house at the end of the road have become key spaces of the horror genre. Even when horror takes place in overpopulated cities the action may be confined solely within the walls of an apartment. However, horror has also sought to take advantage of the intrinsic human fear of the contaminated, dark, crowded, alienating city itself (Latham 2007) and the pathogeneses linked to the contemporary metropolis that have ultimately taken over the discourse of urbanity in the twentieth century (Vidler 2000). A paradigm of a film attempting to exploit the very idea of the scary city in its narrative is Bernard Rose's *Candyman* (1992), which can be seen as a landmark feature of the urban horror subgenre. *Candyman* appears in many must-see horror films lists (Schneider 2009) and its commercial success led to two sequels: *Candyman: Farewell to the Flesh* (Bill Condon, 1995) moved the action to the carnival in New Orleans while *Candyman: Day of the Dead* (Turi Meyer, 1999) transformed Candyman into yet another slasher flick icon.

Candyman returned to cinema screens more recently in Nia DaCosta's requel, *Candyman* (2021).

Rose's film has been the subject of a plethora of academic examinations, with scholars adopting different points of inquiry. Hill (1997) and, more recently, Blouin (2016) discuss the racial tensions of the film and Candyman's character. Wyrick (1998) examines the transformation of the myth in relation to specific cultural histories. Kuhn (2000) and, later, Hoeveler (2007) focus on the film's gender roles and Ni Fhlainn (2008), Donaldson (2011) and Means Coleman (2011: 188–91) highlight the intersectional aspects of the social stakes depicted in the film. In the same line of investigation, Briefel and Ngaî (1996) and Thompson (2007) add to discussions about the social conflicts depicted in the film while also focusing on the importance of the film's spatial setting and architectural space.

The distributor's promotion of *Candyman* as a slasher flick – seemingly an attempt to capitalize on the trend set by *Halloween* (John Carpenter, 1979) and similar franchise-leading films – has resulted in scholars examining the film as part of this subgenre (see Abbot 2015). However, Thompson (2007: 59) notes that Candyman is not actually an incarnation of pure evil who slaughters teenagers and so is not really a slasher film character as such. Also, the extensive literature on the film which underlines its urban element contradicts Maccabe's view that the film is an 'articulation of fundamental emotions in generalised settings' (Rose and Maccabe 1993: 24) and highlights the important role played by Cabrini Green, the low-income Black neighbourhood situated in Chicago's Near North. When DaCosta's *Candyman* requel was announced, many press articles revisited the film and its link to the urban setting of Chicago's infamous housing project and the gentrification process it subsequently underwent. In this chapter, I build upon earlier literature but I argue that contrary to the focus of previous work on providing background details about Cabrini Green, knowledge of the urban context is not the overriding reason for the suspense and tension generated in *Candyman*. Instead, I suggest that Rose's film captures the more expansive essence of the 'scary city' (Kern 2010) by showing the ways that urban boundaries in large cities divide communities and groups, based on income, race and gender. By framing its action within a complicated urban structure, the film actually links to a universal spatial connotation of higher-income white areas, lower income areas populated by 'Others' and the fear of crossing the invisible but constantly present boundaries found between them.

The first part of the Candyman franchise works on the idea of a constantly transforming urban legend which is generated by tensions relating to the possible or actual encounter of subjects from different areas of Chicago. For the film death is the price paid by anyone crossing those well-established socio-spatial borders. In order to support this argument, the chapter examines the narrative and the structure of the film, in juxtaposition to the discourse of fear of the city. The chapter constructs the mental map of Chicago set by the film and examines how it creates a 'notional place' (Rowley 2015) of fear, which reflects the global urban condition of cities with mixed cultures and races. The film raises questions on the response to those issues through gentrification strategies and the way new developments ignore existing communities. The actual urban fear, similar to the transformation of the Candyman myth throughout the film (Wyrick 1998), prevails as long as there is an oppressed group of people, dislocated or marginalized by the forces of the market, and despite any investments in higher security measures.

Social and spatial borders

Andrea Kuhn (2000) argues that *Candyman*'s polarized filmic world is obvious even from the official synopsis of the film. Helen Lyle (Virginia Madsen), the female protagonist, is a member of the WASP upper class community of the city's university, while Candyman (Tony Todd) comes from the other side, the place of the urban myths, the Black community and the lower income families confined in the housing projects of Cabrini Green. In this filmic version of Chicago, the social, racial and spatial segregations become key narrative tools, and analysis of the film demonstrates how the urban context is intrinsic to the filmic version of Candyman.

The Candyman myth has taken on multiple versions (Wyrick 1998) and its origin is not actually linked to Chicago. Clive Barker's original story 'The Forbidden' (2001) takes place in a similarly demonized urban context, a decaying council housing estate in Liverpool. The decision for the film to be set in America led its producers to Cabrini Green, because during a location scouting visit Bernard Rose 'realized that this was an incredible arena for a horror movie because it was a place of such palpable fear' (in Horrorella 2015). Similarly, Virginia Madsen, who grew up in Chicago, remembered that 'you did not even drive by Cabrini Green' (in Schwarz 2004), highlighting the suspense created in the film by having a white female character walking in the area alone.

Cabrini Green has long been a contested area and historically had a negative reputation. The slum area in the north part of Central Chicago was once called Little Sicily and was also known as Little Hell (Zorbaugh 1929). The Cabrini Green project was supposed to rebrand the area and upgrade the living conditions for the workers living there (Ruiz-Tagle 2014). Not long after its construction started in 1940, the closing of the factories following the end of the Second World War created an area with many unemployed residents. In the late 1950s, the first residential towers were constructed, changing an initially smaller scale approach in order to host more families. However, budget limitations resulted in an undesired area: planned green spaces were paved, streetlights were not maintained, and by the 1980s damaged apartments would be sealed instead of being fixed up (Maudlyne 2010). In addition, the segregation strategies of the city authorities led to a change of population and subverted the original plans for a mixed-income community. By 1962 the majority of residents were Black and when people's financial situations improved they would move away from the area (Austen 2018).

The area became synonymous with drugs, gangs and crime, and during the end of the 1980s and the early 1990s – the time that the film was going into production – the press were reporting incidents such as the death of a woman who was murdered when someone broke into her flat through a mirror (Bogira 1987) and the killing of a seven-year-old boy by gang crossfire (Terry 1992). Both of these cases affected the overall reputation of the area and they were duly integrated into the film (Bogira 2014). The inclusion of these events in the film's narrative are key, since their association with the area requires some local knowledge, which the majority of the audience did not possess. Rose by not being local understood the need to go beyond the Cabrini Green name and he states that he wanted to address the universal idea of 'being in the wrong part of the city' (in Schwarz 2004). The challenge then is to map and define the different parts of the city and to examine why people cross the lines that divide them.

Chicago's racial maps visualize why Cabrini Green has been such a contested place and a key scene in the film draws the social and racial borders of the city, making sure that *Candyman*'s Chicago embodies the tensions found in reality. While racial segregation in housing is one of the key issues in the city, even fifty years after the Fair Housing Act (Insalaco 2018), racial mappings of the area of Near North never seem to have a high concentration of Black citizens (maps by Paul Jogn Higgins in Bogira 2011). However, a more detailed representation of segregation (Rankin 2009) which looks within each smaller area within Near North reveals that Cabrini Green was an enclave of poverty with a high concentration of a Black citizens, in great proximity to affluent and mainly white areas, especially Gold Coast (see Figure 5.1). The housing projects disrupt the urban order because Gold Coast residents may not be able to avoid an element of contact with Cabrini Green. For example, they may have to cross the area on a daily basis if they need to travel across the city in a Westward direction. Contrary to the segregation policies that attempt to make the less affluent areas invisible, Cabrini Green's location makes it difficult to overlook. The film draws on that contradiction and the narrative gradually interweaves the two parts of the city.

A key scene of the film is when Helen and Bernadette (Kasi Lemmons) discuss the findings of their research and they draw the boundaries of the filmic map of Chicago. The two women are sitting in the living room of the apartment at the fictional Lincoln Tower owned by Helen and her husband Trevor (Xander Berkeley), a university professor. Looking at the window and the privileged view of the city, Helen explains that her research revealed that Lincoln Tower was originally planned as a social housing project. However, the building's location was outside the urban borders that allowed the separation of the upper-middleclass area from the projects. Figure 5.1 overlays the filmic map on Chicago's urban map and shows what Helen means when she says 'the city soon realized that there was no barrier between here and the Gold Coast. Unlike over there, where you got the highway and the L train to keep the ghetto cut off'. For this reason, they refurbished Lincoln Tower, plastered the walls and sold them 'as condos'.

Until this moment when this mental map is clearly drawn the narrative stays within the affluent world of the University and Gold Coast. The first intersection of the city's two worlds is not spatial. It comes about through contact with a group of people who are part of the University world but who are usually overlooked, the cleaners. Helen has a discussion with one of the cleaners in the University who mentions that her friend Ruthie Jean lived in Cabrini Green and was allegedly murdered by Candyman. This first intersection of the city's two worlds is the reason that Helen starts her research into Cabrini Green, convinced that there lies the truth behind the urban legend of Candyman. The headline Helen's research turns up – 'What Killed Ruthie Jean? Life in the Projects' – and Bernadette's reaction – 'I won't even drive

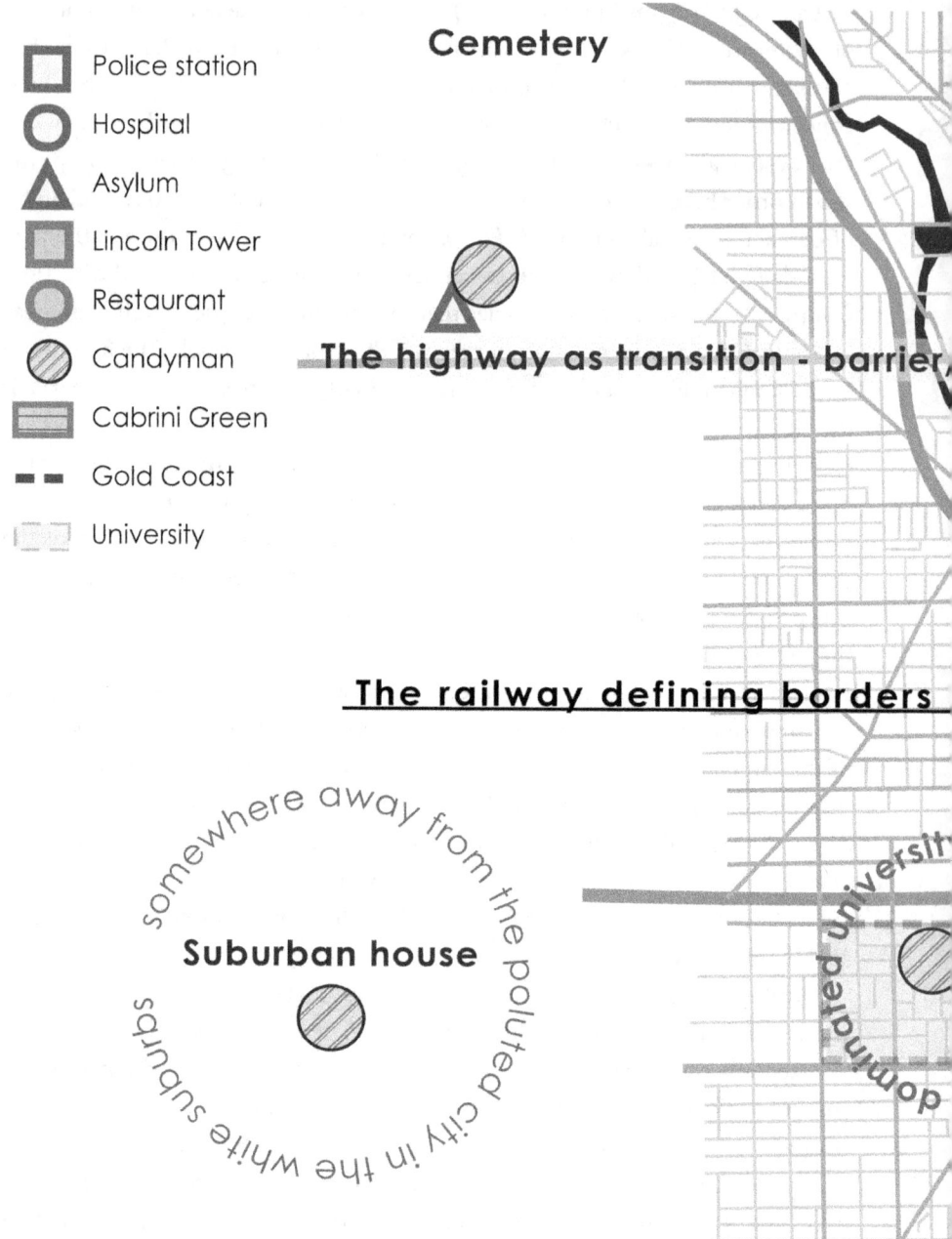

Figure 5.1 *Candyman*: Chicago as presented in *Candyman* (1992). Image © 2022 Phevos Kallitsis.

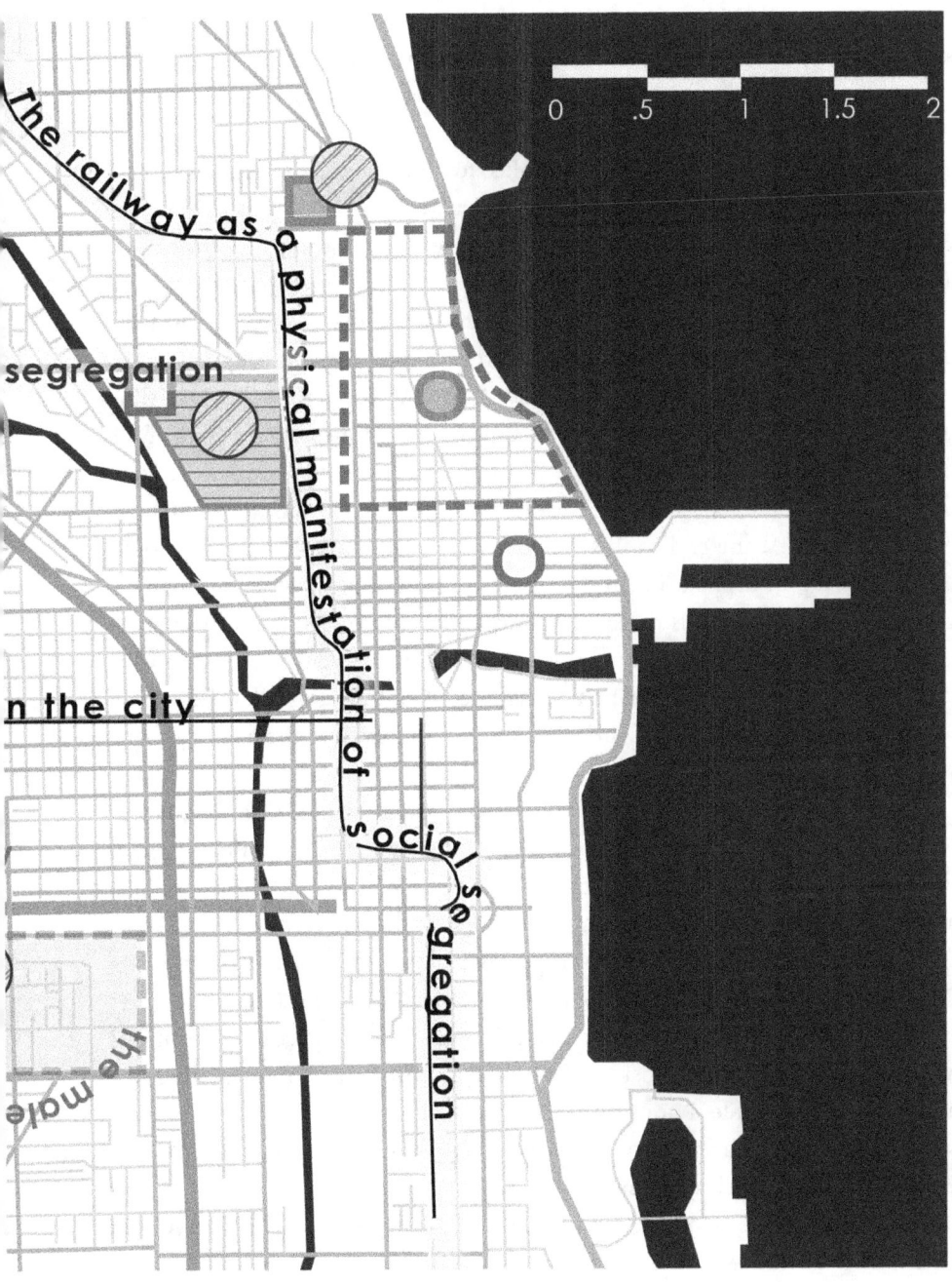

past there, heard a kid got shot there the other day' – are inferences to local stories which constitute the very idea of a dangerous part of the city. Thus, the two researchers need to overcome their fears and to cross the boundary of the highway.

According to Lysaght (2007), fear is linked to space, because it is the awareness of a possible threat connected to the way the subject reads the space. Thus, Nan Ellin (1997) explores architecture as a response to a constant need for safety and a response to feelings of vulnerability. Kuhn (2000) argues that the highway mentioned by Helen is the manifestation of the divide that allows the residents of Gold Coast to feel safe and it plays a key role in the narrative as a transitional pathway which crosses districts in the city. As we can see in the spatial timeline of the film (see Figure 5.2) the highway appears three times. At the start of the film a long overhead shot (with the film's titles and credits overlaid) travels from the east (Gold Coast) to the west (Cabrini Green, the unknown territory of the 'Other'). At the end of this sequence Rose cuts to a shot of what looks like a close-up of asphalt, but the music fades into a buzzing sound and the camera zooms into what is revealed to be a swarm of bees. In the next shot the swarm – a sign of Candyman's presence – hovers over the city and a voice-over acts as a warning that the whole city is haunted. Contrary to Helen's belief that Candyman is an issue for the Cabrini Green community only, the opening scene signals the much larger scale of the problem.

The film's production design showcases the extent of the issue. The layout of Helen's and Ruthie Jean's apartments are identical in plan, with the main differences being the uncovered cinder block and the furniture. This superficial approach to what it means to regenerate and alter an area or a building shows the tendency of dealing with the symptoms and not the reasons of scary city syndrome and reflects the literature on urban safety. De Souza (2010) identifies two solutions, which he defines as liberal and conservative respectively. The liberal approach (Mitchell 2003) considers fear to be a consequence of social divisions and inequalities, while a conservative approach seems to recycle older ideas such as defensible space theory (the idea that architectural and environmental designs can effect levels of crime) (Newman 1972), the broken windows theory (the idea that visible signs of crime encourage more crime) (Kelling & Wilson 1982), zero tolerance policies and the creation of excluding environments to sanitize the urban experience and remove unwanted encounters with the 'Other' (Smith 1996). Despite living in a sanitized environment, if Helen and Bernadette aspire to progress their research, they need to deal with the fact that urban space intrinsically implies a possibly fearful, virtual or actual, meeting with the 'Other' (Abu-Orf 2012).

The second time the highway appears signifies the crossing of the spatial and social boundary. The two women are worried about what they are wearing and about visiting the area on their own and Bernadette carries a pepper spray. Once in the projects, wide and middle shots show an abandoned place, a greenless desert with high-rise buildings. The women see a group of boys and the frame's point-of-view perspective gives the feeling that the women are entering a fortress. Indeed, within the frame a fenced corridor works like a bridge to a fortress and the boys are placed in key positions as if they are guards. The boys' suspicion that the women are cops, a broken elevator and the lack of lights on a staircase create a sequence of events which increases the tension, but things never escalate to what the characters or the audience are expecting. Rather quickly Helen and Bernadette are left alone to explore the building. The interior of the building contradicts the sanitized pastel colours of Lincoln Tower: graffiti on the walls, a lack of light and abandoned apartments. Helen and Bernadette take photos, enter the deserted flats and act as if no permission is required. It is a tenant, Anne-Marie (Vanessa Williams), who at some point, opens her door and says 'You have no right to do whatever you want', reminding the two women (and the audience) that there are people who live here who have to be respected. This moment reveals that Helen's care stems from a position of privilege about 'the daily horrors of their [the Cabrini Green community's] lives' and that she needs to treat the subjects of her research with respect (Gibbs 2006).

For Helen's second visit to Cabrini Green there is no transitional shot of the highway (see Figure 5.2). The transition is done through a simple cut from Helen in a restaurant with her husband and other academics to Helen taking photos again in Cabrini Green. This time though she meets Jake (DeJuan Guy), an eleven-year-old boy, who becomes her guide. Jake leads her to some public toilets where the last attack of the alleged Candyman took place. Once again, the shots express the abandonment and the lack of maintenance of the area's communal and public spaces. The outdoor space in Cabrini Green is a wasteland, contrary to that of Lincoln Tower, which looks like a park. However, the interior of Anne-Marie's apartment is a warm space, and the film highlights that people have made their homes there despite the challenges. Thus, they need to be respected and as Helen understands this, her transition towards Cabrini Green becomes more direct and easier. On the other hand, her way out of the projects becomes more challenging.

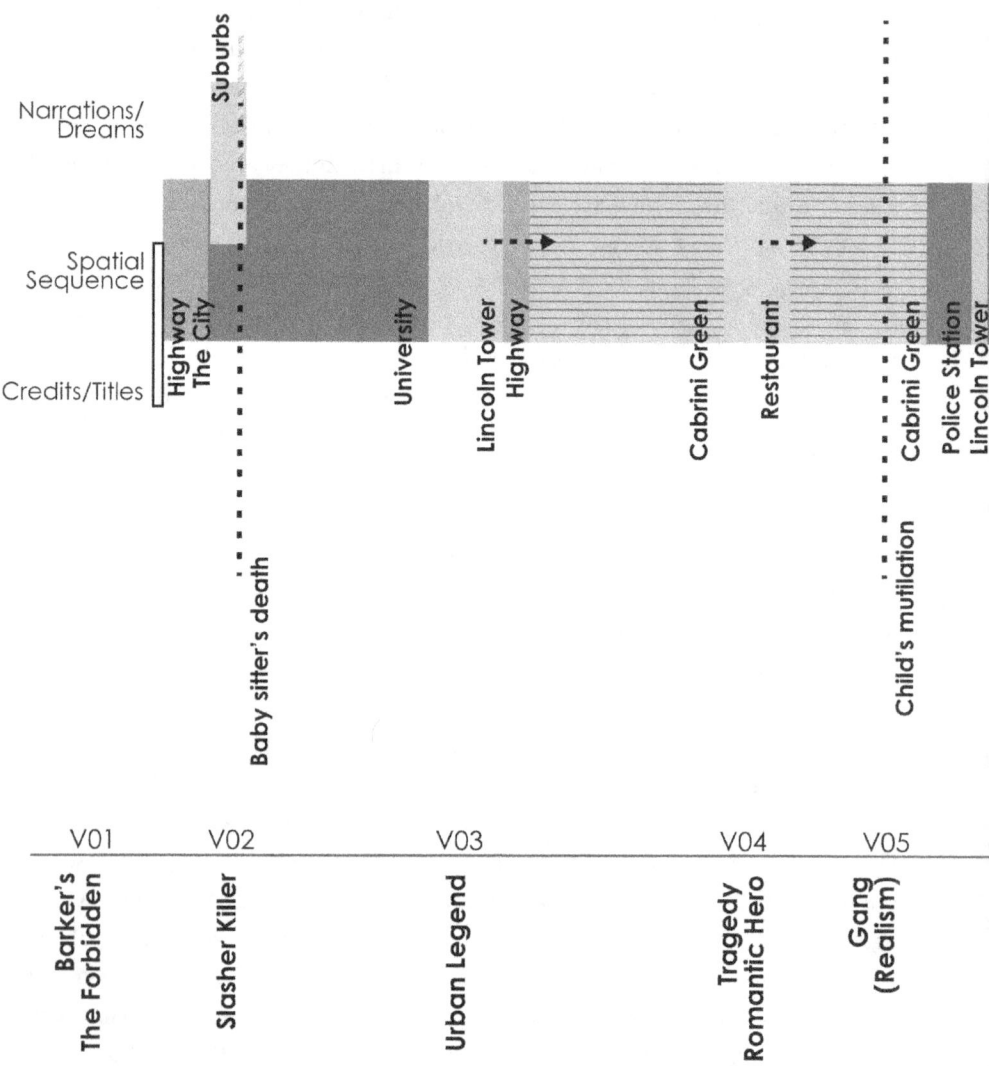

Figure 5.2 *Candyman*: The sequence of spaces in *Candyman* (1992) juxtaposed to key events and the evolution of the Candyman myth. Image © 2022 Phevos Kallitsis.

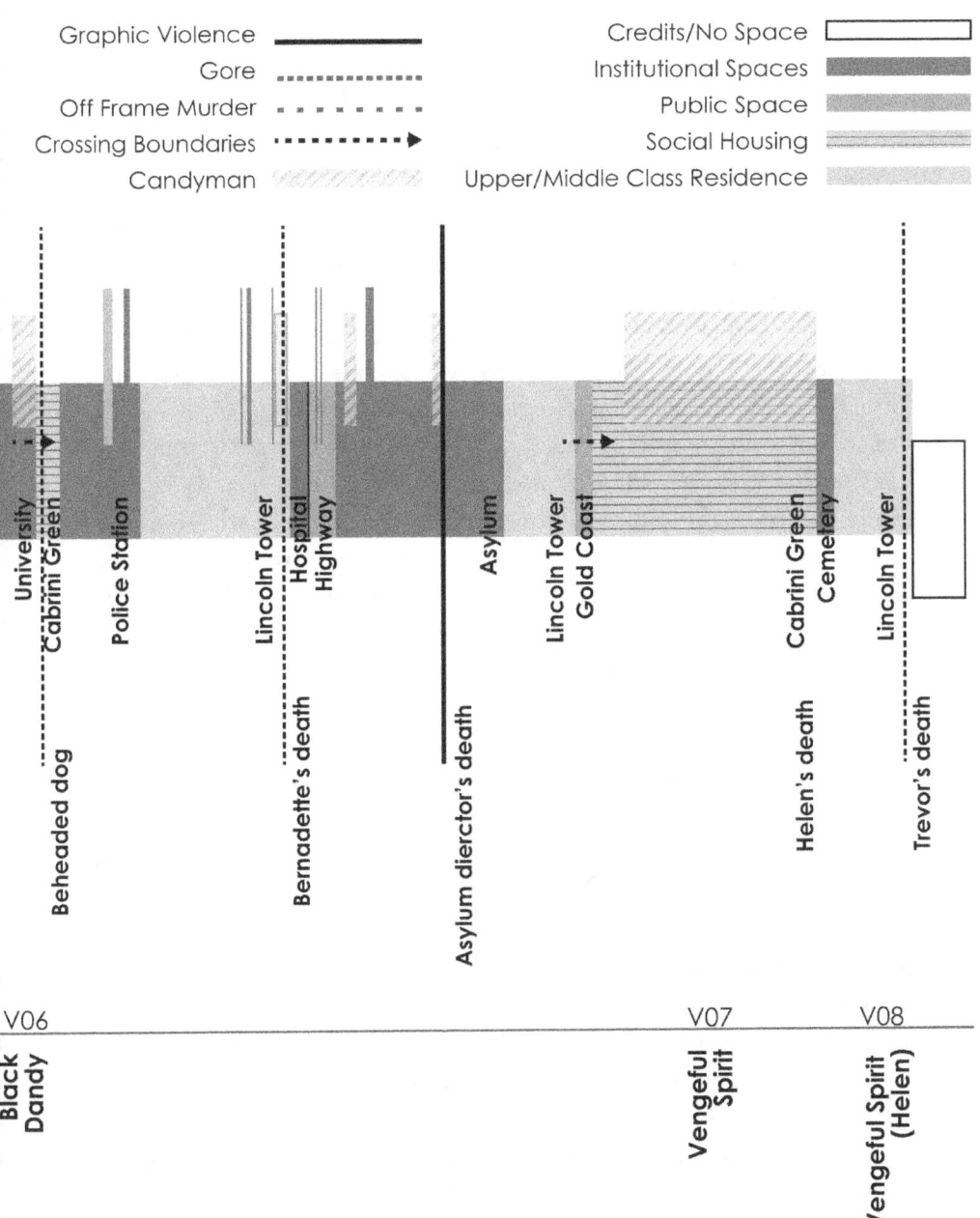

From the suburbs to the soon-to-be gentrified city

Wyrick (1998) highlights the continued transformations of the Candyman myth from Barker's story and throughout Rose's film, which subsequently changes direction in the two sequels, but is picked up again by the 2021 requel. If we overlay the versions of the Candyman myth over the spatial set up of Rose's film (see Figure 5.2) it becomes clear that the spatial set up changes alongside the myth. Barker's original Candyman (a blond figure wearing a colourful coat) operates solely within a rundown housing estate in Liverpool, but in the film there is a cycle of locations for Candyman, which takes in the white suburbs, Cabrini Green and the upper middle-class area of Chicago.

The city as a link to fears is underlined from the opening scene, following the titles. After the overhead highway shot, Candyman's voice sounds over the city and then the shot transitions slowly to Helen's close-up. Moreover, this transition underlines how Helen and Candyman are linked from the beginning (Kuhn 2000); the image of the city reveals the common ground where they will meet. However, when the myth first manifests in Barker's story, it follows the slasher flick narrative of a ghost killer attacking a teenager in a suburban house. Barker's story is narrated by a student but this version does not resonate with the film's student, Helen. Helen questions the mediated experience of the film's white students, while the story of Ruthie Jean seems more plausible and realistic, especially as it links to an infamous area of the city. Until the moment when Jake guides her to the public toilets, Helen believes that there is a rational explanation for the Candyman legend. In the toilets, Helen is attacked by a gang that has taken advantage of the myth to terrorize people. The injured Helen ends up at the police station, recognizes the gang leader and the gang is arrested.

Following the resolution of the mystery, Helen talks with Bernadette about the social inequality that is evidenced when the police choose not to act when two Black people are murdered, but soon 'tear the place up' when a 'white woman gets attacked'. This comment reflects not only social inequalities but also the idea that the importance of safety only becomes a priority after the affluent classes have themselves moved from the periphery to the deteriorating central urban areas of a city (Atkinson 2006). The safety of these newly identified dangerous areas require political action (Lees 2003) because the land offers investment opportunities. The dangerous city becomes a tool to promote urban regeneration creating a reciprocal relation between these interventions in the city and fear, because the affluent classes do not want to encounter what has been defined as the dangerous 'Other'.

At this moment, when a rational explanation has been offered, Helen goes to her car in the empty University parking lot and Candyman appears. His outfit has invariably been described as one belonging to an urban pimp or a metaphorical prince or, as Donaldson (2011) more accurately suggests, a Black Dandy. The Black Dandy interpretation reflects the romantic version of the myth that Professor Purcell (Michael Culkin) described earlier during the restaurant scene, and it is also adopted in the sequels. In this scene, Rose uses the stereotypical horror-thriller scenario of a stranger appearing in an empty parking lot, but Helen does not have the expected reaction. Instead of panicking and running, she remains magnetized by his presence. In part, both her and the audience did not expect Candyman's first actual appearance to be outside the borders of Cabrini Green. Contrary to the gangs, Candyman is not just a problem of the Black community, and the highway does not prevent him from carrying out attacks outside of the poverty enclave. At the end of the parking lot scene, Candyman embraces Helen and transports her back to Cabrini Green.

After this scene, Helen is constantly drawn to the projects and dives headlong into Candyman's world; the wrong part of the city which needs external intervention to be saved, or to be regenerated. The narration leaves things open to interpretation, since Helen is the only person who witnesses Candyman's killings. Helen slowly draws away from her own community and her status fluctuates but ultimately becomes reduced while Candyman's power continues to grow stronger. Helen, based on the context, is aligned with both the oppressed and the oppressors in different sections of the film. Helen needs to stand up and question the limits of her gender within the male-dominated University (Hoeveler 2007), while her professor husband and the urban legend specialist Purcell question her research and her abilities. Her research and ambitions are actually interrupted by the brief period in which she assumes the housewife role after the gang attacks her. However, when in Cabrini Green she is a white middle-class woman who has many privileges (on this note it is worth mentioning also that Bernadette's blackness is erased when she is in Cabrini Green, because of her class status). So, Helen's presence constantly highlights and questions the spatial divisions that are set by gender, race and class.

Helen's privileges are revealed after her first meeting with Candyman. She wakes up in Anne-Marie's apartment covered in blood. A dead dog is next to her and Anne-Marie's baby has gone, but she just goes to the hospital and then goes home to wait for the results of the police investigation. The audience may know about Candyman's existence but the police do not, so their decision to allow Helen to remain at liberty is based on her class and race. Candyman continues haunting her and he appears in the Lincoln Tower to kill Bernadette. Accused of killing the middle-class Bernadette in Gold Coast, Helen is subsequently transferred to an asylum and the loss of status for Helen results in Candyman becoming stronger. After Candyman kills the asylum director, Helen escapes and runs to her apartment only to discover that Trevor is having an affair with one of his students. At this moment, she decides to quit her world and to return to the projects to save Anne-Marie's baby from Candyman.

Spatial sequences and the consequences of crossing

The diagram of the sequences of *Candyman*'s spaces (see Figure 5.2) reveals Helen's journey throughout the film. There are two levels depicted, the actual space where Helen is located and the mental spaces which are created when Helen is listening to a narration or imagining something. The spaces are divided into private, communal and public spaces, institutional spaces and Cabrini Green (the wrong part of the city). The diagram reveals the presence of some key notional links. The role of the highway in a transitional shot that travels from Gold Coast to Cabrini Green has already been discussed. The highway appears again to link Helen's journey from Gold Coast to a new unknown space, the asylum, where she is held after being arrested for Bernadette's murder. Thus, the highway once again signifies this journey to the unknown. The other key observation that comes out of the diagram is the places that Helen ends up after a visit to the wrong part of the city. With the exception of her first visit, every other visit to Cabrini Green is followed by a visit to a space which underlines the warning that she should not have been to Cabrini Green. Indeed, after crossing the boundaries of Cabrini Green, Helen ends up in the police station, once as an injured victim and once as a suspect, and after her last visit she winds up at a cemetery. Furthermore, as she crosses these boundaries she loses her status, ultimately being considered to be a murder suspect. Furthermore, she is removed from the public space, becoming trapped in her apartment, or the asylum, or handcuffed, limited and adrift to the decisions of various men: her husband, the detective, the doctors, the asylum director and of course Candyman.

Before responding to Candyman's call to save Anne-Marie's baby, she wanders in Gold Coast, completely disconnected before a simple cut shows her in her final visit to Cabrini Green. She moves through the cracks of the urban space, always finding openings that lead her deeper into the uncharted territories of the area's decay. This sequence reflects the reports in newspapers about the poor maintenance of the projects, with damaged apartments being boarded up and left to rot instead of being repaired and re-inhabited (Maudlyne 2010). In a manifestation of the much contested 'broken windows' theory (Kelling and Wilson 1982), the lack of maintenance results in the damaged space expanding and the decaying projects become the temple of Candyman. The wall paintings and graffiti found there are not just the stereotypical signs of gang culture. The wall paintings portray Candyman's tortured history and mark a sacred place. The symmetry of the frames and the production design portray an altar for an urban legend who aspires to become a god and requires a blood sacrifice.

Helen saves Anne-Marie's baby, but she is not the one who will stop the killings. At the film's end the previously absent Black community, who had remained terrorized behind locked doors, is finally forced to reappropriate its own public space because they cannot expect any help to come from outside of Cabrini Green. Led by Jake who realizes that Candyman hides in a huge pile of garbage that is situated in a nearby courtyard, the local residents act as an empowered community when they elect to stop Candyman by torching the garbage pile. This collective action puts Anne-Marie's baby (who has been hidden in the garbage pile by Candyman) in danger, but Helen rescues him before she dies. Helen must sacrifice herself, paying the price for ignoring established urban boundaries but she is redeemed for her earlier lack of respect. However, the fact remains that she is not the one who faces Candyman and saves the day.

Conclusion: Subverting spatial fears and borders

Twenty years after the film's release, when the last tower of the projects was demolished in the name of urban regeneration, some of the residents remained opposed to the whole demolition and relocation plan (Austen 2018). The demolition of the Cabrini Green buildings was reported by newspapers as being 'the end of an ugly era' (Hawkings 2010) and the start of a gentrified future for the city of Chicago. Rose actually celebrates the possibility that the film led to the demolition of the area (Schwarz 2004). Contemporary to *Candyman*, Diane

Ghirardo (1996: 43–4) writes how public space seems to obtain two qualities: on one hand it becomes a consumer's space and on the other hand it becomes fragmented and easily controlled. The future of a community and its existing networks can be disregarded because, at an emotional level, it is deemed that the wrong part of the city needs to be sanitized so that it can function as a reassurance for every insecurity.

The new face of Cabrini Green demanded a change of population. Despite the promises of affordable housing as part of the new development, most of the existing community was dislocated and moved to other parts of the city, making space for those with higher incomes to move into the new buildings (Vale 2012), just like Helen and Trevor had done in Lincoln Tower. The new Cabrini Green was purified from the evils of those with lower incomes, as real estate maps of crimes committed in Chicago show (CrimeGrade.org n.d.). As a result, despite the celebration of the end of an ugly era, the reality is that inequalities always generate violence and fear, and prosthetic approaches to security are insufficient tools.

Despite the film's various clichéd shock tactics to make its audience jolt, gory scenes do not dominate *Candyman* (see Figure 5.2). Helen and Candyman both remain characters of ambivalent nature and they both pay a price for trying to change their place on the social map. Helen's presence highlights questions about the spatial divisions that are set by gender, race and class and her status shifts between that of oppressor and oppressed. Candyman changes constantly and is presented in different forms. At the start of the film Candyman is simply an urban legend, narrated by white students as part of a typical suburban horror story; Professor Purcell offers the back story of the hook handed man, as a romantic avenging spirit of the past; Helen rationalizes the myth by uncovering the 'fake Candyman' gang, which leads to Candyman himself manifesting as the stranger in the parking lot. The fearful retreat of the Cabrini Green community nurtures the myth and the projects become his temple. Helen and Candyman's crossings from one area of the city to the other destabilize both Cabrini Green and Gold Coast and ultimately provide the foundation of fear. But even when the residents burn down Candyman's hiding place, the fear felt by those citizens with higher incomes is far from over.

Rose's film includes different facets of repression that underlie the various crystallizations and de-crystallizations that form today's concept of public space. The connection between the threat (them, the 'Other') and the threatened (us) is a major trope of horror films and it can be linked to Wood's (2004: 69–84) concept of the 'return of the repressed'. The exclusion of a particular community leaves a space for the creation of new legends and violent reactions. Before the end credits roll Helen, the repressed and excluded female figure of the white middle-class community, becomes the next incarnation of the myth. She turns into an avenging entity and kills Trevor; an indication that the danger can also be 'us' rather than just the 'Other'. Interestingly, Da Costa's requel builds upon the idea of the rebirth of the myth and its altering nature, something that the two sequels failed to do.

Still the turning point of the film is not the conclusion of Helen becoming the killer. The pivotal moment in *Candyman* comes after Candyman is burnt and Helen is dead and the fear felt by the Cabrini Green community is ended. The Cabrini Green residents appear at Helen's funeral and, as they walk together and look more engaged than Helen's friends, they demonstrate that despite our beliefs about decaying neighbourhoods and areas, within those notional places of fear there are actual communities formed and relations forged that cannot be overlooked or neglected. These social networks and communities are linked to places and sometimes this is a greater safety net than the isolated, polished and sealed spaces favoured by those who fear the city and hide behind their higher security measures. Anyway, Candyman just needs one person to say his name five times and he will be back regardless of where that person is located.

Bibliography

Abbot, Stacey. 'Candyman and Saw: Reimagining the Slasher Film through Urban Gothic'. In *Style and Form in the Hollywood Slasher Film*, edited by Wickham Clayton, 67–78. London: Palgrave Macmillan, 2015.

Abu-Orf, Hazem. 'Fear of Difference: "Space of Risk" and Anxiety in Violent Settings'. *Planning Theory*, 12, no. 2 (2012): 158–76.

Atkinson, Rowland. 'Padding the Bunker: Strategies of Middle-class Disaffiliation and Colonisation in the City'. *Urban Studies (Routledge)* 43, no. 4 (2006): 819–32.

Austen, Ben. *High-Risers: Cabrini-Green and the Fate of American Public Housing*. New York: Harper, 2018.

Barker, Clive. 'The Forbidden'. In *The Books of Blood*, 597–629. Toronto: Stealth Press, 2001.

Blouin, Michael J. 'Candyman and Neoliberal Racism'. In *Magical Thinking, Fantastic Film, and the Illusions of Neoliberalism*, edited by Michael J. Blouin, 81–107. New York: Palgrave Macmillan, 2016.

Bogira, Steve. 'They Came in Through the Bathroom Mirror: A Murder in the Projects'. *Reader*, 3 September 1987. Available online at: https://chicagoreader.com/news-politics/they-came-in-through-the-bathroom-mirror/ (accessed 15 June 2017).

Bogira, Steve. 'Separate, Unequal, and Ignored'. *Reader*, 10 February 2011. Available online at http://www.chicagoreader.com/chicago/chicago-politics-segregation-african-american-black-white-hispanic-latino-population-census-community/Content?oid=3221712 (accessed 15 February 2015).

Bogira, Steve. 'How a Story About the Horrors of Housing Projects Became Part of a Horror Movie'. *Reader*, 14 March 2014. Available online at https://chicagoreader.com/blogs/how-a-story-about-the-horrors-of-housing-projects-became-part-of-a-horror-movie/ (accessed 15 May 2017).

Briefel, Aviva and Sianne Ngaî. '"How Much Did You Pay for This Place?": Fear, Entitlement, and Urban Space in Bernard Rose's *Candyman*'. *Camera Obscura* 13, no. 1 (1996): 69–91.

Cherry, Brigid. *Horror*. London: Routledge, 2009.

de Souza, Marcelo Lopes. 'The Brave New (Urban) World of Fear and (Real or Presumed) Wars'. *City* 14, no. 4 (2010): 457–63.

Donaldson, Lucy Fife. '"The Suffering Black Male Body and the Threatened White Female Body": Ambiguous Bodies in Candyman'. *Irish Journal of Gothic and Horror Studies* 9 (2011): 32–43.

Ellin, Nan. 'Shelter from the Storm or Form Follows Fear and Vice Versa'. In *Architecture of Fear*, edited by Nan Ellin, 13–47. New York: Princeton Architectural Press, 1997.

Ghirardo, Diane. *Architecture after Modernism*. London: Thames & Hudson, 1996.

Gibbs, John. 'What Killed Ruthie Jean?: Architectural Design in Candyman (1992)'. In *Close-Up 01: Filmmakers' Choices/The Pop Song in Film/Reading Buffy*, edited by John Gibbs, Deborah Thomas, Ian Garwood, and Dougles Pye, 69–82. New York: Wallflower, 2006.

Hawkings, Karen. 'Chicago Shutters Infamous Public Housing Complex'. *NBCNews*, 1 December 2010. Available online at: http://www.nbcnews.com/id/40450463/ns/us_news-life/t/chicago-shutters-infamous-public-housing-complex/#.WbJTDbKGOM8 (accessed 12 February 2014).

Hill, Mike. 'Can Whiteness Speak? Institutional Anomies, Ontological Disasters, and Three Hollywood Films'. In *White Trash: Race And Class In America*, edited by Annallee Newitz and Matt Wray, 155–73. New York: Routledge, 1997.

Hoeveler, Diane Long. 'The Postfeminist Filmic Female Gothic Detective: Reading the Bodily Text in Candyman'. In *Postfeminism Gothic: Critical Investigations in Contemporary Culture*, edited by Benjamin A. Barbon and Stéphanie Genz, 99–113. London: Palgrave Macmillan, 2007.

Horrorella. 'Horrorella Talks Tolstoy, Beethoven and Candyman with Writer-Director Bernard Rose!'. *Ain't it Cool News*, 12 August 2015. Available online at: http://www

.aintitcool.com/node/72689?utm_source=full-feed&utm_medium=feed&utm_term=coolnews&utm_campaign=1310_RSS (accessed 15 May 2017).

Insalaco, Amanda. 'Fifty Years Since Passage of the Fair Housing Act: Rent-to-income Ratios in the Persistence of Residential Racial Segregation in Chicago'. *John Marshall Law Review* 51, no. 3 (2018): 551–88.

Kelling, George L. and James Q. Wilson. 'Broken Windows: The Police and Neighborhood Safety'. *The Atlantic*, March 1982: 29–38.

Kern, Leslie. 'Selling the "Scary City": Gendering Freedom, Fear and Condominium Development in the Neoliberal City'. *Social & Cultural Geography* 11, no. 3 (2010): 209–30.

Kuhn, Andrea. '"What's the Matter, Trevor? Scared of Something?" Representing the Monstrous-feminine in Candyman'. *Erfurt Electronic Studies in English* 1 (2000). Available online at: http://webdoc.sub.gwdg.de/edoc/ia/eese/artic20/kuhn/kuhn.html (accessed 15 May 2017).

Latham, Rob. 'The Urban Horror'. In *Icons of Horror and the Supernatural: An Encyclopedia of Our Worst Nightmares*, edited by S. T. Joshi, 591–618. Westport: Greenwood Publishing Group, 2007.

Lees, Loretta. 'Visions of "Urban Renaissance": The Urban Task Force Report and the Urban White Paper'. In *Urban Renaissance?: New Labour, Community and Urban Policy*, edited by Rob Imrie and Mike Raco, 61–82. Bristol: Bristol University Press, 2003.

Lysaght, Karen D. '"Catholics, Protestants and Office Workers from the Town": The Experience and Negotiation of Fear in Northern Ireland'. in *The Emotions. A Cultural Reader*, edited by Helen Wulff, 93–100. Oxford: Berg, 2007.

Maudlyne, Ihejirika. 'Cabrini-Green's Last Stand: Families Prepare to Move Out'. *Chicago Sun-Times*. 23 October 2010. Available online at: https://chicago.suntimes.com/news/metro/2246720-418/cabrini-housing-cha-residents-public.html (accessed 16 May 2015).

Means Coleman, Robin. *Horror Noire: Black in American Horror Films from the 1890s to the Present*. London: Routledge, 2011.

Mitchell, Don. *The Right to the City: Social Justice and the Fight for Public Space*. New York: Guilford Press, 2003.

Newman, Oscar. *Defensible Space: Crime Prevention Through Urban Design*. New York: Macmillan, 1972.

Ni Fhlainn, Sorcha. 'Sweet, Bloody Vengeance: Class, Social Stigma and Servitude in the Slasher Genre'. In *Hosting the Monster*, edited by Holly Lynn Baumgartner and Roger Davis, 179–96. Amsterdam: Rodopi, 2008.

Rankin, Bill. 'Chicago Boundaries'. *Radical Cartography*, 2009. Available online at http://www.radicalcartography.net/index.html?chicagodots (accessed 19 February 2015).

Rose, Bernard and Collin Maccabe. 'More Things in Heaven and Earth + Reflections on the Serial Killer Film "Candyman"'. *Sight and Sound* 3, no. 3 (1993): 22–4.

Rowley, Stephen. *Movie Towns and Sitcom Suburbs: Building Hollywood's Ideal Communities*. New York: Palgrave Macmillan, 2015.
Royer, Carl and B. Lee Cooper. *The Spectacle of Isolation in Horror Films: Dark Parades*. New York: Taylor and Francis, 2005.
Ruiz-Tagle, Javier. 'The Broken Promises of Social Mix: The Case of the Cabrini Green/Near North Area in Chicago'. *Urban Geography*, 37, no. 3 (2014): 352–72.
Schneider, Stephen J. *101 Horror Movies You Must See Before You Die*. London: Cassell, 2009.
Smith, Neil. *The New Urban Frontier: Gentrification and the Revanchist City*. New York: Routledge, 1996.
Terry, Don. 'Even a Grade School is No Refuge from Gunfire'. *The New York Times*, 17 October 1992. Available online at: https://www.nytimes.com/1992/10/17/us/even-a-grade-school-is-no-refuge-from-gunfire.html?sec=&pagewanted=print (accessed 16 May 2017).
Thompson, Kirsten Moana. *Apocalyptic Dread: American Film at the Turn of the Millennium*. Albany: State University of New York Press, 2007.
Vale, Lawrence. 'Housing Chicago: Cabrini Green to Parkside of Old Town'. *Places Journal*, February 2012. Available online at: https://placesjournal.org/article/housing-chicago-cabrini-green-to-parkside-of-old-town/ (accessed 7 January 2023).
Vidler, Anthony. *Warped Space: Art, Architecture and Anxiety in Modern Culture*. Cambridge: MIT Press, 2000.
Wood, Robin. 'An Introduction to the American Horror Film'. In *Planks of Reason: Essays on the Horror Film*, edited by Barry Keith Grant and Christopher Sharrett, 107–41. Maryland: Scarecrow Press, 2004.
Wyrick, Laura. 'Summoning Candyman: The Cultural Production of History'. *Arizona Quarterly: A Journal of American Literature, Culture, and Theory* 54, no. 3 (1998): 89–117.
Zorbaugh, Harvey Warren. *The Gold Coast and the Slum: A Sociological Study of Chicago's Near North Side*. Chicago: University of Chicago Press, 1929.

Filmography

Candyman (1992), [Film] Dir. Bernard Rose, USA / UK: PolyGram Filmed Entertainment / Propaganda Films / Candyman Films.
Candyman (2021), [Film] Dir. Nia DaCosta, Canada / USA: Universal Pictures / Metro-Goldwyn-Mayer (MGM) / BRON Studios.
Candyman: Farewell to the Flesh (1995), [Film] Dir. Billy Condon, USA: Propaganda Films.
Candyman 3: Day of the Dead (1999), [Film] Dir. Turi Meyer, USA: Universal Pictures.
Halloween (1979), [Film] Dir. John Carpenter, USA: Compass International Pictures.
Sweets to the Sweet: The Candyman Mythos (2004), [DVD extra] Dir. Jeffrey Schwarz, USA: Columbia Tristar Home Entertainment.

6

Decide for yourself

Cult, controversy and anti-capitalism in *The Hunt*

Craig Ian Mann

Introduction: 'Hunting Season Open'

The Hunt (Craig Zobel, 2020) is a hybrid of horror, action and thriller elements: a 'human hunting' film, and one of many that can be traced back to the pre-Code horror picture *The Most Dangerous Game* (Irving Pichel and Ernest B. Schoedsack, 1932). Its concentration on humans hunting other people for sport is a contemporary variation on an old idea, and one that has been employed in genre cinema many times before. However, what sets *The Hunt* apart (and what gives it a claim to cult status) is the controversy that has surrounded it. That controversy can be attributed to who occupies the roles of 'hunter' and 'hunted'; this is a film in which wealthy 'liberals' (Democrats) stalk and kill what they term 'deplorables' – in reference to Hilary Clinton's description of Trumpian Republicans (Reilly 2016) – as part of a conspiracy dubbed 'Manorgate'. Having been described as a 'political Rorschach test' (Sims 2019), the film has been accused of being either too liberal or too conservative. At best, it has been considered centrist or even apolitical, a satirical critique of vicious divisions in the contemporary United States.

In this chapter I will first outline the troubled history of *The Hunt* and its claim to cult status, before investigating the controversy surrounding it and a critical tendency to interpret it using a rigid ideological spectrum. I will show that these readings stand only if the film is understood to be engaging with a political system that it entirely rejects and argue that it is less concerned with partisan politics than it is with the economic inequality that has been a consequence of free-market capitalism – an issue that can no longer be resolved at the ballot box. I will make a case for *The Hunt* as an indictment of a nation that increasingly offers no alternative to capitalism and suggest that it is symptomatic of a contemporary 'desire to simply refuse the system' (Phillips 2021: 7). To conclude, I will illustrate that *The Hunt*'s anti-capitalist subtext continues a thematic tradition in human hunting films that can be traced back to *The Most Dangerous Game*.

'Manorgate'

Given that it is a mainstream film produced by Blumhouse Productions and distributed by Universal Pictures, *The Hunt* seems an unlikely cult movie if not for the fact that it was nearly never released at all. Shot on location in New Orleans in early 2019 (Chow 2020), it was originally planned for release on 18 October that year before Universal brought it forward to 27 September. On 12 July, Universal released its first poster – designed to resemble a warning sign stating that 'Only designated people may be hunted at the Manor' – along with a short teaser: a mock advertisement for a hunting retreat. A more substantial trailer began playing exclusively in theatres that same day (Squires 2019) before it was made available online at the end of the month, generating a great deal of buzz on entertainment news websites (see Schaffstall 2019).

Marketing for *The Hunt* was off to a good start – albeit only for a matter of days. The trailer was released online on 30 July; on the following weekend, two mass shootings took place in El Paso, Texas, and Dayton, Ohio. ESPN pulled ads for the film (Masters and Siegel 2019), and on 6 August the *Hollywood Reporter* published an exclusive in which it quoted incendiary lines from its screenplay, erroneously claimed that its original title was *Red State vs. Blue State* and questioned how wise it was to release *The Hunt* 'Given the fraught political climate' (Masters and Siegel 2019). In the aftermath of these events and further news coverage, Universal paused its marketing campaign on 8 August. In a statement, the studio asserted that this decision was made to show 'sensitivity to the attention on the country's recent shooting tragedies', though the film's release was still scheduled to go ahead (quoted in Watson and Schwartzel 2019). That quickly changed. The next day, Donald Trump posted two vitriolic tweets about *The Hunt* via his personal Twitter feed. Now deleted following the permanent suspension of Trump's account on 8 January 2021, they read [*sic*]:

> Liberal Hollywood is Racist at the highest level, and with great Anger and Hate! They like to call themselves 'Elite,' but they are not Elite. In fact, it is often the people that they so strongly oppose that are actually the Elite. The movie coming out is made in order ... (Trump 2019a)
>
> ... to inflame and cause chaos. They create their own violence, and then try to blame others. They are the true Racists, and are very bad for our Country! (Trump 2019b)

These comments from the president of the United States – on a movie that he had not seen – caused a further media frenzy and sparked responses from both ends of the political spectrum. With this new furore on top of the marketing campaign's proximity to two instances of real-world gun violence, Universal pulled the picture from its release schedule. As *Variety* reported on 10 August, a spokesperson announced: 'after thoughtful consideration, the studio has decided to cancel our plans to release the film' (quoted in Nickolai 2019). Its shelving prompted further responses from critics and cultural commentators; *Variety* itself ran a piece on Universal's decision the next day, praising the studio for not releasing a movie that might have been received as 'less a provocation than a brazen act of insensitivity' (Gleiberman 2019).

However, Universal made clear in its statement that it did not intend to withhold *The Hunt* indefinitely: 'We stand by our filmmakers and will continue to distribute films in partnership with bold and visionary creators, like those associated with this satirical social thriller, but we understand that now is not the right time to release this film' (quoted in Nickolai 2019). The studio decided that the time had come in February 2020, when it launched a fresh marketing campaign that directly referenced the political debates surrounding the film and illustrated 'Blumhouse's willingness to engage with controversial material' (McCollum, Clasen and Platts 2022: 4). Its newest poster featured a tagline reading 'The most talked about movie of the year is one that no one's actually seen' and a challenge to viewers: 'Decide for yourself'. The marketing tactic worked; several outlets framed their coverage around the 2019 controversies when the film's new release date was announced (see Collis 2020).

The Hunt finally arrived in theatres on 13 March 2020. However, the onset of the Covid-19 pandemic meant that most cinemas began to close a few days later. Universal was left with no choice but to shelve the film (again) or release it for home viewing via video-on-demand services. Along with *The Invisible Man* (Leigh Whannell, 2020), it became available to stream as a 'premium rental' on 20 March. Devised in 2011, this distribution model was initially designed to allow for new movies to be released digitally only sixty days after they left theatres (Tryon 2013: 37), but the pandemic reduced that already brief period to a single week. Not surprisingly, it was not the success that either Blumhouse or Universal was hoping for. Its theatrical run generated a gross of $12.4 million against a budget of $14 million, and it did not fare particularly well via streaming platforms either. In total, the four films that Universal made available for premium rental in March 2020 had made only $48 million for the studio by the end of April (Schwartzel 2020). For all the controversy it created, *The Hunt* was a failure by any commercial measure – but the political discourse around it continued regardless.

'Everyone is lying'

So *The Hunt* had met several roadblocks before reaching its audience, hampered by real-world tragedies, vicious partisan debates and the onset of a global pandemic. Its complicated history and commercial failure are reason enough to consider it a cult movie; as Ernest Mathijs and Xavier Mendik state, cult films 'invariably have complex, confused, controversial or bumpy origins' (2008: 7). But the film's perceived transgressions against good taste constitute a more important reason. Many cult movies are defined by their transgressive qualities, or their 'challenging of one or more "conventions" of filmmaking, which may include stylistic, moral or political qualities' (Mathijs and Mendik 2008: 2). *The Hunt* has been widely accused of having transgressive morals and politics, but one of the most interesting things about it is that – while there is an agreement that it is in some way transgressive – there is no consensus on what its morals or politics are.

That is likely because commentary on those elements of the film began before anyone could watch it. Fox News was an early detractor. In response to the release of the first trailer and the *Hollywood Reporter*'s article, Fox News and Fox Business Network covered it extensively (Barr 2019). Over the days leading up to Trump's tweets, right-wing anchors and commentators on Fox's various programming unambiguously presented the film as anti-conservative. For example, actor Zachery Ty Bryan – appearing as a guest on *Fox & Friends First* on the morning of 9 August – opined: '[Liberals] look at us as racists and bigoted evil people. When you can dehumanise a side or a group that supports

Trump in this case . . . you can do anything, so why not hunt them like you would animals?' (quoted in Barr 2019). The film's apparently anti-conservative politics were also reported by notoriously far-right and conspiracy-led outlets such as the *Epoch Times* (Stieber 2019) and *Breitbart*, which uncharacteristically reserved judgement on *The Hunt* until its release but still suggested that 'the movie looks like murder porn for leftists' (Nolte 2019).

Breitbart's coverage was tempered by a possibility that the film's conservative characters might be its 'heroes' (Nolte 2019), an assumption that characterized another set of responses to it from all sides of the political spectrum. For example, the right-wing *National Review* lamented Universal's decision to shelve *The Hunt* because its hunters 'hate the president' and 'For once, a genre movie was built around an anti-progressive premise' (Smith 2019). In keeping with its 'non-partisan' editorial stance, the *Daily Beast* mocked Trump for his reaction to the picture on the basis that it appeared to be 'lampooning well-off, angry liberals, portraying them as villainous psychos' (Suebsaeng 2019). The liberal *Vanity Fair* also felt that it depicted its hunters as villains through their 'caviar-munching, jet-setting indifference' and suggested that conservative commentators had purposely misread its trailer to create 'bad faith reporting designed to foment another battle in the culture wars' (Fitzpatrick 2019). *Variety* then claimed to have obtained an early draft of its script, one that revealed its 'original intention . . . to depict working-class conservatives as the heroes' (Maddaus 2019), though all of the content it picked out from this supposedly 'early draft' appears in the film.

Commentary of this type continued until *The Hunt* was released (see Tucker 2020) and was both fuelled by and fed into similar responses to it on social media. When critics began to publish their reviews (all of them referencing the controversy in one way or another), something of a muddled critical consensus finally began to emerge: *The Hunt*, it seemed, attacked everybody. The *Boston Globe* gave it lukewarm praise for making clear that 'When we turn other people into cartoons of our worst fears, the only thing left to do is kill each other' (Burr 2020: G1). The *New York Times* surmised, 'Its satirical fire is aimed not from the left or the right, but at both . . . from an unmapped middle, an unpolarized, perhaps imaginary place' (Scott 2020). In a far less favourable review, *The Washington Post* called it 'an infantile, pox-on-both-your-houses rant'. It continued: 'The put-downs and arguments serve only as so much verbal scaffolding for the film's real purpose, which is to shoot, impale, blow up and otherwise gruesomely dispatch as many of its loathsome characters as possible' (Hornaday 2020).

Even the eventual critical responses to *The Hunt* were divided. The only thing that is common among them is a sense that it directs its ire indiscriminately: it is either a politically neutral film that uses satirical humour to make a centrist plea for civility and an end to partisan squabbling, or an apolitical, impassive one that aims to exploit bitter divisions for cheap genre thrills. Both interpretations arise from filtering *The Hunt* through its controversies. Its true politics are better represented by its original teaser trailer, released before the backlash against the film occurred, which makes no mention of partisanship. Instead, it attacks the decadence of the super-rich through a mock advertisement promising 'the ultimate in luxury': a 'five-star boutique experience' for those wishing to hunt other human beings. Before coming to analyse *The Hunt* itself, though, it is necessary to outline its political context.

'No sentimentality, comrade'

For many decades, scholars, critics and cultural commentators have explored the politics of cinema on an understanding that movies, in James Combs's words, 'operate across an ideological spectrum' that stretches from the left to right. As Combs notes, this has often produced readings that function 'as a way of "locating" ideological conflicts between liberals and conservatives' (1993: 12). Traditionally, 'liberal' has been understood to denote the mainstream social and economic left, while 'conservative' is accepted as a synonym for the mainstream right. As Douglas Kellner suggests, though, since the 1980s those distinctions have become less clear, and ideological readings of cinema now must account for 'neo-liberal and neo-conservative' movements (1993: 70). While 'liberalism' and 'conservatism' (in as much as these terms are useful at all in a modern context) have remained opposed on social issues, 'liberal' and 'conservative' approaches to the American economy have moved ever closer together.

Free-market capitalism is generally considered a pursuit of the political right in the United States. However, the financial deregulation and mass privatization that began under the Jimmy Carter administration in the 1970s before accelerating under Ronald Reagan in the next decade created a situation in which 'markets are superior to government when it comes to serving people's needs, thus facilitating the adoption of policies that strengthen capitalism's grip over democratically elected governments' (Panayotakis 2020: 49). The result is that 'the political survival of even left-wing governments depends on capitalist accumulation. This dependence stems from the importance of capitalist investment for employment and the strength of the economy' (Panayotakis 2020: 50). As Costas Panayotakis argues, this process has steadily disenfranchised a working class that now views 'the political system as unresponsive to their needs' (2020: 56) and has given left-leaning parties only two viable strategies to gain power in a democratic election: 'by either giving up on politically alienated low-income groups' and adopting pro-market policies that appeal to wealthier demographics, 'or by discrediting democracy through promises that even a left-wing government will not be able to honor' (2020: 49).

In the United States, the result of this shift is that the Democratic Party has moved to the centre under Bill Clinton (who famously embraced a neoliberal 'Third Way' that married fiscal conservatism with social liberalism), Barack Obama and Joe Biden. Meanwhile, it has made pledges that have either not come to fruition or have been significantly watered down in their final application, including Obama's healthcare reforms and Biden's promise to cancel student loan debt. Since 1980, America has pursued pro-market policies under Republican and Democratic administrations from Reagan to Biden; economically, the distinction between the parties has become unclear as they have both embraced the same 'macroeconomic paradigm' (Palley 2011: 4). It was a bipartisan commitment to the interests of business that led to the bursting of the housing bubble, the financial crisis of 2007–8 and the Great Recession (Palley 2011: 5). But even this economic shock did not stop the march of capitalism. In fact, 'the most perverse legacy of the global crisis has been a further entrenchment' of policies and legislation that protect capital (Peck, Theodore and Brenner 2012: 265). After all, Obama's response to the financial crisis was to loan over $700 billion in public funds to financial institutions via the Emergency Economic Stabilization Act of 2008 rather than offering any meaningful assistance to ordinary people suffering the fallout of their near collapse (see Hanan and Chaput 2013: 26–31).

In America, then, the left has moved to the centre as the right has moved to the far-right, eroding democratic choice for voters in a political system that now offers no alternative to a government that will work to advance the interests of the market. As Kendall R. Phillips argues, this has contributed to a 'state of political discord and rancor that has become the new normal in the United States' (2021: 1). Importantly, this feeling is one that transcends party politics: 'Even as the two ends of the political spectrum differ in so many ways, they do share this core feeling that the system is deficient and has failed' (Phillips 2021: 7). Phillips suggests that American genre films have come to echo this feeling by articulating a desire to completely refuse 'systems that can no longer be tolerated' (2021: 21). *The Hunt* is one such film: a movie so dedicated to refusing the American political system that it disrupts any attempt to interpret its themes on a partisan binary.

'The jackrabbit always wins'

The Hunt follows Crystal May Creasey (Betty Gilpin), though she is not initially established as the film's protagonist. Following a prologue, several strangers awake in a forest – apparently in Arkansas – with their mouths gagged. They locate a large wooden box that contains a cache of weapons, but as soon as they arm themselves they begin to die in gruesome fashion: some are killed by armed hunters, while others fall victim to landmines and pitfall traps. The few survivors surmise that they are victims of 'Manorgate', a right-wing conspiracy theory that has been circulating about a group of rich liberals who kidnap, hunt and kill conservatives. Before long, all are dead aside from Crystal and Don (Wayne Duvall), who may or may not be a 'liberal elite' in disguise. Having discovered that she is not in Arkansas at all, but Croatia (where, it is implied, the hunters have bribed officials to overlook their activities), Crystal sets out to turn the tables on her pursuers. By the film's end, she has killed most of the hunting party (including Don, just in case), and sets out for a final showdown with their leader: the formidable Athena Stone (Hilary Swank).

It is not difficult to understand why *The Hunt* has been interpreted as it has; the majority of its characters are rendered as stereotypes. Trumpian Republicans are depicted as pro-gun, anti-Semitic, racist, opposed to immigration and prone to believing in wild conspiracy theories that affirm their warped views. One, Gary (Ethan Suplee), links Manorgate to the so-called 'deep state', which Trump and his supporters claim is a 'shadowy network of unelected bureaucrats that illegitimately holds the levers of *real* power' (Horwitz 2021: 473). This is actually a play on the real-world conspiracy theory 'Pizzagate', which suggested that 'a cabal of Democratic Party leaders . . . were involved in ritual Satanic abuse of children at a pizza parlour in Washington' (Bleakley 2021: 2). Meanwhile, the hunters are caricatures of affluent and performative Democrats, who are more concerned with policing language than recognizing the vast power, privilege and impunity their wealth affords them. They chastise each other for cultural appropriation and failing to use inclusive language, all while they hunt the less fortunate (who they refer to as 'hicks' and 'rednecks' among other classist terms) with no awareness of how their actions contradict their words. The film pits these groups against one another, but not to communicate a centrist cry for civility nor to exploit political divisions for entertainment. Rather, the film satirically points out that far-right Republicans and 'Third Way' Democrats are increasingly the *only* options available to American voters.

The Hunt largely communicates this idea through Crystal, who does not belong to either side and is defined solely by her working-class identity. This is established through her costume early in the film, when 'Yoga Pants' (Emma Roberts) calls out to her for help upon awakening in the game reserve. Crystal is dressed in boots, canvas trousers and an orange shirt with a name tag pinned to it; it is immediately apparent that she is wearing her work uniform. It later becomes clear that she once served in the military and toured Afghanistan – something she is not proud of, given that she describes it as having been 'in the shit' – and now lives in Mississippi, where she works a low-paid job as a desk clerk for a car rental company. The film makes clear that she possesses few financial resources when she pulls a $20 bill from her sock, which she states is hidden there for 'emergencies'. Her lifestyle is, in short, far removed from the group of millionaires who are hunting her.

Importantly, though, Crystal also feels no alignment with the rest of the people the hunters have chosen as their prey. At the beginning of the film, she completely ignores Yoga Pants when she pleads for assistance and later shows little interest in working together with either Gary (whose attempt to introduce himself is met with a stern 'Shut the fuck up, Gary') or Don. She ignores them when they launch into racist tirades or try to engage her in their conspiratorial thinking (and rejects any attempt to find reasons for the hunters' actions, because 'they're trying to kill me, I don't give a shit why'). Eventually, it is revealed that Crystal was kidnapped in a case of mistaken identity. She is not a Trumpian Republican at all, but an ordinary working American who is unrepresented by both factions, trapped within a political system that offers no meaningful support for working people regardless of how they vote. As she openly states, she does not trust anyone, 'because everyone is lying'.

Crystal's lack of allegiance to either side of this ideological battle could be used as evidence to aid a 'centrist' interpretation of the film, and even screenwriter Damon Lindelof suggests that he and his co-writer Nick Cuse intended for her to unify viewers regardless of their political affiliation: 'If you identify as super right wing or super left wing but can agree Crystal is awesome, that is her purpose: to be the overlap in whatever Venn Diagram exists' (quoted in Chow 2020). However, any centrist interpretation of *The Hunt* is dependent on the idea that a traditional political spectrum *does* still exist in the United States, and that one side of this conflict represents the progressive left wing. Writing on the film often refers to the 'left' (Scott 2020), the 'far-left' (Goldberg 2020) or, in Lindelof's words, the 'super left', but the hunters are not 'left wing' in any conventional sense of the word. They are characterized as neoliberal capitalists: stand-ins for the modern Democratic mainstream.

The prologue, in which the hunters are using a private jet to transport those they have kidnapped to Croatia, makes it clear that they hold nothing but contempt for working people; even before the hunt commences, class divides are more important to the film's narrative than partisanship. The scene begins as Richard (Glenn Howerton) smugly asks a flight attendant (Hannah Alline) whether she has ever tried caviar, before reacting with incredulity when he is told that the plane is not equipped to satisfy his entitled request for 'a grilled vegetable thing, with some figs or even, like, any kind of small fish'. He is rudely expressing his disappointment at the champagne selection on offer – having hoped that he might be able to drink the rare 1907 Heidsieck, which Athena Stone is rumoured to have purchased for a quarter of a million dollars per bottle – when Randy (Jason Kirkpatrick) escapes from the rear of the plane, where he and the rest of the hunters' quarry have been confined for the journey. Before Randy even enters the scene, a clear sense of class conflict has been established; Richard's dismissive attitude towards the attendant communicates his disregard for those he considers to be socially and economically inferior, worthless beyond their ability to serve his needs.

Richard's interaction with the attendant informs the rest of the scene, as Randy stumbles into the cabin under the effects of sedatives. He is costumed in distinctly working-class attire – a lumberjack shirt and denim jacket – that creates a stark visual disparity between him and the well-dressed hunters who immediately respond to their intended prey as a *thing* rather than a person. 'One of them's awake', Richard cries, while another hunter, repulsed by his presence, simply says 'gross'. He is treated by the hunters as the attendant has been treated by Richard: as an inferior being. Both Randy and the attendant are then further positioned as victims of the hunters. Ted (Steve Coulter) orders the attendant to fetch towels before asking to borrow her pen, which – to her horror – he uses to puncture Randy's neck. He survives, but not for long; Athena enters the cabin, claiming her first victim by stabbing him in the eye with the stiletto heel of an expensive designer shoe, a potent symbol of her wealth. To reinforce the disdain the hunters have for the working class, Ted then hands the bloodied pen back to the traumatized attendant, before Martin (Dean West) insolently asks her to fetch him 'a little seltzer water or something'. The attendant is not a Trumpian 'deplorable', but the hunters do not treat her much better than one.

These class dynamics are replicated in the film's final scenes, when Crystal confronts Athena in her Croatian mansion. She enters through an ornate gate, before marvelling at the decadence of the place, the camera pointedly lingering on its fountains and gardens, its expensive furniture and state-of-the-art kitchen. Once Crystal is inside, Athena launches into a classist tirade, only stopping to echo Richard in flaunting her culinary taste ('You know, most people think that you should use cheddar in a grilled cheese, But I use Gruyère'). Before learning that she has kidnapped the wrong Crystal, she judges what she believes to be her lifestyle at length, concentrating on her economic status: 'You bounced from part-time job to part-time job, to welfare and back. . . . You fail, we pay.' So Athena might pretend to have noble ideals – as evidenced by her pretentious and confused obsession with George Orwell's *Animal Farm* (1945), from which she earlier appropriates the revolutionary words 'no sentimentality, comrade!' (Orwell 2021 [1945], 29) – but in truth she loathes the working class and believes it is acceptable to hunt them because they are a drain on capitalist America.

Furthermore, while the film makes it clear that the hunters' quarry hold truly abhorrent beliefs, that is not the primary reason that Athena and her colleagues thirst for their blood. As is revealed in a series of flashbacks, 'Manorgate' was once just a conspiracy theory based on a leaked thread of text messages between Athena and other high-profile businesspeople, in which she joked about 'slaughtering a dozen deplorables' at 'The Manor'. They have decided to bring the conspiracy to life only because that 'joke' led them to lose their positions as corporate CEOs, the heads of charitable foundations and hedge-fund managers. As Miranda (Amy Madigan) comments, the hunters are aggrieved because they 'lost their jobs and their reputations'. In theory, their actions are motivated by irreconcilable ideological differences. In practice, the hunters care less about the political views held by their prey and more about seeking violent reparation for a loss of economic and social capital.

So the battle that ultimately occurs in Athena's manor is not one fought between left and right, but haves and have-nots. Crystal reveals that she is not who Athena thinks she is, before the two launch into a fight that destroys the mansion and its contents. In a frenetic sequence that represents a metaphorical attack on the economic elite, vases and lamps are broken, bookcases collapse, glass dividers are smashed and expensive household items (a Bluetooth speaker, a kitchen blowtorch, the blade from a food-mixer and even a bottle of the champagne that Richard was so desperate to sample) are all used as weapons. Athena is dying when the dust settles, symbols of her material wealth lying in ruins all around her. Crystal's victory, then, is a victory for working people unserved by centrist neoliberalism. This is further reinforced after she leaves the mansion wearing a stolen designer dress and clutching the 1907 Heidsieck; boarding Athena's jet, she drinks the champagne straight from the bottle and shares caviar with the long-suffering flight attendant in a symbolic redistribution of the hunters' wealth.

However, while *The Hunt* renders wealthy Democrats as antagonists, that does not mean that its right-wing characters are heroes or even blameless victims; their bigoted views are consistently framed as risible, senseless and absurd. But it is important to note that the rise of far-right populism is another outcome of the left's shift to the centre and the economic crash that resulted from decades of pro-market policies under both Republicans and Democrats. As Paul Sanders notes, 'A populist backlash occurs each time there is a confluence of five factors: a major financial crisis, an increase in inequality, and the emergence of demagoguery, whose targets are immigration and the perceived corrupt political elites' (2020: 16). These are precisely the conditions that led to the election of Trump, who gained power by exploiting America's economic discontent, discrediting the political establishment – the 'liberal elite' – and directing the ire of his supporters towards scapegoats, particularly immigrants (Panayotakis 2020: 61–4). The irony of this is that Trumpian populism primarily acted 'as a diversion' to further entrench capitalism (Sanders 2020: 19). Once elected, Trump set about 'scrapping government regulation of business' and delivered a tax package that 'disproportionately favoured the wealthy elite, including Trump himself' (Gamble 2019: 31).

At the level of government, then, far-right populism and centrist neoliberalism both pursue pro-market policies that favour corporations and the rich. Economically, there is little material difference between the 'left' and 'right' in the contemporary United States; a vote for either a Republican or Democratic candidate is a vote for capitalism. Importantly, this is something that *The Hunt* acknowledges. It does so most obviously during a flashback sequence in which Athena is asked to step down as the CEO of a large company. Her superior, Paul (J. C. MacKenzie), chastises her and her colleagues for those leaked messages – in which they refer to an unnamed Trump as 'our ratfucker-in-chief' – and warns her against criticizing the government. As Athena attempts to defend herself, Paul cuts her off and delivers the film's most important line of dialogue:

'It's not a country, it's a business.' In this, *The Hunt* laments that capitalism has supplanted democracy. No matter who occupies the White House, the interests of business will be served before those of working people.

This idea is also articulated by a story that Crystal recounts to Don before confronting Athena. In a twisted version of Aesop's 'The Tortoise and the Hare', the hare (or, in Crystal's version, the 'jackrabbit') refuses to accept losing a race to the tortoise (the 'box turtle'), because the jackrabbit always wins. Enraged, he bursts into the box turtle's home, killing his family and eating their dinner. Don is confused: 'Who's the rabbit? Is it us or them?' Crystal does not answer because her story has two meanings: both she and the hunters are the jackrabbit. In that moment, Crystal imagines herself as the rabbit. Refusing to be beaten, she intends to find Athena, kill her and eat her dinner (or, rather, drink her champagne). But, more importantly, the fable functions as a potent allegory for the contemporary United States, where no matter how hard ordinary people work or how they vote (as the box turtle tells his wife and children before the rabbit kills them all, 'never give up, just keep crawling forwards'), capitalism will prevail – because Republican or Democrat, the jackrabbit *always* wins.

The Hunt is thus neither 'liberal' nor 'conservative'. Rather, it allegorizes a nation in which there is no meaningful avenue for progressive economic change and, through Crystal, communicates the rage that has been created by an erosion of democratic choice. It is her disconnection from both Republican and Democratic forces that clearly illustrates *The Hunt*'s wilful rejection of the partisan binary, while her cathartic victory over Athena expresses a frustrated 'desire to refuse the system' entirely (Phillips 2021: 7). *The Hunt* attacks both sides – which co-writers Lindelof and Cuse (Chow 2020), director Craig Zobel (Maddaus and Lang 2019) and producer Jason Blum (Lang 2020) have all indicated was their intention – but primarily to point out that those 'sides' are moving ever closer together in their legislative support for business and the wealthy. It is also not accurate to suggest that the film is 'centrist', then. The term that best describes *The Hunt* and its politics is anti-capitalist.

Conclusion: 'You're hunting human beings'

That *The Hunt* proves to be more interested in critiquing capitalism than lampooning social divisions should not be surprising. As Cuse has stated, it is a modern retelling of *The Most Dangerous Game* (quoted in Crucchiola 2020).

Based on the 1924 short story of the same name by Richard Connell, *The Most Dangerous Game* not only launched a tradition of genre pictures concerned with human hunting but also established its long-standing anti-capitalist themes. Connell's tale takes place on an isolated South Pacific island, where General Zaroff hunts human beings for sport. Connell paints Zaroff as 'the epitome of Old World aristocracy' (Thompson 2019: 321), a former Russian nobleman who was forced to flee his homeland following the October Revolution. His latest quarry is Bob Rainsford, a big-game hunter who ironically finds himself stalked through the jungle after a shipwreck. He is an 'American-born harbinger of the current century which Zaroff hates, resists and denies, all while living on his private island, a veritable Potemkin village of what nineteenth-century Europe used to be' (Thompson 2019: 321).

By the time the cinematic adaptation was released in 1932, America was suffering through the worst of the Great Depression. Restyled as Count Zaroff (Leslie Banks) in the film, Connell's hunter was thus a perfect villain for the times. He is a symbol of excess who resides in a cavernous hillside castle, using a vast inherited fortune to sustain his appalling lifestyle. But given the economic climate of the time, Rainsford (Joel McCrea) – a wealthy globetrotter who spends his days tracking big game – must have seemed far less virtuous than his literary counterpart. In fact, his lifestyle is questioned in the film's opening scene, when he is pointedly asked how he would feel if he were 'the tiger instead of the hunter'. Unperturbed, he states that there are two types of people: 'the hunter and the hunted'. For an audience ravaged by recession (likely to count themselves among life's 'hunted'), seeing Rainsford find out what it is like to be the tiger is part of the film's appeal – even if he does triumph over a far more abhorrent representation of the elite.

The Most Dangerous Game set the template for human hunting films to follow. In *Bloodlust!* (Ralph Brooke, 1961), another wealthy hunter – this time an American – stalks teenagers who have wandered onto his private game reserve. *Savages* (Lee H. Katzin, 1974) sees an affluent lawyer turn his gun on a young gas-station attendant he has hired as a guide for a hunting expedition in the Mojave Desert. *Turkey Shoot* (Brian Trenchard-Smith, 1982) and *The Running Man* (Paul Michael Glaser, 1987) cast these class-conscious themes into dystopian futures, where dissidents against authoritarian capitalist regimes are hunted for entertainment. In both *Hard Target* (John Woo, 1993) and *Surviving the Game* (Ernest R. Dickerson, 1994), the unhoused are kidnapped from the street to be tracked by super-rich hunters who have paid for the pleasure of killing them.

And *The Hunt* is only one of several films to rework the anti-capitalist human hunting narrative for the twenty-first century; the deranged hunters in *Desierto* (Jonas Cuaron, 2015), *Happy Hunting* (Joe Dietsch and Louie Gibson, 2016), *Bacurau* (Kleber Mendonça Filho and Juliano Dornelles, 2019) and *Hounded* (Tommy Boulding, 2022) all target the economically disadvantaged.

So the controversy that has surrounded *The Hunt* has obscured both its nuanced subtext and its cinematic lineage. It is best understood as one of many genre films that have used the human hunting narrative to indict the horrors of capitalism, and it is ironic that its message – that capitalism is no longer a partisan issue in America – has been lost in a decidedly partisan debate.

Bibliography

Barr, Jeremy. 'Trump's Apparent Interest in "*The Hunt*" Follows Heavy Fox News Coverage'. *Hollywood Reporter*, 9 August 2019. Available online at: https://www.hollywoodreporter.com/news/politics-news/trumps-apparent-interest-hunt-follows-heavy-fox-news-coverage-1230601/ (accessed 23 August 2022).

Bleakley, Paul. 'Panic, Pizza and Mainstreaming the Alt-Right: A Social Media Analysis of Pizzagate and the Rise of the QAnon Conspiracy'. *Current Sociology* 71, no. 3 (2021): 1–17.

Burr, Ty. 'After All that Controversy, "*The Hunt*" Arrives to Blast Away at Partisan Stereotypes'. *Boston Globe*, 13 March 2020: G1.

Chow, Andrew R. 'Inside the Making of *The Hunt*, From Conception to Controversy'. *Time*, 6 March 2020. Available online at: https://time.com/5796100/the-hunt-movie-blumhouse/ (accessed 13 August 2022).

Collis, Clark. '*The Hunt* to be Released in Theaters Next Month Despite Criticism from Donald Trump'. *Entertainment Weekly*, 11 February 2020. Available online at: https://ew.com/movies/2020/02/11/the-hunt-new-release-date-trailer/ (accessed 22 August 2022).

Combs, James. 'Introduction'. In *Movies and Politics: The Dynamic Relationship* (Lib. ed.), edited by James Combs, 3–25. London: Routledge, 2014.

Connell, Richard. *The Most Dangerous Game* [Wisehouse Classics ed.]. Ballingslöv: Wisehouse Publishing, 2020 [1924].

Crucchiola, Jordan. 'Untangling the Politics of *The Hunt* with Damon Lindelof and Nick Cuse'. *Vulture*, 17 March 2020. Available online at: https://www.vulture.com/2020/03/the-politics-of-the-hunt-with-damon-lindelof-nick-cuse.html (accessed 13 September 2022).

Fitzpatrick, Kevin. 'Universal Cancels The Hunt Release After Trump's "Hollywood is racist" Criticism'. *Vanity Fair*, 10 August 2019. Available online at: https://www

.vanityfair.com/hollywood/2019/08/the-hunt-movie-canceled-deplorables-trump (accessed 20 August 2022).

Gamble, Andrew. 'Globalization and the New Populism'. In *The Crisis of Globalization: Democracy, Capitalism and Inequality in the Twenty-First Century*, edited by Patrick Diamond, 27–41. London: I. B. Tauris, 2019.

Gleiberman, Owen. 'Why Canceling "*The Hunt*" Was the Right Call (Column)'. *Variety*, 11 August 2019. Available online at: https://variety.com/2019/film/news/the-hunt-universal-right-call-1203298926/ (accessed 22 August 2022).

Goldberg, Matt. '"*The Hunt*" Review: Toothless Satire Offers the View from Nowhere'. *Collider*, 11 March 2020. Available online at: https://collider.com/the-hunt-review-betty-gilpin-hilary-swank/ (accessed 23 August 2022).

Hanan, Joshua S. and Catherine Chaput. 'Stating the Exception: Rhetoric and Neoliberal Governance During the Creation and Passage of the Emergency Economic Stabilization Act of 2008'. *Argumentation and Advocacy* 50, no. 1 (2013): 18–33.

Hornaday, Ann. 'Controversial Thriller "*The Hunt*" is Finally in Theaters. Don't Waste Your Time'. *Washington Post*, 11 March 2020. Available online at: https://www.washingtonpost.com/goingoutguide/movies/the-hunt-movie-review/2020/03/11/7d97f3a0-6091-11ea-b014-4fafa866bb81_story.html (accessed 23 August 2022).

Horwitz, Robert B. 'Trump and the "Deep State"'. *Policy Studies* 42, no. 5–6 (2021): 473–90.

Kellner, Douglas. 'Films, Politics and Ideology: Towards a Multiperspectival Film Theory'. In *Movies and Politics: The Dynamic Relationship*, edited by James Combs, 55–92. London: Routledge, 2014 [1993].

Lang, Brett. '"*The Hunt*" Producer Jason Blum and Writer Damon Lindelof Speak Out: "This Is Not a Dangerous Movie"'. *Variety*, 11 February 2020. Available online at: https://variety.com/2020/film/news/the-hunt-jason-blum-damon-lindelof-the-hunt-trump-1203500608/ (accessed 13 September 2022).

Maddaus, Gene and Brett Lang. '"*The Hunt*" Director Breaks Silence on Film's Cancellation'. *Variety*, 19 August 2019. Available online at: https://variety.com/2019/film/news/the-hunt-universal-craig-zobel-1203299514/ (accessed 13 September 2022).

Masters, Kim and Tatiana Siegel. 'Ads Pulled for Gory Universal Thriller "*The Hunt*" in Wake of Mass Shootings (Exclusive)'. *Hollywood Reporter*, 6 August 2019. Available online at: https://www.hollywoodreporter.com/news/general-news/ads-pulled-hunt-wake-mass-shootings-1229829/ (accessed 3 January 2023).

Mathijs, Ernest and Xavier Mendik. 'Editorial Introduction: What is Cult Film?'. In *The Cult Film Reader*, edited by Ernest Mathijs and Xavier Mendik, 1–11. Maidenhead: Open University Press, 2008.

McCollum, Victoria, Mathias Clasen, and Todd K. Platts. 'Introduction'. In *Blumhouse Productions: The New House of Horror*, edited by Todd K. Platts, Victoria McCollum, and Mathias Clasen, 1–10. Cardiff: University of Wales Press, 2022.

Nickolai, Nate. 'Universal Cancels "*The Hunt*" Release'. *Variety*, 10 August 2019. Available online at: https://variety.com/2019/film/news/the-hunt-canceled-universal-betty-gilpin-hilary-swank-emma-roberts-1203298774/ (accessed 22 August 2022).

Nolte, John. '"Elites" Kill "Deplorables" in New Horror Film "The Hunt"'. *Breitbart*, 7 August 2019. Available online at: https://www.breitbart.com/entertainment/2019/08/07/elites-kill-deplorables-in-new-horror-film-the-hunt/ (accessed 22 August 2022).

Orwell, George. *Animal Farm* [Collins Classics ed.]. Dublin: William Collins, 2021 [1945].

Palley, Thomas. 'America's Flawed Paradigm: Macroeconomic Causes of the Financial Crisis and Great Recession'. *Empirica* 38, no. 1 (2011): 3–17.

Panayotakis, Costas. 'Neoliberalism, the Left, and the Rise of the Far Right: On the Political and Ideological Implications of Capitalism's Subordination of Democracy'. *Democratic Theory* 7, no. 1 (2020): 48–72.

Peck, Jamie, Nik Theodore, and Neil Brenner. 'Neoliberalism Resurgent? Market Rule after the Great Recession'. *South Atlantic Quarterly* 111, no. 2 (2012): 265–88.

Phillips, Kendall R. *A Cinema of Hopelessness: The Rhetoric of Rage in 21st Century Popular Culture*. London: Palgrave Macmillan, 2021.

Reilly, Katie. 'Read Hillary Clinton's "Basket of Deplorables" Remarks About Donald Trump Supporters'. *Time*, 10 September 2016. Available online at: https://time.com/4486502/hillary-clinton-basket-of-deplorables-transcript/ (accessed 3 January 2023).

Sanders, Paul. 'Populism Discourse and "Trouble in Democracy": A Critical Approach'. In *Leadership, Populism, and Resistance*, edited by Kristin M. S. Bezio and George R. Goethals, 8–28. Cheltenham: Elgar, 2020.

Schaffstall, Katherine. 'Betty Gilpin Fights for Her Life Against Hilary Swank in "*The Hunt*" Trailer'. *Hollywood Reporter*, 30 July 2019. Available online at: https://www.hollywoodreporter.com/movies/movie-news/hunt-trailer-betty-gilpin-fights-hilary-swank-survival-1227912/ (accessed 22 August 2022).

Schwartzel, Erich. '"*Trolls World Tour*" Breaks Digital Records and Charts a New Path for Hollywood'. *Wall Street Journal*, 28 April 2020. Available online at: https://www.wsj.com/articles/trolls-world-tour-breaks-digital-records-and-charts-a-new-path-for-hollywood-11588066202/ (accessed 22 August 2022).

Scott, A. O. '"*The Hunt*" Review: The Culture War, With Heavy Casualties'. *New York Times*, 11 March 2020. Available online at: https://www.nytimes.com/2020/03/11/movies/the-hunt-review.html/ (accessed 23 August 2022).

Sims, David. 'How *The Hunt* Became a Political Rorschach Test'. *The Atlantic*, 13 August 2019. Available online at: https://www.theatlantic.com/entertainment/archive/2019/08/confused-politics-canceled-release-hunt/596008/ (accessed 13 August 2022).

Smith, Kyle. 'Pro-Trump Movie Cancelled, Thanks to Trump'. *National Review*, 11 August 2019. Available online at: https://www.nationalreview.com/corner/pro-trump-movie-cancelled-thanks-to-trump/ (accessed 23 August 2022).

Squires, John. 'While "*The Hunt*" Trailer Plays in Theaters, Here's a Teaser for Blumhouse's "Private Hunting Experience" [Video]'. *Bloody Disgusting*, 12 July 2019. Available online at: https://bloody-disgusting.com/movie/3572446/trailer-plays-theaters-heres-first-poster-blumhouses-hunt/ (accessed 13 August 2022).

Stieber, Zachary. 'Movie Showing Elites Hunting Down "Deplorables" Slated to Hit Theaters in September'. *Epoch Times*, 7 August 2019. Available online at: https://www.theepochtimes.com/movie-showing-elites-hunting-down-trump-supporters-slated-to-hit-theaters-in-september_3033214.html (accessed 23 August 2022).

Suebsaeng, Asawin. 'Trump Freaks Out Over "*The Hunt*," a Satirical Film He Doesn't Understand, as U.S. Reels from Mass Shootings'. *Daily Beast*, 9 August 2019. Available online at: https://www.thedailybeast.com/trump-freaks-out-over-the-hunt-a-satirical-film-he-doesnt-understand-as-us-reels-from-mass-shootings/ (accessed 23 August 2022).

Thompson, Terry W. 'A Tale of Two Centuries: Richard Connell's "The Most Dangerous Game"'. *Midwest Quarterly*, 59, no. 3 (2019): 318–30.

Trump, Donald [@realDonaldTrump]. 'Liberal Hollywood . . .'. *Twitter* [deleted], 9 August 2019a. Available online at: https://https://www.thetrumparchive.com/ (accessed 22 August 2022).

Trump, Donald [@realDonaldTrump]. 'To Inflame and Cause Chaos. . .'. *Twitter* [deleted], 9 August 2019b. Available online at: https://www.thetrumparchive.com/ (accessed 22 August 2022).

Tryon, Chuck. *On-Demand Culture: Digital Delivery and the Future of Movies*. New Brunswick: Rutgers University Press, 2013.

Tucker, James. 'Let's Talk About "*The Hunt*," Blumhouse's New "Centrist" Political Thriller'. *Rue Morgue*, 5 March 2020. Available online at: https://rue-morgue.com/lets-talk-about-the-hunt-blumhouses-new-centrist-political-thriller/ (accessed 13 August 2022).

Watson, R. T. and Erich Schwartzel. 'Universal Pictures Halts Marketing of Movie After Mass Shootings'. *Wall Street Journal*, 8 August 2019. Available online at: https://www.wsj.com/articles/universal-pictures-halts-marketing-of-movie-after-mass-shootings-11565229642/ (accessed 22 August 2022).

Filmography

Bacurau (2019), [Film] Dir. Kleber Mendonça Filho and Juliano Dornelles, Brazil / France: Vitrine Filmes / SBS Distribution.

Bloodlust! (1961), [Film] Dir. Ralph Brooke, USA: Crown International Pictures.

Desierto (2015), [Film] Dir. Jonas Cuaron, Mexico / France: Cinépolis / Version Originale.

Happy Hunting (2016), [Film] Dir. Joe Dietsch and Louie Gibson, USA: Vertical Entertainment.

Hard Target (1993), [Film] Dir. John Woo, USA: Universal Pictures.
Hounded (2022), [Film] Dir. Tommy Boulding, UK: Signature Entertainment.
The Hunt (2020), [Film] Dir. Craig Zobel, USA: Universal Pictures.
The Invisible Man (2020), [Film] Dir. Leigh Whannell, USA: Universal Pictures.
The Most Dangerous Game (1932), [Film] Dir. Irving Pichel and Ernest B. Schoedsack, USA: RKO Radio Pictures.
The Running Man (1987), [Film] Dir. Paul Michael Glaser, USA: Tri-Star Pictures.
Savages (1974), [TV Movie] Dir. Lee H. Katzin, USA: ABC.
Surviving the Game (1994), [Film] Dir. Ernest R. Dickerson, USA: New Line Cinema.
Turkey Shoot (1982), [Film] Dir. Brian Trenchard-Smith, Australia: Roadshow Film Distributors.

Part II

Cult horror directors

7

'We are going to do something nasty'
The cult horror films of Harry Kümel

Mark Goodall

Introduction

The filmography of the Belgian director Harry Kümel, born in Antwerp in 1940, is brief but potent. Kümel's films blend the tropes of the decadent supernatural film and the short-form TV series together with thematic, visual elements from the Belgian tradition of the fantastic and the surreal, to explore the 'split between the real and the imaginary' (Mathijs 2005: 317). This unusual and inconsistent blend of styles and genres has made Kümel something of a cult director. Kümel's most famous film *Daughters of Darkness* (1971) retains a reputation as one of the best examples of European trash cinema and is both an affirmation of the vampire horror film and a reworking of that particular genre from an entirely new and highly original perspective. The film, based on the legend of Erzsébet Báthory (the 'bloody countess'), features violent deaths and erotic scenes of bloodlust, set in a glorious crumbling Ostend hotel (instead of a remote castle) and stars one of the most eminent European art house actresses of the age, Delphine Seyrig. Forever associated with Alain Resnais's masterful puzzle film *Last Year at Marienbad* (*L'Année dernière à Marienbad*, 1961), Seyrig's presence in *Daughters of Darkness* led to one critic to dubbing the film Dracula in Marienbad (Mathijs 2005b: 462).

Malpertuis (1972), the follow-up to *Daughters of Darkness*, was an adaptation of the infamously decadent novel of the same name by Jean Ray (1998) [1943] and is set in the haunted house of the film's title. Kümel managed to persuade Orson Welles to appear in the film, alongside French chanteuse Sylvie Vartan and British actress Susan Hampshire, who plays three different roles. The irrational nature of Ray's novel is retained in the film; it is a work governed 'only by the logic of dreams' (Soren 1979: 44). Difficulties in the completion of the production process resulted in several different versions of the film being issued. Following the 'commercial disaster' (Soren 1979: 63) of *Malpertuis*, Kümel's TV series *The Coming of Joachim Stiller* (*De Komst van Joachim Stiller*, 1976) reinvents the sixty-minute TV serial format as a bizarre string of incidents. It is essentially a psychological mystery drawn from the tradition of 'magic realism'.

Kümel's work manages to combine the practice of the auteur and the experimentation of the avant-garde with those of the film showman and TV entertainer. This chapter will discuss the three productions introduced earlier and the generic conventions found in Kümel's work to reveal how the director skilfully manipulates these conventions to create a stylistic and highly original mode of filmmaking. I will also situate Kümel's work within the decadent tradition of Belgian culture as the grounding the director had in this realm of expression is crucial to the appreciation of the unique nature of his vision as a cult film director. While Kümel's films are often perverse and lurid they are at the same time beautiful and poetic. Kümel is not afraid to assault the viewer (such as with the sensational opening sex scene of *Daughters of Darkness*) and yet can at the same time display tenderness and lyricism in equal measure. As a Belgian artist, Kümel worked in a site that was 'sympathetic to Symbolist and Decadent developments' (Milner 1978: 98) and his films conform to certain aspects of these traditions in which European modernism is steeped.

Belgian cinema and Harry Kümel

The old (and inaccurate) joke about there being no famous Belgians is echoed in the general ignorance towards to the country's national cinema. Critical reflection on Belgian film is either negligent (there are only a handful of English-language books on the subject) or merged with that of the Netherlands as the cinema of 'le plat pays' (the 'low countries'). This appears to be something of a long-standing problem. The *International Film Guide* in 1969 for example contains a single page on new Belgian cinema and that focuses mainly on the Czech director Věra Chytilová. Kümel's first feature *Monsieur Hawarden* (1968) features in the Netherlands section, presumably as it was a co-production between Parkfilm in that territory and Sofidoc in Belgium. Subsequent issues of the *International Film Guide* paint a gloomy picture of too many international co-productions and meagre state funding. Home audiences 'suffer an inferiority complex . . . and an anti-national *snobisme* when it comes to domestic films' (Davay 1970: 68) and Belgian cinemas needs to find a middle ground between 'erotica' and the 'hyper-intellectual kind of movie' (Davay 1971: 84). Mathijs has identified this cinema as being 'overloaded with self-doubt' (2004: 1), further exacerbating the problem.

Thankfully, the success of Fons Rademakers' *Mira* (1972) was a game-changer for Belgian cinema, grossing over $1.3 million in box office receipts and paving the way for Belgian film to be taken seriously. It is a strange state of affairs because while Belgian directors may not be world-famous their films have certainly left a mark. Examples of this 'one-off' type of success include Thierry Zéno's *One Man and His Pig* (*Vase de Noces*, 1974), Chantal Akerman's *Jeanne Dielman, 23 quai du Commerce, 1080 Bruxelles* (1975), Dominique Deruddere's *Crazy Love* (1987), Jaco van Dormael's *Toto the Hero* (*Toto le Héros*, 1991), Rémy Belvaux, André Bonzel and Benoît Poelvoorde's *Man Bites Dog* (*C'est arrive pres de chez vous*, 1992), Jan Bucquoy's *The Sex Life of the Belgians* (*La Vie sexuelle des Belges 1950-1978*, 1994) and Fabrice du Welz's *Calvaire* (2004). None of this work contributes to a collective canon of any sort, but then since artists such as Henri Magritte, James Ensor and Félicien Rops there has been a resistance to conventional 'ways of seeing' in Belgian culture. Even the recent political crisis in the country, as Steele (2019) notes in the introduction to his study on the subject, was reimagined in Isabelle Christiaens, Philippe Dutilleul and Nathalie Jacobs's TV docudrama *Bye Bye Belgium* (*Tout ca [ne nous rendra pas la Belgique]*, 2006) in the form of an artistic subversive rupture.

Belgium is a nation divided by French and Dutch-speaking regions leading to what has been called a 'split screen' version of cinema where the French-speaking work only is presented as 'auteristic' (in the French New Wave sense of the word). Steele (2019) defines a specifically 'Wallonian' regional dimension (itself a part of the wider 'francophone' cinema) to Belgian national film production while problematizing and questioning any notions of a 'national' cinema and what that might mean anyway in a 'transnational' epoch. Steele (2019) argues that transnationalism is an important and topical lens to look at these films through as it encourages the dissolving or blurring of cultural, social, political and aesthetic boundaries. Moreover, Belgian cinema is defined here as 'small cinema'– film at the 'periphery' – contributing to a flexible reception of what cinema is where the local can be as significant, or more significant, than the national. Yet despite the small size and marginalization of Belgian cinema, the nation has produced some startling and important film works and it is these that Steele's work seeks to explore, along with the films' contributions to what one critic cited by Steele calls 'a nation in search of itself' (2019: 12).

Film criticism nevertheless tends to marginalize certain kinds of Belgian cinema, with the many excellent genre/underground films by Belgian directors (several of which have attained cult status internationally) shunned in favour of more serious 'arthouse' works. This is odd when one thinks that one of the exciting new directors briefly mentioned all those years back in the *International Film Guide* was Kümel, who has had to innovate between the realms of feature film, TV drama, commercials and pop videos with funding drawn from a variety of international sources, to make ends meet. Mathijs (2005a) makes this explicit in relation to genre films, where there is a limited sense of what horror as a genre is, a lack of interest in directors making horror films, and 'no tradition of discussing Belgian horror cinema' to be found (Mathijs 2005a: 316). Strangely, in relation to Mathijs, there seems to be a critical reluctance in Belgium to label films such as those by Harry Kümel as 'horror', while a film such as *Man Bites Dog*, with its darkly comic interactive documentary style, is considered a horror film. Either way, when films such as *Daughters of Darkness* are well received elsewhere, they are largely ignored at home.

The influence of visual arts on Belgian cinema is evident. As Michael Richardson states, 'the visual mark of Rene Magritte and Paul Delvaux has left such a striking impression that film directors cannot fail to be aware of it' (2006: 168). From the very start of his career Harry Kümel defined a distinctive aesthetic expressing the key dimensions of decadence with a visual style that drew on impressionistic/surrealist cinema. Kümel was a member of the Film Group 58, a gathering of amateur filmmakers in Belgium. From this group Kümel went on to produce semi-professional films such as *Aether* (1960), one of his early engaging shorts that exemplifies an early fascination with colour (particularly the colour red). After this experimental period Kümel moved, like many of his contemporaries, into television. Kümel made a documentary about one of his cinematic heroes Josef von Sternberg and dedicated his first feature *Monsieur Hawarden* to the great director with whom he shares a talent for films that are 'poetic without being symbolic' (Sarris 1966: 8). As Cowie observes, 'there is scarcely an orthodox shot in this film; nor is there a pretentious one' (1969: 125). This remark would undoubtedly please Kümel, suspicious as he is of film critics and is typical of what the critic Simon Leys described as the Belgian 'fear of pretentiousness' (2013: 212). Despite Kümel's own dismissive attitude (at least in public) to his films we can judge them as important contributions to cult cinema. As Mathijs argues, his films, especially *Daughters of Darkness*, have forced 'new perspectives' (2015: 331) on not just Belgian genre films but also Belgian film criticism. This is a remarkable achievement for something Kümel (2008) once called 'a piece of trash'.

Kümel's films have their own distinct 'language' and are situated in their own hermetic worlds. His films are set 'elsewhere', a place 'self-consciously created out of cinematic effects' (Grant 2000: 64) that the art of film, with its reference to reality and deviation from it into dreams, is especially adept at providing. *Monsieur Hawarden* broke new ground (for Belgian cinema) by adopting a rich tonal palette and expressing Freudian dream symbolism, thus offering an atmosphere and a pervasive psychological dimension generally only found in the horror or supernatural genres. The film on release was described as 'extraordinary' and confirmed Kümel's place as 'one of the best directors in Europe' (Cowie 1969: 125). The film opens with a beautifully composed shot of a peasant in a wheat field that owes much to the art of the silent cinema, both European and American, and closes with a series of 'screen test' like shots of Hawarden (Ellen Vogel), facing the camera in grief and pain. Scenes in the film resemble the set-pieces of the early European horror classics that utilized the decadent/surrealist methodology such as Carl Theodor Dreyer's *Vampyr* (1932).

But while some aspects of *Monsieur Hawarden* drew on established signs from horror films, Kümel managed to create something new with his distinct settings and staging. Kümel exhibited in this first film a talent for *photogénie*, the technique beloved of early impressionistic and surrealist filmmakers for endowing everyday objects with an 'extreme poetic aspect of beings and things' (Morin 2005: 15). Black gloves, playing cards, pocket watches, a roulette wheel and a glass are all imbued with a poetic value, making them appear 'luminous and spellbinding' (Ray 2001: 4). By bringing an intense elegance to his unusual narrative cinema Kümel was developing a modern decadent style of filmmaking. With exquisite framing, movement and lighting, augmented by a discreet and mannered score by Pierre Bartholomée, *Monsieur Hawarden* looks very much like a classic of modern European art cinema and one can see why this first feature so excited critics. How disappointed the same critics must have been then to see the director's switch to the lowbrow horror genre.

Decadence: *Daughters of Darkness*

As noted earlier, the films of Harry Kümel incorporate elements that can be identified as emerging from the symbolist and decadent tradition. Artists such as Felicien Rops with his obsession with gothic death imagery, skill at depicting the 'cruel aspect of contemporary woman' (Praz 1933: 369) and 'dubious eroticism' (Milner 1971: 115) and Fernand Khnopff's precise and cool depictions of mystic sexuality find echo in Kümel's filmic scenarios. Kümel's flair for theatrical settings reflects the decadent tradition's preoccupation with the 'cult of the artificial' (Milner 1971: 8) and the symbolist poet's fascination with the mystical 'time before the world' where the 'happening' of the artwork is the work itself (Grant 2000: 64). This is particularly evident in *Daughters of Darkness* where the hotel becomes a space of its own, beyond the 'real world' and where every appearance of the countess (Delphine Seyrig) is imbued with an exotic luxury (see Figure 7.1).

Another Belgian decadent artist James Ensor grew up in Ostend and the oppressive nature of his art is echoed in Kümel's use of the town as a gloomy backdrop to the strange events depicted in *Daughters of Darkness*. Kümel

Figure 7.1 *Daughters of Darkness*: The countess (Delphine Seyrig) connotes exotic luxury. Image courtesy of Harry Kümel.

once stated that 'it is not the reflected thing that counts but the reflection itself' (Mathjis 2004: xviii), which is a fitting methodology for the creation of fantastical cinematic imagery and the appreciation and incorporation of a wide range of stylistic elements into a new and original ensemble. Often, any discussion of 'decadence' in relation to cinema has negative connotations, the most famous being Susan Sontag's article 'The Decay of Cinema' (1996), which criticizes the degeneration of film in the late twentieth century, due to rampant commercialization and the onset of television. Here in Kümel's aesthetic, cinematic decadence relates to Pitirim Sorokin's concept of decadence as a 'sensate art', one that 'seeks to amuse, to entertain and to provide pleasure in every imaginable form' (Winthrop 1971: 523). As sensate art is divorced from religious, moral or social concern it is able to celebrate artistic expression in a pure form and explore 'cultural shock' (Winthrop 1971: 523) as an imaginative technique. Kümel uses these elements to create a cinematic style resistant to realist 'new wave' cinema, prefiguring the recent 'neo-decadent' movement, where the spirit of the original fin-de-siècle tendency is modernized via a 'shift in aesthetic consciousness' (Corrick 2018: 8). *Daughters of Darkness* epitomizes this being a work that is 'an attempt to combine aesthetic and exploitation elements in one film' (Mathijs 2004: 97) and to be 'exploitative and artistic at the same time' (Mathijs 2004: 100). A well-made film that continues to be difficult to categorize, Joan Hawkins asserts that *Daughters of Darkness* 'occupies a contested critical site' because it successfully functions as both 'a poetic art film and an affective horror movie' (2000: 66).

Emerging as the European fascination with sex/horror films reached a high point, *Daughters of Darkness* is a 'haunting and sensuous vampire story fully within the trajectory of surrealism' (Richardson 2006: 168). To summarize the plot, a honeymooning couple, Stefan (John Karlen) and Valerie (Danielle Ouimet) check in at a hotel in Ostend, where they appear to be the only guests. One night, a countess arrives with her companion Ilona (Andrea Rau). The concierge is convinced that the countess stayed there forty years ago, though he cannot explain how her appearance remains totally unchanged. The countess takes an interest in the young couple recounting to them the grisly exploits of her ancestress, who killed eight hundred virgins so as to preserve her youth and beauty by bathing in their blood. Later that night, after a violent quarrel with Stefan, Valerie leaves the hotel but is persuaded to return by the countess, who has followed her to the railway station. It soon becomes clear that the countess has plans for the couple that will place them in extreme danger.

The film's chic eroticism was designed in from its inception. It has been likened by Kümel in interviews to the subsequent aesthetic of *Emmanuelle* (Just Jaeckin, 1974), but the film's erotic grace represents a much more skilful deployment of sexuality. Kümel himself describes his style as 'iconic' and 'allegorical' (Kümel 2003). The film opens with a perfect depiction of Kümel's cool eroticism as the newly weds Stefan and Valerie make love in a train carriage. The scene is overlaid with a vivid blue filter and the music combines effectively with the physical exertions of sexual intercourse. Kümel works within what Raymond Durgnat calls the 'orchestration of sexual desire', a bodily obsession, whereby the 'sublime and the disgusting, the rhapsodic and the lucid, the altruistic and the grossly selfish, find their most rewarding unison-in-tension' (1966: 8). Sexuality in Kümel's films is drawn from the uneasiness and 'erotic quickening' (Durgnat 1966: 8) of surrealist art where an intense atmosphere creates a sensual and cruel tableau, ceremonial in its precision.

The cool winter exterior shots of Ostend (although filmed in late summer) and the crumbling baroque buildings are presented starkly against the setting winter sun. Further exteriors (shot at dusk or dawn in the grounds of the Astoria Hotel in Brussels) blend with the film's lush interiors wherein artificial hues, especially the blue, red and gold of the bedroom scenes, preside. Kümel's designs for the film are exquisite, be it the staging more generally or the costumes and hairstyles developed for Seyrig and Rau. Actors appearing in his films consistently praised Kümel's formalist direction for being extremely detailed and precise and in *Daughters of Darkness* this approach enabled his actors to develop their actual sense of isolation in the empty seaside town while also helping them to establish the characters that they play. With the Ilona character Kümel manages to create a powerful sense of evil despite a somewhat limited performance from Rau, whose work onscreen contrasts with that of Seyrig.

Although Kümel references older directors such as Josef von Sternberg (as seen in the countess's sensational entrance into the film and the stylistic Dietrich-esque flourishes that Kümel applies to her) and G. W. Pabst (as seen in Ilona's Louise Brooks-inspired looks) there are also more contemporaneous Hitchcockian moments such as Valerie's scream at a window and Ilona's blood-soaked death, where the close-up shots of the mouth and the eye respectively echo the shower scene in *Psycho* (Alfred Hitchcock, 1960). Seyrig provides an especially striking and versatile screen presence. Her appearance, especially in a close-fitted Paco Rabanne-style silver dress, represents a cult film-1960s art/fashion sensibility which Soren calls 'chic camp' (1979: 32). Then again, the film's formalist stylistics sometimes break down, as in the scenes where Valerie tries to flee by train and the moment when Ilona's body is removed from the house, since both were shot using a hand-held camera in order to give an occasional jolt of realism.

The score for *Daughters of Darkness*, composed by multi-instrumentalist François de Roubaix, also echoes the baroque and decadent atmosphere of the film. The arrangement used by the composer incorporates a varied tonal approach, akin to the best work of other contemporaneous genre composers such as Manfred Hübler and Ennio Morricone. De Roubaix's flair for contemporary grooves and strong melodic progressions adds much to the feeling and atmosphere of the film while his skill in blending traditional instruments, such as the psaltery which accompanies the appearance of the countess, with the kind of electronic instrumentation found on his other soundtrack work adds a shimmering elegance to the scenes. In general, the use of music in Kümel's films is designed to add to the unreality of the experience, where the 'demand for musicality is at the opposite pole of the demand for objectivity' (Morin 2005: 161). Such is the power of the *Daughters of Darkness* soundtrack that it has since been widely sampled by electronic and hip-hop artists.

The Baroque: *Malpertuis*

Kümel's next film *Malpertuis* was begun before *Daughters of Darkness* but was delayed due to funding issues. *Malpertuis* is a surreal drama that made a conscious effort to again take the audience on a journey outside of reality. The film is visually stunning, taking the cursed house theme (*The Legend of Doom House* was one of its alternative titles) and extending the realms of this kind of cinematic drama into areas of the fantastic and the grotesque. The bizarre look of the film, a sort of medieval surrealism, is echoed in the films of Federico Fellini and Marco Ferreri and in Gualtiero Jacopetti and Franco Prosperi's *Mondo Candido* (1975). Indeed, all of these films deal with the 'realm of dreams'. The style of *Malpertuis* has been described by Kümel as a fairy tale but he explained that the film is a fairy tale 'taking place nowhere' (Kümel 2005) with the imaginary setting (enhanced by the constant switching of locations for the production) adding to the surreal nature of the film.

On docking at a Flemish port, a sailor Yann (Mathieu Carriere) is knocked unconscious and taken to Malpertuis, the vast house where his uncle

Cassavius (Orson Welles) lies dying, surrounded by Yann's sister Nancy (Susan Hampshire), his cousin Euryale (Susan Hampshire, again) and other relatives and employees. On his deathbed, Cassavius explains that they will all receive a fortune but only on condition that they never leave Malpertuis. He also plans that the couple who outlive all the others should marry and inherit everything. The residents idle away their time while Yann begins to explore the mysteries of the fantastic house, including an eerie attic room and Philarete's (Charles Janssens) taxidermist workshop. When the residents of the house begin being killed off in mysterious ways those who remain turn against Yann and the secret of Malpertuis is revealed to revolve around rejuvenated Greek gods clothed in human form and a plan to sire a race of demigods.

Kümel, in adapting Jean Ray's bizarre novel, created a kaleidoscopic picture devised out of a series of incredible and vivid tableaux (see Figure 7.2). There are scenes of horror in the film such as the moment an eagle swoops down to peck out the liver of Lampernisse (Jean-Pierre Cassel) and when Mathias Crook (Daniel Pilon) is killed by being impaled on a door by a metal spike. In an interview Matthieu Carriere described the film as 'shlock/shock' (Martens

Figure 7.2 *Malpertuis*: An incredible and vivid tableau featuring Euryale (Susan Hampshire) and Jan (Mathieu Carriere). Image courtesy of Harry Kümel.

2005) but once again Kümel was able to demonstrate great skill in combining what might be described as high art and trash. Jean Ray himself was connected to the 'Belgian school of the weird', a form of creative expression that is linked to the most important avant-garde movements of the late nineteenth and early twentieth century – impressionism, symbolism, surrealism – where atmosphere and the logic of dreams was of primary importance. Childhood memories and traumas from the past were brought to bear in Ray's stories and characters from that remembered past were made figurative and in three dimensions.

It can be instructive (if risky) to observe the early works of a feature director to ascertain stylistic themes and preoccupations that might shape a subsequent film style. *Aether* (1960), the short experimental film Kümel made with Herman Wuyts, in some ways sets out the style for Kümel's subsequent works. The film opens with a string of hypnotic pulsing red lights, revealed to be part of a subway passage. As a car emerges from the tunnel, we cut to a modern housing block. A red car pulls up in front of it (we see only part of it). The female driver's red gloves match the car. She beeps the horn and a figure appears at a window. The man descends the stairwell and we see him angled from above as he slips on a bright red ball that has been left on the stairs and he falls agonisingly. The ball bounces down the steps. Cut to a nurse walking along a long corridor. The man is now in hospital and a different set of red surgical gloves appear in frame. An operation is about to be performed. The man is now running across water and a field, the red ball always a presence. Is this a monstrous anaesthetized dream? He pauses and a splash of red blood washes across the frame. Suddenly the operation is over; the man appears to have died. Cut to the girl in the red car still beeping the horn. This time there is no one at the window. She drives off, the ball left in the road. The car retreats into the tunnel of pulsing red lights.

The geographical shapes of the staircase as the man descends prefigure shots of the decrepit stairs found in *Monsieur Hawarden* and *Malpertuis*, which are also framed in the same obtuse manner. Kümel's fascination with geometrical space is emphasized in the strange red lines that appear on the screen in *Aether*, mapping the angles of the buildings and objects in the frame. Long corridors, seen sometimes from a point-of-view perspective, also prefigure shots used in the hotel in *Daughters of Darkness* and the crumbling house in *Malpertuis*, albeit in this instance sterile and clinical as opposed to rotten and decaying. The prevalence of the colour red throughout, as both the hue of objects and as a surreal gesture, splashing and drawn over the screen, is a stylistic device that elevates the short film to the level of art and artifice. Similarly, the final shot of

Malpertuis – a freeze-frame of an extreme close-up of Yann's left eye – is overlaid with a Lewis Carroll quote: 'Life, what is it but a dream?'

The 'haunted houses' in both *Daughters of Darkness* and *Malpertuis* are mysterious and suspended, existing in the 'empty space between life and death' (Grant 2000: 70). The actions that take place within the walls of these places enjoy their own dream logic, while the outside world or 'reality' rumbles on, and the characters held within the films' anti-narratives are powerless to control what is happening to them. Moreover, they are trapped in a world with a past but no future, as the events of the films are re-played in a weird time-space for what seems to be an eternity. Kümel's symbolist films represent a consciousness that moves between lucidity and confusion, with scenes in the films moving between a recognizable reality and an occult world of perplexity. This leaves the viewer with the experience of a journey, albeit one whose process and end are impossible to guess. But the experience is a rich and vivid, if disturbing, one to endure. In Kümel's films, the living become the dead and also the undead. Indeed, the countess in *Daughters of Darkness* and the residents of *Malpertuis* 'are conscious of being dead, and so unable to die' (Grant 2000: 71). Again, Kümel makes masterful use of music, on this occasion created by the legendary French film composer Georges Delerue. Delerue's score uses more traditional film orchestration which moves between the dramatic, the romantic and the lush and the creepy, the carnivalesque and the absurd. The deep opening chords of the title sequence are particularly strident. Kümel's setting of the tableaux in film has been compared to certain Belgian painters, most notably Paul Delvaux who shares Kümel's fascination with the human body set against lush yet artificial backdrops. Kümel deploys the elegance, emptiness, even 'silence' of Delvaux's pictures in his portrayals of sex and death as his characters 'sleepwalk' through the cinematic world he created for them. This dimension was later extended into the written text by the British writer Nicholas Royle, with his 2005 novel *Antwerp*, a kitsch *noir* fantasy drawing on a synthesis of Delvaux's paintings and Kümel's films.

Magic realism?: *The Coming of Joachim Stiller*

Kümel's next film was an adaptation of another Belgian experimental novel *De komst van Joachim Stiller* (2019) [1960] by the Flemish writer Hubert Leon Lampo, one of the founders of Belgian magic realism. Magic realism portrays a realistic picture of the world but a world that also includes fantastical elements, one where the lines between fantasy and reality are blurred. The story concerns the mysterious arrival of a figure from the past, Joachim Stiller (Peter Strynckx), who affects present day lives with his eerie presence. With *Joachim Stiller*, Kümel was able to temper what he viewed as the 'mistakes' of *Malpertuis*, these being mainly in relation to the understandable tendency of a director to try to render a fantastical narrative by way of equally fantastical imagery, meaning that the audience experiences 'double' the surrealism. In Kümel's own words 'a fantastic subject should not be treated fantastically' (Thompson 2002: 18). With *Joachim Stiller*, the unusual poetry and lyricism of the novel was created by setting a more realistic tone overall. Interestingly, Lampo's original text even includes cinematic touches. Chapter 4, for example, opens with the line 'In the open window the panorama of the city lay trembling in the sun like a Technicolor shot before the camera starts tracking' (Lampo 2019: 35). The film opens with a long, extreme close-up shot of the protagonist, Freek Groenevelt (Hugo Metsers), staring directly into the camera lens (another affective Kümel trope previously seen in *Monsieur Hawarden* and in the publicity images for *Daughters of Darkness*). This is a minimal and low key, if highly atmospheric, opening by Kümel's standards and similar extreme close-ups of facial elements pepper the film.

The entire opening sequence, where the journalist Freek's world begins to be turned upside-down, has the crisp direction of a 1970s European thriller. Even the music by Pieter Verlinden, with its ominous bass notes and rapid high-hat motif is reminiscent of a score from a French *Polar* or Italian *Poliziotteschi* film. The film's sense of strangeness comes from its everyday events (a tram suddenly stopping; unnecessary roadworks; lunch in a bar while reading Kafka), which make each location suddenly odd and invested with supernatural menace. Kümel cleverly uses the surrealistic technique of rendering the object-fetish (a fountain; a stuffed bird; items on a bureaucrat's desk) magical. The colour red appears symbolically again – Lily's (Willeke van Ammelrooy) coat and umbrella and a kids' ball – recalling the use of bright red in Kümel's short *Aether* and in *Daughters of Darkness*. Often the sky, by way of arresting matte effects, changes lurid colour and rolls across the city scape in an ominous and strange manner, again reflecting the original text where the world seems out of joint and the city sky is described as having 'displayed unreal contrasts of light and shade' (Lampo 2019: 110). The alderman's dull office suddenly becomes like Dracula's castle, made up of dark shadows set against a thunderstorm and lit only by flashes of lighting. A vivid blue hue covers the town, indicating Stiller's occult grip over everything. The ordinary apartments, lit with atmospheric hues and Kümel's meticulous but unusual framing, are reminiscent of the peculiar gothic sense of the house in *Malpertuis*. The cathedral bells hypnotize the bewitched inhabitants of the city in the darkness of night while the uninitiated hear nothing. A climactic scene takes place in a fairground, usually a symbol of 'fun' but actually filled with horror and fright here. A dinner scene is filmed with a hand-held camera creating the vibrant energy of a documentary, despite the oddness of the subject. *Joachim Stiller* also has its moments of crude comic absurdity and fantastical characterization – the scenes with the ridiculous art dealer Zijlstra (Ward de Ravet) and his perverted protegee Siegfried (Charles Janssens) – which combines with quotidian events to create a persistent unsettling mood. *Joachim Stiller* ends with an incredible flashback montage sequence, representing Freek's childhood trauma, that is both surreal and tragic.

Conclusion

Harry Kümel works successfully within the realms of 'popular cinema' but has added layers of artistry and sophistication to his genre films. Working within what Jean Rollin has called 'B-Series' films, Kümel has produced works in a manner which regardless of the 'quality' of the concept 'allows for the creation and development of a director's personality' (2004: xi). Like Rollin, Kümel drew on surrealism and imagination, eschewing the fashionable trend for the realism of *nouvelle vague* cinema. In Kümel's films the landscape and the territory of the setting is brought to life with magic and illusion, the ordinary becoming extraordinary, a 'cinema of the imaginary' (Rollin 2004: xi). Critical opinion views Kümel's career, after the success of *Daughters of Darkness*, as relatively disappointing although this is explained by certain writers as an example of the difficulties facing a highly individualistic director, 'unafraid of offbeat or provocative materials but quite unwilling to compromise his vision for the sake of ministerial commissions, producers and audiences alike' (Mosley 2001: 113).

Kümel's cinematic works have been previously discussed as good examples of cult films and fan criticism has helped to 'assist in the rediscovery' (Mathijs and Sexton 2011: 54) of Kümel as a cult film director worthy of attention. Mathijs (2005b) argues that *Daughters of Darkness* in particular, through a variety of incidences relating to pre-production, marketing and reception, has ensured its 'bad (cult) reputation' and has acknowledged that the film is 'highly praised in cult reception' (Mathijs and Sexton 2011: 114). Mathijs indicates that this process of rediscovery and praise involves a set of 'extrinsic references . . . pointing to different interpretive communities', the very uncertain status of the film and how it is received by different audiences being what makes it so fascinating in the first place (Mathijs 2005b: 471). The same can be said of *Malpertuis* with the numerous unsatisfactory edits of the film, since its inception, in circulation. The uncaring treatment of the completed films and the rights to them; the screenings of the films in a variety of contexts; the constant changing of their titles; the snobbishness of film critics and even the mixed messages of the director himself about the worth of the films, are all common components in the creation of a cult film (in contrast to a work of cinematic 'art' which is revered from the start). But the concurrent shift in academic film studies to encompass trashy film genres and styles has also helped the rehabilitation of Kümel's works, as is evidenced by this latest collection.

Kümel (2003) once stated that 'films are not reality, they are dreams'. But Andrew Sarris's description of Josef von Sternberg's method – 'the colourful costumes, the dazzling decors, the marble pillared palaces merely underscore by ironic contrast the painfully acquired wisdom of the all too human prisoners of grandiose illusions' (1966: 8) – reads like an appropriate description of Kümel's method too. The three Harry Kümel films discussed here are all concerned with the same individual struggle of all humankind: that to live happily with yourself you have to comprehend yourself fully and honestly, be the 'proud hero who ventures into his own intimacy . . . the visionary of his own soul' (Bertellini 1997: 12). These Kümel films 'take the viewer backwards and forwards in time' like cinematic representations of 'Huysman's dream of Spiritual Naturalism . . . fixated all the while on transcendence through style' (Corrick 2018: 10). The 'brittle elegance' (Pirie 1977: 113) of Harry Kümel's entire visionary oeuvre ensures that his contribution to the cinema of the fantastical will endure for some time. Meanwhile, Kümel's ongoing plan to finally complete a sequel to *Daughters of Darkness*, with the crumbling edifice of Northern England as the backdrop, continues to be eagerly anticipated.

Bibliography

Bernheimer, Charles. *Decadent Subjects: The Idea of Decadence in Art, Literature, Philosophy, and Culture of the fin de siècle in Europe*. Baltimore: Johns Hopkins University Press, 2002.

Bertellini, Girogio. 'A Battle d'arrière-garde: Notes on Decadence in Luchino Visconti's *Death in Venice*'. *Film Quarterly* 50, no. 4 (1997): 11–19.

Corrick, Daniel. 'Introduction'. In *Drowning in Beauty: The Neo-Decadent Anthology*, edited by Justin Isis and Daniel Corrick. Sacramento: Snuggly Books, 2018.

Cowie, Peter. *International Film Guide 1969*. London: Tantivy Press, 1969.

Davay, Paul. 'Belgium'. In *International Film Guide 1970*, edited by Peter Cowie, 67–70. London: Tantivy Press, 1970.

Davay, Paul. 'Belgium'. In *International Film Guide 1971*, edited by Peter Cowie, 83–6. London: Tantivy Press, 1971.

Durgnat, Raymond. *Eros in the Cinema*. London: Calder and Boyars, 1966.

Grant, M. 'Fulci's Wasteland: Cinema, Horror and the Dreams of Modernism'. In *Unruly Pleasures: The Cult Film and its Critics*, edited by Xavier Mendik and Graeme Harper, 63–72. London: Fab Press, 2000.

Hawkins, Joan. *Cutting Edge: Art Horror and the Horrific Avant-Garde*. Minneapolis: University of Minnesota Press, 2000.

Kümel, Harry. 'Director Commentary' for *Daughters of Darkness*. DVD. Los Angeles: Blue Underground, 2003.

Kümel, Harry. 'Audio Commentary' for *Malpertuis*. DVD. Brussels: Kroniek van de Vlaamse Film, 2005.

Kümel, Harry. *7th Fantastic Films Weekend*. Bradford: The National Media Museum, 13–15 June 2008.

Kümel, Harry. 'Harry Kümel'. *Alchetron*, 24 October 2022. Available online at: https://alchetron.com/Harry-Kümel (accessed 6 November 2022).

Lampo, Hubert Leon. *The Coming of Joachim Stiller / De komst van Joachim Stiller*. Richmond, Virginia: Valancourt Books, 2019 [1960].

Leys, Simon. *The Hall of Uselessness: Collected Essays*. New York: New York Review of Books, 2013.

Martens, Erik. 'De Malpertuis archieven' for *Malpertuis*. DVD. Brussels: Kroniek van de Vlaamse Film, 2005.

Mathijs, Ernest (ed.). *The Cinema of the Low Countries*. London: Wallflower Press, 2004.

Mathijs, Ernest. '*Man Bites Dog* and the Critical Reception of Belgian Horror (in) Cinema'. In *Horror International*, edited by Steven Jay Schneider and Tony Williams, 315–35. Detroit: Wayne State University Press, 2005a.

Mathijs, Ernest. 'Bad Reputations: The Reception of "Trash" Cinema'. *Screen* 46, no. 4 (Winter 2005b): 451–72.

Mathijs, Ernest and Jamie Sexton. *Cult Cinema*. Chichester: Wiley-Blackwell, 2011.

Milner, John. *Symbolists and Decadents*. London: Studio Vista/Dutton, 1971.

Morin, Edgar. *The Cinema or the Imaginary Man*. Minneapolis: University of Minnesota Press, 2005.

Mosley, Philip. *Split Screen: Belgian Cinema and Cultural Identity*. Albany: State University of New York, 2001.

Pirie, David. *The Vampire Cinema*. London: Quarto Press, 1977.
Praz, Mario. *The Romantic Agony*. London: Humphrey Milford, 1933.
Ray, Jean. *Malpertuis*. London: Atlas Press, 1998 [1943].
Ray, Robert B. *How a Film Theory Got Lost and Other Mysteries in Cultural Studies*. Bloomington: Indian University Press, 2001.
Richardson, Michael. *Surrealism and Cinema*. Oxford and New York: Berg, 2006.
Rollin, Jean. 'Foreword: For an Illogical and Nonsensical European Cinema'. In *Alternative Europe: Eurotrash and Exploitation Cinema Since 1945*, edited by Ernest Mathijs and Xavier Mendik, xi–xiii. London: Wallflower, 2004.
Royle, Nicholas. *Antwerp*. London: Serpent's Tail, 2005.
Sarris, Andrew. *The Films of Josef von Sternberg*. New York: The Museum of Modern Art, 1966.
Sontag, Susan. 'The Decay of Cinema'. *The New York Times*, 25 February 1996. Available online at: https://www.nytimes.com/1996/02/25/magazine/the-decay-of-cinema.html (accessed 12 January 2020).
Soren, David. *Unreal Reality: The Cinema of Harry Kümel*. Columbia: Lucas Brothers, 1979.
Steele, Jamie. *Francophone Belgian Cinema*. Edinburgh: Edinburgh University Press, 2019.
Thompson, David. 'Auteur of Darkness'. *Sight and Sound* 12 (August 2002): 16–18.
Winthrop, Henry. 'Variety and Meaning in the Concept of Decadence'. *Philosophy and Phenomenological Research* 31, no. 4 (1971): 510–26.

Filmography

Aether (1960), [Film] Dir. Harry Kümel and Herman Wuyts, Belgium: Production Company Not Known.
Bye Bye Belgium (*Tout ca [ne nous rendra pas la Belgique]*, 2006), [Film] Dir. Isabelle Christiaens, Philippe Dutilleul, and Nathalie Jacobs, Belgium: Radio Television Belge Francophone (RTBF).
Calvaire (2004), [Film] Dir. Fabrice du Welz, Belgium / France / Luxembourg: La Parti Productions / Tarantula / StudioCanal.
The Coming of Joachim Stiller (*De Komst van Joachim Stiller*, 1976), [TV series and Film] Dir. Harry Kümel, Belgium: Algemene Vereniging Radio Omroep (AVRO) / Belgische Radio en Televisie (BRT).
Crazy Love (1987), [Film] Dir. Dominique Deruddere, Belgium: Multimedia.
Daughters of Darkness (1971), [Film] Dir. Harry Kümel, Belgium / France / West Germany /USA: Showking Films / Maya Films / Roxy Film / Ciné Vog Films / Gemini Pictures International / Cinépix.
Emmanuelle (1974), [Film] Dir. Just Jaeckin, France: Trinacra Films / Orphee Productions.

Jeanne Dielman, 23 quai du Commerce, 1080 Bruxelles (1975), [Film] Dir. Chantal Akerman, Belgium / France: Paradise Films / Unite Trois.

Last Year at Marienbad (*L'Année dernière à Marienbad*, 1961), [Film] Dir. Alain Resnais, France / Italy: Terra Film.

Malpertuis (1973), [Film] Dir. Harry Kümel, Belgium / France / West Germany: Artemis Film / Les Productions Artistes Associés / SOFLDOC / Société d'Expansion du Spectacle.

Man Bites Dog (*C'est arrive pres de chez vous*, 1992), [Film] Dir. Rémy Belvaux, André Bonzel, and Benoît Poelvoorde, Belgium: Les Artistes Anonymes.

Mira (1972), [Film] Dir. Fons Rademakers, Belgium / Netherlands: Kunst en Kino / Rademakers Productie BV.

Mondo Candido (1975), [Film] Dir. Gualtiero Jacopetti and Franco Prosperi, Italy: Perugia Cinematografica.

Monsieur Hawarden (1969), [Film] Dir. Harry Kümel, Belgium / Netherlands: Parkfilm / Sofidoc.

One Man and His Pig (*Vase de Noces*, 1974), [Film] Dir. Thierry Zéno, Belgium: Zéno Films.

Psycho (1960), [Film] Dir. Alfred Hitchcock, USA: Shamley Productions.

The Sex Life of the Belgians (*La Vie sexuelle des Belges 1950–1978*, 1994), [Film] Dir. Jan Bucquoy, Belgium: Transatlantic Films.

Toto the Hero (*Toto le Héros*, 1991), [Film] Dir. Jaco van Dormael, Belgium / France / Germany: Iblis Films.

Vampyr (1932), [Film] Dir. Carl Theodor Dreyer, Germany / France: Tobis Filmkunst.

8

(Re)positioning Ken Russell as a cult horror auteur

Matthew Melia

Introduction: Ken Russell and horror cinema

The career of Ken Russell is one which defies easy classification. As Kevin M. Flanagan (2015) has noted, Russell was a 'chameleonic' director, and in interrogating his position as a cult horror auteur, we must first recognize that he is also a somewhat awkward fit for the 'box' of horror director. In a nearly sixty-year career he made only a limited number of horror films, most of which were self-reflexive, postmodern and self-parodic productions. It was nearly thirty years into his career and during a brief relocation to work within Hollywood (a period which began with studio interest in his ultimately abandoned *Dracula* project [Melia, 2022: 85–9] and the science fiction horror of *Altered States* [1980]) that his film work would take a more definite turn towards genre cinema. Post 1980, Russell directed three horror films: *Gothic* (1986), *Lair of the White Worm* (1988) and *The Fall of the Louse of Usher* (2002). Despite such an intermittent engagement with the genre, the tropes of horror and the gothic are significant defining, stylistic and narrative components of many of Russell's films (Melia 2022: 85–9). Furthermore, Russell's later repositioning as a cult horror film director was facilitated by the birth of video in the 1980s – a medium that would become increasingly important to him.

This chapter will consider the extent to which Russell became the custodian of his own legacy in the final years of his life. Here the chapter will explore both his film work, *The Lair of the White Worm* and the micro-budget *The Fall of the Louse of Usher*, and his self-reflexive appearance in Keith Fulton and Louis Pepe's punk body-horror 'mockumentary' *Brothers of the Head* (2006). All three of these films are indicative both of Russell's embeddedness in the horror genre and his desire to interrogate his own relationship to it. Thus this chapter will contextualize the ways in which Russell was culturally repositioned as, not just a director of horror cinema, but as a cult director too. The chapter will further explore how Russell's cultural position changed in the 1980s and beyond while arguing that Russell's transition to the status of a cult horror director was catalysed by the VHS home video boom of the early to mid-1980s.

Russell's composer films and his engagement with horror

Russell's *Monitor* film on the British artist, filmmaker and counter-cultural eccentric Bruce Lacey, *The Preservation Man* (1962), marks a starting point for the director's preoccupation with the gothic and the monstrous as channels of creation. Here Lacey's eccentric bric-a-brac automatons are presented as whimsical *Frankenstein*-style creations. Mechanical automated toys would also appear in *Gothic* in the form of a mechanical piano player and a mechanical belly dancer and these toys serve as a link back to the *The Preservation Man*. More engagements with horror can be found in Russell's major composer films of the 1970s. *The Music Lovers* (1971) is a film about the Russian composer Pyotr Illych Tchaikovsky (Richard Chamberlain) and his marriage to Nina Milukova (Glenda Jackson) and is in many ways closer in spirit to being a serious horror film than Russell's later comic horror parodies like *The Lair of the White Worm*. Indeed, the film navigates a variety of traumatic and searing horror images, not least in the attempt to cure the composer's mother of cholera by immersing her in boiling water; or in Nina's final asylum imprisonment during which she is molested by the hands of unseen lunatics from beneath an asylum courtyard grill. *Mahler* (1974) presents a Poe-esque nightmare sequence in which the composer Gustav Mahler (Robert Powell) is depicted encased alive in a coffin, open mouthed and silently screaming. Russell was preoccupied with the works of Edgar Allan Poe, Mary Shelley and Bram Stoker and these authors are part of a structural/organizational framework upon which Russell's own work frequently hangs. Indeed, Russell (2008) once observed that 'another lifelong passion is my fascination with the bizarre and fantastic. On my bedside table is a well-thumbed copy of *Tales of Mystery and Imagination* by Edgar Allan Poe'. The highly stylized *Lisztomania* (1975) is a musical about the composer Franz List (Roger Daltrey) but Russell turns to the *Frankenstein* mythology for inspiration: Rick Wakeman plays Thor as Frankenstein's monster as created by a Nazi Richard Wagner (Paul Nicholas).

The Frankenstein mythos and narratives of rebirth and creation are central underlying themes across Russell's film and television work, in both his horror-oriented and non-horror texts. The mythos is tackled head on in *Gothic*, a postmodern and self-reflexive dramatization, not of the Frankenstein story but of its romantic and gothic origins at the Villa Diodati in 1816. Horror cinema had a catalysing influence across Russell's career from Expressionist and Universal horror films to more contemporary examples. Russell even revealed his own interest in contemporary 'cult' British horror cinema, citing the transgressive and low-budget pleasures of *The Wicker Man* (Robin Hardy, 1973) and *Hellraiser* (Clive Barker, 1987) before adding, 'why we are always tripping off to Transylvania in search of *Dracula* I will never know. As the same author, Bram Stoker, shows us in *The Lair of the White Worm*, when it comes to the crunch, you can't beat British incisors' (1993: 143).

Russell cites the theatrical and camp guignol horror of *Theatre of Blood* (Douglas Hickox, 1973) as being 'one of the most ingenious horror films I have seen' (1993: 143). In it, ham Shakespearean actor Edward Lionheart (Vincent Price) fakes his own death in order to wreak bloody revenge on the critics who have savaged his performances (killing them in the style of gruesome deaths taken from in Shakespeare's plays). We might perhaps recognize the appeal of *Theatre of Blood* for Russell, who as the 1970s wore on was increasingly becoming a pariah to many film critics. These critics perceived Russell to be a director whose work was no longer to be taken seriously, a camp stylistic affront to the politeness, prestige and conservatism of the British cinema of the 1980s. As Russell writes, the conservative critics in *Theatre of Blood* are a 'bigoted lot' who

> receive their just rewards. Criticism has become a blood sport. It makes a refreshing change to see the hunters hunted down instead of hapless quarry ... Having been pursued for years by unspeakable reviewers perhaps I have developed a taste for blood myself ... As Lionheart says to one critic he is about to do away with, 'How many artists have you killed because you lacked the ability to create yourself?' (1993: 149)

Here one cannot help calling to mind Russell attacking the *Evening Standard*'s film critic Alexander Walker with a rolled-up newspaper copy of his review of *The Devils* (1971), live on television! But despite Russell's lifelong identification with the horror genre, it was not until the final decade or so of his life that he would actually be canonized as a *cult* horror director.

Several events are, perhaps, illustrative of this late adoption: early in the first decade of the twenty-first century Russell was forced on the grounds of ill health to turn down an invite from director Mick Garris to contribute to the anthology horror series *Masters of Horror* (2005–7), which included films by a roster of contemporary cult horror auteurs such as Brian Yuzna, Takashi Miike, John Carpenter, Tobe Hooper and Dario Argento. In 2006 he was invited to contribute to the anthology horror film, *Trapped Ashes* (2006, various). This invite came at a time when Russell had turned exclusively to micro-budget 'do-it-yourself' filmmaking. Russell's segment in *Trapped Ashes* – 'The Girl with the Golden Breasts' – was a parodic exercise in camp, comic, low-budget Cronenbergian body horror that featured a pair of vampiric breast implants. The segment can be seen as an exercise in self-parody too since it brings to mind an earlier example of unsettling body horror found in Russell's hallucinatory and surrealist *Gothic*. In that film Claire Clairmont's (Myriam Cyr) breasts are given surrealistic staring eyes. Interestingly, it was Russell who presented the Canadian body-horror director David Cronenberg with a lifetime achievement award from the influential horror magazine *Rue Morgue* at the 'Festival of Fear' in Toronto in 2010. These events imply that if Russell had, in the last decades of his life, been relegated to the margins of the wider mainstream film establishment, he had conversely been accepted as a pioneering figure of immense stature by an alternate cult horror film 'establishment'.

Ken Russell, Vestron Video and the home video boom

Kevin Flanagan has noted that 'though previously known for his eclectic idiosyncratic interests', it was in the 1980s that 'Russell became a maestro of horror cinema' making 'a transition to a more commercial form' (2009: xvii) from the end of the 1970s (although he maintained within this his art house sensibilities). Flanagan comments:

> Russell entered a more commercial phase with *Valentino* (1977) and *Altered States* (1980), both made with the backing of major funding and distribution. Russell's films for the remainder of the 1980s were done for such minimajors as New World Pictures, Virgin Vision, and Vestron Pictures and include *Crimes of*

Passion (1984), *Gothic* (1986), and *The Rainbow* (1989), though this period also saw a refocusing on projects for television, as well as Russell turning to work in the opera. (2009: xvii)

Of these cited titles only *Gothic* presents itself as an obvious genre-defined (and genre-pastiching) horror film (and will be discussed in more detail later). However, Russell's slice of neon drenched LA Noir, *Crimes of Passion,* produced by New World Pictures, plays with and dissolves generic boundaries and style in a typically self-referential way and draws on a clear set of gothic horror tropes (Melia 2022: 75–7). The film deliberately and knowingly casts Norman Bates himself, Anthony Perkins, as the psychotic, obsessive street preacher the Rev Shayne (who carries with him a bag of sex toys including a monstrous, steel, sharpened dildo called 'The Superman') opposite Kathleen Turner's sex worker by night-respected fashion exec by day China Blue. The film's narrative of dual personas and the liberation of the unconscious id is reminiscent of Luis Buñuel's *Belle de Jour* (1967) and Robert Louis Stevenson's *Dr Jekyll and Mr Hyde* (a gothic narrative of duality that also informs aspects of *Altered States*).

Russell's relationship with the mainstream Hollywood studios had faltered after the failures of both *Valentino* and *Altered States* and the collapse of his *Dracula* project – a reimagining of Bram Stoker's tale which sees the vampire feeding on the creativity of the great romantic and modernist artists (the film was abandoned before going into production due to the release of John Badham's *Dracula* [1979]). It was the emergence of these new, independently driven film markets led by the minimajors, however, that afforded Russell a professional lifeline. The video industry had been developing from the mid-1970s and as Johnny Walker (2022: 17) notes, it was from 1978 that the industry really began to take off in the UK (where Russell would return to make *Gothic, Lair of the White Worm* and *Salome's Last Dance* [1988] before returning to the States to make *Whore* [1991] for Trimark Pictures).

Minimajors such as New World Pictures, Virgin Vision and Vestron Pictures were initially working on the peripheries of the mainstream (although some would later go on to produce and distribute some of the most popular mainstream films of the 1980s in conjunction with Hollywood studios). Ken Russell had, from the mid-1970s onwards, also been pushed further towards the margins of what was perceived as mainstream cinema – a trajectory that had begun slowly with *The Devils*, a film which was equally celebrated and reviled by critics. The new industrial landscape of the minimajors would largely provide a spiritual home for Russell. In his study of the emergence of the video industry, Frederic Wasser notes that 'there was an aura of subversion surrounding the VCR' (2001: 91) and Russell found himself drawn into not just a new counter-industry but into a new and subversive video culture that seemed ready to adopt him, and which would provide the creative freedom he was increasingly being denied. It would carve out a space for him and legitimize his cultural repositioning on the margins. These companies (which from an early stage catered to the B-movie/horror crowd) served to provide a new and appreciative audience for Russell's work. The 'subversive' nature of this video culture would of course be exemplified in the UK through the moral panic over the 'video nasties' – a situation that, given Mary Whitehouse's opposition to both *Dance of the Seven Veils* (Ken Russell, 1970) and the panic among the censors and the conservative right caused by *The Devils*, Russell's work might be seen to anticipate.

While Russell's relationship with the minimajors may be seen to go back as far as 1975 and *Tommy* (produced by the Hemdale Film Corporation and distributed by Columbia Pictures), it is his relationship with Vestron Video that is especially important in his repositioning as a cult horror director. Vestron Video was founded by the American filmmaker John Hughes and was borne out of the ashes of the Time-Life Video library. During the 1980s its main business was distributing horror films on VHS and one of its key releases was John Landis's *An American Werewolf in London* (1981). Prior to 1986 Vestron Video had been operating exclusively in the United States distributing films by Cannon and other companies on the peripheries of mainstream Hollywood. From 1986 the company moved into film production too and rebranded itself as Vestron Pictures, the banner under which it released Russell's *The Lair of the White Worm* in 1988.

To understand Russell's relationship with the company however we must go back to 1986 and *Gothic*, which was produced by Richard Branson's Virgin Vision and distributed on video by Vestron. The script for the film had already been written by a then unknown and emergent screenwriter, Steven Volk (who would go on to become one of the UK's foremost horror writers for both page and screen). As reported in an article in *The New York Times*, the script had come to Al Clark, head of acquisitions for Virgin Vision, who immediately recommended Russell for the job of director (Ackerman 2022). Like Russell, Volk had come from an advertising background and had a lifelong preoccupation with both Poe and Mary Shelley. This collaborative, postmodern, fever dream of a film is based on the fateful meeting of Mary Shelley (Natasha Richardson),

Percy Shelley (Julian Sands), Dr John Polidori (Tim Spall) and Mary's half-sister Claire Clairemont at Byron's (Gabriel Byrne) Villa Diodati on the shores of Lake Geneva in 1816. This is the moment that – as Volk expressed to me in interview – twentieth-century horror culture was born (Author interview 2022). The film premiered at the London Film Festival in 1986 but was received poorly by critics and was a disaster for Virgin Vision on the big screen. *Gothic*'s theatrical release coincided with Vestron's entrance into film production and home video distribution in the UK and the film subsequently became a notable success when it was released on home video by Vestron Video.

Vestron was at that time under the stewardship of head of acquisitions Dan Ireland, who would become an ally and champion of Russell's work. Indeed, Ireland is at the centre of a shift in perceptions of Russell as a filmmaker. Ireland had made his name as a producer of films such as John Huston's *The Dead* (1987). He had also co-founded the Seattle Film Festival and had been responsible for bringing another European art cinema director, Paul Verhoeven, to the attention of American audiences and turning him into a cult success. In some ways Vestron's repositioning of Verhoeven for a new audience may be taken as a model for its repositioning of Ken Russell – both directors had previously been associated with the British and European art house cinema and now they were being identified as being marketable to a new cult video market. Ireland would also produce *Salome's Last Dance*, *The Rainbow* and *Whore*.

The Lair of the White Worm

According to Ireland (2012), it was on the strength of *Gothic*'s success on home video that he offered Russell a three-film deal with Vestron, having been mandated by the company to produce a horror film prior to *The Rainbow*. This was to be *The Lair of the White Worm*, and the director would frequently quip in interviews that he could not get Stoker's best novel made so he filmed his worst instead.

The Lair of the White Worm would offer a variety of transgressive, hallucinatory and paracinematic pleasures: a naked and fanged Amanda Donohoe (painted blue from head to toe and wearing only a vicious looking strap-on dildo) and a roman orgy of ravished nuns are two such examples. The film is also a parody of the sort of prestige Merchant-Ivory-styled British heritage cinema that was pushing Russell's own style of cinematic excess to the margins. *The Lair of the*

White Worm even stars Hugh Grant, fresh from his role in the Merchant-Ivory film *Maurice* (1987). J. Hoberman duly noted of the film that:

> Like Russell's comparably entertaining *Altered States*, albeit with more endearing tackiness, *Lair of the White Worm* is rabidly hallucinatory. Not only does the resident vampire sprout eight-inch fangs at will, the merest drop of her venom plunges [Catherine] Oxenberg into a psychedelic delirium of screaming nuns, rampaging serpents, bloody crucifixions, confused Roman soldiers and impaled eyeballs. (1988: 65)

The film also exhibits a folk-punk sensibility typical of the mid-1980s with groups like The Oysterband. At one point Russell repurposes an old English folk song called 'The Lampton Worm' which he claims to have unearthed in the archives of Cecil Sharp House, a location that he dubbed a 'treasure trove of folklore' (1993: 144). In the film a folk-punk band play the song at a party thrown by Lord James D'Ampton (Hugh Grant). Furthermore, the film evidences Russell's love of and awareness of British folk horror – its opening scene of the uncovering of an ancient monstrous skull is similar to the opening of *The Blood on Satan's Claw* (Piers Haggard, 1971). IQ Hunter has commented of Russell's film:

> In its own delightfully bonkers way, *The Lair of the White Worm* is a near perfect trash movie. Sharply self-parodic but locked into key themes of British cinema (and indeed culture), knowing and surreal, ridiculous but tightly controlled, it is a fine example of 'heterosexual camp', a compromise solution by a director exiled from the art house who is using a low genre as a vehicle for 'mad' imagery in the absence of any other commercial outlet. (2013: 152)

Consolidating the film's cult appeal, *The Lair of the White Worm* has lent itself more readily than Russell's other films to fan engagement and practices. This was in evidence at the Offscreen Film Festival, Brussels, in 2014 which included a full retrospective of Russell's work complete with *The Lair of the White Worm* cosplayers.

It is also interesting to note another potential provenance of the film. We might hypothetically draw a line from Russell's childhood experience of seeing the 1934 film *The Secret of the Loch* (Milton Rosmer, 1934), which he described as being 'the most horrific film I ever saw' since it featured a monster that was represented by what turned out to be a 'naked chicken, plucked and very much alive' (Melia 2022: 76), to a potential project (reported in *Variety* in 1979) called *The Monster of Loch Ness*, 'a contemporary tale of the 300ft monster, in this case mutated by ecological disaster and radiation' (Melia 2022: 76), to *The Lair of* the *White Worm*. Across the publicity for the film, Russell would turn again to discussion of the Loch Ness Monster – as if *Lair* was the monster movie – and the *Dracula* film he had been trying to make for many years.

The Fall of the Louse of Usher: Ken Russell, 'Garagiste'

Increasingly across the course of his career Ken Russell would rely on a matrix of friends and associates to support and collaborate on his creative endeavours – not only Dan Ireland but also figures like the broadcaster Melvyn Bragg (who throughout the 1990s supported Russell's return to television and his films via *The Southbank Show* [ITV]) and the film critic Mark Kermode (who would find and restore previously lost footage from *The Devils*). In his later years his wife Elize (and other family members), friends and neighbours and would play a major role in Russell's work as he turned increasingly to micro-budget filmmaking. Russell performed in, wrote, produced and edited his final films himself, which were made at home and in his garden via his own Gorsewood Productions.

During the 1980s the home video industry had provided a new market and audience for Russell's work, providing him with an increased popularity among horror film-collecting fans via releases of his films on the labels of small but emergent video production and distribution companies such as New World Pictures, Virgin Vision and Vestron Video. But in the last two decades of his life, the use of hand-held video cameras and camcorders became an increasingly important artistic outlet for Russell. These cameras and the technology that developed alongside them allowed Russell to wrest back creative control, to regain control of the editing suite and the final cut of his films and to self-promote and self-release his work (Hoyle 2009: 59). In other words Russell was at liberty to make the films he wanted to make free of budgetary, financial and industrial constraints. Video camera and camcorder technology thus provided a new and liberating canvas for him to work on. Indeed, Russell (2008) stated his preference for this medium:

> All you have to do is press a red button. And there's nobody telling you what to do, it's also nice to have control over what I'm doing now, like I had in my early films such as *Amelia and the Angel* [1958]. It's free and easy and anything that comes into one's mind is achievable. There's a way to achieve without resorting to money.

In his book *Directing Film: From Pitch to Premiere* (2000), Russell also observed that 'for years I'd listened to film buffs extolling the virtues of celluloid over tape, but as I'd always suspected this just wasn't so . . . Film may have a wonderful transparency but tape has a bright compulsive . . . richness of colour and a unique ability to jump out of the screen and hit you' (quoted in Hoyle 2009: 59).

Russell's Gorsewood Productions or 'Garagiste' films were shot on a digital video camcorder in the grounds of his home in East Boldre, UK. These films have, perhaps unsurprisingly, garnered relatively little in the way of critical discussion and are often regarded by critics of his work as an insignificant coda to a once great career. This chapter would like to recognize, however, the legitimacy and importance of these projects. Of a small number of commentators, Brian Hoyle (2009) provides perhaps the most objective and serious consideration of these later works. The most well-known of these films was the home-made comic horror, *The Fall of the Louse of Usher* (hereafter *Usher*), which was also the last of his films to be given an official release on home video. These 'Garagiste' films were not simply an attempt to pass the time making chaotic and ultra-low-budget home movies, but were (as I have argued elsewhere [Melia 2022a]) serious attempts not only to return to his amateur film making roots by circumnavigating a continuous lack of funding to get the films he wanted to make made, but also to take his deconstructive postmodern preoccupations with horror cinema and the act of creation to their logical and furthest conclusion. *Usher*, we may argue, brings to a conclusion an experiment in self-reflexive creation that began with *Gothic*. Christophe Van Eecke offers an analysis of *Gothic*, in which he observes 'the parallels between the film's structure and a funhouse ride; the film's use of the tableau vivant; the film's engagement with nineteenth-century celebrity cults; and the film's representation of heritage tourism' (2019: 140). Van Eecke adds that 'the film is structured as a ride through the booby-trapped funhouse of the Villa Diodati. Just like a dark ride in a modern theme park, where spectators move from one view to the next, so too the spectacular geography of the Villa Diodati is that of a series of rooms furnished with attractions that await us' (2019: 140).

In a similar way Russell self-reflexively turns his very own East Boldre home into a disorienting and disquieting 'funhouse' in *Usher*. Russell even cast himself in the mad scientist/head of the house role of Dr Calahari (a self-reflexive move that brings to mind his role as Dr Lucy in *Trapped Ashes*). Thus this real-world domestic space is transformed into a chaotic and sometimes disturbing Edgar Allan Poe-themed carnival space in which the writer's stories are rendered through Russell's do-it-yourself and punk aesthetic: a space of cavorting inflatable dolls and dinosaurs, penis-threatening pendulums, saucy nurses and writhing nuns (played by gothic group The Medieval Babes). As Van Eecke notes of *Gothic*:

> The Villa Diodati, Byron's rented home on the shores of Lake Leman, Switzerland, is a haunted funhouse . . . full of mechanical automatons, disorienting corridors and passages – metonyms for the haunted and traumatised gothic psyche where the viewer is drawn ever further into its nightmarish complexities as the frenzy of the evening crescendos. (2019: 140)

In *Usher*, Russell employs shop bought inflatable dolls (instead of automatons) and other home-made props (he wears a doctor's head-mirror made from a head band and a compact disc). The micro-budget aesthetic allows Russell to strip his previous work in – and ongoing preoccupations with – horror down to their bare essentials in an act of self-interrogation. As such the film's content appears to offer a fascinating glimpse into the director's own psyche.

Russell (2007), who coined the term 'garagiste' (one who makes films in their garage or at home, independently and with materials that are to hand), noted that he

> First became a garagiste more than 50 years ago – long before I could afford a garage, let alone the budget to indulge in home movie making. . . . In my youth I saved up pennies I earned as a freelance press photographer and over a period of several years made three home movies, which I showed to the BBC. The rest is history.

As Hoyle has observed (citing Russell), 'Russell had to give up on the idea of a "multi-million-dollar blockbuster to be shot in Hollywood [for] a (more or less) no budget underground film to be shot in my back garden, conservatory or garage"' (2009: 58). This turn towards micro-budget filmmaking situates Russell within an overlooked milieu of cult horror filmmaking and allows comparisons with another similar micro-budget cult horror auteur and contemporary of Russell, Michael J Murphy.

Joseph Lanza (2007) has suggested that Russell had intended to make *Usher* ten years earlier, in Hollywood, casting both Roger Daltrey and Twiggy. Its origins however, date back further than this to the point at which Russell left the United Kingdom to work in the United States and prior to his adoption by Vestron. As I have discussed elsewhere (Melia 2022), this no-budget underground film has its roots in the script for an unmade feature which was pitched to Columbia

Pictures in the late 1970s, with which the studio had wanted to 'out-Corman Corman' (Author interview 2019). Indeed, *Ten Times Poe* was a script by Russell which he had developed in collaboration with studio executive Michael Nolin as *Horrible Beauty*. With *Usher*, Russell revived this postmodern experiment in horror: an anthology horror film which collates a variety of Poe stories within one overarching narrative – an updating of *The Fall of the House of Usher*. Here Roderick Usher becomes Roddy Usher (James Johnson, the lead singer of the cult Goth punk band Gallon Drunk), an LA rock star who is condemned to an asylum for the murder of his sister. As he travels on his picaresque journey through the film's narrative, Usher encounters a set of inmates whose back stories correspond to other tales of terror written by Poe.

Usher bears its minimal budget as a badge of pride. Furthermore, it might also be argued that the film is an exercise in what might be termed video expressionist horror. As Hoyle notes:

> It is a film of strong colours, particularly reds and purples, and video does indeed give them a vibrancy and texture that would have been far more muted on celluloid, particularly a 16mm blown up to 35mm, a common recourse of low budget film makers. Russell also takes advantage of modern video-editing technology to lend the film some additional production value. Using a system called Casablanca, described as a 'Pandoras box of editing marvels' Russell is able to enhance his images and manipulate his colour palate. . . . Russell pushes these already bold colours to the point of saturations. The leaves on the trees behind the castle move from bright emerald to autumn brown and deep purple, while the castle itself changes between fuchsia, acid green, crimson and aquamarine. This for next to no money, gives the scene an appropriately dreamlike, hallucinatory quality, and provides the film with a fitting coda. (2009: 59)

Usher is thus illustrative of a director who was not only continuing to experiment with horror as a cultural form, playing with its palate, narratives and aesthetic. It is also illustrative of a filmmaker who had gleefully adapted to his cult and paracinematic status.

Brothers of the Head

Keith Fulton and Louis Pepe's cult punk-body horror 'mockumentary' *Brothers of the Head* sits among a body of work by a set of contemporary directors for whom Russell is a stylistic and thematic cornerstone. The film, which is an adaptation of a novel by the British science fiction author Brian Aldiss (1977), concerns a pair of conjoined twin brothers, Tom and Barry Howe (Luke and Harry Treadways), who are taken from their family and groomed for punk rock stardom by an unscrupulous record company and an abusive manager. This is a contemporary gothic narrative concerning the spectacular and monstrous body and its exploitation. The 'mockumentary' not only frames Aldiss's story as a 'Ken Russell film' but in a variety of ways may also be said to be *about* Russell himself. Indeed, the film presents an interesting set of concentric narratives circles: first, the narrative of the 'mockumentary' film itself that the audience are watching (the first layer); second, the narrative of the purposely degraded 'documentary' footage of the 'real' Tom and Barry that makes up parts of the overarching 'mockumentary' (the second layer); and third the narrative of the outtakes from an 'abandoned' Ken Russell dramatization of *Brothers of the Head* that also make up part of the overarching 'mockumentary' (the third layer). The film dissolves the boundaries between these layers and Russell even appears as himself during an early talking-head sequence.

Fulton and Pepe switch between to-camera dialogue and interview footage; the 'documentary' film footage of the twins; and outtakes of Russell's 'abandoned' 'film'. To borrow Mark Sinker's term, their approach evidences a knowing 'mutant' or Frankenstein style of filmmaking (2006: 44). Russell's involvement with the film adds a further level of self-awareness and knowing irony to the proceedings. His presence at the 'head' of the film, and the film's incorporation of different styles and modes of narrative, surely prompts Russell savvy viewers to associate *Brothers of the Head* with different but significant aspects of the director's earlier work: his gothic infused early bio-documentaries, his musical films of the 1970s and the gothic body horror shocks of his work from the 1980s. In his first talking-head sequence Russell states of his 'film' that 'It's really about innocence and the loss of innocence, the exploitation of innocence always appeals to me because, again, that happened in *Tommy,* and it began to happen with Tom and Barry, the way they were bought'. The reference to *Tommy* here provides an intertextual link to his own 'Gothic' depiction of the music industry as played out during the film's 'Sally Simpson' sequence, in which the young groupie Sally (Victoria Russell) eventually marries a rock musician from California who is played by a child actor (Gary Rich) dressed as a Rock and Roll Frankenstein's Monster.

Further levels of self-awareness are revealed when Russell reappears in the film for a second time towards the end (he actually bookends the film as if he is its Alpha and Omega) during a section in which it is revealed that a tumour in one of the twins heads turns out to be a mutant third sibling, a narrative turn that resonates with the film's concern with authorship and creation: Russell himself is the 'third twin' in the film's structure, hidden beneath the surface. An 'outtake' from Russell's 'abandoned' 'dramatization' subsequently presents the third sibling as a monstrous, glistening, living appendage that Russell describes as being a manifestation of the twin's genius. Significantly, the notion of 'artistic genius' found in Ken Russell's artist biopics is commonly associated with the monstrous, the parasitic and the vampiric. It is something that feeds on the artist leading them to their downfall or death. For example, in *Song of Summer* (Ken Russell, 1968) the composer Frederick Delius (Max Adrian) is presented as a monstrous, parasitic figure who is cruel and demanding. Russell not only venerates the artist/composer but also recognizes the innately vampiric/monstrous qualities of the artist and the burden of his genius on those around him.

Ultimately, Russell is positioned as the stylistic and imaginative centre of *Brothers of the Head*, even displacing Brian Aldiss as the creative fulcrum. Indeed, in the 'talking head' interview sequences, Aldiss is actually played by British television actor James Greene. As Kevin Flanagan observes with regard to *Gothic* and *Lisztomania*, *Brothers of the Head* also readily offers a Russellian 'Gothic Mashup' both literally (given its lead characters' condition) and textually (given the nature of the footage that makes up the three narrative layers previously discussed). Furthermore the 'monstrous' presence of the conjoined twins is suggestive of not only 'Romantic [and Gothic] discourses on creation' but of a textual preoccupation with the senses of 'individual creativity and adaptation' which flourish across Russell's film and television work (2022: 34).

Conclusion: Russell's legacy as cult horror director

Before concluding, I would like to add that Ken Russell's legacy as a cult horror film director is also to some extent tied to his adoption by other filmmakers. Indeed, this adoption has served to consolidate his position as a cult horror film director. For example, Anna Biller's *The Love Witch* (2017) starts with a deliberate homage to the opening of *The Lair of the White Worm*, pastiching its title font and the image of Thor's cave found in its opening shot. But – as this chapter has argued – Russell's initial repositioning as a cult horror film director came about because of his relationship with the home video industry and his later move into micro-budget, do-it-yourself, postmodern filmmaking. To conclude, this chapter asserts that in the last decade or so of his life, Russell curated his own legacy as a cult horror film director and genre personality. His turn to microbudget filmmaking, his involvement with and appearances in contemporary cult horror cinema (*Trapped Ashes* and *Brothers of the Head*), his links to *Rue Morgue* magazine and its 'Festival of Fear' and so on led to a cultural repositioning that was in many ways a design of Russell's own, a way of claiming a legacy and reclaiming control.

Bibliography

Ackerman, Diane. 'Why Horror Movies Still Gnaw at Us'. *New York Times*, 5 April 1987. Available online at: https://www.nytimes.com/1987/04/05/movies/film-why-horror-movies-still-gnaw-at-us.html (accessed 26 July 2022).

Aldiss, Brian. *Brothers of the Head*. London: Pierrot Publishing Ltd, 1997.

Author interview, Michael Nolin, May 2019.

Author interview, Stephen Volk, February 2022.

Flanagan, Kevin M. 'Introduction'. In *Ken Russell: Re-Viewing England's Last Mannerist*, edited by Kevin M. Flanagan, ix–xxv. Plymouth: Scarecrow Press, 2009.

Flanagan, Kevin M. 'Nuancing Ken Russell'. *EUP*, 13 October 2015. Available online at: https://euppublishingblog.com/2015/10/13/nuancing-ken-russell/ (accessed 13 July 2022).

Flanagan, Kevin M. 'Adapting Monstrous Creation: *Lisztomania* (1975) and *Gothic* (1986) as Gothic Mash-Ups'. In *Gothic Mashups: Hybridity, Appropriation and Intertextuality in Gothic Storytelling*, edited by Nathalie Neil, 21–36. Vauxhall: Lexington Books, 2022.

Hoberman, J. 'Blood and Guts'. *Village Voice*, 1 November 1988: 65.

Hoyle, Brian. 'In Defence of the Amateur'. In *Ken Russell: Re-Viewing England's Last Mannerist*, edited by Kevin Flanagan, 40–62. Plymouth: Scarecrow Press, 2009.

Hunter, IQ. *British Trash Cinema*. London: BFI, 2013.

Ireland, Dan. 'The Lair of the White Worm'. *Trailers from Hell*, 15 May 2012. Available online at: https://trailersfromhell.com/the-lair-of-the-white-worm/ (accessed 26 July 2022).

Lanza, Joseph. *Phallic Frenzy. Ken Russell and His Films*. London: Aurum Press, 2007.

Melia, Matthew. 'Ken Russell's Gothic Modernism'. In *ReFocus: The Films of Ken Russell*, edited by Matt Melia, 69–95. Edinburgh: Edinburgh University Press, 2022a.

Melia, Matthew. 'The Shared History of Stanley Kubrick's *A Clockwork Orange* (1971) and Ken Russell's The Devils (1971)'. *Historical Journal of Film, Radio, and Television* 42, no. 1 (2022b): 10–15.

Rose, Bernard. 'Hi Ken – Sorry I Stole Your Movie'. *The Guardian*, 15 September 2008. Available online at: https://www.theguardian.com/film/2008/sep/15/biography (accessed 26 July 2022).

Russell, Ken. *Fire Over England: The British Cinema Comes under Friendly Fire.* Hutchinson: London, 1992.

Russell, Ken. *Directing Film: From Pitch to Premiere.* London: Batsford, 2000.

Russell, Ken. 'Coming Soon from a Garage Near Me'. *The Times 2*, 19 July 2007. Available online at https://www.thetimes.co.uk/article/coming-soon-from-a-garage-near-me-sgt0996zv3r (accessed 26 July 2022).

Russell, Ken. 'A Ban Apart'. *Garageland: Art, Culture and Ideas*, Issue 6: Supernatural, 2008. Available online at: https://www.transitiongallery.co.uk/htmlpages/editions/g_land6_russell.htm (accessed 28 July 2022).

Russell, Ken. 'The Lifelong Reading Spree that Inspires my World'. *The Times 2*, 16 December 2008. Available online at: https://www.thetimes.co.uk/article/the-lifelong-reading-spree-that-inspires-my-world-ppbgk8dfp2b (accessed 26 July 2022).

Sinker, Mark. 'Fabulous Freak Brothers'. *Sight and Sound* 6, no. 11 (2006): 44.

Van Eecke, Christophe. 2019. 'Phantasmagoria: Ken Russell's "Gothic" as a Neo-Victorian Meta-Heritage Film'. *Journal of Neo-Victorian Studies* 12, no. 1 (2019): 135–56.

Walker, Alexander. 'Review of The Devils'. *Evening Standard*, 22 July 1971. Press archive, British Film Institute.

Walker, Johnny. *Rewind, Replay: Britain and the Video Boom, 1978–92.* Edinburgh: Edinburgh University Press, 2022.

Wasser, Frederick. *Veni, Vidi, Video: The Hollywood Empire and the VCR.* Austin: University of Texas Press, 2001.

Filmography

Altered States (1980), [Film] Dir. Ken Russell, USA: Warner Bros.
Amelia and the Angel (1958), [Film] Dir. Ken Russell, UK: BFI Experimental Film Fund.
American Werewolf in London (1981), [Film] Dir. John Landis, UK/USA: Polygram Pictures.
Belle de Jour (1967), [Film] Dir. Luis Buñuel, France/Italy: Paris Film Productions.
The Blood on Satan's Claw (1971), [Film] Dir. Piers Haggard, UK: Tigon.
Brothers of the Head (2006), [Film] Dir. Keith Fulton and Louis Pepe, UK: Potboiler Productions.
Crimes of Passion (1984), [Film] Dir. Ken Russell, USA: New World Pictures.
Dance of the Seven Veils (1970), [Film] Dir. Ken Russell, UK: BBC.
The Devils (1971), [Film] Dir. Ken Russell, UK: Russo Productions.

Dracula (1979), [Film] Dir. John Badham, UK: Universal Pictures.
The Fall of the Louse of Usher (2002), [Film] Dir. Ken Russell, UK: Gorsewood Productions.
Gothic (1986), [Film] Dir. Ken Russell, UK: Virgin Vision.
Hellraiser (1987), [Film] Dir. Clive Barker, UK: New World Pictures.
Lair of the White Worm (1988), [Film] Dir. Ken Russell, UK: White Lair.
Lisztomania (1975), [Film] Dir. Ken Russell, UK: Goodtimes Enterprises.
Mahler (1974), [Film] Dir. Ken Russell, UK: Goodtimes Enterprises.
Masters of Horror (2005–7), [TV series] Dir. Various, Canada/Japan/USA: Showtime.
The Music Lovers (1971), [Film] Dir. Ken Russell, UK: Russ-Arts.
The Preservation Man (1962), [Film] Dir. Ken Russell, UK: BBC.
The Rainbow (1989), [Film] Dir. Ken Russell, UK: Vestron Pictures.
Salome's Last Dance (1970), [Film] Dir. Ken Russell, UK/USA: Jolly Russell Productions.
The Secret of the Loch (1934), [Film] Dir. Milton Rosmer, UK: Wyndham Productions.
Theatre of Blood (1973), [Film] Dir. Douglas Hickox, UK: Harbour Productions.
Trapped Ashes (2006), [Film] Dir. Sean Cunningham, Joe Dante, Monte Hellman, Ken Russell, and John Gaeta, USA/Japan: Independent Film Fund.
Valentino (1977), [Film] Dir. Ken Russell, UK/USA: Chartoff-Winkler Productions.
Whore (1991), [Film] Dir. Ken Russell, USA/UK: Trimark Pictures.
The Wicker Man (1973), [Film] Dir. Robin Hardy, UK: British Lion.

Part III

Cycles and clusters

Deliverance derivations

Counter constructions of white trash in 1970s horror cinema

Xavier Mendik

Introduction

According to David Bell (1997), horror remains one of the most frequent genres associated with American cinema's representations of the countryside. The author has identified a repeated trope that sees urban outsiders searching for plenitude and serenity in the countryside, only to uncover violence and mayhem that unambiguously reorders this space as the rural 'anti-idyll'. Indeed, Bell observes that the countryside is home to 'societies which appear idyllic, but which are malignant, at a dead end, and viewed in the grip of their own death throes. That condition is the real horror of the rural' (1997: 106). This transition from tranquillity to terror is premised on elements of the natural environment that gradually turn against its visitors or local inhabitants whose entrenched ways of living provoke conflict with the metropolitan dweller.

Images of anti-idyll horror began to circulate during the 1960s, with releases such as *Two Thousand Maniacs!* (Herschell Gordon Lewis, 1964) focusing on unwitting outsiders being sacrificed by supernatural southerners seeking to avenge crimes committed during the American civil war. However, it was the 1970s that saw the peak period of rural anti-idyll horror. Here,

> the film genre of horror began to replace the melodramas and comedies of previous decades . . . small towns and the countryside were increasingly portrayed as sites of contestation and decay, often embodied in those characters living there. (Bell 1997: 106)

As popularized through John Boorman's *Deliverance* (1972) and Tobe Hooper's *The Texas Chainsaw Massacre* (1974), Bell argues that 1970s rural horror projected the American South as a foreboding terrain, whose inhabitants exact retribution for their social and political marginality against a range of unwitting outsiders.

This chapter aims to analyse some of the key features and concerns associated with the 1970s anti-idyll horror narrative. Using Bell's key case study of *Deliverance* as a template, I will analyse what shall be termed as '*Deliverance* derivations', or rural inspired horror narratives that represent those communities 'usually referred to in US horror films as hillbillies, rednecks or mountain men' (Bell 1997: 96). In so doing, this study will also seek to situate these *Deliverance* derivations within existing research devoted to the subject.

The rural anti-idyll and the academy

Bell's (1997) study of rural American horror fits within a body of scholarship that considers the representations, themes and historical constructs associated with rural American communities on screen. *Deliverance* remains a key touchpoint across a wide range of these accounts and they are therefore worthy of opening consideration. For instance, J. W. Williamson situates the film through alternating distinctions between the rustic and inoffensive 'hick', and the more unpredictable and dangerous 'redneck'. Writing in *Hillbillyland: What the Mountains Did to the Movies and What the Movies Did to the Mountains*, Williamson contends that 'in both roles – in safe cartoons and in believable depictions of reality meant to scare us – he's the same hillbilly serving different purposes, our richly symbolic American country cousin' (1995: 2). Across comedic and monstrous renditions, it is the hillbilly's proximity to urban America that remains an 'uncomfortable and unwelcome opening into a history we have tried to forget' (Williamson 1995: 3).

In *Hillbilly: A Cultural History of an American Icon*, Anthony Harkins argues that '*Deliverance's* portrayal of degenerate, imbecile and sexually voracious predators bred fear into several generations of Americans' (2004: 206). In so doing, the film reflected news reports and moral panics that constructed mountain dwellers as potential social problems for urban authorities to contend with. These fears fixated on a post-war influx of poor, transient rural families deemed to be an 'inassimilable and unwanted population' (Harkins

2004: 175). Metropolitan anxieties were furthered by media coverage and policy initiatives that fed notions of a southern 'invasion'. As exemplified by Harkins's (2004) review of the 1956 article 'Down from the Hills and into the Slums', such reports contrasted the immorality of the mountain migrant with the sophisticated norms of urban civility. For Harkins (2004), these socio-economic divisions became mediated through TV comedies such as *The Real McCoys* (1957–63) and *The Beverly Hillbillies* (1962–71). Here, humour was derived from the incongruous clash of rural and urban mannerisms resulting from poor farming families relocating to California (*The Real McCoys*) or intergenerational clans being elevated to the Beverly Hills elite after oil reserves are discovered on their land (*The Beverly Hillbillies*). Both series employed tropes of class conflict and comedy of manners motifs to exploit an existing 'fear and fascination with southern mountaineers much in the news' (Harkins 2004: 186).

John Hartigan Jr.'s *Odd Tribes: Towards a Cultural Analysis of White People* situates *Deliverance* as 'a break from the satirical and comical representations of the "otherness" of poor southern whites which predominated on television shows' (2005: 137). The author traces the film's unsettling imagery to the American eugenics movement of the nineteenth century. As initialized by Richard Dugdale's 1877 account of 'The Jukes', this philosophy postulated a set of links between criminality, heredity, physiology and familial dysfunction, establishing a template for further rural surveys that became known collectively as the 'Eugenics Family Studies' (Hahn Rafter 1988). With indicative titles such as 'The Happy Hickories' (1918) and 'The Mongrel Virginians' (1926), these accounts functioned through a discourse of boundary marking, which sought to separate the intellectually superior white urban American from their seemingly less developed country-based counterpart. However, for Hartigan Jr. *Deliverance* is dominated by a 'white trash poetics' (2005: 136), that blurs the presumed hierarchies separating urban superiority from its debased rural shadow image. Indeed

> the terror and tension in this poetics involves the uncertainty over whether the 'other' is really threateningly there or if it is a projection of a repressed self which class, sexual and racial decorums produce. (Hartigan Jr. 2005: 136)

Beyond eugenics inferences, Michael DeAngelis (2007) has linked *Deliverance* to the toxic political contexts of 1970s America. Through its focus on the countryside concealment of criminal acts, the film mirrors Watergate paranoias surrounding authority figures who knowingly suppressed wrongdoing. Additionally, DeAngelis (2007) notes that the contemporary prominence given to both queer representations and pornographic films (with their emphasis on women's voracious desires) provided an uncomfortable mirror to *Deliverance*'s problematic constructions of heterosexual potency. Masculine tensions are further raised in Isabel Machado's 2017 account, which contextualizes Boorman's film against 1970s Sunbelt planning strategies used to regenerate rural regions through industrial modernization. Machado (2017) divides the film's conflicts along a developmental axis of 'old' versus 'new' south, with its hillbillies representing a violent mode of virility that progress has erased from its overcivilized urban protagonists. More recently, Meredith McCarroll (2018) has convincingly dissected the racialized construction of Appalachia in films such as *Deliverance*, noting that such patterns of representation draw parity with the negative stereotypes often applied to African American and Native American communities. Effectively, these remain 'images that are phonetically white and drawn from nonwhite stereotypes, which seem to categorise Appalachia outside of white normative culture' (McCarroll 2018: 13). McCarroll's (2018) work adds to an existing body of scholarship devoted to *Deliverance*, with the film now worth considering in detail.

Deliverance as anti-idyll master text

Based on James Dickey's best-selling novel from 1970, *Deliverance* outlines the fate of four urban dwellers who seek to explore Georgia's Cahulawassee river prior to its displacement by a new electric dam destined to bring creature comforts to Atlanta. The film's opening scene counterposes shots of placid waterways and the tranquil wilderness with a montage of dusty, dirty, polluted scenes of bulldozing and destruction that the encroaching industrialization entails. This paradox of urban advancement at the expense of the countryside becomes a framing device for the rural environment that the urbanites seek to conquer. For Williamson, this expedition effectively becomes 'a sexual metaphor, a display of penetration driven by the terror of inadequacy' (1995: 157). This quest figures the landscape as a paradoxically enticing and dangerous site of self-discovery, which is described by the group's de facto leader Lewis (Burt Reynolds) as 'just about the last wild, untamed, unpolluted, un-fucked up river in the South'. Lewis's comments and sexualized condemnation of the building work as being destined to 'rape this whole goddam landscape' are later reiterated by his companion Bobby (Ned Beatty) who states, 'It's true what you said Lewis. There is something in the woods and the water that we have lost in the city'.

At the level of production, *Deliverance* was filmed on the Chattooga River in Rabun County, establishing a trend for location shoots that would become a benchmark of realism within later examples of 1970s rural horror films. This actuality filming foregrounds what Williamson terms as a pattern of 'mountain-induced ambiguity' (1995: 19), that recodifies woodland territories as venues of chaos, contagion and the denial of reason. While Williamson has traced the long held and biblical basis to these beliefs, contemporary cultures have continued to imbue the wild landscape with a set of negative physiological characteristics including: 'ills, deformities, excrescences, protuberances, and swellings' (1995: 19).

It is this pathologizing of Georgia's rivers, woodlands and inhabitants that provides the boundary markers for the film's urban explorers. However, while Lewis is coded as an outwardly masculine, 'survivalist' figure, companions such as Ed (Jon Voight) are either ill at ease in these unfamiliar outdoors environments or, in the case of Bobby, openly critical of its traditional rural dwellers. The film's opening interactions detail Bobby's disgust at the ramshackle state of local surroundings and the ill-fitting dress and mannerisms of the elderly men they encounter. Indeed, he snarls, 'Look at all this junk. I think this is where everything finishes up. We just may be at the end of the line!' The protagonist's dismissive attitude is mirrored by Ed's unease when he secretly surveys unsettling images of an aged mother (Andy Webb) tending to an ill and disabled infant through a shanty house window. The documentary style camerawork used to convey Ed's observations provides a pseudo-medical examination of 'abnormal' rural types later verbalized by Bobby: 'Talk about genetic deficiencies. Isn't that pitiful?' These aberrations appear confirmed when fellow traveller Drew (Ronny Cox) strikes up an impromptu banjo duet with a disabled hillbilly teenager (Billy Redden) in one of the film's most iconic interludes. Although often referred to as the 'duelling banjo' sequence, the credits of *Deliverance* appropriately register the theme as from 'an arrangement' entitled 'Feudin' Banjos', which more fully encapsulates the group's feelings of anxiety and intimidation within this unfamiliar environment. Thus, Drew's statement 'I'm lost', when he tries to emulate the banjo player's frenzied style, says more about the group's geographical displacement than any failures of musical mirroring.

These fears of isolation are later actualized by the film's most controversial scene. Here, Bobby is ritualistically humiliated by two mountain men before being raped while Ed is bound to a tree and forced to watch. This brutal encounter proceeds along socio-economic lines, with the mountain men bristling at Ed's suggestion that 'If you gentlemen have a (whisky) still near here that's fine with us'. Their statement that the urban duo has 'don taken a wrong turn' also inferences linguistic markers based on class and educational differentiation, while the use of direct sound within the sequence further renders local dialogue as inaudible 'mumble'. The sexual assault that follows conveys regionally defined physiological distinctions, with the camera dwelling on the rapist's blackened teeth and his accomplice's lack of teeth to suggest inherited deficiencies are aligned to the rural body. These visual alterities confirm Williamson's view that 'The assault . . . is properly understood as a confrontation between mainstream America and its own hidden potentialities' (1995: 157).

As the mainstream American figure 'most condescending to the natives, the one most assured of his superiority' (Williamson 1995: 159), it is pointed that Bobby becomes the main object of the locals' retribution. Paradoxically, this coerced sex scene actualizes much of the prior innuendo associated with the urban group's penetration of the environment (specifically Lewis's doubly coded comment 'You just wait till you feel that white water under you Bobby'). As he is stripped naked and pursued through woodland Bobby is informed that he 'looks just like a hog', before being forced to 'squeal like a pig' as the unwanted penetration takes place. This assault entails not only a masculine violation but the recodification of Bobby's physical appearance from civilized to abject, further eroding the prior distinctions between the two communities. In so doing, Bobby, like his rural attackers, now 'symbolically reminds us of filth, of disgusting bodily functions' (Williamson 1995: 159).

Although Lewis manages to kill the rapist before Ed endures a similar assault, this act fails to restore the group's authoritative status. As Lewis warns, they have just killed 'a mountain man, a cracker. That gives you something to consider'. As John Hartigan Jr. has noted, it is the fear of wider retaliation and revenge from 'a tangle of relations, not clearly delineated or hierarchized' (2005: 142) that leads the group to bury the mountain man's body rather than report the incident to the local police. Concurrent with this illegal act, it is noticeable that the locals and the landscape itself increasingly evoke the rural anti-idyll, with the forest now appearing as a malevolent, personified force, whereby 'A fear of perversity disembodied, having irrupted from the body, infuses into the entire landscape' (Hartigan Jr. 2005: 142). These fears are foregrounded when Drew suddenly falls into the water, leading his colleagues to believe that he has been shot and killed by the surviving mountain man. In the melees that follows, the group's canoes capsize in an increasingly unpredictable river, resulting in Lewis becoming incapacitated. As a result, *Deliverance* enacts a powershift that reconstitutes Ed as 'the nascent masculine primitive ideal hidden under office flab' (Williamson 1995: 159).

In his newly promoted role, Ed proceeds to kill a further mountain man (whose participation in their sexual assault remains unresolved), before coaching Bobby and the badly immobilized Lewis on how to conceal their actions from the town's suspicious sheriff (played by *Deliverance* author James Dickey). The survivors' return to 'normality' remains noticeable for its reversal of prior rural stereotypes: 'The clear bodily distinctions of class . . . are no longer apparent: all of the locals have clean faces and straight teeth' (Hartigan Jr. 2005: 146). This recodification of Georgia's populous as hospitable, articulate and noticeably multiracial positions *Deliverance* as the ultimate urban nightmare. This is confirmed by its closing images where Ed fantasizes the murdered mountain man's hand rising from its watery grave, indicating that rural anti-idyll horror ultimately defies narrative closure.

Reflecting upon the cultural significance of Boorman's film, Williamson has defined *Deliverance* as a seminal text 'in shaping what people think they understand about the southern mountains' (1995: 157). This impact exceeds its fictional narrative to include what the author terms as the 'Deliverance syndrome' (1995: 162), which witnessed a steady stream of urban males venture out to Rabun County seeking to replicate the film's perilous river trips, often with fatal results. For Meredith McCarroll, the enduring symbolism of the film resides in its perpetuation of rural stereotypes across a wider set of popular culture texts whereby 'geographical isolation, inbreeding and the resultant genetic deficiencies, and cultural hatred of outsiders combine in the stereotype most often associated with *Deliverance*' (2018: 24).

Don't look in debasement: The *Deliverance* derivation

The cultural impact of *Deliverance* established an American rural horror imprint that became replicated across a range of subsequent releases. This represents a cycle of '*Deliverance* derivations' which stretched throughout the decade, encompassing both mainstream and 'exploitation' cinema releases. While *Deliverance* anchored its images of amorality within a specific Appalachian geography, the derivations that followed often generalized rurality to 'a fantastic

South where mountains bordered on swamps, and other cities and factories were nowhere to be seen' (Harkins 2004: 211).

These derivations also multiplied *Deliverance*'s focus on a small male group with a platoon of soldiers marooned in harsh rural environments (*Southern Comfort*, Walter Hill, 1981), or vacationing professional women victimized by marauding rural male groups (*I Spit on Your Grave*, Meir Zarchi, 1978). The format additionally exposed upwardly mobile African American women to racial oppression within liminal southern communities (*Poor Pretty Eddie*, David Worth/Richard Robinson, 1975). Representations of predatory rural communities were themselves extended to encompass all-male clans displaced by construction projects (*God's Bloody Acre*, Harry Kerwin, 1975), murderous identical twins (*Just Before Dawn*, Jeff Lieberman, 1981) and backwoods satanists (*Midnight*, John A. Russo, 1982). In terms of national contexts, this trend also included the Canadian titles: *Rituals* (Peter Carter, 1977), where vacationing doctors are hunted by a disfigured veteran and *Trapped/Baker County, USA* (William Fruet, 1982), which repurposed *Deliverance*'s Rabun County locations to depict a maniacal rural patriarch.

Despite these variations, the *Deliverance* derivations retained parity with Boorman's original through the following seven key features that were recycled (either selectively or entirely):

(1) *a dramatic focus on the conflicts between urban and rural communities*
(2) *the paradoxical construction of regional landscapes as both idyllic and threatening*
(3) *the generation of sexual threat as demarcating urban from rural groups*
(4) *a fixation on the physiological deviancy of the rural 'white trash' body*
(5) *documentary techniques that add 'realism' to images of rural underdevelopment*
(6) *audio signifiers employing banjo and harmonica interludes to convey backwoods environments*
(7) *narrative irresolution that prevents closure from rural anti-idyll trauma*

Importantly, when these seven features were adapted by regional filmmakers, narrative alterations were introduced that appear to counter and complicate many of the stigmatizing precepts associated with marginal rural communities. Arguably, one of the most distinctive of these regional derivations was *Scum of the Earth* (AKA *Poor White Trash Part II*, 1974), helmed by Arkansas based filmmaker S.F. Brownrigg. For Charles Kilgore, *Scum of the Earth* represents 'a bitter blend of splatter and sleaze', dominated by 'unsettlingly believable performances' (1992: 14). The film formed part of a quartet of regional horrors that Brownrigg created, confirming his status as a leading light in *Dallas Magazine*'s definition of a localized tradition known as the 'grislies' (Kurrus 1975: 35). However, Stephen Thrower has suggested the director's brand of rural horror failed to garner more widespread appeal:

> Sherald 'S.F.' Brownrigg has received little attention from genre fans, probably because his gloomy little tales lack the extravagant gore and nudity offered by America's better-known horror auteurs of the period. His persistently downbeat approach to the genre has also barred him from wider cult appreciation. (2003: 177)

Scum of the Earth redirects *Deliverance*'s focus on imperilled masculinity towards a young married couple who travel to an unspecified countryside location. The film's opening scenes counterbalance their arrival with rural idyll images of tranquil waters and dazzling sunsets. Here, Helen (Norma Moore) narrates a backstory of returning to this holiday location that was once shared with her parents. However, her husband Paul's (Joel Colodner) ambivalence towards the countryside proves well placed, as he is suddenly killed by an unidentified aggressor, forcing the heroine to flee into the woods during the film's credit sequence.

This violent act shifts the environment into the rural anti-idyll, with mobile camerawork and low-key lighting conveying the woodland as a site of gloomy entrapment, while up-tempo music is replaced by the sombre theme tune 'Death Is a Family Affair'. During her escape, Helen encounters the brutish rural patriarch Odis Pickett (Gene Ross), whom she initially believes to be her husband's assailant. Pickett's mannerisms and dishevelled appearance instantly connotes him as debased rural other as contemporized by titles such as *Deliverance*. Here, socio-economic distinctions between the pair are conveyed linguistically, as in the protagonist's statement: 'I ain'a gonna kill yeh. I ain't killed nobody . . . lately.'

Although immediately uncomfortable with Pickett's licentious inclinations, Helen reluctantly accepts an invitation to return to his family home to seek shelter from the murderer. Upon arrival, she is disturbed by the squalid nature of Pickett's impoverished homestead, as well as the outlandish behaviour of his family members. These include Pickett's aggressive daughter Sarah (Camilla Carr) and his illiterate son Bo (Charlie Dell), whose nickname, 'No Count', conveys his severely limited intellectual abilities. Also present is Pickett's markedly younger and heavily pregnant wife Emmy (Ann Stafford), who is ungraciously introduced as 'That there skinny one with the big belly'. Emmy's passivity to these abusive proceedings belies attempts to keep the fractious clan together. In one of several pointed asides between the two women, Emmy confesses to Helen that her marriage to the much older farmer resulted from a debt that her father owed, leading to her being sold as part of the financial settlement.

Having declared that Helen is now 'one of the family', Pickett sets the traumatized visitor a series of domestic chores to undertake. When the heroine recoils in disgust at Bo's presentation of a newly killed animal for the family's supper pot, Sarah dismissively hisses: 'I guess that city gal don' care too much for possum!' While class and cultural conflicts bristle through these claustrophobic interactions, they also trigger Pickett's descent into a moonshine induced spiral, revealing lustful intentions towards the unwilling guest. These perverse inclinations are shockingly exposed by Sarah, who confronts her father for being a regular abuser throughout her teenage years.

In a contrast to *Deliverance* (where urbanites are forced to consider potential retribution for killing a 'cracker'), in Brownrigg's film it is Emmy who confesses: 'This time it could be real bad! That there's a city gal, and with Pick drinkin' the way he do, we are gonna have big trouble'. In panic, she despatches Bo to a neighbour's house to ring for police assistance. However, Bo is fatally impaled on a graveyard fence railing by the marauding killer, who has been silently staking out the family home. When his corpse is dumped outside the Picketts' front porch, the clan turn their hatred on Helen for bringing bad luck into their homestead. As Sarah lashes: 'She's the one done spelled us all!' Despite Emmy's attempts to shield the visitor from retribution, Pickett uses Bo's death as a ploy to rape and imprison Helen. The heroine awakes from this assault to find herself shackled with Pickett's belt and subject to further threats.

This extended campaign of abuse includes her being forced to wash and prepare Bo's corpse before Pickett sends Sarah to the local preacher's house so that burial rights can be conducted. During the journey, she also encounters the unidentified stranger who responds to an attempted seduction by strangling her with a barbed wire coil. Sarah's continued absence from the home gives Emmy the opportunity to liberate Helen from Pickett, who is in turn violently killed by the mysterious assailant while out searching for his missing daughter. Rather than being an impoverished rural dweller, the finale reveals the true aggressor to be Jim (Hugh Feagin), Helen's first husband who was presumed dead during the Vietnam war. Having been imprisoned in a Vietcong internment camp, Jim hatched an elaborate plan to punish Helen for abandoning him and marrying another suitor. Although Jim's plan to kill Helen provides the culmination of this plot, he is shot dead by the mortally wounded Sarah before he can complete this quest. The film ends with the established device of rural anti-idyll trauma preventing narrative resolution. This sees Emmy committing to look after the traumatized Helen, who reclines on the Pickett porch in a clearly catatonic state.

Scum of the Earth confirms David Bell's definition of countryside horror constructions 'in which the "victim" is coded as urban and both the setting and the "monster" as rural' (1997: 95). Brownrigg's former training as an army combat photographer certainly aids these aberrant representations, providing a documentary feel that is realized through the distorted, pseudo-medical representations of the Pickett family, who frequently address the camera lens directly (see Figure 9.1).

This ethnographic approach extends to the range of male/female rural stereotypes that the director assembles, which remain dominated by Gene Ross's unnerving performance as Pickett. When Helen tells Pickett, 'You are just too brutal and sadistic to be real', she is of course correct, as Brownrigg

Figure 9.1 *Scum of the Earth*: Direct to camera depravity and the pseudo-medical gaze.

has constructed this monstrous figure from long-standing urban anxieties that are traceable across the American eugenics movement to John Boorman's *Deliverance* and beyond. However, by revealing the film's killer to be an educated but alienated former veteran, Brownrigg also seeks to reverse urban versus countryside horror mythologies, effectively reconfiguring this *Deliverance* derivation as a 'hillbillies in peril' entry.

Alongside Brownrigg, Florida-based filmmaker William Grefé is another regional horror auteur whose work adapted existing rural stereotypes with interesting results. For his 1977 release *Whisky Mountain*, Grefé employed Georgia's locations for a focus on two mixed gender biker couples seeking to exploit confederate army treasures contained within a mountain location. As with *Deliverance*, these landscapes evoke alternating states of tranquillity and threat. The bikers' initial journey into the wilderness is accompanied by documentary style footage of regional sunsets and mountain views, while established audio signifiers promoting rurality emphasize a bluegrass song containing the lyric 'Whiskey Mountain rising in the Georgia sunset' to connote transitions from metropolitan to country spaces. The later lyric 'Does your bosom hold a treasure that's for me, and me alone?' introduces a more sexualized construction of the landscape that mirrors emergent tensions found between its depicted communities.

These frictions are first evidenced in an early scene when Bill (Christopher George), his girlfriend Jamie (Linda Borgson) and Dan (Preston Pierce) stop at a rural store for directions. The shopkeeper Rudy (John Davis Chandler) and assembled rednecks take instant offence at the visitors' humorous dismissal of their primitive stock items, with Dan proclaiming a toilet plunger to be 'one of them new under the arm vacuum cleaners!' The playful nature of these interactions soon takes a sinister turn when the hillbillies harass Bill's partner Dianna (Roberta Collins), who is sleeping in their parked car. Rudy then warns the bikers against searching for Whisky Mountain as 'Some of those mountain folk don't take to strangers'.

Following this terse encounter, the landscape markedly moves towards the rural anti-idyll, with the bikers beset by woodland fires that threaten to engulf them, while efforts to cross a raging ravine result in near drowning and a loss of key supplies. As with *Deliverance*, the forest in *Whiskey Mountain* also takes on depersonalized and sinister characteristics, while the hillbillies it harbours echo John Hartigan Jr.'s definition of being 'blurred and diffuse lurking figures, obscured by trees' (2005: 140). When they are exposed, these dwellers depart markedly from metropolitan notions of physiological normalcy. For instance, as the group progress into the wilderness they encounter an elderly itinerant whose sudden appearance causes fright and intimidation for the two women members. His filthy, unkempt appearance and inability to verbally communicate leads Dianne to observe, 'Let's get out of here. This is the worst yet!', especially as the vagrant appears to have been hoarding her missing underwear.

Although this rural dweller laughs hysterically when Bill and Dan further enquire about Whisky Mountain, the group finally uncover the cavern and the film's central enigma. Here, the cave is revealed as concealing a marijuana distribution network, while the 'hillbilly' antagonists led by Rudy are in fact articulate urban dope peddlers masquerading as rednecks. Bill notes, 'You know, there's a change from hillbilly to dope dealer', to which Jamie responds, 'Yeah, even his voice has changed!' When Bill and Dan manage to evade the criminal gang and flee into town to raise help, Jamie and Dianne are captured and subsequently molested at the hands of Rudy's henchmen.

In a further deviation from the *Deliverance* template, the sexual assault that follows is articulated in modern technological terms rather than along rural and archaic lines. Here, a montage of polaroid still images outlines differing stages of the attack while the cackling sounds made by the oppressors are heard on the soundtrack. Although this scene complicates the civilized/primitive paradigm upon which the *Deliverance* template is based, its ambiguities are confirmed when Bill and Dan's requests for assistance are rebuffed by a local sheriff, indicating cross territorial compliance between urban and country-based criminal communities. When the duo returns to rescue the two women, these urban/rural paradoxes continue, with Dan suddenly being killed by the elderly itinerant who had previously assisted them. Although Bill manages to despatch the outlaws in the climactic, bloody gun battle, *Whiskey Mountain* ends on a final ambiguous freeze-frame of the local sheriff arriving by police helicopter to kill the wounded hero and his freed companions.

Derivations and deviant networks

The conclusion of Grefé's film confirms the trope of narrative irresolution that unites *Deliverance* with regional derivations such as *Scum of the Earth*. However, the ending also points to an interesting expansion of the anti-idyll template. Rather than residing in marginal and isolated communities, it intimates an expanded rural network of perversity and corruption, which was itself mirrored by a subsidiary set of films that followed Boorman's film. This strand of *Deliverance* deviation was filtered through incarceration narratives that channelled regional depravity into extreme prison settings dominated by sexual exploitation and racial oppression. Within this variant, violence and transgression are not isolated to backwoods clans, but instead reside across intersecting communities that actively collaborate to ensure the downfall of outsiders. Given his profile in the 1970s 'women in prison' film cycle, it seems unsurprising that producer Roger Corman relocated the geographical focus of some of these entries towards the rural space, most notably with *Jackson County Jail* (1976). The film was directed by Michael Miller and stars Yvette Mimieux as Dinah Hunter, a self-willed Californian advertising executive who embarks on a road trip to evade restrictive professional practices and a philandering partner. The early part of the film sees Hunter dialogue with other articulate women who are undertaking comparable road trips as journeys of discovery. However, the relocation to Jackson County is designed to draw sharp distinctions between urban and rural conceptions of gendered emancipation, as evidenced by the number of local women who seek to deceive Hunter. These figures include a brash restaurant waitress (Betty Thomas) who knowingly attempts to overcharge the heroine, before a strung-out hippy (Nancy Noble) uses her pregnant appearance to manipulate Hunter into giving her and boyfriend Bobby Ray (Robert Carradine) a ride so that they can rob her at gunpoint.

If *Jackson County Jail* exposes the collusion of 'white trash' women in acts of exploitation, the representation of Jackson County's males confirms Mary Mackey's view that

> extreme graphic violence against women in the cinema has been coeval with the growth of the women's movement. One might well see in it a kind of conservative backlash against the real threat of female independence. (1977: 13)

This 'backlash' is actualized through 'a parade of stereotypes' (Mackey 1977: 13) that Hunter encounters following the robbery. These include a lascivious bartender (Britt Leach) who attempts sexual assault following a plea to use his telephone to report the crime. It is Hunter's defiance against these advances that leads to her being arrested by a rural law enforcement official who also warns her to 'shut that tramp yap of yours!'

These aggressive encounters later culminate with the incarcerated heroine being raped by police officer Deputy Hobie (Frederic Cook). Although initially coded as a comical hick, Hobie's assault is predicated on a presumption of urban women being sexually promiscuous, epitomized by his statement that he knows what 'Hollywood women like'. Interestingly, following the assault, his behaviour reverts from a masquerade of confident masculinity to a highly emotive mode of comedic performativity, confirming Williamson's view that 'the hillbilly monster comes from the same threshold territory that produces the hillbilly as fool – the threshold of suddenly ambiguous potential' (1995: 167).

Hobie's assault is witnessed by a local murder suspect Coley Blake (Tommy Lee Jones), who subsequently forces Hunter to go on the run with him following the policeman's death. Through this character, the film provides a counter-cultural construction of rural masculinity: 'a combination [of] guide, father figure, and guru' (Mackey 1977: 14). Under Blake's tutelage, Hunter's reconstruction as 'rural' outsider draws comparison with Bobby's similarly recodified image following the rape scene in *Deliverance*. Here, Hunter's appearance alters from sophisticated urban dweller to badly bruised, rural white trash dweller, who is taken into Blake's outlaw gang before a climactic gunfight with the police during a Bicentennial ceremony. The finale sees Blake gunned down while Dinah Hunter passively looks on from the confines of a police car, further confirming the open endings of other 1970s rural anti-idyll narratives. As Mackey notes, Hunter 'has not escaped, but merely exchanged one cage for another, traded in her old keeper (the convict) for a new keeper (the State)' (1977: 14).

Beyond the example of *Jackson County Jail*, it is interesting to note how 1970s made for television films also modified their content to fit with the prevalent rural horror trends I have been discussing. One example is John Llewellyn Moxey's *Nightmare in Badham County* (1976), which was released in both TV broadcast and 'stronger' cinema variants. The film details the downfall of two interracial college students Cathy Phillips (Deborah Raffin) and Diane Emery (Lynne Moody), whose summer road trip is disrupted when they incur the wrath of a bigoted lawman, Sheriff Danen (Chuck Connors). It is noticeable that Badham County is initially depicted as an example of what David Bell terms as 'an innocent idyll of bucolic tranquillity and communion with nature' (1997: 94). These sentiments are echoed by Diane when she observes, 'This is a far cry from Philadelphia, I will tell you that. I mean that I have never seen so much empty land before in my life'. However, the heroine's statement is immediately contradicted by a camera pan revealing nearby scenes of poverty and racial segregation that will come to dominate the narrative.

These repressive elements surface when the pair's car develops a defect, leading them to be rebuked by Sheriff Danen for letting a local resident of colour assist them. This confrontation makes explicit the Sheriff's sexually aggressive nature, as well as his disdain for the racially integrated nature of modern urban living. Indeed, he comments that 'you people get away with murder' in response to the revelation that Diane is in fact attending UCLA. These sexual and racial tensions are exacerbated when Diane publicly humiliates Danen in a local diner after he attempts to proposition the pair. This results in him arranging for Cathy's vehicle to be impounded before arresting the two women for trespassing on local woodland. As with *Jackson County Jail*, Llewellyn Moxey's film represents rural incarceration as a site of sexual repression, with Danen exploiting the situation to rape Diane while Cathy is forced to passively listen to the assault from an adjacent cell.

As with other examples of the *Deliverance* derivation incarceration strand, Danen's perversions are replicated by a wider network of white authority figures who work to keep archaic systems of exploitation and prejudice in place. These include Badham's County Judge (Ralph Bellamy), who as Danen's cousin uses kin connections to jail the outsiders after the Sheriff's sexual assault becomes public knowledge. As Governor of the correctional work farm where the pair become incarcerated, Superintendent Dancer (Robert Reed) furthers this chain of degradation, while operating the facility as a segregated plantation that sees Diane shunted into the squalid Black living quarters of the camp.

This enforced separation sees Diane taken under the wing of Sarah (Della Rose), a prominent Black matriarch who shields the heroine from the racial injustices that are manifest within the farm and the wider community beyond. As she warns Diane, 'Aint no white man gonna' help you, and ain't no black man can'. These racial divisions are underscored by the audio cues that punctuate *Nightmare in Badham County*: while the white inmates' labour is accompanied by harmonica and banjo interludes, the plight of the Black detainees is referenced via a more melancholic spiritual score. These musical distinctions appear actualized in the film's nihilistic ending, which sees Sheriff Danen shoot Diane dead as she attempts to distract his attention so that Cathy can escape. The surviving heroine's liberation exposes the regimes of violence and racial oppression occurring in Badham County. The film ends with a freeze-frame of the soil where the bodies of Diane and other Black inmates have been discarded, with a closing intertitle indicating that the prison's repressive practices are 'currently under wider investigation'.

Conclusion: Rural reflections

Unlike the other genre texts considered in his study, David Bell considers John Boorman's *Deliverance* as more of a hybrid anti-idyll narrative 'combining rite-of-passage, man-against-nature, thriller and actioner status' (1997: 97). These intersecting elements helped contemporize a range of established stereotypes surrounding disadvantaged regional communities, while heightening the rural space as an 'imagined cultural geography' (Bell 1997: 94) within the urban imagination. For Anthony Harkins, the impact of *Deliverance*:

> not only shaped conceptions of mountaineers for decades to come, but also helped launch a slew of adventure and horror novels and films, all premised on the fatal encounter of modern suburbanites rashly and disrespectfully penetrating raw culture and meeting a bloody end. (2004: 210)

This 'bloody' influence is evidenced by the *Deliverance* derivations that emerged after the film's release and proliferated throughout the remainder of the decade before declining in the early 1980s. The success of these ancillary productions not only contributed to long-standing myths surrounding the rural dweller but also helps explain the emergence of additional film cycles that used the countryside as a locus for violent female vendetta, extreme incarceration narratives and even revolt of nature plotlines. In so doing, the *Deliverance* derivations reflect the 1970s as a key period when American cinema rediscovered its horrific relationship to the countryside.

Bibliography

Bell, David. 'Anti-Idyll: Rural Horror'. In *Contested Countryside Cultures*, edited by Paul Cloke and Jo Little, 94–108. London: Routledge, 1997.

DeAngelis, Michael. '1972: Movies and Confession'. In *American Cinema of the 1970s: Themes and Variations*, edited by Lester D. Friedman, 71–94. Oxford: Berg: 2007.

Dickey, James. *Deliverance*. London: Pan Books, 1971.

Harkins, Anthony. *Hillbilly: A Cultural History of an American Icon*. Oxford and New York: Oxford University Press, 2004.

Hartigan Jr., John. *Odd Tribes: Towards a Cultural Analysis of White People*. Durham and London: Duke University Press, 2005.

Kilgore, Charles. 'Swamp Trash and Bayou Blues Part II'. In *ECCO: The World of Bizarre Video. No. 16* (1992): 8–16.

Kurrus, Theodore. 'Dallas Motion Picture History'. In *Dallas Magazine* 54, no. 3 (March 1975): 32–48.

Machado, Isabel. 'Revisiting Deliverance: The Sunbelt South, the 1970s Masculinity Crisis, and the Emergence of the Redneck Nightmare Genre'. 19 June 2017. Available online at: https://southernstudies.olemiss.edu/study-the-south/revisiting-deliverance/ (accessed 15 October 2022).

Mackey, Mary. 'The Meat Hook Mama, the Nice Girl, and Butch Cassidy in Drag'. *Jump Cut: A Review of Contemporary Media* 14 (1977): 12–14.

McCarroll, Meredith. *Unwhite: Appalachia, Race and Film*. Athens: The University of Georgia Press, 2018.

Rafter, Nicole Hahn, ed. *The Eugenic Family Studies 1877–1919*. Boston: Northeastern University Press, 1988.

Thrower, Stephen. 'S.F. Brownrigg's Southern Blues'. In *Eyeball Compendium*, edited by Stephen Thrower, 177–81. Godalming: FAB Press, 2003.

Williamson, J. W. *Hillbillyland: What the Movies Did to the Mountains and What the Mountains Did to the Movies*. Chapel Hill & London: The University of North Carolina Press, 1995.

Filmography

The Beverly Hillbillies (1962–1971), [TV series], USA: Filmways / CBS Television Networks.

Deliverance (1972), [Film] Dir. John Boorman, USA: Warner Bros. / Elmer Enterprises.

God's Bloody Acre (1975), [Film] Dir. Harry Kerwin, USA: American General Pictures / Crawford / Lane Productions.

I Spit on Your Grave (1978), [Film] Dir. Meir Zarchi, USA: Barquel Creations.

Jackson County Jail (1976), [Film] Dir. Michael Miller, USA: New World Pictures.

Just Before Dawn (1981), [Film] Dir. Jeff Lieberman, USA: Hollywood West Entertainment / Oakland Productions.

Midnight (1982), [Film] Dir. John A. Russo, USA: Congregational Productions.

Nightmare in Badham County (1976), [Film] Dir. John Llewellyn Moxey, USA: ABC Circle Films / Ambroad.

Poor Pretty Eddie (1975), [Film] Dir. David Worth/Richard Robinson, USA: Artaxerxes Productions / Michael Thevis Enterprises Production.

The Real McCoys (1957–63) [TV series], USA: Brennan-Westgate / Materno Productions / ABC / CBS Television Networks.

Rituals (1977) [Film] Dir. Peter Carter, Canada: Astral Bellevue Pathé / Canart Films / Canadian Film Development Corporation (CFDC) / Famous Players.

Scum of the Earth (AKA Poor White Trash Part II, 1974), [Film] Dir. S. F. Brownrigg, USA: Zison Enterprises.

Southern Comfort (1981), [Film] Dir. Walter Hill, USA: Cinema Group Ventures / Phoenix Films.

The Texas Chainsaw Massacre (1974), [Film] Dir. Tobe Hooper, USA: Vortex (A Vortex/Henkel/Hooper Production).

Trapped/Baker County, U.S.A. (1982), [Film] Dir. William Fruet, USA: Verdict Productions.

Two Thousand Maniacs! (1964), [Film] Dir. Herschell Gordon Lewis, USA: Jacqueline Kay (The Jaqueline Kay, Inc.) / Friedman/Lewis Productions.

Whisky Mountain (1977), [Film], Dir William Grefé, USA: Whiskey Mountain Production Company.

10

Hybrid horror from Australia

Pete Falconer

Introduction

In the Australian film *BMX Bandits* (Brian Trenchard-Smith, 1983), Goose (James Lugton) recounts 'this really good movie I saw at the drive-in once: *Kiss the Blood Off My Carburettor*', describing it as 'a horror road movie'. Adding to the mix of genres presented, the lurid title seems to be an allusion to *Kiss the Blood Off My Hands* (Norman Foster, 1948), an American *film noir*. The prospect of this movie is treated as a punchline, but the joke also plays on the understanding that such generic combinations were a recognized feature of Australian popular cinema at that time. Indeed, *Roadgames* (Richard Franklin, 1981), a high-profile Australian production released two years before *BMX Bandits*, could legitimately be called a horror road movie.

Generic hybridity is a prevalent feature in popular cinemas around the world. Rick Altman notes that it is 'a basic Hollywood strategy' for a film to have 'an interlaced, multi-generic plot offering every possible chance for positive audience response' (1999: 139). However, there remains much to be gained from critical attention to hybridity in specific contexts. This chapter examines what Raphaëlle Moine calls 'the causes and particular conditions of various states of hybridity' (2008: 117) in Australian horror and horror-related films from the 1970s and 1980s. I focus on this period partly because of the interesting variety of genre films that it produced, and partly because of the increased availability of these films in recent years, following the documentary *Not Quite Hollywood: The Wild, Untold Story of Ozploitation!* (Mark Hartley, 2008). Affording close attention to these films highlights the varied and complex ways in which genres can combine, the different factors that can bring genres together and the extent to which hybridity can extend beyond genre into other categories, such as national identity.

There are Australian films from the period that belong primarily to the horror genre: among others, *Night of Fear* (Terry Bourke, 1973), *Nightmares* (John D. Lamond, 1980) and *Next of Kin* (Tony Williams, 1982). These films still have connections to other genres, but such connections tend to be more minor and peripheral. In many cases, though, horror is combined overtly with other genres. Some of these combinations are relatively conventional, as in the mixing of horror and science fiction in *Thirst* (Rod Hardy, 1979) and *Dead Kids* (Michael Laughlin, 1981). Others, like the horror-Western *Inn of the Damned* (Terry Bourke, 1975), feature more unusual genre pairings.

Inn of the Damned

Inn of the Damned demonstrates the multiplicity of generic combinations within a single hybrid. There are moments of direct interaction between horror and the Western, for example, when Kincaid (Alex Cord) first visits the titular inn. Kincaid, the film's sole American character and clearest representative of the Western, is shown approaching on horseback. With his hat, neckerchief and waistcoat, Kincaid presents a strongly Western figure. The music, however, consists of a repeating melody on piano and tuned percussion, accompanied by the spectral wailing of a female voice. The instrumentation, repetition and dissonant intervals evoke a creeping menace, placing the Western image into a horror context. Certainly, the narrative situation at this point in the film fits comfortably into the horror genre: Beverly (Carla Hoogeveen) and her abusive stepmother Mrs. Millington (Diana Dangerfield) are asleep at the inn, having been drugged by Caroline Straulle (Judith Anderson). Caroline's husband Lazar (Joseph Furst) has murdered Alfred (Philip Avalon), the Millingtons' driver, with an axe, and is removing all evidence of the guests' presence at the inn. Yet when Kincaid arrives and meets Caroline, his tersely polite greeting of 'Afternoon, ma'am', with a tug of the hat brim, is as Western a gesture as there is in the film.

There are moments in *Inn of the Damned* in which the juxtaposition of genres is translated into literal conflict in the narrative. Adam Knee identifies a similar confrontation between horror and the Western as the basis for the American film *Billy the Kid Versus Dracula* (William Beaudine, 1966): 'two quite distinct sets of generic conventions have been pulled together and forced into a showdown, a fact which the title immediately and self-consciously draws attention to' (1994: 143). Towards the end of *Inn of the Damned*, Lazar approaches Kincaid with his axe and Kincaid shoots the head off the axe with his rifle. Here the 'Western' weapon triumphs over the 'horror' weapon.

While horror and the Western combine in different ways in the film, the genres are first introduced separately and sequentially. The film begins by establishing its Western iconography. The first thing we see is a team of horses pulling a stagecoach down a dirt road. The coach then arrives in a town with wooden buildings and piano music spilling out from its saloon. A title tells us that this is 'Gippsland, Australia' in 1896. While there is an established tradition of Australian Westerns (see Zimmermann 2012), the country remains an unconventional location for the genre. One reason why *Inn of the Damned* establishes its Western components so emphatically, then (and why we get three minutes of stagecoach action playing under the opening credits before the location is revealed), may be to offset the potential incongruity of a Western set in Australia.

The horror side to the film becomes apparent only after the stagecoach arrives, somewhere beyond the town, at the inn. The shift into horror is quite abrupt: night falls and we see the inn's clock striking ten, followed by a close-up shot of a young woman's face in a painting. Cutting to the painting helps create a sudden change of mood. It is not immediately clear where the painting is located or what proportion of it we are actually seeing. The young woman's eyes are narrowed and looking off to the side; introduced quickly and out of context, her expression seems suspicious. The music, which starts at the cut to the painting, is similar to that which accompanies Kincaid when he is approaching the inn later in the film. The scene moves into the guest bedroom, where Martin Cummings (John Morris) and his unnamed companion (Josie Mackay) are killed by something unseen that descends on them from above (this is later revealed to be the bed's canopy, which is weighted with rocks and can be brought down to crush anyone lying underneath it). As she realizes what is happening, Cummings's companion screams. We see the scream, arguably the most characteristic horror movie sound, in an extreme close-up of the woman's mouth. By this point, we have moved decisively into the horror genre.

There are actually some sinister suggestions present before this shift, but because of the film's initial emphasis on Western conventions, these do not necessarily register as horror elements. Before nightfall, as the stagecoach pulls away, Lazar is shown digging a grave-shaped hole. However, in the context of the opening moments, this action feels more like a feature of a Western than a horror movie since graves and gravediggers are common enough in Westerns.

Indeed, the film goes on to evoke aspects of Sergio Leone's Westerns through its inclusion of a comically grotesque undertaker figure (Nat Levison).

Roadgames

As the gravedigging example from *Inn of the Damned* suggests, the balance of generic elements in a film can significantly affect how subsequent developments are understood. In some contexts, the use of a genre's conventions can be harder to recognize. Something similar can be seen in *Roadgames*. While horror is established as relevant by the early scene in which an unnamed hitchhiker (Angie La Bozzetta) is garrotted with a guitar string, the tone of much of the first half of the film is lighter. Suggestions of menace, when reintroduced, thus feel somewhat incongruous.

This incongruity is evident after Patrick Quid (Stacy Keach) stops his truck following an antagonistic game of Twenty Questions with Madeleine 'Sunny' Day (Marion Edward). Madeleine had been left behind by her husband and flagged Quid down by blocking the road with pink toilet paper. With her all-pink outfit and noxious can of hairspray, Madeleine belongs to the Australian tradition of parodic suburban tackiness, famously represented by Dame Edna Everage (Barry Humphries), and seen in other examples such as *Strictly Ballroom* (Baz Luhrmann, 1992) and *Kath & Kim* (ABC/Seven Network, 2002–7). The exaggerated depiction of Madeleine establishes this as a comic episode within the film, but when Quid stops the truck, the horror plot reasserts itself.

Madeleine points out a man (Grant Page) digging a hole by the roadside and Quid recognizes him as the curious van driver that he has nicknamed 'Smith or Jones'. Through binoculars, Quid sees the driver trying to bury some bin bags, and his previously unformed suspicions about the mystery man start to take shape. 'Smith or Jones' sees that he is being watched, packs up and drives away. His greater awareness of Quid brings a sense of danger back into the movie. This is emphasized when the point-of-view shot presented through Quid's binoculars settles on the man and he is shown to be looking directly back at Quid.

However, the scene then veers back towards comedy. As Quid starts expounding on his theory that 'Smith or Jones' might be the murderer mentioned on the radio, Madeleine remains unconvinced: 'You truck drivers take drugs, don't you? You've got the DDTs.' Her malapropism and primly judgemental tone help to maintain a comic dimension, which continues even as Quid's speculations get more gruesome. As Quid is about to suggest that a body can fit in a rubbish bag 'if you cut off the damn . . . ' Madeleine screams, 'Stop it!' and runs from the truck. Unlike the scream of Cummings's companion in *Inn of the Damned*, this development does not mark a shift into the horror genre. Instead, we get a long shot of Madeleine running into the flat and arid landscape. The absurd sight of a pink-clad middle-aged woman running awkwardly across the Nullarbor Plain helps to delay the fuller emphasis on horror that is much more characteristic of the second half of the movie.

At this point, the tone of the scene does get more complicated. As Quid catches up with her, Madeleine comes unexpectedly to the edge of a cliff. The camera zooms out to an extreme long shot, showing the full height of the cliff and the sea below, as the music reaches a crescendo. This scenario is presented as a moment of danger, but the narrative context that it is presented within makes it an anti-climax. The film has already indicated that 'Smith or Jones' is the killer and so we know that Madeleine has nothing to fear from Quid. The comedy in the preceding scenes also makes it harder to take any suggested threat seriously. Subsequently, however, an additional context emerges. Madeleine reveals that she and her family have been caught up in a situation relating to the meatworkers' strike in Perth, mentioned elsewhere in the film: 'They threatened my children – horrible phone calls, late at night. They killed our dog'. Madeleine's comical presentation and the apparently trivial reason for her flight act as a kind of misdirection, obscuring the real fears that make her unwilling to be involved in anything that might require talking to the police. By bringing this context to light, the apparent anti-climax at the cliff functions as a way of reintroducing more uncertainty and menace into the film.

Quid's experience gets more nightmarish in the second half of *Roadgames*. At one point, he hallucinates a fanged, bulging-eyed kangaroo lunging towards him. He also starts to suspect that 'Smith or Jones' has broken into his truck and concealed sections of human torso among the sides of pork that he is transporting. Prior to this more sustained shift, the lighter sections of the movie never fully abandon horror, preserving it as a viable direction to take eventually. Despite the killing of the dog, the political violence faced by Madeleine and her family is not the type that is conventionally depicted in horror movies. However, by evoking the possibility of any kind of violence, the film maintains a proximity to horror, which eases the subsequent transition. Similarly, in the next scene, as Quid is trying to call the police at the Yellowdine Roadhouse, we see a mural, titled 'Hunting natives', which shows uniformed soldiers shooting, stabbing and chaining up Aboriginal Australians. Again, this helps to keep violence on the agenda and to emphasize the cruelty of the surrounding environment.

The presence of horror in the first half of the film is maintained most explicitly by the appearances of 'Smith or Jones'. When Quid first encounters him on the road (having previously seen him at a motel) guitar harmonics on the soundtrack point back to the first killing, which featured the nefarious use of a guitar string. Later, after Quid has picked up Pamela 'Hitch' Rushworth (Jamie Lee Curtis) and they are camping out at an abandoned settlement, the van driver appears again. When Hitch steps away from the campfire, she sees him sitting on the side of his van, playing the guitar. The guitar again recalls his signature killing method, but the horror dimension is especially evident in the flashes of lightning that reveal him before he disappears back into darkness. The sudden onset of gothic weather is juxtaposed with the rainbow that appears the following morning. In moments like this, before *Roadgames* moves more fully into horror conventions, 'Smith or Jones' seems like a horror character in a non-horror film.

Horror contained and unleashed

Horror elements in non-horror contexts can signal a generic shift, but they can also be kept relatively contained. This distinction can be seen across two films by British-Australian director Brian Trenchard-Smith. In a night-time scene in *BMX Bandits*, the three main characters hide from two criminals in a cemetery. *BMX Bandits* is a teen action comedy, and while the scene makes extensive use of horror conventions, these are inflected in ways that preserve the tone of the wider film. The criminals chasing the young protagonists are wearing monster masks. While this emphasizes the scene's horror dimension, the best the villains can manage is to embody a cheap, ready-made monstrosity – 'the sort of thing you get in joke shops', as Goose describes it. Goose's friend Judy (Nicole Kidman) falls into an open grave, but rather than compounding the danger, this helps to conceal her from her pursuer. Later, Judy's hand shoots out and grabs Goose by the ankle, pulling him down into the grave with her. While this moment evokes the ending of *Carrie* (Brian De Palma, 1976), it is presented more as a punchline than a shock; Judy grabs Goose just as he is confidently telling P.J. (Angelo D'Angelo) that 'there's nothing to be scared of'.

Most of the horror elements in *BMX Bandits* are treated comically and kept within the graveyard scene. After that, the presence of horror in the film is negligible.

Figure 10.1 *Turkey Shoot*: The fanged and furry Alph (Steve Rackman).

Closer to *Roadgames* in tone is *Turkey Shoot* (Brian Trenchard-Smith, 1982). Like *Roadgames*, *Turkey Shoot* has a character who initially seems like a horror figure in a non-horror context: Alph (Steve Rackman), a large, hairy man in the service of the wealthy and decadent Tito (Michael Petrovitch). Alph's eyes, with vertical slit pupils like those of a cat or a fox, are picked out in an extreme close-up shortly after he is introduced. In his overall appearance, the fanged and furry Alph, who Tito claims to have found in a circus, resembles a werewolf (see Figure 10.1).

As with 'Smith or Jones' in *Roadgames*, Alph is part of what pushes *Turkey Shoot*'s generic identity closer towards horror as the film progresses. *Turkey Shoot* presents a variation on the human hunting scenario made famous in *The Most Dangerous Game* (Irving Pichel and Ernest B. Schoedsack, 1932), though in this case the action is set in a fascistic future where the hunted are the inmates of a 're-education and behaviour modification' camp. In its early stages, the film is primarily a dystopian action thriller; the camp, with its CCTV cameras and automated gun turrets, combines the militaristic with the futuristic. A connection to horror is suggested through an investment in the grotesque – the inmates are made to gut fish; the guards, led by Ritter (Roger Ward), are leering monstrosities – but this is not fully developed until later. The introduction of elements like Alph, however, tips the generic balance and the presence of horror registers more strongly. From the mid-point of the film, where the hunt begins, we get more instances of gruesome spectacle. Examples include Alph catching Dodge (John Ley), tearing off his little toe and eating it; Alph's eventual death, cut in half by a bulldozer; Chris (Olivia Hussey) chopping off Ritter's hands with a machete. In moments like these, the film's horror component becomes much more prominent.

Turkey Shoot's shift in the direction of horror may have been partly prompted by the circumstances of its production. Trenchard-Smith claims that the film lost 'half the budget' at an advanced stage. His response was 'to make it into a high-camp splatter movie. Stunts may be expensive, but blood is cheap' (*Not Quite Hollywood*, 2008). The shift in emphasis from stunts to blood also implies a shift in genre, from action towards horror. This points to an interesting relationship between the two genres, both of which often involve the presentation of violent spectacle. The spectacles in horror tend to be more intimate, more focused on corporeal harm than on larger-scale force. When lower-budget action films depict their violence on a more personal level and emphasize relatively inexpensive make-up effects over, for example, stunts, they can start to resemble horror movies. The connection between horror and lower-budget action films can be seen in examples including *The Terminator* (James Cameron, 1984), which has a slasher-influenced narrative and a scene in which a man's heart is ripped out, and the more recent *Brawl in Cell Block 99* (S. Craig Zahler, 2017), which features deliberately low-tech prosthetic effects.

As the example of *Turkey Shoot* suggests, genre shifts can be side-effects of other factors. This is also arguably the case in *Snapshot* (Simon Wincer, 1979). Here, the horror dimension is brought out by what seems more like imprecise storytelling than a deliberate strategy. For most of its duration, *Snapshot* is a thriller combined with a realist drama, in which nineteen-year-old Angela (Sigrid Thornton) becomes a model and is thrown out of the family home by her mother. Much of the film is given over to Angela's efforts to establish an independent life and career, against the ordinary, subdued backdrop of Melbourne in winter. The thriller component revolves around stalking: Angela is repeatedly followed and accosted by her ex-boyfriend Daryl (Vincent Gil). At one point, Angela returns to her bedroom to find that one of her dresses has been torn to pieces. Later, she also finds a pig's head in her bed. It is eventually revealed that multiple characters in the film are obsessed with Angela. As well as Daryl, there is also Madeline (Chantal Contouri) and her husband Elmer (Robert Bruning). Elmer locks Angela in a room and forces her to undress; she escapes, aided by Daryl, who resumes his controlling behaviour but is then killed by Madeline. At no point is it clear how much of the earlier stalking was done by Daryl and how much was done by the other two; Daryl denies any knowledge of the pig's head, and the matter is left unresolved. This makes it difficult to give an accurate and coherent account of the narrative, but it retrospectively imbues the film with a more malevolent atmosphere. As the additional stalkers are revealed (to the extent that they form half the film's top-billed cast) and it becomes less clear who did what to Angela, the threat to her seems to come less from particular people in her life than from people in general. By the end of *Snapshot*, the world that Angela inhabits seems more like that of a horror film.

Ozploitation and Australian genre movies

For some of my examples, then, part of what connects them to horror comes from narrative vagaries or budgetary expediency. At this point, it is useful to consider some wider contexts of Australian popular cinema in the 1970s and 1980s, the period now associated with 'Ozploitation'. This term was popularized by *Not Quite Hollywood*, which also prompted a renewed interest in some of the films under discussion. However, an over-emphasis on Ozploitation promotes a misleading view of Australian genre filmmaking. Adrian Martin argues that the retrospective identity 'carries an element of wish-fulfilment fantasy' that 'gives Australia the raw, vibrant, popular cinema it has never actually had' (2010: 11). Australian popular film in the 1970s and 1980s was more fragmentary than the Ozploitation label implies, with little support at home and uneven opportunities for export.

As Mark David Ryan points out, conditions in the Australian film industry have rarely supported the sustained production of genre movies:

> Cultural policy (as well as public subsidy), in the way that has been practised in Australia since the 1970s, has fostered a certain type of film industry: it circumscribes certain notions of value; it mandates a particular film culture; and it limits the types of films produced in Australia, favouring art house films emphasising Australianness and social realism in opposition to genre films . . . Cultural policy's narrowness 'shuts out' genres such as horror from funding environments and mainstream film culture. (2009: 47)

The Australian Film Development Corporation (AFDC hereafter) provided some funding for genre filmmaking in the first half of the 1970s, but this largely ended in 1975 when the AFDC was superseded by the Australian Film Commission (AFC hereafter). The latter body became associated with 'so-called AFC films' (Heller-Nicholas 2016: 170), prestige movies that were targeted at international film festivals. There was also Division 10BA of the Income Tax Assessment Act, designed to encourage the private financing of Australian films. While 10BA helped to generate 'a fleeting increase' (Balanzategui 2017: 21) in genre film production, it had its own problems, including that 'the tax incentive did not depend on anybody actually seeing these films' (Martin 2010: 13). French-Australian director Philippe Mora described the scheme as being 'basically anarchy', in which 'anything could get funded' (Pedler 2009: 96) but little attention was paid to the resulting movies.

Across the two decades, Australian popular filmmaking went from some government support, to little government support, to some private investment coupled with an often very limited interest in the films themselves. It is unsurprising, then, that the genre films from this period lack the shared identity that the idea of Ozploitation tries to impose upon them. This also helps to account for the looseness and inconsistency evident in some of the movies; intermittent opportunities, variable resources and limited quality control are unlikely to foster a robust popular cinema. It is for this reason, however, that the term 'Ozploitation' remains critically useful. While it overstates its case by implying that films from the period form an identifiable movement, it also highlights the pertinent context of exploitation cinema.

Australian horror movies from the 1970s and 1980s do not fulfil all the criteria set out in stricter definitions of exploitation (see Schaefer 1999: 4; Waddell 2018: 5), but various features remain relevant. Eric Schaefer describes 'classical' American exploitation films as 'a form that lacked stability and order' (1999: 341). This would seem an overly harsh way to describe something like *Snapshot*, or other films like *Thirst* (the ending of which is similarly difficult to parse) but both reflect contexts in which 'the demands of narrative intelligibility' (Schaefer 1999: 340) were not always prioritized or adequately resourced. Crucially, the context of exploitation (or something quite like it) also helps to explain some of the forms of hybridity found in these movies.

Snapshot exemplifies a key, perhaps defining, aspect of exploitation cinema:

> The term exploitation film is derived from the practice of exploitation, advertising or promotional techniques that went over and above typical posters, trailers and newspaper ads.... A kind of carnivalesque ballyhoo became integral to their success. (Schaefer 1999: 4)

Snapshot was subject to sales tactics of this sort, including being misleadingly presented as a slasher film:

> *Snapshot* was released in the United States as both *The Day After Halloween*, *The Day Before Halloween*, and *The Night After Halloween*, making no attempt to

disguise its desire to profit from the recent success of John Carpenter's *Halloween* the year before (in spite of the fact that *Snapshot* is not set on Halloween, and makes no reference to it). (Heller-Nicholas 2016: 176)

The exploitation-like ballyhoo in the advertising of *Snapshot* adds another dimension to the film's mixed generic identity. At least part of its connection to the horror genre is extra-textual, more related to its marketing than to the film itself. Similarly, aspects of the promotion of *Roadgames* presented it as more fully a horror film than it was. The posters for the film's US release were based around an image of a woman's neck and chest, with two hands in driving gloves (like those worn by 'Smith or Jones') reaching over her shoulders. One hand is pulling a guitar string around the woman's neck, while the other holds the zip on the front of her top, poised to pull it open (the stripes down the middle of the top are made to look like road markings). While the poster draws mostly on material from the film, it does so in a way that particularly emphasizes the combination of sex and violence that was associated with horror films, and particularly slasher films, in the early 1980s. The cover of the Charter Entertainment video release used a variation of the same poster design with the woman's face visibly that of Jamie Lee Curtis (despite the fact that her character is not strangled with a guitar string). This video cover image also establishes an intertextual connection to horror since, at this early stage in her career, Curtis had featured almost exclusively in horror films.

Even if a film was only partially or intermittently a horror movie, it might be marketed as one if that seemed to give it the best chance commercially. Calum Waddell refers to 'the exploitation-horror film's calculated opportunism' (2018: 119) and this description also seems to fit the production and release strategies of many Australian horror films from this period. It is apparent, for example, that *Nightmares* is an attempt to capitalize on the popularity of slasher films following the success of *Halloween* (John Carpenter, 1978). Indeed, Alexandra Heller-Nicholas describes the film as being a '*Halloween* fan-fic slasher' (2014: 39). *Night of Fear*, the first notable Australian horror film released after the relaxation of censorship and the introduction of the R-rating in 1971 (Brandum 2016: 55) was originally the pilot episode for a television series, to be called *Fright*. When the series fell through, *Night of Fear* was repurposed for cinema release (Heller-Nicholas 2016: 173).

At under an hour in length, and without dialogue, *Night of Fear* is an unusual feature film (between its origins in television and resemblance to both a silent movie and a short film, it could be considered an example of medium hybridity). Again, though, variances in running time and narrative style are more typical of exploitation cinema:

> The narrative elements of many exploitation movies were truncated at best, almost nonexistent when carried to the extreme. To create feature-length movies, many producers were forced to add additional material – padding – to expand a film to fifty or more minutes. (Schaefer 1999: 68)

Exploitation films often have a makeshift quality, with disparate components brought together to fit available resources and commercial circumstances. Multiple films can be edited together, or new footage introduced into existing films, as in *Voyage to the Planet of Prehistoric Women* (Pavel Klushantsev and Peter Bogdanovich, 1968). Less drastically, exploitation films can combine elements from different genres, as a source of marketable novelty or as a way to offer multiple forms of spectacle. While Schaefer argues that belonging to a mainstream genre would disqualify a film from the exploitation category (1999: 5), genre mixing can nonetheless be a product of similar impulses. Whether we define 1970s and 1980s Australian horror as exploitation, films from the period did operate under similar conditions to other forms of sensationalistic low-budget filmmaking.

International relations

One way in which Australian horror movies were able to succeed in these conditions was through international sales. The narrowing of government funding reduced some opportunities for genre production but increased others through a greater emphasis on exports (Heller-Nicholas 2016: 169). International exhibition and, increasingly in the 1980s, home video markets, provided pathways to profit for Australian genre films.

This commercial focus prompted some movies to adopt a deliberately international address. Australian horror films in this period were often national as well as generic hybrids. A prevalent strategy was to bring in actors from the United States, the United Kingdom and elsewhere. Examples of this practice include Stacy Keach and Jamie Lee Curtis in *Roadgames* and David Hemmings and Henry Silva in *Thirst*. The period also produced some curious international blends. Screenwriter Everett DeRoche recalls that a version of *Patrick* (Richard

Franklin, 1978) was dubbed for US release, resulting in an Australian film in which several British actors were given American accents (Testro 2009: 92).

Elsewhere, attempts to evoke an American milieu generated some unusual effects. A widely discussed example is the fantasy-horror-thriller *Harlequin* (Simon Wincer, 1980):

> The film wears its intent to woo foreign markets on its sleeve, with its myriad accents, international cast, American slang ('the feds' for police, 'the slammer' for gaol) and political system (talk of 'senators' and 'governors'), the incongruous inclusion of right-hand drive cars, and even a Dixie band. (Heller-Nicholas 2009: 101)

The setting of *Harlequin* is neither America nor Australia, but a strange combination of both. More emphatically American in setting is *Dead Kids*, a co-production shot in New Zealand. *Dead Kids* is set in Galesburg, Illinois, a real town. However, the film's version of Galesburg, made up of locations in Auckland, becomes a showcase of exaggerated Americana. Old Glory flies prominently outside of the local high school. In front of the police station is a billboard-sized schedule of Little League Baseball games, decorated with a cartoon Native American holding a tomahawk.

After several young people are killed, Detective Shea (Scott Brady) comes in from Chicago to assist the local police. Shea arrives in the stereotypical Hollywood detective trench coat and fedora, almost immediately asks for bourbon and mentions that he came via 'Route 66'. The concentrated accumulation of motifs from American popular culture is evident here and elsewhere in the film. The hyperbolic assertions of Americanness, alongside the electronic soundtrack from Tangerine Dream, help to give the film an unreal, dreamlike atmosphere. The film's hallucinatory depiction of its setting supports the narrative, in which it is revealed that the killings are the result of chemically induced mind control.

Dead Kids displays its international make-up self-consciously. However, the Australian horror film that most emphasizes its international identity may be *Howling III: The Marsupials* (Philippe Mora, 1987). In Heller-Nicholas's summary, *Howling III* 'brings an over-the-top "Australianness" to a subgenre marked precisely by its foreign origins' (2020: 118). The second sequel to *The Howling* (Joe Dante, 1981), the film is explicitly about hybridity, featuring humans and werewolves (both marsupial and the more familiar variety) strengthening their species through the breeding of mixed offspring. Within its first five minutes, the film includes scenes set in three different countries: Australia, Russia and the

United States. At the film's end, Dame Edna Everage (Barry Humphries) presents an Oscar-like award to marsupial werewolf Jerboa (Imogen Annesley) who has escaped persecution in Australia and become Loretta Carson, a Hollywood star. The film celebrates cultural exchange – for example in the romance that develops between the Australian Professor Beckmeyer (Barry Otto) and the Russian werewolf ballerina Olga Gorki (Dasha Blahova) – but also highlights the damage that can be done in less equitable intercultural encounters. In the film's backstory, lycanthropes were victims of nineteenth-century colonial genocide, directly ordered by Queen Victoria and US president Benjamin Harrison. The depiction of distinctively Australian marsupial werewolves facing threats from Britain and America seems itself to be a comment on Australian identity. Heller-Nicholas refers to the 'dual cultural colonial pressures' between which much Australian culture finds itself, 'implying that (white) Australian identity was marked by its physical and cultural distance from Britain and America' (2016: 170).

Both of these international relationships have shaped Australian horror movies. The influence of Hollywood is inescapable in mainstream narrative filmmaking, especially in English-speaking countries. As Australia sought to develop a prestige art cinema in the late 1970s, national identity and genre became increasingly intertwined, with genre movies being associated with a specifically American foreignness: 'the commercial was necessarily defined by its oppositional status as un-Australian due to the "Hollywood-ness" (a synonym for mainstream, popular cinema as a whole) of its commercial motive' (Heller-Nicholas 2016: 170). In *Howling III*, *Dead Kids* and other examples, engagement with genre conventions also entails engagement with American popular culture and Australia's relation to it.

Because of Australia's colonial history, however, the stronger cultural influence is often British. Robert Hood (2002) notes the popularity of Hammer horror films in Australia; elements of Hammer-style gothic can be seen in films like *Thirst* and *Next of Kin*, and Hammer star Shane Briant features (and is billed first) in *Cassandra* (Colin Eggleston, 1987). The closer historical and cultural connection to Britain also generates more direct criticism. In *Alison's Birthday* (Ian Coughlan, 1981), Britain is associated with the past, and represents an unwelcome, even parasitic burden on modern Australia. Alison Findlay (Joanne Samuel) has been raised to be the new vessel for an ancient Celtic demon, brought to Australia by its previous host, her English grandmother (Marion Johns). Alison's aunt and uncle (Bunney Brooke and John Bluthal) have a Stonehenge-like circle at the bottom of their garden where the transference ritual ultimately takes place, and the film plays on the incongruity of this feature in a suburban garden and in Australia more generally. *Alison's Birthday* ends with Alison's consciousness waking up in her 104-year-old grandmother's body; the horror of loss of identity and premature ageing is linked to a change in nationality, from Australian to British.

In *Turkey Shoot*, monstrous Britishness is more explicitly colonial. The camp commander, Charles Thatcher, played by British actor Michael Craig, wears safari suits and decorates his residence with what appear to be Aboriginal wood carvings. His surname is also an allusion to the British Prime Minister at the time the film was made and released. Somewhat in keeping with the marketing practices of exploitation filmmakers discussed earlier, David Michael Brown notes that 'The film was re-released on video later as *Blood Camp Thatcher* in an effort to further milk the controversial name' (2009: 96).

Conclusion

In many of the examples I have discussed, generic hybridity and national hybridity are intertwined. In *Inn of the Damned*, Kincaid is an imported American character embodying the Western, an imported American genre. In *Turkey Shoot*, the interplay of action, science fiction and horror is supported by a deliberately ambiguous cultural and geographical setting and international cast. However, these films also demonstrate that we cannot align generic and national identity too schematically. Horror plays different roles in different generic mixes and connects to national contexts in ways that change from film to film. Categories like genre and national identity are useful – they help us to recognize what different examples might have in common – but their parameters can often shift and realign. This is highlighted when different categories interact. As this chapter has shown, even the relatively narrow context of Australian horror movies of the 1970s and 1980s can demonstrate the variety and complexity of these interactions.

Bibliography

Altman, Rick. *Film / Genre*. London: BFI, 1999.
Balanzategui, Jessica. '*The Babadook* and the Haunted Space Between High and Low Genres in the Australian Horror Tradition'. *Studies in Australasian Cinema* 11, no. 1 (2017): 18–32.

Brandum, Dean. 'Temporary Fleapits and Scabs' Alley: The Theatrical Dissemination of Italian Cannibal Films in Melbourne, Australia'. In *Grindhouse: Cultural Exchange on 42nd Street, and Beyond*, edited by Austin Fisher and Johnny Walker, 53–71. London: Bloomsbury, 2016.

Brown, David Michael. 'The Cheap Thrill of the Hunt: *Turkey Shoot*'. *Metro* 162 (2009): 94–6.

Heller-Nicholas, Alexandra. 'Dark Forces: Excess and Absence in *Harlequin* and Beyond'. *Metro* 162 (2009): 98–102.

Heller-Nicholas, Alexandra. 'The Black Hole: Remembering 1980s Australian Horror'. *Metro* 180 (2014): 38–41.

Heller-Nicholas, Alexandra. 'From Opera House to Grindhouse (and Back Again): Ozploitation in and Beyond Australia'. In *Grindhouse: Cultural Exchange on 42nd Street, and Beyond*, edited by Austin Fisher and Johnny Walker, 163–79. London: Bloomsbury, 2016.

Hood, Robert. 'Killer Koalas: Australian (and New Zealand) Horror Films'. *Tabula Rasa*, 2002. Available online at: https://tabula-rasa.info/AusHorror/OzHorrorFilms1.html (accessed 6 May 2022).

Knee, Adam. 'The Compound Genre Film: *Billy the Kid Versus Dracula* Meets *The Harvey Girls*'. In *Intertextuality in Literature and Film: Selected Papers from the Thirteenth Annual Florida State University Conference on Literature and Film*, edited by Elaine D. Cancalon and Antoine Spacagna, 141–56. Gainesville: University Press of Florida, 1994.

Martin, Adrian. 'Ozploitation Compared to What? A Challenge to Contemporary Australian Film Studies'. *Studies in Australasian Cinema* 4, no. 1 (2010): 9–21.

Moine, Raphaëlle. *Cinema Genre*, translated by Alastair Fox and Hilary Radner. Oxford: Blackwell Publishing, 2008.

Pedler, Martyn. '"Good Taste is the Enemy of Art": An Interview with Philippe Mora'. *Metro* 161 (2009): 96–8.

Ryan, Mark David. 'Whither Culture? Australian Horror Films and the Limitations of Cultural Policy'. *Media International Australia* 133 (2009): 43–55.

Schaefer, Eric. *'Bold! Daring! Shocking! True!': A History of Exploitation Films, 1919–1959*. Durham: Duke University Press, 1999.

Testro, Lucas. 'Master of Darkness: Everett DeRoche'. *Metro* 162 (2009): 89–93.

Waddell, Calum. *The Style of Sleaze: The American Exploitation Film, 1959–1971*. Edinburgh: Edinburgh University Press, 2018.

Zimmermann, Stefan. 'I Suppose it has Come to this. . . How a Western Shaped Australia's Identity'. In *Crossing Frontiers: Intercultural Perspectives on the Western*, edited by Thomas Klein, Ivo Ritzer, and Peter W. Schulze, 134–48. Marburg: Schüren, 2012.

Filmography

Alison's Birthday (1981), [Film] Dir. Ian Coughlan, Australia: 7 Network / David Hannay Productions / Fontana Films Pty. Ltd. / The Australian Film Commission.

Billy the Kid Versus Dracula (1966), [Film] Dir. William Beaudine, USA: Circle Productions.

BMX Bandits (1983), [Film] Dir. Brian Trenchard-Smith, Australia: Nilsen Premiere.

Brawl in Cell Block 99 (2017), [Film] Dir. S. Craig Zahler, USA: Assemble Media / CINESTATE / IMG Films.

Carrie (1976), [Film] Dir. Brian De Palma, USA: Red Bank Films.

Cassandra (1987), [Film] Dir. Colin Eggleston, Australia: Cassandra Films Pty. Ltd. / Parallel Film Productions.

Dead Kids (1981), [Film] Dir. Michael Laughlin, Australia / New Zealand / USA: Hemdale / Fay Richwite / South Street Films.

Halloween (1979), [Film] Dir. John Carpenter, USA: Compass International Pictures.

Harlequin (1980), [Film] Dir. Simon Wincer, Australia: F.G. Film Productions.

The Howling (1981), [Film] Dir. Joe Dante, USA: AVCO Embassy Pictures / International Film Investors / Wescom Productions.

Howling III: The Marsupials (1987), [Film] Dir. Philippe Mora, Australia: Bancannia Holdings Pty. Ltd.

Inn of the Damned (1975), [Film] Dir. Terry Bourke, Australia: Terryrod.

Kath & Kim (2002–2007), [Television Programme] ABC / Seven Network.

Kiss the Blood Off My Hands (1948), [Film] Dir. Norman Foster, USA: Harold Hecht / Norma Productions.

The Most Dangerous Game (1932), [Film] Dirs. Irving Pichel and Ernest B. Schoedsack, USA: RKO Radio Pictures.

Next of Kin (1982), [Film] Dir. Tony Williams, Australia / New Zealand: Filmco Australia / Film House / SIS.

Nightmares (1980), [Film] Dir. John D. Lamond, Australia: Bioscope / John Lamond Motion Picture Enterprises / Movityme Pty.

Night of Fear (1973), [Film] Dir. Terry Bourke, Australia: Terryrod.

Not Quite Hollywood: The Wild, Untold Story of Ozploitation! (2008), [Film] Dir. Mark Hartley, Australia: AFFC / City Films Worldwide / Madman Entertainment.

Patrick (1978), [Film] Dir. Richard Franklin, Australia: Anthony I. Ginnane / Filmways Australasia.

Roadgames (1981), [Film] Dir. Richard Franklin, Australia: Essaness Pictures.

Snapshot (1979), [Film] Dir. Simon Wincer, Australia: AIFC / Filmways Australasia / F.G. Film Productions.

Strictly Ballroom (1992), [Film] Dir. Baz Luhrmann, Australia: Beyond Films / M&A.

The Terminator (1984), [Film] Dir. James Cameron, USA: Hemdale / Pacific Western Productions / Euro Film Funding / Cinema '84.

Thirst (1979), [Film] Dir. Rod Hardy, Australia: New South Wales Film Corporation / F.G. Film Productions / Film Victoria.

Turkey Shoot (1982), [Film] Dir. Brian Trenchard-Smith, Australia / UK: Hemdale / FGH / Filmco.

Voyage to the Planet of Prehistoric Women (1968), [Film] Dirs. Pavel Klushantsev and Peter Bogdanovich, USA: The Filmgroup.

'I can't believe so many horror fans aren't watching *Inside*'

The cult status of twenty-first-century French horror cinema

Alice Haylett Bryan

Introduction

It is easy enough to conclude that *The Sunday Times* journalist Peter Whittle was not a fan of Pascal Laugier's *Martyrs* (2008). Indeed, Whittle (2009) said of the film:

> Profoundly depressing in every way, this slab of blood-soaked sadism is the latest example of a new kind of French horror, which in its extreme brutality leaves Hollywood standing. . . . The air of pretentiousness and the whiff of Lesbian chic suggests that the bunch of nihilists who produced this garbage will claim something for it. All it really demonstrates is that there is something seriously rotten in the state of France.

Whittle (2009) manages to deride the film, make a sly wink to his own (highbrow) knowledge via a reference to Shakespeare, and cast aspersions about France, all in one pithy 120-word review. In contrast, a few weeks later Brad Miska (2009) wrote about the film for *Bloody Disgusting* in a very different tone: 'It begins with a whisper – then there's some buzz – then there's a friend who knows someone who knows someone else who has seen it. Word has it that the movie is awesome, and that is when it transforms into something more than another horror flick, that is when it becomes a legend'. Miska argued that *Martyrs* was that year's *Inside* (*À l'intérieur*), referring to Alexandre Bustillo and Julien Maury's 2007 film about an expectant mother attacked in her home by a woman who wishes to steal the baby from her womb. Miska's excitement is palpable as he labels these two French horror films 'legendary'. As with Bustillo and Maury the year before, *Martyrs* rocketed Laugier into horror-notoriety, attracting to the director not only the attention of fans across the world, but also several big-time American producers including (the now disgraced) Harvey Weinstein. French horror became synonymous with extreme imagery and gore; horror films for the 'true' horror fan as opposed to faint-hearted interlopers.

These sharply differing evaluations of *Martyrs* are not exactly surprising given their contexts. A horror fan site like *Bloody Disgusting* is obviously going to be more receptive to such a film than a mainstream centre-right newspaper with the majority of its readership in the thirty-five to sixty-four age bracket (Hurst Media 2020). Whittle (2009) and Miska (2009) are reviewers on opposite ends of the spectrum, but both go to great lengths to refer to *Martyrs* as a 'French' film. So it is not just a horror film, but a French horror film. For the former this speaks to something corrupt about or within the nation, for the latter it positions it as different, exciting and part of a cycle of horror films that only those 'in the know' are aware of. During the early 2000s horror filmmaking in France went from being a relatively rare occurrence, to producing a small body of work that attracted international attention for its high levels of gore and imaginative takes on traditional horror tropes and narratives. Nevertheless, these films remained part of a niche market, even if their directors often went on to bigger, and more mainstream, American projects. This chapter will explore the potential cult status of this corpus of early twenty-first-century French horror films, taking *Inside* as a case study due to it being one of the first big hits of the cycle. I do not intend to make a case for *Inside* as a cult object (because this in and of itself would have little value), but instead to evaluate the degree to which its country of origin plays a part in the cult practices that surround the film.

On the hunt for French horror

At the dawn of the twenty-first century, French horror cinema experienced a bloody rebirth. Preceded by *Deep in the Woods* (*Promenons-nous dans les bois*, Lionel Delplanque, 2000) and *Brotherhood of the Wolf* (*Le Pacte des loups*, Christophe Gans, 2001), this new cycle of French horror was kick-started with Alexandre Aja's *High Tension/Switchblade Romance* (*Haute Tension*) in 2003. In the years that followed, a stream of gory and politically engaged films were released, such as *Them* (*Ils*, David Moreau and Xavier Palud, 2006), *Satan* (*Sheitan*, Kim Chapiron, 2006) and *Frontier(s)* (*Frontière(s)*, Xavier Gens, 2007), as well as the aforementioned *Inside* and *Martyrs*. Dubbed 'Sarkozy horror' by the critic Neil Young (2008), these films explicitly and implicitly responded to the political climate of the period, which was overshadowed by the 2005 riots and the anti-immigration rhetoric of Nicolas Sarkozy (see Haylett Bryan 2021). Ben McCann writes that this body of filmmaking was 'engaged in a fascinating dialogue with [concurrent] political and social events in France, grafting metaphors of border porosity and domestic invasion onto their narratives of visual excess' (2008: 226). These early works were often made on shoe-string budgets, were excessively gory and tapped into American horror subgenres and tropes such as the home invasion narrative, the slasher film and hillbilly horror. Despite their limited financial success, many were well received by horror critics and fans, and a significant number of the directors were swept off to work on American projects. Consequently, the cycle lost much of its momentum, but then reappeared with renewed force after the release of Julia Ducournau's aesthetically in-keeping *Raw* (*Grave*) in 2016.

It is worth stressing that these French horror films were neither big-budget affairs nor box office successes. As Bustillo and Maury, and Laugier (as well as many others) have noted, during this period it was very difficult to get funding to produce a horror film in France. It was believed (and to some extent proved) that while French horror fans would go in their hundreds of thousands to see the latest instalment of an American horror franchise, they had little time for home-grown horror. Indeed, Bustillo observed that there is 'no French community of horror. For foreign cultures France seems like the new El Dorado of horror, but it's not true. In France, there are only a few guys who try to shoot horror movies with a low budget' (Brown 2011). But outside of France among Anglophone horror communities, French horror found a loving home that celebrated its willingness for excessive gore. In his review of *Martyrs* Miska (2009) writes, 'The one thing that makes being a horror fan so awesome is the hunt, the search for the holy grail of gore', suggesting that *Martyrs* and *Inside* are just that. This idea of having to 'hunt' speaks to the cult practices that surround certain horror films; a process and experience to uncover something hidden, not easily locatable, not mainstream. The hunt forms part of the 'communal' experience of watching these films that adds to their potential cult status, with critics *and* fans sharing reviews and recommendations on dedicated horror websites, in horror publications, or at film festivals. For an Anglophone audience in the era preceding digital streaming, the foreign status of French horror demanded that films had to be hunted down. Screenings beyond film festivals were unlikely and rental versions (as was infamously the case with *Inside*) were sometimes cut to conform to local classifications and censorship rules. In some cases DVDs had to be purchased from abroad (often necessitating the downloading of subtitle files) or poor-quality pirated copies had to be watched online.

Martyrs and *Inside* went on to be reasonably accessible, especially as their general release coincided with a boom in the DVD sales and rental markets. However, many more French horror films went unreleased outside of mainland Europe with fans left waiting years to acquire physical copies of their favourite movies. For example, despite a significant number of major producers courting Bustillo and Maury after *Inside*, their 2011 follow-up *Livid* (*Livide*) never received an American release, and only became readily available in the country in 2022 when it was platformed on *Shudder*. In line with Miska's (2009) suggestion of a hunt, another post on *Bloody Disgusting* lists *Livid* as a 'Hidden Halloween Gem', again positioning this French film as something clandestine that had to be tracked down and uncovered (even though it was actually reasonably easy to acquire by then via import or illegal download), that would ultimately reward the dedicated horror fan (Navarro 2021). Such websites play a key role in disseminating knowledge about French horror, especially for a non-French speaking audience. For example, when writing for *Dread Central*, Andrew Kasch (2007) waxed lyrical at the release of *Inside*: 'To call this the most visceral slasher film of all time is an extreme understatement. Birthed in the minds of two twisted individuals, *Inside* is a masterwork of horror so savage and disturbing, I'm careful who to recommend it to. One thing's for sure: Hollywood won't be remaking this anytime soon.'[1] Kasch's sentiment that he was careful who to recommend the film to was echoed in a later *Dread Central* review of the film's DVD release, when Steve Barton (2008) stated that although the film would make it into his 'best of the year list', he 'wouldn't know who to recommend it to . . . This is not for the easily offended, not for the squeamish, and definitely not for the general public'. If horror critics liked to label French horror films as gems

---

[1] Unfortunately, Hollywood did remake *Inside*, and *Martyrs*, both of which were generally derided and financial flops. For example, Matt Glasby (2016) writes in his *Total Film* review of the American remake of *Martyrs* (K. Goetz and M. Goetz, 2016): 'Where Pascal Laugier's 2008 horror can make a decent claim to the word "masterpiece", Kevin and Michael Goetz's Blumhoused update can barely justify its existence. Not what you could call bad – just depressingly pointless . . . the addition of a softer ending and some CG fire (perhaps because it has none of its own) suggest you can't remake art, only diminish it'.

to be hunted out, they were also keen to differentiate them as notorious works that were not for the ordinary film viewer, or even for the average horror fan.

Cult horror cinema

This cycle of French horror films can therefore be described as excessively gory, not widely known nor easily available (although this has changed with the advent of VOD platforms, especially *Shudder*) and only enjoyable for the self-appointed hardcore horror fan. It is these elements that position this corpus as being ripe for classification under the category of cult cinema. It is not within the scope of this chapter to attempt to define what cult cinema is. This has been done many times before and often – if any conclusion is reached – it is that such a definition must be broad, fluctuating and intangible (see Mathijs and Mendik 2008; Grant 1991; Gorfinkel 2008). On a very basic level the cycle of French genre films under review here lends itself to a cult classification as it features horror films, and, as is often noted in cult film studies, horror and cult cinema are 'kindred spirits' (Hantke 2019: 50). The genre can be seen to fit easily within cultdom via the necessity for it to be transgressive; whether ultimately progressive or conservative, horror must go against the norms of society in order to 'be'. A film such as *Inside* could be classed as transgressive purely for the intense amount of gore that it contains, due to the various stabbings and mutilations that take place using items such as knitting needles, scissors, kitchen knives and home-made flame-throwers. However, there are further elements that mark this quintessential French horror film as one that goes against the norms and expectations of society.

Set on Christmas Eve, the film centres on heavily pregnant Sarah (Alysson Paradis), at home alone waiting to have a caesarean which is booked in for the following day. Earlier on in her pregnancy she and the baby's father (Jean-Baptiste Tabourin) were involved in a car crash that took his life, so she is faced with going through the birth of her child on her own. An unnamed woman (Béatrice Dalle) appears at her door before breaking in and attacking Sarah. Sarah's mother (Nathalie Roussel), her boss (François-Régis Marchasson), three police officers (Ludovic Berthillot, Emmanuel Lanzi and Nicolas Duvauchelle) and a young man (Aymen Saïdi) in their custody, all enter the house over the course of the evening and are killed by either the woman or accidentally by Sarah. During the prolonged battle both women become increasingly mutilated and bloodied, especially the pregnant Sarah, who goes into labour due to her injuries, threatening the life of her child. It is revealed that the unnamed woman was also involved in the car crash that took Sarah's husband's life, and she lost her own baby in the event. She has now come to take Sarah's baby as a replacement, and the film ends with her cutting the child out of Sarah's womb with a pair of scissors, killing Sarah in the process. Subsequently, continuous extreme violence against a pregnant woman – and therefore a child – dominates the near entirety of the film's eighty-two-minute runtime, challenging the limits of acceptability. Horror is obviously rife with attacks and killings, but very few films have babies as victims. Babies are considered to be innocents who must be protected and their peril or injury is rarely shown on screen. Thus, the baby in *Inside* presents an opportunity to shock or challenge even the most hardened horror fan.

Inside's narrative would be very hard to sell to a mainstream audience, an idea arguably proved by the content of the film's subsequent remake. After Bustillo and Maury turned down the opportunity to do an American remake of their own film, *Inside* (2016) was helmed by two figures from Spanish horror cinema: co-writer Jaume Balagueró, who had enjoyed huge success with his film *[Rec]* (2007), and director Miguel Ángel Vivas. Although this remake was a Spanish production, it was intended for an American audience, set in Chicago with an American cast. Not only is the violence far less extreme in this version, but the ending is completely different. Instead of the bleak nihilism of the original's closing sequence of Sarah's visibly empty womb and the now heavily deformed woman rocking the newborn baby, in the remake the woman (Laura Harring) dies and Sarah (Rachel Nichols) survives, giving birth to her a baby in the swimming pool as help arrives. Therefore, the remake, in its attempts to appeal to a more mainstream audience, has scaled back on the transgressive elements of the original. It is not as gory, the antagonist is punished through death, and the pregnant protagonist keeps her baby. Transforming the film's ending from an image of the penetrated and incomplete maternal body to that of a successful birth and 'complete' mother child union changes the overall nature of the film.

The resounding commercial failure of the remake of *Inside* illustrates Steffan Hantke's argument that 'Fans of the horror film genre might suspect that mainstream horror's inclusiveness, its appeal to a mass audience beyond fandom, must be achieved by, paradoxically, compromising on exactly that transgressiveness which defines the appeal of its genre in the first place' (2019: 51). So, to be a horror film in and of itself is not enough for cult status to be allotted. As Hantke notes, in horror as much as elsewhere in filmmaking, in order to be readily accepted as cult cinema, such films must exhibit more classically cultist traits: being made with small budgets by independent auteurs and attracting a minority of dedicated viewers who actively seek out such films. It is this minority of viewers which is key here. What really distinguishes cult cinema is that it is demarcated as much by the audience as the filmmaker. Mathijs and Sexton argue that cult cinema is a phenomenological experience, where meaning is created in the relationship between film and viewer and between the viewer and other viewers: 'The cult film experience is indeed often described as one of close proximity to the screen (enthrallment with the giant canvas), to fellow viewers (huddled together in communion), and to the subject matter (overly close-reading of themes and motives)' (Mathijs and Sexton 2011: 17). Therefore, even if gore 'is a sure way to grant films cult status' (Mathijs and Mendik 2008: 3), it is not simply gore that makes French horror a cult object. It is the way that audiences experience the gore, respond to the gore, celebrate the gore, hunt out the gore, distribute the gore and become gatekeepers of the gore that is key.

From the new wave to the new extremism

It is in this interplay between fan and film where French horror takes on its own set of very specific elements. France has a long-standing and complicated relationship between auteurism and genre filmmaking, a relationship bound closely to the ideas and practices of cult cinema and cinephilia. As Elena Gorfinkel writes in 'Cult Film or Cinephilia by Any Other Name', French cinephilia and (usually American) cult practices are an 'apt pairing' (2008: 33). Gorfinkel (2008) argues that the connections between cinephilia and cultism run throughout French cinematic history, from the Surrealists to the *cahiers du cinéma* critics via Bazin. She writes that within French cinephilic culture there is a celebration of the bad, and a 'reclamation and resuscitation' of the overlooked, and as such there is a degree of cultism at work (2008: 34). While the directors of the French New Wave championed the work of well-respected and 'artistic' filmmakers they also celebrated directors who were often dismissed as mere purveyors of popular entertainment. Thus their influences might include a mix of American B-Movies, French noirs from the likes of Jean-Pierre Melville and the works of *cinéma verité* directors such as Jean Rouche. Yet, Gorfinkel is quick to add that cult appreciation and cinephilia are not one and the same thing: 'cult in its approach appears more cynical, *using yet refusing* the parameters of artistic value and the idea of the hallowed masterpiece' (2008: 34). This relationship between cinephilia and cult, and the way that the two are fundamental elements of French cinematic history, is an important factor in the discussion of French horror as it speaks to the cultural baggage that these films come with. This cultural baggage affects the consumption of French horror in two ways. First, the critical role that France has played in cinematic history is well-known, especially among film fans, but even in quotidian life. The term 'French cinema' brings to mind not the action blockbuster, but Jean-Luc Godard's glasses and cigarette; the trademark image of the auteur. The general (non-French) public associate (however wrongly) French cinema with art cinema. But compounding this association is the fact that those likely to engage with French horror texts in a cultist way often have some degree of film knowledge, and as I will demonstrate, are often keen to exhibit it. Therefore, French horror becomes connected with artistry and creativity via an imaginary link to the New Wave.

The second item of cultural baggage that comes with French horror is a little more niche and even troubles the statement just made concerning the simplistic connection between French horror and artistry: the impact of what was dubbed the New French Extremism and the celebration of the auteur. With its start predating the cycle of French horror under discussion by about ten years, the New French Extremism was the label given to the work of a group of auteurs such as Gaspar Noé, Catherine Breillat, François Ozon and Philippe Grandrieux, who were producing highly graphic and transgressive art cinema that borrowed themes and imagery from horror and pornography. In his infamous diatribe against the movement, James Quandt wrote: 'Bava as much as Bataille, Salò no less than Sade seem the determinants of a cinema suddenly determined to break every taboo, to wade in rivers of viscera and spumes of sperm, to fill each frame with flesh, nubile or gnarled, and subject it to all manner of penetration, mutilation and defilement' (2004: 127). These films were often critically well received, or at least accepted as being part of a lineage of rebellious French artistry.

However, there is a tendency among some film scholars to place key twenty-first-century French horror films within the more highbrow category of New French Extremism. For example, in her book *Films of the New French Extremity*, Alexandra West (2016) classifies all French horror under the label without any real justification nor discussion around the potential issues arising from doing so. And these potential issues are numerous. For instance, there is the long-standing divide between auteurism and genre filmmaking in France. The directors of the French New Wave may have been inspired by, and borrowed from, genre filmmakers, but their own films are seen as highbrow works of individualism, not genre films. In the same manner, New French Extremism directors such as Noé, Breillat and the like may borrow elements from horror cinema for their works, but they too are seen as auteurs, not genre filmmakers. Their films are regularly screened at prestigious art cinema festivals such as Cannes and Berlin, and as such the directors of the New French Extremism bring with them the caché of film festival exhibition to access funding streams not open to your average horror genre filmmaker.

Consequently, interviews with the directors of the New French Extremism rarely contain references to how difficult it is to get their films funded. As Maxime Bey-Rozet writes 'this perceived gap between auteurism and genre cinema is nothing new, and has been a staple of conversations about genre film production in France. At the core of such a division is the pervasive belief that genre cinema in general, and horror in particular, are the province of Hollywood, and that French productions cannot hope to compete' (2021: 191). Bey-Rozet notes how in order to challenge this gap, in 2018 the *Centre National du Cinéma et de l'image animée* (CNC) announced that it would be looking to offer financial support for genre films, with a special committee headed by Julia Ducournau that would focus on fantasy, science fiction and horror filmmaking. In her statement for the committee Ducournau declared, 'An auteur is a person who has a vision, who knows how to express that vision in their art, whatever its grammar. Genre – horror, fantasy, etc. – is a grammar in the same way that comedy and drama are' (quoted in Bey-Rozet 2021: 199). Here Ducournau is pointedly stating that genre filmmakers can be auteurs too, which actually contradicts the CNC's previous position of prioritizing funding to screenplays that 'demonstrate an auteur's point of view, . . . move away from familiar codes and show singularity' (Bey-Rozet 2021: 200). By subsuming all French horror titles under the categorization of New French Extremism, scholars ignore this long and difficult relationship between auteur and genre filmmaking in France and more importantly, erase the real difficulties that French horror directors have experienced when seeking funding for their work.

Beyond these production differences, French horror and the New French Extremism are also fundamentally different in intent. The films of the latter 'borrow from' horror as part of a wider project of transgression and audience manipulation, they are not horror works in and of themselves. As is well documented, the New French Extremism is driven by a willingness to engage the spectator in an active and embodied response that often has philosophical and/or ethical implications (see Beugnet 2007; Palmer 2011; Horeck and Kendall 2011). Yes, these works may borrow from horror, and horror might move spectators in a similar way, but this does not mean they are the same thing, nor that they come from the same set of intentions. Even at the most basic level, horror is a genre, while the New French Extremism is a style or mode of practice. In her influential work on this period in French cinema, Martine Beugnet argues that one of the key works of the New French Extremism, *Trouble Every Day* (Claire Denis, 2001), is precisely *not* a horror film for this very reason. She writes 'in spite of its knowing reworking of the conventions and traditions of specific genres, Denis' is a film of "terror" rather than a horror or gore feature, a work that elaborates an aesthetic of dread or angst rather than one of systematic, plethoric shock and disgust' (2007: 37). Subsequently, French horror brings with it cultural baggage of varying degrees of weight. While not every person who watches *Inside* will be aware of the New French Extremism, simplistic associations between French cinema and (highbrow) 'art' are commonplace outside of France and arguably still exist within French institutions to this day. The result is that viewers are more likely to approach a French horror film with a set of positive and/or negative pre-conceived ideas about its content and style, from the pretentiousness that Whittle (2009) scoffs at, to the artistry that Miska (2009) delights at.

'French horror seems to be all the rage among fellow genre fans these days' (Cujo1083 2010)

In order to understand the extent to which *Inside*'s French heritage impacts on the way that viewers regard the film, and by extension whether it contributes to its cult status, I carried out an analysis of 322 reviews of the film submitted to the website *International Movie Database* [*IMDB* hereafter] (2022). *IMBD* hosts user-generated reviews, supplied by the general public rather than film critics. It is not a horror-specific website, so the range of contributor tastes is varied. Of these 322 reviews I took a sample of 200 for closer analysis, which were selected from a range of years falling between 2008 and 2022. Statistics from all 322 reviews are presented as numbers and those from the sample are presented as percentages. I looked for a number of factors: whether the review was positive, if it referred to France, if the reviewer mentioned or recommended other films they had seen, whether they displayed knowledge about the horror genre (its history/conventions/technical aspects and so on), if they compared *Inside* favourably or unfavourably to other French or American films, if they mentioned gore or violence as a measure of some kind, if they mentioned the New French Extremism or described the film as extreme, and finally whether they took part in what I will call gatekeeping – saying whether the film is, or is not, suitable viewing for certain groups of people. This is not a comprehensive analysis but intended more to provide an overview of how public reviewers responded to the film. The sample revealed that roughly 46 per cent of reviewers referred to the French origin of *Inside*. This may not seem like a significant figure, but when it is noted that a significant number of the 54 per cent of reviews that did not refer to the film's country of origin were very short (e.g. 'The most awful movie I have ever see Splatter so much blood I could beraly watch it!' [*sic*] [dorakont15 2021]) it begins to carry more weight.

It is interesting to note that contributors were far more likely to mention *Inside*'s national origin the earlier the date of the review's submission. Taking two sample years – 2008 and 2020 – I found that 67 per cent of reviewers referred to the nationality of the film in 2008, compared to just 26 per cent in 2020. There was not a noticeable difference in the overall number of favourable reviews between the years (66 per cent in 2008 versus 53 per cent in 2020), but what is noteworthy is that reviewers in 2008 were far more likely to refer to other films they had seen (48 per cent versus 5 per cent in 2020), display a level of genre knowledge (32 per cent versus 0 per cent in 2020), and talk about the levels of gore in the film (66 per cent versus 26 per cent in 2020). Part of this disparity might relate to the average length of the reviews. 2008 was not long after the film had been released, and there were eighty-eight reviews in total that year, with an average length of 327 words (all word counts include the *IMDB* disclaimer). This dropped to nineteen reviews in 2020 with an average length of 126 words. This undoubtedly reflects a change in the way that people have interacted with *Inside* over time. Viewers in 2008 would have had to go to greater lengths to see the film (even if that was just a trip to a DVD rental store). Time has not overtly affected the overall popularity of the film, but the length of the earlier reviews, their reference to other films and displays of genre knowledge – as well as their more common reference to its nationality – suggest that these early viewers had a more in-depth engagement with it, and were potentially a more active part of the horror community, choosing to give their feedback on an area which they were knowledgeable about as a kind of service to other fans.

This idea of a community is supported further when considering the instances of gatekeeping in the reviews: stating whether the film is suitable viewing for someone (usually a horror fan), or not suitable viewing for someone. This was done in both favourable and unfavourable reviews, and with regard to the favourable reviews was presented in both a positive and negative sense, with reviewers claiming that *Inside* should *only* be watched by certain people or should *not* be watched by certain people. Across the sample of 200 reviews which I looked at in depth, there were forty-five instances of gatekeeping. For example, Indyrod26 (2008) wrote, 'Every gorehound, or fan of graphic violent cinema, will want a copy of this movie'. Such a comment is at once both welcoming, but also suggests that if you are not a fan of gore, you should steer well clear. Conversely, some instances of gatekeeping were negative, but could also work to encourage a sense of an 'outsider' community among those who did like the film. These reviews tend to associate those who enjoyed *Inside* with mental illness, with comments such as 'avoid at all costs if you're not a gorie loony!' (Vonp1r316 2021) or 'definitely one of the worst horror movies I've seen, but the mentally ill may like it' (Flekoun6 2021). These comments recreate in part the contrast that was evident between Whittle (2009) and Miska (2009), one side in utter disbelief that anyone could like such content (and therefore suggesting that there is something 'seriously wrong' with them), the other seeing the fact that some people will not like the film (while they do) as a marker of identity.

The gatekeeping exhibited here by fans of *Inside* illustrates the active 'imagined' community that scholars have argued is an integral part of cult cinema appreciation, for example, 'we like it, you will not'. Indeed, as I Q Hunter writes, 'Cult requires a sense of difference from . . . [the] imagined Other of clueless consumers of mainstream Hollywood' (2016: 4). Additionally, these gatekeepers reinforce their sense of 'oppositional identity' (see Sconce 1995; Jancovich 2002) even further, by positioning themselves against the 'average' horror fan. For example, fredfontein15's (2008) positive review reports that 'this film is sickeningly nauseating. If you like the occasional horror film, I would stay away from this film it may be too much . . . I get the feeling this film is for the die hard horror fans who are always looking for the film that takes it one step further'. Across the sample, gatekeeping was far more likely to be present in positive reviews (82 per cent). Of these reviewers, 65 per cent referred to the nationality of the film, and were more likely to demonstrate genre knowledge, recommend films or compare *Inside* to other French or American productions. Across the sample, the split between those who compared the film positively or negatively to other French films was fairly even, but of those who compared the film to US horror, 85 per cent did so in a favourable light. These reviews tend to praise the film (and/or French horror in general) for its originality and extremity.

One way that reviewers displayed their genre knowledge was through reference to the New French Extremism. Across all the reviews, the New French Extremism was mentioned twelve times, usually as part of long reviews which referenced multiple films. The earliest reference to the New French Extremism is in 2013, but from 2018 onwards the movement is referenced more frequently. These reviews are evenly split between the positive and negative, suggesting that a fan of the New French Extremism might not always be a fan of French horror cinema. For example, giantjott26 (2022) asks:

> I just don't get it. What is so great about this film? It's supposed to be representative of the so-called New French Extremity, which includes some truly original, ambitious films (*Irreversible* [*Irréversible*, Gaspar Noé, 2002], *Fat Girl* [*À ma soeur!*, Catherine Breillat, 2001], *Baise-Moi* [Virginie Despentes and Coralie Trinh Thi, 2000]), so why does this unoriginal, unsurprising, uninteresting take on the home invasion subgenre get all the attention? [*sic*].

The five-year gap between the first review and the primary mention of the New French Extremism also suggests that French horror is not really such a natural part of the latter categorization as some might believe. As noted earlier, early reviews were significantly more likely to reference the nationality of the film, and many speak of a new cycle of French horror, but any reference to the New French Extremism comes much later. In comparison, thirty-four reviews (over 10 per cent) mention *Haute Tension*, so it is far more likely that a reviewer will position *Inside* in relation to other French horror films than films classically regarded to be part of the New French Extremity.

These findings point to several conclusions, some of which are specific to *Inside*, and others that could be seen as part of a wider pattern within user-generated review sites. I discovered that the average length of the review grew shorter the further from the release date it was written, likely due to the increased availability of the film. Early reviewers of *Inside* would have had to actively seek it out, suggesting a pre-existing desire to see the film, rather than casually stumbling across it on a VOD platform. This is often confirmed in the reviews, regardless of whether they are being positive or negative about the film. Earlier reviews were more likely to show other elements of cult practice too – such as exhibiting wider knowledge, recommending other films and gatekeeping. These fans were knowledgeable about the subject matter and used this knowledge to position themselves as connoisseurs of extreme horror. Interestingly, these reviews generally do *not* attempt to make French horror sound highbrow by seeking to align the film with the New French Extremism. Instead these reviews celebrate *Inside* purely as a horror film to be enjoyed by horror fans. However, what is key is that these earlier, more detailed reviews are substantially more likely to refer to the film as French. Such reviews are also likely to compare *Inside* favourably against American horror cinema, positioning French horror as something new and different and reinforcing the 'us and them' sense of a non-mainstream community of knowledgeable and discerning fans. Combining this with the frequency of reference to other French horror films, the country of origin of *Inside* does appear to be an important factor in the way that reviewers engaged with the film.

Conclusion

It feels fitting to end this chapter with a quote from the first ever *IMDB* review of *Inside*. In 2007 alaccheo16 wrote: 'Europe, particularly France has got the knack for creating horror films that are actually scary and yes a little excessive but they succeed in creating scares. If you are pregnant or have a weak stomach, this ride is not for you!!!' Such a review demonstrates the intersection between cult practices and French horror fandom. The country of origin of the film (and therefore its foreignness for an Anglophone audience) is singled out and positioned as a marker of meaning. Knowledge is exhibited, and a defined body of work is suggested. Finally, there is a sense of gatekeeping, and therefore again the shoring up of a line between those who will like and appreciate the film, and those who will not. The knowledge exhibited by the reviewer reinforces the idea that those who will like the film are the informed ones, and that those who will not are uninformed, uninitiated and unable to deal with 'actually scary' films. Such fan reviews of *Inside* replicate the cult practices that are also at play in the critical reviews of the film in dedicated horror media outlets. All work to position the fan of French horror as being somebody who actively seeks out these hidden gems and is able to withstand their extreme levels of gore, which typically exceed those tolerated by 'normal' horror fans. It is through such fan identity making and activity that the (Anglophone) cult status of French horror is achieved.

Bibliography

Barton, Steve. 'Inside (DVD)'. *Dread Central*, 8 April 2008. Available online at: https://www.dreadcentral.com/reviews/6753/inside-dvd/ (accessed 9 June 2022).

Beugnet, Martine. *Cinema and Sensation: French Film and the Art of Transgression*. Edinburgh: Edinburgh University Press, 2007.

Bey-Rozet, Maxime. 'Cycles of Death and Rebirth in Twenty-First Century French Horror'. *French Screen Studies* 21, no. 3 (2021): 191–203.

Brown, Phil. 'Exclusive: Directors Alexandre Bustillo and Julien Maury Talk Livid and Their Abandoned Hellraiser Remake'. *Collider*, 15 September 2011. Available online at: https://collider.com/alexandre-bustillo-julien-maury-livid-hellraiser-remake-interview/ (accessed 9 June 2022).

Glasby, Matt. 'Movies to Watch this Week at the Cinema'. *Total Film*, 28 March 2016. Available online at: https://www.gamesradar.com/movies-to-watch-1-april-2016/ (accessed 9 June 2022).

Gorfinkel, Elena. 'Cult Film or Cinephilia by Any Other Name'. *Cinéaste* 34, no. 1 (2008): 33–8.

Grant, Barry Keith. 'Science Fiction Double Feature: Ideology in the Cult Film'. In *The Cult Film Experience*, edited by J. P. Telotte, 122–37. Austin: University of Texas Press, 1991.

Hantke, Steffan. 'Cult Horror Cinema'. In *The Routledge Companion to Cult Cinema*, edited by Ernest Mathijs and Jamie Sexton, 50–8. London: Routledge, 2019.

Haylett Bryan, Alice. 'Inhospitable Landscapes: Contemporary French Horror Cinema, Immigration and Identity'. *French Screen Studies* 21, no. 3 (2021): 224–38.

Horeck, Tanya and Tina Kendall. 'Introduction'. In *The New Extremism in Cinema: From France to Europe*, edited by Tanya Horeck and Tina Kendall, 1–17. Edinburgh: Edinburgh University Press, 2011.

Hunter, I.Q. *Cult Film as a Guide to Life: Fandom, Adaptation and Identity*. London: Bloomsbury, 2016.

Hurst Media. 'The Times Profile'. Available online at: https://www.hurstmediacompany.co.uk/the-times-profile/ (accessed 9 June 2022).

IMDB. 'Inside User Reviews'. Available online at: https://www.imdb.com/title/tt0856288/reviews?ref_=tt_urv (accessed 9 June 2022).

Jancovich, Mark. 'Cult Fictions: Cult Movies, Subcultural Capital and the Production of Cultural Distinctions'. *Cultural Studies* 16, no. 2 (2002): 306–22.

Kasch, Andrew. 'Inside'. *Dread Central*, 19 November 2007. Available online at: https://www.dreadcentral.com/reviews/5534/inside-2007/ (accessed 9 June 2022).

Mathijs, Ernest and Xavier Mendik. 'Editorial Introduction: What is Cult Film?'. In *The Cult Film Reader*, edited by Ernest Mathijs and Xavier Mendik, 1–11. Maidenhead: Open University Press, 2008.

Mathijs, Ernest and Jamie Sexton. *Cult Cinema: An Introduction*. Oxford: Wiley-Blackwell, 2011.
McCann, Ben. 'Pierced Bodies, Punctured Borders: The Contemporary French Horror Film'. *Australian Journal of French Studies* 45, no. 3 (2008): 225–37.
Miska, Brad. '[Review] Brutal "Martyrs" is Immensely Uncomfortable'. *Bloody Disgusting*, 27 April 2009. Available online at: https://bloody-disgusting.com/reviews/111179/martyrs-v-2/ (accessed 10 January 2022).
Navarro, Meagan. 'Hidden Halloween Gem: "Livid" Uses Halloween Folktale Roots for Horror Fairy Tale'. *Bloody Disgusting*, 29 October 2021. Available online at: https://bloody-disgusting.com/movie/3689840/hidden-halloween-gem-livid-uses-halloween-folktale-roots-horror-fairy-tale/ (accessed 10 January 2022).
Palmer, Tim. *Brutal Intimacy*. Middleton, CT: Wesleyan University Press, 2011.
Quandt, James. 'Flesh and Blood: Sex and Violence in Recent French Cinema'. *Art Forum International* 42, no. 6 (February 2004): 126–32.
Sconce, Jeffery. 'Trashing the Academy: Taste, Excess and an Emerging Politics of Cinematic Style'. *Screen* 36, no. 4 (1995): 371–93.
West, Alexandra. *Films of the New French Extremity: Visceral Horror and National Identity*. Jefferson: McFarland and Company, 2016.
Whittle, Peter. 'Martyrs'. *The Sunday Times*, 29 March 2009. Available online at: https://www.thetimes.co.uk/article/martyrs-93kmrn0w5b2 (accessed 9 June 2022).
Young, Neil. 'Triblinz'. *Neil's Young's Film Lounge*, 2008. Available online at: https://www.jigsawlounge.co.uk/film/reviews/triblinz/ (accessed 10 January 2022).

Filmography

Brotherhood of the Wolf / Le Pacte des loups (2001), [Film] Dir. Christophe Gans, France: Metropolitan Filmexport, Canal+.
Deep in the Woods / Promenons-nous dans le bois (2000), [Film] Dir. Lionel Delplanque, France: Canal+.
Frontier(s) / Frontière(s) (2007), [Film] Dir. Xavier Gens, France / Switzerland: Cartel Productions, BR Films, EuropaCorp.
High Tension / Switchblade Romance / Haute Tension (2003), [Film] Dir. Alexandre Aja, France: Alexandre Films, EuropaCorp.
Inside (2016), [Film] Dir. Miguel Ángel Vivas, Spain / UK / USA / France: Inside Producción, Embankment Films, Grand Piano Productions.
Inside / À l'intérieur (2007), [Film] Dir. Alexandre Bustillo and Julien Maury, France: BR Films, La Fabrique de films.
Livid / Livide (2011), [Film] Dir. Alexandre Bustillo and Julien Maury, France: La Fabrique 2, SND Films, La Ferme! Productions.

Martyrs (2008), [Film] Dir. Pascal Laugier, France: Eskwad, Wild Bunch, TCB Film.

Martyrs (2015), [Film] Dir. Kevin Goetz and Michael Goetz, USA: Blumhouse Productions, The Safran Company, Temple Hill Entertainment.

Raw / Grave (2016), [Film] Dir. Julia Ducournau, France / Belgium / USA: Petit Film, Rouge International, Frakas Productions.

[Rec] (2007), [Film] Dir. Jaume Balagueró, Spain: Castelao Producciones, Filmax.

Satan / Sheitan (2006), [Film] Dir. Kim Chapiron, France: 120 Films, La Chauve Souris, StudioCanal.

Them / Ils (2006), [Film] Dir. David Moreau and Xavier Palud, France / Romania: Eskwas, StudioCanal, Castel Film Romania.

Trouble Every Day (2001), [Film] Dir. Claire Denis, France / Germany / Japan / Luxembourg: ARTE, Arte France Cinéma, Canal+.

12

Vertical violence

Horror cinema's terrible towers

Kev Bickerdike

Introduction

Few buildings have come to symbolize the post-industrial city as much as the high-rise tower. These structures have become connotative of economic growth, technological advancement and industrial progress, and yet at the same time they are representative of problematic social housing solutions. Indeed Kim Duff suggests that 'in many respects, the high rise concentrates the social discontent of the city into the smaller container of the tower block' (2014: 11). As a key visual component of the modernist city, tower blocks have inevitably become part of the cinematic landscape. Often, their presence is simply an element of a wider urban topography; at other times their spatial particularities (the peculiar experience of insularity and seclusion once inside their corridors; their domineering visual aspects) lend themselves to a variety of narrative tensions. Given this propensity for generating spatial tension (both internally and in their external contrast to other structures within the city), tower blocks are well suited to genre narratives. From the industrial futurism of *Metropolis* (Fritz Lang, 1932), the adrenalized thrills of *The Towering Inferno* (John Guillermin, 1974) to the claustrophobic dystopia of *Dredd* (Pete Travis, 2012), tower blocks generate significant tension through their status as antagonistic devices that serve as much more than mere backdrops for narrative events.

This chapter will explore representations of tower blocks within cult horror cinema (and offer ancillary glances at their appearances within cinema at large) and consider how these structures have been used to express cultural ideas and social tensions. After briefly looking at examples from various moments on the cinematic timeline, it will offer three close readings of horror films in which tower blocks are shown to be claustrophobic spaces that foster isolation and internal conflict: Jaume Balagueró and Paco Plaza's *[Rec]* (2007), David Cronenberg's *Shivers* (1975) and James Nunn and Ronnie Thompson's *Tower Block* (2012).

A brief history of tower blocks

Tower blocks have become recognized as symbols of urban growth and the modernist city, in both their commercial and residential forms. In Britain, the latter became a ubiquitous feature of post-war cities and towns; the protruding, concrete masses were designed to replace the dilapidated housing of the Victorian era (or at least the housing designated for working-class residents), and to accommodate the increasing swell of population following the Second World War. The economics involved in creating affordable housing for a growing citizenship meant that concrete would be the preferred material for state sponsored building projects, including schools and public spaces. Partly due to a shortage of traditional building materials, the use of concrete allowed for the rapid manufacture of a variety of structures, and the remote fabrication of various built elements that could be delivered to construction sites where they would be pieced together to form new buildings (Hughes 2022). Many of these structures would come to be recognized as belonging to the architectural style known as Brutalism, a term that was 'coined in the 1950s by architects Peter and Alison Smithson to describe the style of Modern Architecture that was completely stripped of all unnecessary elements' (Kopec and Lord 2010: 448). However, the architects most closely associated with British Brutalism did not strip away these 'unnecessary elements' as an economic concession (regardless of whether the cost effectiveness of their designs ensured their popularity), but rather as an aesthetic decision that very deliberately celebrated the concrete formality of their work.

Clearly, then, the regeneration project that saw the design and implementation of mass re-housing was, initially, the result of creative aesthetics and the sort of forward thinking that was part and parcel of wider welfare state policies. However, what problematized the regeneration project was the fact that these new tower blocks and 'council' estates were not opened up as utopian spaces that would communally house residents from a variety of socio-economic backgrounds (as was their original intention). Tim Tinker, designer of South London's Heygate estate, suggested that 'it was the indexing of potential residents in terms of social deprivation that ensured an increasing bias towards a less homogenous, mainly working-class makeup of populace' (Duff 2014: 56). What this meant, in terms of spatial distribution, was a concentration of residents from the poorest section of society. The housing was affordable, but housing authorities ensured that residents dependent upon help from the welfare state were offered prioritized places within these new forms of communal living, in what amounted to a deliberate act of social separation. The residents of the estates and high-rises had little choice but to live in imposed communities predicated on socio-economic standing.

This stratification written upon architectural space was not always the case with tower block projects in other countries. Nicholas Dagen Bloom suggests that within New York City, tower block tenants were less stigmatized than their British counterparts, because the city's 'public housing projects' were 'similar in appearance to many middle-income housing projects' (2012: 419). However, public housing towers in both the United Kingdom and the United States suffered from high incidences of crime, partly because the secluded nature of the towers resulted in them often becoming 'microenvironments of poverty and crime' (Goetz 2011: 269). There followed a trend within both countries wherein some towers that had formerly housed social housing tenants were gentrified, in the belief that mixed-income living arrangements would have an aspirational effect on lower income residents. The truth of the matter is that the increased housing prices that gentrification inevitably brings would price out many tenants, ensuring that a homogenized group of more affluent tenants would come to occupy these particular spaces.

Towers on film

Cinematic representations of tower blocks have tended to engage with the ideological complexities that the structures have come to embody; symbols of architectural and social progress; metaphors for apparent social degradation; representations of isolation and exclusion. *Metropolis* spatializes its class system in terms of a confluence between social and capital standing and access to elevated architecture. The same is true of *Blade Runner* (Ridley Scott, 1982), where the powerful industrialist Eldon Tyrell (Joel Turkell) lives within a huge pyramid that dominates the Los Angeles skyline and serves to symbolize his wealth and influence. George Romero's *Land of the Dead* (2005) even has this social stratification survive into its post-zombie-apocalypse landscape; while the cataclysmic nature of the zombie apocalypse might be expected to sweep away ideas of class structure, the scarcity of food and security enables those who are able to afford these essentials to enjoy a better quality of life, living as they do within Fiddler's Green, a lavish high-rise tower, while those who pragmatically gather the food and provide the security on their behalf live at ground level in squalid camps. Romero explicitly illustrates the ways in which power, via capital, is encoded into space, through the use of the tower block as a gated community.

Romero had earlier explored the problem of close-quarters communal living, this time through the demonization of the residents of a low-rise apartment block, within his seminal zombie film *Dawn of the Dead* (1978). The film is more readily associated with the space of the indoor shopping mall but, after introducing the state of play within a TV studio, the film offers some social commentary via the space of the low-rise apartment block. A SWAT team have surrounded a building where members of a Latino community have gathered together in order to resist both being transferred to refugee sites (the TV broadcast states that citizens are no longer permitted to occupy private residences) and to prevent the removal of their dead. This act of spatial resistance is borne out of a need to collectively affirm a group identity. Tim Cresswell states that 'place is a kind of "necessary social construction" – something we have to construct in order to be human' (2015: 51) and the forcible removal of the residents from their collective space disenfranchises and dehumanizes them, even if it is presented as a necessary police act that is not discriminatory. This latter idea is problematized when one SWAT member, Wooley (Jim Baffico), repeatedly offers racist caveats and demonstrates a peculiar spatial envy when he states, 'how the hell can we stick these lowlife bastards in these big-ass fancy hotels anyway? Shit, man, this is better than I got'. Wooley's spatial resentment is linked to ideologies of prejudice. What is it that he resents? Is it the unified sense of community within the building? Wooley's racism fails to recognize the importance of the expression of a collective cultural identity on the part of the Latino group, precisely because the collective identity of his own group (white Americans) is ubiquitously expressed on every level in such a way as to be systemically invisible.

It is difficult, then, to view the assault on the apartment block as anything but an act of state violence against a minority group, and the resistance by this group must consequently be viewed as a protection of both a collective, and autonomous identity, and the space in which that identity can exist. Indeed, this idea is visually expressed inasmuch as the first zombies that we see are deceased members of this group, housed in the basement of the building. As the police gain entry to this lower level and break away the boards separating the living from the dead, a mass of undead arms surge forward to grasp the invading authority figures, wrestling away their guns and literally disarming the representatives of the state in what is a struggle for spatial occupation. In having its first zombies be drawn from this group, the film suggests a demonization (on the part of the authorities) and disempowering of apartment block tenants and especially those from minority groups. These tenants refuse to submit either culturally or spatially to the police, and their resistance challenges the conflation of people and place that is imposed upon apartment blocks and other spaces where social control is practised.

Stanley Kubrick's *A Clockwork Orange* (1971), like Anthony Burgess's source novel (1962) before it, is seemingly scathing of the concrete environment and the generation who have grown up among its looming towers and tenebrous underpasses. The tower in which the film's protagonist Alex (Malcolm McDowell) lives resembles a municipal building, inasmuch as there is little that immediately marks it as a domestic space. Indeed, the high-rise aesthetic often led to this visual ambiguity because of the lack of ornamentation the buildings displayed, and because of the newness of the form; the break from traditional structures meant that the buildings were recognized as being avant-garde constructs far more than they were viewed as being functioning hospitals, residences or office blocks. Inside the lobby of Alex's building there is a mural that seems to depict various people working together, in the style of classical art, which has been modified by local youths to include crude slogans and puerile depictions of genitalia. The mural gestures towards the socialist thinking that saw the creation of the welfare state, and the construction of the new concrete forms of living spaces, and indeed it suggests the state art of the Soviet Union and East Germany. The subversion of the artwork signifies the lack of investment in the idea on the part of those who have grown up in this concrete environment and suggests a failure on the part of the state to maintain its initial altruism. The degeneration of these living spaces, un-homely as they seem to be, reveals a corresponding atrophy of the communities that have been forcibly confined within these structures, and indeed the film suggests the idea that the family unit is fundamentally threatened by the spatial configuration of the tower block, dependent as it is upon state intervention and social control.

Roman Polanski's *Rosemary's Baby* (1968) uses the claustrophobia of its New York apartment block setting to great effect, inasmuch as there is a pervading sense of isolation throughout the film that suggests a paradox present within communal forms of living; residents live within tightly formed spatial arrangements that *should* foster increased social bonds, and yet there is a tendency to retreat into one's own space and to limit contact with others. Because of the reduced opportunities for movement that Rosemary (Mia Farrow) has access to, she is subject to both surveillance and control from her Satanist neighbours. Polanski had previously explored this specific phenomenon in *Repulsion* (1965), where the central character (Catherine Deneuve) suffers from a form of delirium that results from her isolation within a low-rise apartment block that is set in London, and she subsequently develops a mistrust of her fellow tenants because of this. And a similar scenario would subsequently be explored in Polanski's later film, *The Tenant* (*Le locataire*, 1976). Here Trelkovsky (Roman Polanski) is increasingly troubled by paranoid delusions after moving into an old apartment block in Paris. Within all three films, isolation and reduced access to space is figured as a loss of control and personal agency that engenders horror via the splintered states of mind that the protagonists duly suffer.

Bernard Rose's *Candyman* (1992) explores the effects of gentrification and the 'whitening' of socially deprived housing projects within Chicago's Cabrini Green, an infamously crime plagued district. Similar to Polanski's films, *Candyman* demonstrates the sense of claustrophobia and surveillance that is found within low- and high-rise forms of living, but where Rosemary was subject to paranoia and reduced personal movement, Cabrini Green's mostly Black tenants are subject to far more explicit forms of horror through the threat of violence from drug gangs and the fear of the mythical Candyman (Tony Todd). The drug gangs control the tower blocks' communal spaces and exert a ubiquitous threat of reprisals against anyone speaking out against them while Candyman can exert his supernatural powers within the blocks' communal and private spaces. It is significant that the police only take action against the gangs when they target a white graduate student (Virginia Madsen) who is exploring the mythology of Candyman for her PhD.

The remainder of this chapter will focus on three close readings of films from within the horror genre, providing an examination of the ways in which they use tower blocks to generate horror and express ideas relating to isolation, class stratification and identity.

[Rec]

Jaume Balagueró and Paco Plaza's Spanish production *[Rec]* generates significant spatial tension and horror through its greatly exaggerated representation of the conflicts that arise when people share the communal space of an apartment block. The two factors that markedly contribute to the film's sense of unease are the ways in which the tenants of the block share a cloying familiarity due to their habitational proximity, and the isolation that results from the particular spatial configuration found within tower blocks. The film was one of many that drew influence from *28 Days Later*'s (Danny Boyle, 2002) viral dystopia narrative; itself influenced greatly by both George A. Romero's *Dawn of the Dead* and the novel that influenced Romero's zombie mythos, Richard Matheson's *I Am Legend* (1954). The narrative follows a TV film crew who are accompanying a fire service team, answering an emergency call in an apartment building. Central to *[Rec]*'s story is the idea of a contagion that is spread incredibly rapidly and locks anyone it infects into a state of murderous rage. Dahlia Schweitzer suggests that within outbreak narratives, 'fear of infection makes one especially aware of the distance between bodies, making a suspected carrier feel uncomfortably close. Metaphorical lines are drawn between those who are not infected and those who are deemed infectious or more likely to be infectious' (2018: 48). Because of the increased proximity resulting from the apartment block's spatial organization, the building's tenants are hyper-aware of their potential exposure to infection once the viral threat becomes apparent. They congregate in the building's main foyer not only to wait for the emergency services, but also to separate the hygienic from the infected and the potentially infected and there is significant tension because of the reduced ability to create space between the healthy and unhealthy bodies present. However, it becomes clear that there are also pre-existing lines of division that are based not on health concerns but on social and cultural factors.

It transpires that the initial emergency call related to an elderly tenant who was apparently behaving in an erratic way, and a police officer attending the scene tells the fire crew that 'the neighbours say she's really weird'. It is not unreasonable to suggest that *any* community exercises similar judgements in terms of members of their spatial group, but with the increased proximity of apartment and tower block living comes an exaggerated sense of observation and judgement, and the corresponding degrees of inclusivity and exclusivity that result from those determinations. This elderly woman is therefore treated with far more suspicion and discrimination because the space she occupies overlaps so greatly with that of the other residents; in a neighbourhood that contains individually partitioned properties, the residents can simply lock their doors and observe others from the safety of their own singular homes, whereas those living in apartment blocks are continually forced to navigate shared spaces. The same hyperbolized judgement is exercised upon a Chinese family living in the building. Once the elderly woman's behaviour is identified as having resulted from a viral threat, the residents start to turn on each other and some are quick to suggest that the virus originated from the Chinese family. The argument is that the family have unhygienic habits; one resident complains that the family 'eat raw fish . . . they always leave the door open', but the issue seems to be that the family are culturally and linguistically separated out from the Spanish members of the community. Again, this sort of xenophobia undoubtedly exists within any community that is dominated by one particular ethnic group, but within the apartment block those prejudices are surely heightened because of spatial compression.

Edward Krupat observes that urban spatial arrangements engender a 'close physical proximity, coupled with great social distance, (that) gives rise to a sense of loneliness, nervous tension, and mutual irritation' (1985: 51). Apartment and tower blocks facilitate a peculiar paradoxical sense of isolation; while the clustering of so many tenants into a single building should, theoretically, foster an increased sense of community, that commonality is somewhat imposed upon the collective, and the particular spatial design of such buildings means that residents are essentially locked away within separated dwelling units. Apartment blocks may have windows that look out onto the larger town or city, but the doors to their properties effectively shut out the rest of the building and isolate individual apartments. To an extent, it is necessary to exercise a degree of separation from other urban residents because, as Fran Tonkiss suggests, 'refusing interaction is not . . . merely a matter of social withdrawal but is instead a primary condition for urban social life, securing individual calm together with relative social peace' (2015: 11).

However, apartment and tower blocks, more than other spaces within the city that enable a greater degree of personal space, lack the truly public spaces that are found within housing estates and streets, and any co-mingling necessarily takes place in shared corridors and foyers which are designed to be transitory and functional areas rather than social spaces. Interestingly, Schweitzer argues that while 'isolation always exists in contemporary society . . . (infectious) outbreaks enhance this existing isolation with fears' (2018: 93). *[Rec]* exaggerates the isolating factors that are inherent within tower block forms of living to amplify the sense of tension and horror that results from the personal danger experienced by the apartment block's residents. Coupled with this internalized segregation is a wider sense of separation from the world outside of the apartment block. This latter factor is viewed as either a positive or a negative state, depending on the nature of the community living within an apartment or tower block. As Constance Smith and Saffron Woodcraft suggest, 'vertical isolation of elites is assumed to be a voluntary self-cocooning, while the isolation of public tower block residents is taken as a form of state-sanctioned segregation in "sink estates"' (2020: 6). While *[Rec]*'s apartment block seems to house fairly middle-class tenants, and bears no signs of aesthetic or structural degradation, it and the tenants within are quickly deemed to be potentially biohazardous threats, and therefore kept at a distance from the healthy city and its, presumably, healthy citizens.

Because of the presence of a contagion within the building, it has a hazardous status inferred upon it and its residents, as extensions of the building, share that status. Within outbreak and zombie narratives, Schweitzer suggests that 'there is a constant emphasis on the need to barricade, to isolate and protect in order to keep others at bay. This arguably reflects our anxiety over our inability to contain things' (2018: 162). As noted earlier, this urge to protect the healthy from the unhealthy is seen in the way that the tenants congregate in the building's main foyer, in order to create some distance between themselves and the tenant who is behaving erratically. But there is a further and more severe separation enforced by the city authorities once the contagion is identified. The building is placed under house arrest, and this political and judicial barrier is enforced via armed police officers and a biohazard team. This act of separation by the city's authorities is little different to the way in which the residents of the building socially include or exclude each other on the basis of shared cultural practices. But it is also an exaggeration of the ways in which tower block residents are routinely viewed as a totalized group: any negative qualities that are assumed to be endemic of that type of communal habitation are routinely reasoned to be shared by *all* residents of such a community. In this sense, individual blocks can be viewed as being units of social standing, in much the same way that distinct areas within any town or city are invested with socio-economic status due to the value of local properties, and the overarching class standing of the people residing within them.

If, as Schweitzer suggests, there is an anxiety concerning our 'inability to contain things' (2018: 162), then *[Rec]* demonstrates spatial horror in the form of containment justification, insofar as the city authorities isolate the apartment block's residents because of the wider health threat that they pose. *[Rec]* shows the ability of the authorities to both culturally and physically exercise this level of containment and exaggerates the trauma of this disconnection in order to generate its particular take on spatial tension and horror.

Shivers

David Cronenberg's Canadian film *Shivers* was released in the same year as J.G. Ballard's novel *High-Rise* (1975), and there is much that connects the two. Both stories concern an exclusive residential tower block, advertised as a revolutionary living space that takes care of all of its residents' needs, in such a way that the towers become safe retreats from the world at large. Both chronicle the gradual erosion of a veneer of hyper-civility, and the degeneration of behavioural mores. Where Ballard's (1975) novel has internal class conflicts (so befitting a British story) strip away the facade of civility and inspire the tenants to commit cathartic acts of violence upon each other, Cronenberg's film has a monstrous parasite infest his tower's residents with an uncontrollable impulse towards sexual voracity that dissolves the social and spatial barriers that separate the residents of his high-rise.

The film's opening sequence is accompanied by a voice-over, delivering Starliner Towers' advertising pitch which adopts, quite overtly, the language associated with cruise holidays: 'Explore our island paradise, secure in the knowledge that it belongs to you and your fellow passengers alone'. Such language denotes a prestigious experience that is simultaneously inclusive and exclusionary. It flatters the potential buyer, inasmuch as it suggests an attainment of status, but equally important is the intimation that the tower excludes as much as it includes, and the fact that the tower is situated on its own island further separates its inhabitants from the other citizens of Montreal. The language used to advertise the tower is jarring, given that it seeks to sell domestic space and yet alludes to the sales pitch typically associated with high-cost holidays. And therein lies the problem with Starliner Towers; the phrasing of the advertisement, along with the living spaces themselves, suggests a temporary spatial arrangement, rather than the 'irreplaceable centre of significance' that Edward Relph argues is the exemplary quality of the space of the home (1976: 39). The apartments are actually very small and contain the bare minimum living requirements (a tiny bathroom; a cramped kitchen). They are essentially little more than hotel rooms (and perhaps not even as luxurious).

There is little room to entertain, or exercise (although the tower boasts a golf course and tennis court for that purpose), and the reduced living space, along with the tower's complete lack of relational history (it is newly built and situated on its own island) means the tower conforms to Marc Augè's (1995) concept of the non-place. In such a space, the individual is 'relieved of his usual determinants. He becomes no more than what he does or experiences in the role of passenger, customer or driver' (Augè 1995: 83). The residents of Starliner Towers do indeed more closely resemble passengers or guests when the lack of opportunity for individualism (that results from the homogenous spatial arrangement of their apartments), and the tower's claim to provide everything its residents require (thus prescribing so much of their behaviour in doing so) are taken into account. One imagines that had the residents chosen to buy more conventional properties within the city, they would have access to more space, more privacy and the opportunity to express their individuality upon their living spaces. As it is, the residents of Starliner Towers are subject to the same spatial compression that plagues those within Ballard's novel. They may be able to claim membership of the exclusive tower, but that membership is cloistering.

The residents clearly enjoy the interactions they share, demonstrating familiarity with each other and conversing in the tower's grounds and even in the waiting room of the medical centre (the fact that the tower *has* its own medical facilities reinforces the idea that it wants to fulfil as many of the tenant's needs as possible). Regardless of the congeniality of these exchanges, though, they more closely resemble the sorts of conversations that could take place in any shared space within the city, rather than within a domestic sphere. That is, there is an element of distance to them, of the merely familiar rather than the intimate. The few glimpses we have into the inner lives of the residents demonstrate a lack of the harmony promised by the opening advertisement (revealing the ubiquitous superficiality of advertisements in general) and suggested by the courteous interactions within the tower's shared spaces. A young couple, Nick (Allan Kolman) and Janine (Susan Petrie), go through the motions of domestic life; the wife tries to engage her husband in conversation, but he is distant and disinterested. Janine's single friend, Betts (Barbara Steele), sits alone in her apartment, seemingly suffering from ennui, a wine bottle always at hand. The most extreme subversion of the veneer of harmony occurs within one apartment, where an elderly doctor strangles a young woman, slices open her abdomen, pours in acid and then cuts his own throat. It is later revealed that this sudden and jarring sequence details an attempt to eliminate a genetically engineered parasite that locks its host into a permanent state of sexual arousal.

The parasite has already found hosts in several of the tower's male residents, who have all been infected through sexual contact with the young woman. These men then go on to either directly transmit the parasite to others, or else expel the phallus-like parasites from their bodies. Once expelled, the parasites are able to find and infect other residents and the communal plumbing that links the tower's apartments aids them in this regard, leading to some scenes of truly visceral horror. As more and more tenants become infected, the behavioural boundaries that enable the residents to experience some limited separation from one another are violently broken down, as the infected attack the uninfected and forcefully engage them in sexual contact. The spatial compression that results from living in such close proximity to others enables the infected to rapidly move around the building, now no longer conscious or mindful of the barriers that civility insists be observed and, in some cases, literally tearing down the walls and doors that physically separate the private spaces of apartments and the shared hallways. The end result of the mass infection is that the surface level bonds that connect the residents, predicated as they are on economic status, social separation from the wider idea of the city and a carefully managed distance between one another are violently stripped away and replaced by a hugely exaggerated intimacy that is based on a lascivious merging of the flesh.

Tower Block

While *High-Rise* and *Shivers* suggest that tower blocks have the potential to become vertically figured gated communities, James Nunn and Ronnie Thompson's 2012 offering *Tower Block* embodies the other side of the argument. This British film suggests that tower blocks have the potential to become as problematic as the previous forms of housing they were designed to replace if investment in the infrastructure of the buildings themselves, and the lives of the people who reside within them, is not maintained. While it would be a stretch to suggest that the film's narrative is hugely nuanced, it does manage to avoid a scathingly clichéd representation of the working-class residents within its titular structure and addresses the negative labelling that is levelled at both high-rise residents and social housing tenants more generally.

The film opens with a young man being chased through a largely deserted tower block, banging on doors to find help. He is eventually caught by his pursuers, two masked men, who administer a fatal beating, but not before one of the residents, a young woman named Becky (Sheridan Smith), attempts to help him but is herself assaulted in the process. The narrative then picks up a few months later, after a fruitless endeavour by a frustrated detective (Steven Cree) to get the tenants to make statements, and a property development company are shown discussing their attempts to get rid of the tower block's last few tenants so they can get on with demolishing the block and gentrifying the area. The building's tenants, then, are viewed as being both uncooperative by the police, and as hindrances to the pursuit of profit by private investors. This demonization of the tenants is made more explicit when a gunman starts to pick off the residents though the windows of their flats, and this marksman is later revealed to be the detective investigating the death of the young man within the tower block.

In the eyes of the property development company, the residents of the tower block are subject to two processes of reductionism: they are viewed as inconveniently slowing down the gentrification process and implicitly viewed as being unsuitable residents for the intended new building. Furthermore, both the property development company and the police subject the residents of the tower block to a totalizing gaze that uniformly attributes them with a tendency towards deviancy and criminality. There is an irony here insofar as tower blocks were adopted as a solution to the inadequate housing situation that saw millions of working-class Britons living in unhygienic homes (Grindrod 2013: 3), and yet these buildings have often become dangerous spaces to live in, due to inadequate investment in their infrastructure and a failure to adequately address the social problems that often occur within them.

A further irony is the fact that older forms of housing were cleared to make way for the new concrete towers and council estates, often resulting in the erasure of communal ties. While the new form of housing was largely viewed in positive terms by those taking up places within tower blocks, their construction involved the dispersal of communities that had to adapt to new forms of collective living (Grindrod 2013: 48). This process is repeated wherever tower blocks that are deemed unfit for habitation purposes are demolished or gentrified, and the communities that have coalesced around their shared spatial ties are dissipated yet again. Tower blocks that were designed to provide affordable housing for large numbers of mainly working-class tenants are completely demolished to make way for higher rent, and therefore higher status, buildings. As Stephen Graham suggests, 'very often . . . the processes through which new housing towers are constructed amount to programmes of engineered gentrification' which 'forcibly evict or sweep away the remnants of earlier periods where housing was at least to some extent organised collectively based on criteria of social need' (2016: 178). Instead, what is left is a marked division of spatial separation that is demarcated on lines of financial resources. There is little wonder, then, that the residents of the tower block in Nunn and Thompson's film find little commonality, given their proximity is based not on choice, or cultural simpatico, but rather on the basis of fiscal limitations.

A more immediately threatening position is the way in which the residents are uniformly viewed as being delinquent. Certainly, there is a pronounced element of antisocial behaviour within the tower, but any resistance to this criminality would require a strong sense of unity on the part of the other residents. Unfortunately, because the tenants are a fractured group, mingling only when they share an elevator or pass each other in their shared hallways, there is a lack of collective identity and communal action to be found here. Indeed the building is subject to a protection racket, orchestrated by a young man named Curtis (Jack O'Connell), who collects money from each resident on a weekly basis, to guarantee their homes are not subject to theft or criminal damage. However, once the gunman has begun his assault on the building and the tenants within, the residents retreat into the relative safety of their shared hallway, where they find themselves rapidly forming a communal identity in order to make sense of their situation. This coming together allows them to resist Curtis's bullying and uncover the fact that two of the tower block's residents were responsible for the young man's death and the ensuing assault on the building. The fact that such unity could not happen earlier is reflective of how splintered the tenants are, and how their well-being is neglected by both the housing authorities and the police.

The gunman views the tower block's tenants as being complicit in the death of the young man, either through direct action (the fact is that two of the residents *were* responsible for the young man's death) or through their failure to either protect the victim or assist the police with their enquiries. At the end of the film, as the gunman is subdued by Becky and two other residents, she angrily says 'you murdered a load of innocent people, for nothing' to which he replies 'Innocent? Those fucking scumbags murdered him. You should've helped him! None of you would talk so the killers got away with it. Where's the fucking justice?' The gunman's point of view echoes a larger reactionary opinion that is directed, in a more generalized manner, towards social housing tenants and the spaces in which they live. Just as the authorities within *[Rec]* applied a totalizing gaze onto the residents of that film's apartment block, *Tower Block*'s gunman, symbolic of the judgemental gaze exercised by those who comment upon the social problems occurring within tower blocks and estates, refuses to acknowledge any notion of the factors at play that mean the residents are unable to actively resist the criminal behaviour occurring within their space, and are unable to help the police because of the threat of reprisals. This attitude ensures that the gunman is ultimately coded as a monstrous figure, who views the tower's residents as being unredeemable, and therefore justifiable targets for his anger.

Conclusion

Tower blocks continue to express ideas of class stratification; from their beginnings as a means of saving millions of people from slum housing, to the recognition that maintaining the structures required a heavy financial commitment on the part of local authorities, to the contemporary practice of gentrifying former social housing buildings, pricing apartments well out of the reach of those who would previously have found themselves living in these cities in the sky. Given the social tensions resulting from the changing use of towers, and the spatial tension the looming structures impose upon the urban landscape, it is surprising how few films make them the centre of their narratives and especially films from within the horror genre, where spatial tension is an effective means of generating fear, anxiety and terror.

The films examined throughout this chapter demonstrate how effectively these concrete monoliths express concerns that arise from prolonged exposure to the built environment, and the anxieties that stem from living among potentially overwhelming numbers of urban residents. For many people, high-rise living is antithetical to the idea of community, but while the spatial configurations the towers offer are non-traditional, communities do nevertheless coalesce wherever groups of people share space. And the *fear* of a loss of community and a dispossession of personal territory is sufficiently present to enable an exaggeration of these concerns to imbue a film's narrative with a wealth of tensions. Given the fact that tower blocks remain a key component of our cities, it might be prudent for filmmakers to utilize their unique (and often terrifying) presence to their fullest more often.

Bibliography

Augé, Marc. *Non-Places: Introduction to an Anthology of Supermodernity*. London: Verso, 1995.

Bloom, Nicholas Dagen. 'Learning from New York'. *Journal of the American Planning Association* 78, no. 4 (2020): 418–31.

Burgess, Anthony. *A Clockwork Orange*. London: William Heinemann, 1962.

Cresswell, Tim. *Place: An Introduction*. Chichester: Blackwell, 2015.

Duff, Kim. *Contemporary British Literature and Urban Space: After Thatcher*. Basingstoke: Palgrave Macmillan, 2014.

Goetz, Edward G. 'Where Have All the Towers Gone? The Dismantling of Public Housing in U.S. Cities'. *Journal of Urban Affairs* 33, no. 3 (2012): 267–87.

Graham, Stephen. *Vertical: The City from Satellites to Bunkers*. London: Verso, 2016.

Grindrod, John. *Concretopia: A Journey Around the Rebuilding of Postwar Britain*. London: Old Street Publishing, 2013.

Hughes, Nicky. 'A Brief History of Reinforced Concrete Buildings'. *The Historic England Blog*, 22 September 2022. Available online at: https://heritagecalling.com/2022/09/22/a-brief-history-of-reinforced-concrete-buildings-in-england/ (accessed 6 April 2023).

Kopec, Dak and Natalie Lord. 'Scares of Communism: Architectural and Design Remnants of an Ideology'. *Space and Culture* 13, no. 4 (2010): 436–454.

Krupat, Edward. *People in Cities: The Urban Environment and its Effects*. Cambridge: Cambridge University Press, 1985.

Matheson, Richard. *I Am Legend*. New York: Gold Medal Books, 1954.

Relph, Edward. *Place and Placelessness*. London: Pion, 1976.

Schweitzer, Dahlia. *Going Viral: Zombies, Viruses, and the End of the World*. New Brunswick: Rutgers University Press, 2018.

Smith, Constance and Saffron Woodcraft. 'Introduction: Tower Block "Failures"? High-Rise Anthropology'. *Focaal: Journal of Global and Historical Anthropology* 86 (2020): 1–10.

Tonkiss, Fran. *Space, the City and Social Theory: Social Relations and Urban Forms*. Cambridge: Polity Press, 2015.

Filmography

A Clockwork Orange (1971), [Film] Dir. Stanley Kubrick, UK: Warner Bros.

Blade Runner (1982), [Film] Dir. Ridley Scott, USA: Warner Bros.

Candyman (1992), [Film] Dir. Bernard Rose, USA / UK: PolyGram Filmed Entertainment / Propaganda Films / Candyman Films.

Dawn of the Dead (1978), [Film] Dir. George A. Romero, USA: United Film Distribution Group.

Dredd (2012), [Film] Dir. Pete Travis, UK: Entertainment Film Distributors.
Land of the Dead (2005), [Film] Dir. by George A. Romero, USA: Universal Pictures.
Metropolis (1932), [Film] Dir. Fritz Lang, Germany: Parufamet.
[Rec] (2007), [Film] Dir. Jaume Balagueró and Paco Plaza, Spain: Casteleo.
Repulsion (1965), [Film] Dir. Roman Polanski, UK: Compton Films / Tekli British Productions.
Rosemary's Baby (1968), [Film] Dir. Roman Polanski, USA: William Castle Productions.
Shivers (1975), [Film] Dir. David Cronenberg, Canada: Cinépix Film Properties.
The Tenant (Le locataire, 1976), [Film] Dir. Roman Polanski, France: Marianne Productions / World Wonder Ring Stardom.
Tower Block (2012), [Film] Dir. James Nunn and Ronnie Thompson, UK: Earth Star Entertainment.
The Towering Inferno (1974), [Film] Dir. John Guillermin, USA: 20th Century Fox.
28 Days Later (2022), [Film] Dir. Danny Boyle, UK: Fox Searchlight Pictures.

13

The Investigative Outsider and the use of *Nemein* as a narrative state change driver in cult horror cinema

James Shelton

Introduction

This chapter will explore the way in which selected cult horror texts generate terror through the employment of both the archetype of the 'investigative outsider' (Rigby 2000: 209) and the concept of *nemein* – the 'due portion required to restore the equilibrium of the cosmic order when it had been imbalanced' (Booker 2004: 329) – in their role as change drivers that alter narrative states. To undertake this analysis the chapter utilizes a narrative framework put forward by Todorov (1969) referred to as the 'minimal complete plot':

> The minimal complete plot can be seen as the shift from one equilibrium to another. This term 'equilibrium,' which I am borrowing from genetic psychology, means the existence of a stable but not static relation between the members of a society; it is a social law, a rule of the game, a particular system of exchange. The two moments of equilibrium, similar and different, are separated by a period of imbalance, which is composed of a process of degeneration and a process of improvement. (1969: 5)

As this chapter will explore, Todorov's (1969) framework serves as the basis for an exploration of narrative agency and the role of retribution as a narrative change driver. Within this analysis 'Similar Equilibrium' is used here to identify the state of the narrative at the beginning of a film and 'Different Equilibrium' is then identified as the state of the narrative at its end. The period of 'Imbalance' represents the events and/or actions taken that effect the transition of a film narrative between Similar Equilibrium and Different Equilibrium states. As such, this analysis is centred on the concept of two sets of change drivers – those that effect the transition between Similar Equilibrium and Imbalance and those that facilitate the transition between Imbalance and Different Equilibrium – the latter being the different, newer state of narrative equilibrium found at the close of the film.

Nemein and the Investigative Outsider

The position this chapter takes is that the protagonists of the four selected cult horror texts – *The Wicker Man* (Robin Hardy, 1973), *Apostle* (Gareth Evans, 2018), *The Guest* (Adam Wingard, 2014) and *Last Night in Soho* (Edgar Wright, 2021) – conform to the archetype of the Investigative Outsider and, in turn, believe that it is their responsibility to allot the 'due portion' to the antagonists of their narrative. This is based on the concept of the Greek mythological Goddess whose name is drawn from the same root word (*Nemesis*; Νεμεσις), whose role within the Greek pantheon was to maintain equilibrium and to rectify excesses caused by either an excess of luck (personified by Tyche, Τύχη) or acts of hubris. As this chapter will analyse, a key characteristic of the Investigative Outsider is that they believe it is their role to punish hubris or repair a state of equilibrium damaged by nefarious forces. As this chapter will then establish, the generic conventions of the horror film mean that this desire is sometimes frustrated, often with self-damaging consequences. This idea of hubris is initially drawn from a definition identified by Ronfeldt, who describes the concept in the following terms:

> hubris is the capital sin of pride, and thus the antithesis of two ethics that the Greeks valued highly: aidos (humble reverence for law) and sophrosyne (self-restraint, a sense of proper limits). (1994: 2)

Ronfeldt identifies a number of hubristic qualities, such as 'overweening pride', 'arrogance', 'insolence' and – crucially for the purposes of this chapter – the 'overstepping [of] boundaries' (1994: 2). When discussing the concept of nemesis, Kershaw refers to 'a mechanical, nonmoral principle of equilibrium whose disturbance . . . must be restored by compensatory acts' (1986: Sections 4:6–4:7). When such a disturbance occurs, 'nemesis does not rest until the right proportion on which the world order depends is re-established' (Kershaw 1986: Sections 4:6–4:7). As such, the four films analysed within this chapter have been selected on the basis that in the first instance they exhibit this specific set of interactions with the concept of narrative equilibrium and, concurrently, the selected narratives also evidence the specific nature of retribution that has been outlined and will be referred to by reference to the concept of *nemein*.

Previous work (Shelton 2020, 2022, 2023) has identified the way in which narratives apportion the responsibility for the first status change – from Similar Equilibrium to Imbalance – to the antagonist of the narrative. In this form the responsibility for the transition from Imbalance to a new or Different state of equilibrium is then apportioned to the protagonist; in effect, the antagonist creates a problem which the protagonist must then 'fix'. During this a process occurs by which the narrative agency of the antagonist wanes while that of the protagonist waxes. However, the concept of 'power parity' – a concept recently advanced by Shoard (2021) – becomes important as, within the four narratives selected for analysis, the narrative agency of the protagonist is in fact inconstant and unstable, often providing, in and of itself, a source of terror. For Shoard (2021), the concept of power parity refers to the ability of other characters within a narrative to take on narrative agency – a scenario most notably seen within the recent James Bond film *No Time to Die* (Cary Fukunaga, 2021), in which the actions of the female characters Madeleine Swann (Léa Seydoux) and Nomi (Lashana Lynch) directly affect the film's narrative progression. For the purpose of this analysis agency is therefore defined as the ability of characters within a narrative to have a direct impact on the transitioning between the different narrative states outlined earlier. However, the films selected for analysis here are particularly noteworthy because it is the process by which the Investigative Outsider experiences an unexpected deterioration of their agency that constitutes a major source of terror.

Equally, while the protagonist in their role as an Investigative Outsider may believe that they have the responsibility for 'solving' the problem posed to them, the horror in the narratives selected for analysis here is also derived in large part from the realization that this is not actually the case. At the same time the selected texts exhibit a specific trait of psychological horror identified by Selbo: in these specific narratives the audience feels 'that just under the outward appearances of ordinariness evil exists and causes havoc where peace and rationality were the norm' (2015: 60). Over and above this, the psychological horror film leads to a state wherein

> The evil force is taking a mental toll on its victim, usually creating a great sense of paranoia, distrust, fear of the unknown or demise of the spirit. Psychological horror films go beyond merely the demise of the flesh. . . . In a psychological

horror narrative, the excess may be in constant and accelerating paranoia and/ or sense of entrapment. . . . The horror genre features a villain who is not a straightforward antagonist but an agent of an excessively deep and dark evil force focused on an excessively malevolent goal with no possibility of a change of heart. (Selbo 2015: 128–9)

Selbo argues that many psychological horror films 'do not focus on body count'; they instead focus on 'the dissolution of peace of mind and relationships due to evil intent or action' and scenarios that lead to the slow erosion of the 'status quo' (2015: 128-9), and this is true of the films selected for analysis here.

Neale notes that the presence of this type of narrative within the horror genre

tends to be marked by a search for that discourse, that specialised form of knowledge which will enable the human characters to comprehend and to control that which simultaneously embodies and causes its 'trouble'. (1980: 22)

The Wicker Man, *Apostle*, *The Guest* and *Last Night in Soho* evidence both the usage of the archetype of the Investigative Outsider and states of Similar Equilibrium where the erosion of the *status quo* has already begun. In each narrative an outsider enters a community with the aim of investigating the nature of the shift in equilibrium and with the purpose of facilitating the shift from the state of Imbalance to a newer, Different state of narrative equilibrium. In each of the selected films, this is unsuccessful – or if there is success, it comes at a terrible price. While the protagonist may believe it is their moral or legal duty to investigate the state of Imbalance and facilitate the change to the next state of equilibrium, they find that their narrative agency waxes and ultimately wanes. At the same time, the distinctive nature of these narratives is that their horror is drawn from a recognition by the protagonist that they have both overstepped their boundaries and have at the same time stepped outside of what they recognize to be their own moral frameworks. They enter a state – akin to the one described by Crane – wherein

all collective action will fail; knowledge and experience have no value when one is engaged with the horrible; and the destruction of the menace (should it occur) carries no guarantee that the future will be safe. (1994: 10)

It is on this basis that the films selected for analysis have been divided into two sections. In the first instance *The Wicker Man* and *Apostle* will be used to draw together a specific understanding of the ways in which the Investigative Outsider acts as a concept within horror narratives. This is undertaken through a recognition that narrative agency is the primary issue – and that a shift of this agency precipitates the move towards explicit horror in narrative terms. Having established a narrative model in which the deterioration of the protagonist's agency is a key element, the second set of films selected for discussion – *The Guest* and *Last Night in Soho* – are then used to further interrogate this model.

The Wicker Man and *Apostle*

The narrative of *The Wicker Man* concerns the investigation into the disappearance of Rowan Morrison (Geraldine Cowper), a young girl on the remote island of Summerisle, by Sergeant Howie (Edward Woodward). As Sergeant Howie continues his investigation he discovers that the islanders have adopted a religion based around the Celtic gods – something that proves to be at direct odds with Howie's Christian faith. Howie grows increasingly unsettled with not only the beliefs and practices of the islanders but with their tendency to obfuscate and dissemble when questioned on the status of Rowan. When Howie eventually meets with Lord Summerisle (Christopher Lee) a debate about comparative religion ensues in which Summerisle makes it clear that the islanders firmly believe that 'the old gods aren't dead'.

Howie believes that it is his responsibility to allot *nemein* to those responsible for the disappearance of Rowan, but, at least initially, he is unable to establish whether a crime has actually taken place. The film's initial minimal complete plot fosters an expectation that the Similar Equilibrium to Imbalance transition is precipitated by the disappearance of Rowan, meaning that Howie must then investigate and trigger the Imbalance to Different Equilibrium transition, which under normal narrative circumstances would lead to a new state of equilibrium – one wherein the mystery has been resolved and the perpetrators identified and punished. Equally, as Catterall and Wells state:

> Much of the power of the film lies in the audience's identification with Howie: he is the outsider, the butt of jokes, and the community in the film knows what he does not – that he is doomed. Yet as Howie approaches ever closer to his martyrdom, his intolerant, unerring faith never wavers. (2002: 141)

The Wicker Man fosters a growing sense that Howie's expectation that good morals and Christian practice should be upheld is increasingly hubristic in nature. As the Investigative Outsider Howie believes he has the right – both moral and legal – to investigate the disappearance of Rowan. Howie attempts to justify this in a variety of ways – for example, he reminds Lord Summerisle that he remains 'the subject of a Christian country' regardless of the beliefs that are fostered on his island – but over time a concern for the legal gives way to moral outrage. When the supposed grave of Rowan Morrison is exhumed, Howie finds only the body of a hare. Confronting Summerisle with this, Howie declares, 'I think that Rowan Morrison was murdered under circumstances of Pagan barbarity, which I can scarcely bring myself to believe is taking place in the twentieth century'. Howie then notes that he will return to the mainland to demand a full enquiry.

Following this encounter the horror of *The Wicker Man* transitions to being derived from the slow removal of narrative agency from Howie; he finds that he is unable to return to the mainland and his ongoing investigations are obstructed further by the islanders. More crucially, Howie's investigation is undertaken in the face of a community whose religious beliefs mean that they believe that nothing untoward has occurred. Indeed, Howie is placed in a set of circumstances that chime with Dickstein's observation that

> civilized man, as he grows out of childhood and adolescence, is taught to subdue his fears and superstitions, and to accept the notion that society will protect him. We are told that if we behave with rational self-restraint others will do likewise. But on some level we never really believe this. (1984: 70)

Howie – a Police Sergeant and the embodiment of the law – finds himself within a society that has no active stake in protecting him or in obeying the law, order and morality of which he is the designated representative. It is Howie's firm belief that as the Investigative Outsider he must establish what has happened to Rowan and then allot *nemein* to the offender in the name of the law; however, as there is no hard evidence present to confirm that a crime has actually taken place, Howie then resorts to attempting to apportion a *nemein* based on moral and religious concerns instead. Howie behaves with 'rational self-restraint' at all times but this is something that ultimately proves to be his undoing as it is his status as both a representative of authority and a virgin that makes him a worthy sacrifice.

The narrative of *The Wicker Man* is therefore based on conflicting ideals of hubris. Howie, in representing legal authority, has the right to investigate the disappearance of Rowan based on the report that the police have received. The issue is that Howie, in the conviction of his beliefs, exhibits a righteousness that places him in opposition to the beliefs of the islanders, making him come across

Figure 13.1 *The Wicker Man*: Howie (Edward Woodward) comes across as condescending and arrogant.

as condescending and arrogant (see Figure 13.1). Howie's agency is initially based solely on the precept that the islanders have respect for the law, but his growing sense of religious intolerance – however seemingly justified by the suggestion that Rowan is soon to be sacrificed by Pagans – warps Howie's righteousness. As such Howie's attempts to position himself as nemesis in order to facilitate a transition from Imbalance to a Different Equilibrium based on the legal and moral principles that he embodies actually lead to *him* becoming the sacrifice – albeit one undertaken in the potentially equally hubristic belief of Lord Summerisle that this sacrifice will ensure the return of fertility to the island's apple crops the following year and cement his position as lord of the island. Howie's assertion that the people of Summerisle will turn on Lord Summerisle himself when the sacrifice fails to produce its intended results in a year's time – in turn giving the Lord his due – ultimately offers little comfort to Howie or the viewer.

The Wicker Man therefore embodies the type of horror narrative where the Investigative Outsider evidences the potential agency to undertake an investigation of the circumstances portrayed within the film – only for this agency to slowly be stripped away and apportioned to either an antagonist or positioned as part of a wider breakdown of 'rational self-restraint'.

Apostle engages with similar elements of this formula while altering them in certain dynamic ways. Echoing the central narrative of *The Wicker Man*, *Apostle* concerns the efforts of Thomas Richardson (Dan Stevens) to investigate the kidnapping of his sister, Jennifer (Elen Rhys), by a religious cult who are based on an isolated island. Equally similar are the motivations of the film's cult – they are seeking to restore fertility to the island by appeasing a local deity. Key differences do emerge, however. While Thomas represents the Investigative Outsider he does not represent a legal authority or, necessarily, a religious authority. Indeed, he was once a Christian missionary but an experience during the Boxer Rebellion in China led to the loss of his faith. Equally, while the pagan gods of Summerisle were never directly manifested, the goddess of the island in *Apostle* is explicitly shown as an elderly female form imprisoned within tree roots who, when fed sacrifices in the form of blood, causes the flora of the island to blossom and bloom.

The narrative of *Apostle* also interacts with the concept of hubris in a different manner to *The Wicker Man*. While in both cases the isolated community invites the Investigative Outsider in through their own actions, within *Apostle* this act is portrayed, initially, as being directly related to their need for immediate financial gain. Although the deity of the island – the *genius loci* – must be appeased with ritual sacrifice, the islanders no longer have the financial capacity to purchase animals for this purpose and instead resort to kidnapping Jennifer in order to extort a cash ransom. However, a representative of Thomas's father instructs him not to pay this ransom until Jennifer is verified to be alive.

The Similar Equilibrium to Imbalance transition in the narrative of *Apostle* on one level follows the traditional pattern – that where the transition is manipulated by the actions of the antagonist. However, the authority structure of the island – a religious leader with two subordinates ruling over the wider community – does not hold the same sway as that of Lord Summerisle in *The Wicker Man*; the narrative of *Apostle* diverges from the 'community uniting against the outsider' scenario depicted in *The Wicker Man* when it is revealed that power struggles exist between the leader of the cult, Malcolm Howe (Michael Sheen), and his second-in-command, Quinn (Mark Lewis Jones). Equally, the fertility issues of the island are greater than the single lost harvest season of Summerisle; in *Apostle* the island's crops are toxic and lambs are born deformed, requiring their immediate destruction. Howe, Quinn and – to a seemingly lesser extent – the third of the founders Frank (Paul Higgins) – have become hubristic in believing that they are able to tame a god and force it to keep the land fertile. Their hubris, in turn, has overspilled to the point of inviting outside intervention with their attempt to ransom Jennifer.

Thomas therefore becomes an appropriate agent to effect the Imbalance to Different Equilibrium transition. But while *nemein* may be allotted by him – and

Thomas may be an appropriate agent – narrative and generic constraints suggest that to do so would not necessarily lead to a 'happy ending'. The ultimate descent of the film into visceral horror – rather than purely psychological horror – is precipitated by the hubristic actions of Quinn, actions which ultimately lead to the Imbalance to Different Equilibrium transition over and above the presence and actions of Thomas. This transition is precipitated by the desire of Frank – the third of the founders – to leave the island, thus breaking the partnership of the founders. Frank plans to take his son Jeremy (Bill Milner) and Quinn's daughter Ffion (Kristine Froseth), who is now pregnant by Jeremy, with him.

Before this can occur, however, Quinn discovers Ffion's pregnancy and murders her; Quinn then frames Jeremy for Ffion's death and subsequently kills him during a 'purification ritual'. Quinn commits hubris on a massive scale not only in attempting to seize power from the cult's leader Howe but also in planning to then appease the deity of the island by initiating a regime where ongoing sexual assaults will result in children who will be sacrificed rather than animals. Quinn's rationale is that human sacrifice will be powerful enough to fully ensure the fertility of the island.

Where in *The Wicker Man* Howie loses his agency as an Investigative Outsider, within *Apostle* Thomas retains it, although only to a certain degree. Within both *The Wicker Man* and *Apostle,* however, it is possible to see the ways in which Crane's 'central axes' of horror operate:

> [The] central axes, about which horror now makes itself known, are as follows: All collective action will fail; knowledge and experience have no value when one is engaged with the horrible; and the destruction of the menace (should it occur) carries no guarantee that the future will be safe. (Crane 1994: 10)

While Thomas is able to effect a rescue of his sister he suffers mortal wounds while fighting Quinn to do so. Equally, while Thomas is able to effect the 'destruction of the menace' in burning the deity of the island, the final frames of *Apostle* show that Thomas then assumes the place of the deity, with Howe still present as the cult's leader.

While *The Wicker Man* and *Apostle* do share some common cinematic DNA – as confirmed by Gareth Evans's *Rue Morgue* interview (Gingold 2018) – the key difference is found in the embodiment of nemesis as a narrative change driver. While Howie begins his investigation full of righteousness and transitions to fury, he is denied the role of nemesis. His eventual fate is to be forced into the role of sacrifice in the place of Rowan, who was originally appointed to that role by

Summerisle's wider community of pagans. Thomas, by contrast, embraces the role of nemesis and punishes the hubris of the cult leaders that he encounters; in doing so, however, he dies fighting – even if he then appears to be 'rewarded' for his sacrifice when he is duly assigned the role of the island's new deity. Thomas, as the protagonist of *Apostle* and in taking on the role of nemesis, does indeed manage to reset the equilibrium of the island. However, in both the Similar Equilibrium and Different Equilibrium states of the film's narrative there is a deity present and there is a cult leader present. Thus the actual significance of the outcome presented by the Different Equilibrium state is open to interpretation by the audience.

Both *The Wicker Man* and *Apostle* follow the framework where audience expectations are potentially set by the boundaries of the myth of nemesis outlined by Ronfeldt:

> Hubris above all is what attracted Nemesis, who then retaliated to humiliate and destroy the pretender, often through terror and devastation. Thus she was an agent of destruction. The battle won, she did not turn to constructive tasks of renewal and redemption – that was for others to do. (1994: 3)

Howie, however, is unable to humiliate or destroy Lord Summerisle; Thomas is able to destroy the more malignant elements of the island's cult community as an agent of destruction, but has no agency in relation to renewal or redemption as he dies in the process.

It is in the overlapping of these two areas – the 'central axes' of Crane (1994) and the hubris-nemesis complex of Ronfeldt (1994) – that the horror found in the narratives of *The Wicker Man* and *Apostle* is generated. In both instances the protagonists are Investigative Outsiders with a mission justified by righteousness – legal and Christian in the case of Howie and familial in the case of Thomas. Equally, both protagonists believe that they have the knowledge and the experience needed to successfully undertake their given tasks. Both Howie and Thomas become agents appointed to punish the hubris of the charismatic but antagonistic cult leaders; both agents attempt to effect the Imbalance to Different Equilibrium transition by completing their investigation; both agents die in doing so. The horror in these narratives stems in part from the growing realization on the part of the protagonist – and, by extension, the audience – that, in their efforts to take on the role of the agent of destruction against the horrible, they are becoming increasingly powerless. No matter how effectively their fears and superstitions are subdued (as per Dickstein [1984]) they will neither complete their task nor survive.

The Guest and *Last Night in Soho*

The model outlined so far – that of the Investigative Outsider who believes that they are there to allot *nemein* for perceived crimes or social issues and who then come to realize that they are powerless to effect narrative change – can be applied to the second set of texts selected for this chapter, *The Guest* and *Last Night in Soho*, with the acknowledgement that these films interact with the model in certain key different ways. Within *The Guest* an outsider arrives with the intention of restoring equilibrium for a family whose son has been killed while serving in the US military; in *Last Night in Soho* a student travels from Cornwall to London in the present day and becomes the Investigative Outsider for a murder that seemingly took place in the 1960s. In both cases the model of the Investigative Outsider is significantly altered, and it is the ways in which these alterations result in horror being generated differently that will form the focus of the next section of this chapter.

The narrative of *The Guest* concerns the arrival of David Collins (Dan Stevens) at the home of the Peterson family. David explains that he was friends with and served alongside their son Caleb, who, they were told, died in an engagement in the war in Afghanistan; David now considers it his duty to help the family. The narrative of the film initially portrays David as the Investigative Outsider – one who examines the situation of the Peterson family and seemingly attempts to help them. As such, where the Peterson family are in a state of Imbalance following the death of Caleb, David appears to be the character tasked with effecting the Imbalance to Different Equilibrium transition; the family, having received negative luck, are to be shepherded to a new state of equilibrium. While Nemesis is often considered an 'avenging or punishing divinity' (Atsma 2017) the goddess was responsible for all great injustices in equilibrium; as such the *nemein* of the Peterson family is to receive positive fortune commensurate to their loss. Within the narrative of *The Guest* David is initially represented as the appropriate agent to allot this due portion.

Over time, however, David's attempts to give the family positive outcomes grow increasingly violent and sociopathic. When Luke Peterson (Brendan Meyer) is bullied at school David orchestrates a confrontation with the perpetrators, severely injuring them and intimidating the witnesses into silence. When Luke's father, Spencer Peterson (Leland Orser), complains of being passed over for promotion his manager and their partner are found dead, seemingly having committed suicide by overdose. The boyfriend of Luke's older sister, Anna Peterson (Maika Monroe), is arrested in relation to his involvement in selling drugs but is then accused of the murder of Craig (Joel David Moore) – a friend of Anna's – and

Higgins (Ethan Embry), a local man who had access to guns. But it was David who actually committed the murders. During the course of the narrative it emerges that David is the result of military 'medical experiments' designed to create a soldier with an unwavering dedication to the mission they are tasked with – a dedication that David, on escaping from the program, transfers to the ongoing well-being of the Peterson family. Elements of this are shown during David's interactions with the family; in talking to Luke about bullies, David advises him that killing the bullies and their families is an acceptable course of action.

David represents a problematic form of nemesis in that his actions are initially designed to compensate the Peterson family for their loss and to assist in moving them towards a new equilibrium. The horror in *The Guest* thus stems from the extents to which David goes in order to generate what he perceives to be the best possible outcomes for the family. When Anna begins to investigate David she triggers the intervention of Major Richard Carver (Lance Reddick) of KPG (a fictional private corporation). Carver and a team of mercenaries arrive in town and attempt to neutralize David unsuccessfully; his identity now known, David first kills Luke and Anna's mother, Laura Peterson (Sheila Kelley) and then her husband Spencer. The issue, Carver later explains to Anna, is that David's conditioning has begun to break down under conflicting priorities:

> Major Carver: David has a neurological condition, Miss Peterson. Designed to protect both him and the experiment. If he feels like his identity may be compromised, he – he's programmed to clean up all loose ends. I doubt he could stop himself now even if he wanted to.

Hence it is the eventual inversion of the Investigative Outsider's character and motivations that generates the horror found in *The Guest*. The Petersons initially believe that David is a good person who simply wishes to help them but it is revealed that his actions are merely a symptom of David's sociopathic devotion to his self-appointed mission. David – in his self-appointed role as the apportioner of *nemein* – takes increasingly violent and/or sociopathic actions in order to bring good fortune to the Petersons. But – upon the triggering of his conditioning – this primary objective becomes secondary to his need to eliminate any trace of his identity and presence. Most concerningly, at the conclusion of *The Guest* the 'destruction of the menace' does not occur; David is shown to escape the climactic showdown, limping away in a stolen fireman's uniform. In this respect *The Guest* differs from the model so far discussed in that David retains agency throughout the narrative – but this agency is only allowed in service of the mission to which he has conditioned devotion and, once this is compromised, David's agency transitions entirely to clearing up the evidence of his presence and actions, with fatal consequences.

The Guest's treatment of devotion and the desire of the Investigative Outsider to have the responsibility for effecting the Imbalance to Different Equilibrium transition is shared, in part, by *Last Night in Soho*. Ellie (Thomasin McKenzie) travels to London in order to attend the London College of Fashion but, after not fitting in at her halls of residence, she moves into a private room in a property owned by Ms Collins (Diana Rigg). At night Ellie begins to experience dreams involving Sandie (Anya Taylor-Joy), an aspiring singer whose manager, Jack (Matt Smith), charms her before forcing her into prostitution. The dreams are actually closer to visions in which Ellie has some presence, physically interchanging with Sandie at points; for example, after an initial encounter with Sandie and Jack, Ellie wakes to discover that she has a 'love bite' on her neck. Over the course of the narrative Ellie becomes devoted to solving what she believes is the murder of Sandie by Jack, having seemingly witnessed this in a vision; however, her mental state also deteriorates due to constant exposure to Sandie's horrific past.

Ellie, in the role of Investigative Outsider, however, is provided with misleading or incomplete information. It is clear that Ellie believes it is her responsibility to allot the *nemein* for Sandie's murder to Jack, who Ellie believes to still be alive and present in the modern era. Ellie believes Jack to be a regular – the Silver Haired Gentleman AKA Lindsey (Terence Stamp) – at the bar that she works in. But when Lindsey dies in a road traffic accident, it transpires that he was actually an undercover vice officer who had briefly interacted with Sandie in one of Ellie's visions. The conclusion of the film reveals that Ms Collins and Sandie are one and the same and that, rather than being the victim, Sandie/Ms Collins murdered Jack and went on to murder many of her former clients, storing their bodies in the walls and floors of her property. Ms Collins attempts to murder both Ellie and her investigative accomplice, John (Michael Ajao), but a fire breaks out and in her pursuit of Ellie, Ms Collins is then assaulted by the spirit of Jack; Ms Collins then attempts suicide rather than be arrested and face prison, but is stopped by Ellie. Ms Collins then encourages Ellie to escape and save John, but resigns herself to her fate of dying in the fire at the house that was her victims' last resting-place.

Last Night in Soho conforms to the model of the protagonist representing an Investigative Outsider who believes that they have a legal and moral duty to provide justice and allot *nemein*; it also confirms the aspect of this model whereby the protagonist believes that it is their moral obligation to effect a narrative shift from the Imbalanced Equilibrium state to the Different Equilibrium state. However, Ellie experiences the erosion of her agency, as protagonist, on two counts; in the first instance this agency is based on what appear to be dreams, visions or hallucinatory episodes that cause Ellie to become obsessed with the case, to the detriment of her physical and mental health. In the second instance Ellie is acting on erroneous information. Her belief that it was Sandie who was murdered by Jack and that she must bring the killer to justice impacts on her narrative agency precisely because she is misaligned in her role as the allotter of due portion. The Different Equilibrium state of *Last Night in Soho* is one where the physical presence of the 'monster' – Sandie/Ms Collins – has been destroyed. However, the last scene of the film shows that Ellie – who had previously demonstrated the ability to see the spirit of her mother in mirrors – now sees Sandie as a similar shade in a mirror.

Conclusion

This chapter has provided an analysis of the ways in which the Investigative Outsider enters a given narrative following a disturbance with the initial aim of establishing the reasons for the transition between the Similar Equilibrium and the current Imbalanced state. The Investigative Outsider then – on legal, moral or religious authority, in the examples selected – attempts to precipitate the transition from Imbalance to a state of Different Equilibrium where all those concerned have been allotted their due and where justice, of whatever form, has been satisfied. This desire can perhaps be seen to reflect a yearning for justice and retribution that is felt more generally by society at large. After all, Tudor observes that

> There is no doubt that the modern horror movie, like all popular culture, tells us something about the society in which we live. That it is a society in which we have become more aware of risks; a society in which we are less convinced by the systems of expertise that surround us and institutions that seek to regulate our lives; a society in which the concept of the self is unreliable; and a society in which anxiety and fear have become ubiquitous. (2002: 116)

The films analysed within this chapter demonstrate a concern over both the systems of expertise and the regulatory institutions of normal everyday life. Howie believes he is investigating a routine disappearance in *The Wicker Man*, but finds both his legal and moral authority have no power in the isolated circumstances of Summerisle; his agency wanes in conjunction with his authority until he is forced to accept his fate as the sacrifice. Thomas, within the narrative of *Apostle*, by contrast, retains his agency until the end of the narrative and manages to effect the change to a state of Different Equilibrium wherein his sister survives – but Thomas gives his life to effect this change and, in making this sacrifice, also takes the place of the island's deity. David, within the narrative of *The Guest,* has the agency to effect the changes between equilibrium states and uses this to do so but, crucially, is actually the antagonist of the film. David attempts to create a positive state of Different Equilibrium for the Peterson family, but does so through violent means – a violence which he then turns on the Petersons when his identity is compromised and his conditioning kicks in. Finally, Ellie, within the narrative of *Last Night in Soho,* believes passionately that she must investigate – and solve – the murder of Sandie, but her conviction is based on incorrect information; her physical and mental health suffer as a result and while she survives the final confrontation it is made clear that Sandie is still present in her life, even if Ms Collins is not.

This chapter has highlighted the ways in which horror is generated in the selected narratives where the Investigative Outsider, as the protagonist, believes with total conviction that they must solve a specific mystery only to discover that their legal, moral or religious concerns do not grant them the relevant narrative agency to effect the desired set of changes. Instead, the Investigative Outsiders of *The Wicker Man, Apostle* and *Last Night in Soho* find themselves feeling a growing sense of terror at the hands of a society, a social group or a powerful individual that removes their agency with complete disregard to their rights, beliefs or, in the first two cases, their very lives. The exception to this is David, of *The Guest,* who investigates the situation and then attempts to effect change through violence and murder. In the final analysis the horror of the Investigative Outsider narrative is found in the growing realization, by both character and viewer, that the protagonist is losing their agency; it becomes not their duty to allot the due of their antagonists but, instead, to receive the inescapable allotted to them.

Bibliography

Atsma, Aaron J. 'Nemesis'. *Theoi Project,* 2017. Available online at: https://www.theoi.com/Daimon/Nemesis.html (accessed 22 March 2022).

Booker, Christopher. *The Seven Basic Plots: Why We Tell Stories.* London: Continuum, 2004.

Catterall, Ali and Simon Wells. *Your Face Here: British Cult Movies Since the Sixties.* London: Fourth Estate, 2002.

Crane, Jonathan Lake. *Terror and Everyday Life: Singular Moments in the History of the Horror Film*. London: Sage Publications Ltd, 1994.

Dickstein, Morris. 'The Aesthetics of Fright'. In *Planks of Reason: Essays on the Horror Film*, edited by Barry Keith Grant, 65–75. London: Metuchen, 1984.

Gingold, Michael. 'Exclusive Interview: Writer/Director Gareth Evans on the Religious Horrors of Netflix's "Apostle"'. *Rue Morgue*, 11 October 2018. Available online at: https://rue-morgue.com/exclusive-interview-writer-director-gareth-evans-on-the-religious-horrors-of-netflixs-apostle/ (accessed 12 June 2021).

Kershaw, S. P. *Personification in the Hellenistic World*. Doctoral Thesis. Bristol: University of Bristol, 1985.

Rigby, Jonathan. *English Gothic: A Century of Horror Cinema*. Richmond: Reynolds and Hearn Ltd, 2000.

Ronfeldt, David. *Beware the Hubris-Nemesis Complex: A Concept for Leadership Analysis*. Santa Monica: RAND, 1994.

Selbo, Julie. *Film Genre for the Screenwriter*. Abingdon: Routledge, 2015.

Shelton, James. '"You are Not a Wolf, and this is the Land of Wolves Now": Nemesis, Narrative and the *Norteamericano* in the *Sicario* Films'. *iMex Revista* 9, no. 18 (2020): 49–60.

Shelton, James. '"Every now and then a Trigger has to be Pulled": Narrative, Nemesis and the Function of Retributive Justice in the *James Bond* Films'. *International Journal of James Bond Studies* 5, no. 1 (2022). Available online at: https://jamesbondstudies.ac.uk/articles/10.24877/jbs.80 (accessed 2 March 2022).

Shelton, James. '"Commodus is not a Moral Man": Nemesis, Narrative Construction, and Historical Reconstruction in Gladiator'. In *A Hero Will Endure: Essays at the Twentieth Anniversary of Gladiator*, edited by Rachel Carazo, 159–88. Wilmington: Vernon Press, 2023.

Shoard, Catherine. 'James Bond was "basically" a Rapist in Early Films, Says No Time to Die Director'. *The Guardian*, 23 September 2021. Available online at: https://www.theguardian.com/film/2021/sep/23/james-bond-no-time-to-die-cary-fukunaga-thunderball (accessed 1 March 2022).

Todorov, Tzvetan. 'Structural Analysis of Narrative', translated by Arnold Weinstein. *NOVEL: A Forum on Fiction* 3, no. 1 (1969): 70–6.

Tudor, Andrew. 'From Paranoia to Postmodernism? The Horror Movie in Late Modern Society'. In *Genre and Contemporary Hollywood*, edited by Steve Neale, 105–16. London: British Film Institute, 2022.

Filmography

Apostle (2018), [Film] Dir. Evans Gareth, USA: Netflix.
The Guest (2014), [Film] Dir. Adam Wingard, USA: Picturehouse.

Last Night in Soho (2021), [Film] Dir. Edgar Wright, UK: Focus Features / Universal Pictures.

No Time to Die (2021), [Film] Dir. Cary Fukunaga, UK: Eon Productions / Metro-Goldwyn-Mayer.

The Wicker Man (1973), [Film] Dir. Robin Hardy, UK: British Lion Films.

Index

Abbot, Stacey   90
Aboriginal Australians   193
Abu-Orf, Hazem   97
Ackerman, Diane   154
Ackerman, Forrest J.   5
Adrian, Max   162
Aether (1960)   134, 141, 143
Afghanistan   117, 250
Ahmed, Ahmed L. M.   36, 37
Aja, Alexandre   207
Ajao, Michael   252
Alan, Ray   42
Aldiss, Brian   161, 162
The Alf Garnett Saga (1972)   41
Alison's Birthday (1981)   201–2
All Hallows Eve (2013)   85
Alline, Hannah   118
Allis, Tim   29
Allmer, Patricia   6
Altered States (1980)   149, 152, 153, 156
Altman, Rick   188
Amelia and the Angel (1958)   157
American civil war   169
American eugenics movement   171, 180
An American Werewolf in London (1981)   154
America/United States   5–7, 10, 22, 40, 46, 47, 72, 73, 79, 80, 84, 85, 91, 109, 111, 114–23, 135, 154, 155, 159, 169–72, 174, 175, 177, 180, 185, 197, 199, 201, 225
Amicus Productions   1
Anderson, Judith   189
Animal Farm (1945)   119
Annesley, Imogen   201
anti-capitalism   110, 121
Antwerp (2005)   142
Apostle (2018)   12, 241, 243, 244, 246–9, 254
Appalachia   172, 175
Argento, Dario   152

Arkansas   116, 176
Arnold, Jack   83
Arosteguy, Susan   31
Askey, Arthur   42
Astoria Hotel (Brussels)   138
Atkinson, Rowland   100
Atlanta   172
Atsma, Aaron J.   250
Au Pair Girls (1972)   39
Auckland   200
Augé, Marc   233
Augustine   63–4, 68
Austen, Ben   92, 103
Australia   1, 10, 11, 37, 188–91, 193, 196–202
Australian Film Commission   196
Australian Film Development Corporation   196
Australian Westerns   190
Avalon, Philip   189
avant-garde   10, 132, 141, 227

Bacurau (2019)   123
Badham, John   153
Baffico, Jim   226
Baise-Moi (2000)   218
Baker, Roy Ward   8, 35, 46
Bakhtin, Mikhail   22
Balagueró, Jaume   11, 211, 224, 229–32
Balanzategui, Jessica   197
Banks, Leslie   122
Barker, Clive   78, 91, 100, 151
Barr, Jeremy   112, 113
Barry Lyndon (1975)   55
Bartholomee, Pierre   135
Bartók, Béla   65
Barton, Steve   209
Bathory, Erzsebet   131
Batman   79
Bazin, Andre   212
Beatty, Ned   173

Beaudine, William   189
Beauty and the Beast/La belle et la bete (1946)   32
Belgian cinema   132–4
Belgium   132–4
Bell, David   169, 170, 179, 183, 185
Bellamy, Ralph   184
Belle de Jour (1967)   153
Belvaux, Rémy   133
Berenson, Marisa   55
Berger, Sidney   22, 30
Bergman, Ingmar   27, 29, 32
Berkeley, Xander   93
Berlioz, Hector   67
Bertellini, Girogio   145
Berthillot, Ludovic   210
Beugnet, Martine   215
The Beverly Hillbillies (1962–71)   171
Bey-Rozet, Maxime   214
Bickerdike, Kev   11
Biden, Joe   115
Bienk, Alice   67
Bierman, Courtney   32
Biller, Anna   162
Billson, Anne   32
Billy the Kid Versus Dracula (1966)   189
Black Feet tribe   67
Blade Runner (1982)   225
Blahova, Dasha   201
Bleakley, Paul   116
the 'Blind Dead' films   35
The Blob (1958)   72, 77, 80–2, 84
The Blood on Satan's Claw (1971)   156
Bloodlust! (1961)   122
Bloody Disgusting   206, 207, 209
Bloom, Nicholas Dagen   225
Blouin, Michael J.   90
Blum, Jason   121
Blumhouse Productions   110–12
Bluthal, John   201
B-movies   72, 73, 79–82, 85, 154, 212
BMX Bandits (1983)   188, 193
Bogdanovich, Peter   199
Bogira, Steve   92
Bonzel, André   133
Booker, Christopher   240
Boorman, John   10, 170, 172, 175, 176, 180, 182, 185

Booth Walter R.   1
Borges, Jorge Luis   8, 56, 57, 59–61, 63–5, 68
Borgson, Linda   180
Boston Globe   113
Boulding, Tommy   123
Boulting, Roy   40
Bourdieu, Pierre   85
Bourke, Terry   11, 189
Boyle, Danny   229
Brady, Scott   200
Bragg, Melvyn   57
Bramwell, Tony   41
Brandum, Dean   198
Branson, Richard   154
Brawl in Cell Block 99 (2017)   195
Brazil   1
Breillat, Catherine   213, 214, 218
Breitbart   113
Brenner, Neil   115
Brenon, Herbert   78
Briant, Shane   201
Brick, Emily   6
Bridel, David   77
Briefel, Aviva   90
the British Commonwealth of Nations   36
the British Empire   35
British Leyland   44
British Motor Holdings   44
the British press   39–41, 43
British Westerns   37
broken windows theory   96, 103
Brooke, Bunney   201
Brooke, Ralph   122
Brooks, Louise   138
Brotherhood of the Wolf/Le Pacte des loups (2001)   207
Brothers of the Head (2006)   10, 149, 160–3
Broughton, Lee   2, 8, 35, 37, 46
Brown, David Michael   202
Brown, Phil   208
Brownrigg, S. F.   10, 176–80
Bruning, Robert   195
Brussels   138, 156
Brutalism   224
Bryan, Zachery Ty   112

Buckland, Danny   41, 43
Bucquoy, Jan   133
Buñuel, Luis   153
Burgess, Anthony   227
Burr, Ty   113
Buscombe, Edward   47
Bustillo, Alexandre   11, 206–9, 211
Bye Bye Belgium/Tout ca [*ne nous rendra pas la Belgique*] (2006)   133
Byrne, Gabriel   155
Byron, Glennis   47

Cabrini Green (Chicago)   9, 90–3, 96–7, 100–5
cahiers du cinema   212
Cahn, Edward L.   72
Calabrese, Omar   55, 59
California   171
Calvaire (2004)   133
Cameron, James   195
Campbell, Jimmy   60
Candyman (1992)   9, 89–105
Candyman (2021)   90
Candyman: Farewell to the Flesh (1995)   89
Candyman 3: Day of the Dead (1999)   89
Cannon Films   154
Cardiff, Jack   42
Carlos, Wendy   67
Carnival of Souls (1962)   7, 19–33
Carpenter, John   90, 152, 198
Carr, Camilla   177
Carradine, Robert   182
Carreras, James   40
Carreras, Michael   37
Carrie (1976)   193
Carriere, Mathieu   139, 140
Carroll, Lewis   142
Carter, Jimmy   114
Carter, Peter   178
Cassandra (1987)   201
Cassel, Jean-Pierre   140
Catterall, Ali   244
Cecil Sharp House   156
Centre National du Cinema et de l'image animee   214
Centron Corporation/Productions (Kansas)   19, 21, 23, 27

Chaffey, Don   40
Chamberlain, Richard   150
Chan, Shen   51
Chandler, John Davis   180
Chaney Sr., Lon   78, 79
Chang, Joseph   43
Chapiron, Kim   208
Chaput, Catherine   115
Charter Entertainment   198
Chattooga river (US)   173
Cherry, Brigid   89
Chiang, David   8, 37, 38
Chicago   9, 90–2, 100, 104, 211
Child's Play (2019)   85
China   37, 43, 52, 247
Chiodo brothers   75, 79, 82–4
Chiodo, Charles   76, 82
Chiodo, Edward   82
Chiodo, Stephen   8, 72, 82, 84, 85
Chow, Andrew R.   110, 121
Christiaens, Isabelle   133
Christopher, Ian   8
Chytilova, Vera   132
Ciment, Michel   66
cinema verite   212
cinephelia   212–13
Clampett, Robert   76
Clark, Al   154
Clark, Jim   38, 41
Clasen, Mathias   111
class   77, 91, 93, 100–2, 104, 105, 113, 115, 117–19, 122, 171, 174, 175, 178, 224–6, 228, 231, 232, 234, 235, 237
classical Hollywood cinema   46, 47
Clifford, John   7, 19–23, 28–30, 32
Clinton, Bill   115
Clinton, Hilary   109
A Clockwork Orange (1962)   227
A Clockwork Orange (1971)   227
Clover, Carol   7
Clown (2014)   85
clowns in popular culture   77–9
Cocteau, Jean   27, 29, 32
Collins, Roberta   180
Collis, Clark   111
Colodner, Joel   177
the colonial gaze   49

Columbia Pictures   40, 154, 159–60
Combs, James   114
Combs, Richard   66
The Coming of Joachim Stiller/De Komst van Joachim Stiller (1976)   9, 132, 142–4
commedia dell'arte   77
Condon, Bill   89
Connell, Richard   122
Connelly, Reg   60
Connors, Chuck   183
the consumer society   35
Contouri, Chantal   195
Cook, Frederic   182
Cook, Jan   5
Cook, Roger   5
Cooney, Ray   45
Cooper B. Lee   89
Cooper, Merian C.   84
Cord, Alex   189
Corman, Roger   160, 182
Cornwall (UK)   250
Corrick, Daniel   137, 145
Corsault, Aneta   81
Coughlan, Ian   201
coulrophobia   85
Coulter, Steve   118
Covid-19 pandemic   111–12
Cowie, Peter   134, 135
Cowper, Geraldine   244
Cox, Ronny   173
Craig, Michael   202
Cramer, Grant   73
Crane, Jonathan Lake   243, 248, 249
Craze (1974)   42
Crazy Love (1987)   133
Creatures the World Forgot (1971)   40–1
Cree, Steven   235
Creed, Barbara   7, 21, 22
The Creeping Terror (1964)   83
Crimes of Passion (1984)   153
Criterion Collection   31, 32
Croatia   116, 118, 119
Croft, David   45
Cronenberg, David   11, 152, 224, 232
Crothers, Scatman   58
Cuaron, Jonas   123
Culkin, Michael   101

The Curse of the Living Corpse (1964)   23
Curtis, Jamie Lee   193, 198, 199
Cuse, Nick   117, 121
Cushing, Peter   8, 35, 37, 38, 43, 44
Cyprus   42
Cyr, Myriam   152

DaCosta, Nia   90
Daffy Duck   76
Daily Beast   113
Dallas Magazine   177
Dalle, Beatrice   210
Daltrey, Roger   150, 159
Dance of the Seven Veils (1970)   154
D'Angelo, Angelo   193
Dangerfield, Diana   189
Dano, Royal   74
Dante, Joe   200
Daughters of Darkness (1971)   9, 131, 132, 134–9, 141–5
Davay, Paul   133
Dawn of the Dead (1978)   226, 229
Dayton (Ohio)   110
de Ossorio, Amando   35
De Palma, Brian   193
de Ravet, Ward   144
de Roubaix, Francois   139
de Souza, Marcelo Lopes   96
The Dead (1987)   155
Dead Kids (1981)   189, 200, 201
DeAngelis, Michael   171, 172
'Death is a Family Affair'   177
the Decadent movement/Decadence   9, 51, 114, 119, 131, 132, 134–7, 139
Decimalisation Day (UK)   42
Deep in the Woods/Promenons-nous dans le bois (2000)   207
defensible space theory   96
Delerue, Georges   142
Deliverance (1972)   10, 170–8, 180–5
Dell, Charlie   177
Delplanque, Lionel   207
Delvaux, Paul   134, 142
Democratic Party   115, 116
Democrats   9, 109, 117, 118, 120, 121
Deneuve, Catherine   228
Denis, Claire   215

DeRoche, Everett   199
Deruddere, Dominique   133
Desierto (2015)   123
Despentes, Virginie   218
The Devil's Messenger (1962)   27
The Devils (1971)   151, 153, 154, 157
Dickerson, Ernest R.   122
Dickey, James   172, 175
The Dickies   80
Dickstein, Morris   245, 249
Dies Irae (1980)   67
Dietrich, Marlene   138
Dietsch, Joe   123
Different Equilibrium   240–4, 246–50, 252–4
Division 10BA of the Income Tax Assessment Act (Australia)   196–7
Donaldson, Lucy Fife   90, 101
Donohoe, Amanda   155
Dornelles, Juliano   123
Dr. Jekyll & Sister Hyde (1971)   46
Dr. Strangelove or: How I Learned to Stop Worrying and Love the Bomb (1964)   55
Dracula (1958)   43
Dracula (1979)   153
the *Dracula* mythos   151
Dread Central   209
Dredd (2012)   223
Dreyer, Carl Theodor   135
du Welz, Fabrice   133
Ducournau, Julia   208, 214
Duff, Kim   223
Dullea, Keir   57
Durgnat, Raymond   138
Dutilleul, Philippe   133
Duvall, Shelley   56
Duvall, Wayne   116
Duvauchelle, Nicolas   210

Earth vs. the Spider (1958)   80
East Boldre (UK)   158
East Germany   227
Eco, Umberto   85
Edward, Marion   191
Eegah (1962)   80
Egan, Kate   39
Ege, Julie   8, 35, 37–43

Eggleston, Colin   201
El Paso (Texas)   110
Elkind, Rachel   67
Ellin, Nan   96
Ellis, Grant   29
Ellison, Art   22, 30
emasculation   35–7, 44–6, 48–51, 173–4, 184
Embry, Ethan   251
the Emergency Economic Stabilization Act 2008 (US)   115
Emmanuelle (1974)   138
Ensor, James   133, 136
Epoch Times   113
Equal Pay Act of   1970 (UK)   36
ESPN   110
eternity   58, 63–9
Europe   6, 28, 35, 36, 41, 42, 45, 52, 122, 131, 132, 135, 137, 143, 155, 209, 219
the European Economic Community   36, 41, 45, 46, 52
European Speedway Championship   42
Evans, Gareth   12, 241, 248
Evening Standard   151
Every Home Should Have One (1970)   38, 40
exploitation films   5, 7, 10, 11, 83, 137, 175, 197–9, 202

The Faces   42
the Fair Housing Act   1968 (US)   92
Falconer, Pete   10, 11
The Fall of the Louse of Usher (2002)   10, 149, 157–60
Famous Monsters of Filmland   5
Farrow, Mia   228
Fat Girl/A ma soeur! (2001)   218
Faust   69
Feagin, Hugh   178
Feldman, Marty   38
Fellini, Federico   139
feminism   7, 21, 22, 35, 37, 46, 52
Ferreri, Marco   139
Festival of Fear (Toronto 2010)   152
'Feudin' Banjos'   173
Filho, Kleber Mendonça   123
Film Group 58   134

The Final Programme (1973)   46
financial crisis of 2007–8   115, 120
Firth, Vincent   39
Fisher, Terence   43
Fitzpatrick, Kevin   113
Flanagan, Kevin M.   149, 152, 162
Fleischer, Ruben   85
Fleming, Victor   76
Foix, Vicente Molina   56
folk horror   156
Forbes-Robertson, John   51
Forbidden Planet (1956)   83
Forster, Laurel   36, 46
Foster, Norman   188
Fox & Friends First   112
Fox Business Network   112
Fox News   112
France   206–8, 212–15, 219
Francis, Freddie   42
Frank, Alan G.   5
Frankenstein mythology   150–1, 161
Franklin, Richard   11, 188, 199–200
free market capitalism   109, 114, 115
the French New Wave   133, 212–14
Freud, Sigmund   78, 135
Frontier(s)/Frontiè(s) (2007)   208
Froseth, Kristine   248
Fruet, William   176
Fuest, Robert   46
Fukunaga, Cary   242
Fulton, Keith   10, 149, 160, 161
Furst, Joseph   189

Gacy, John Wayne   73, 79
Gainsborough, Thomas   55
Galesburg (US)   200
Galley, Michael   5
Gallon Drunk   160
Gamble, Andrew   120
Gans, Christophe   207
Garagiste films   157–9, 163
Garris, Mick   152
gated communities   226, 234
gatekeeping   11, 212, 216, 217, 219
gender   7–9, 21, 22, 35–7, 47, 49, 50, 52, 90, 101, 104, 172, 180, 182
generic hybridity   6, 8, 11, 37, 109, 185, 188–90, 192, 194–5, 197–9, 202

Gengaro, Christine Lee   61, 67
Gens, Xavier   208
gentrification   9, 90, 91, 103, 225, 228, 235–7
George, Christopher   180
Georgia (US)   172, 173, 180
Getty Images   42
Ghirardo, Diane   103–4
The Giant Gila Monster (1959)   83
Gibbs, John   97
Gibson, Louie   123
Gifford, Denis   5
Gil, Vincent   195
Gilpin, Betty   116
Gingold, Michael   248
'The Girl with the Golden Breasts' (2006)   152
Glasby, Matt   209
Glaser, Paul Michael   122
Gleiberman, Owen   111
Głowiński, Michał   56, 57
Godard, Jean-Luc   213
God's Bloody Acre (1975)   176
Goetz, Edward G.   225
Goetz, Kevin   209
Goetz, Michael   209
Gold Coast (Chicago)   93, 96, 102–4
Goldberg, Matt   118
Goodall, Mark   9, 10
Gordon, Bert I.   80
gore   27, 177, 207, 208, 210, 212, 215–17, 219
Gorfinkel, Elena   210
Gorsewood Productions   157, 158
the gothic   8, 47, 136, 144, 149–51, 153, 161, 162, 193, 201
Gothic (1986)   149–55, 158, 159, 162
Graham, Stephen   236
Grandrieux, Philippe   213
Grant, Barry Keith   210
Grant, Hugh   156
Grant, M.   135, 136, 142
Great Britain/United Kingdom   1, 5, 35–46, 51, 52, 153–5, 158, 159, 199, 201, 224, 225
the Great Depression   122
The Great Piggy Bank Robbery (1946)   76
the Great Recession   115, 120

Great Yarmouth (UK)   42
Greene, James   162
Grefé, William   10, 180, 181
Grindrod, John   235
The Guest (2014)   12, 241, 243, 244, 250–2, 254
Guest, Val   39
Guillermin, John   223
Gulliver's Travels (1726)   55
Gurley, George H. Jr.   32
Guy, DeJuan   97

Haggard, Piers   156
Hall Sr., Arch   80
Halloween (1979)   90, 198
Hammer Films   1, 8, 37, 40, 43, 201
Hampshire, Susan   131, 140
Hanan, Joshua S.   115
Hani, Jean   67–8
Hanna, Robert   44
Hantke, Steffan   210, 211
Happy Hunting (2016)   123
Hard Target (1993)   122
Hardy, Robin   12, 151, 241
Hardy, Rod   189
Harkins, Anthony   170–1, 176, 185
Harlequin (clown)   77
Harlequin (1980)   200
Harper, Sue   36, 46
Harring, Laura   211
Hartigan Jr., John.   171, 174, 175, 180
Hartley, Mark   188
Harvey, Herk   7, 19–33
The Haunted Castle/Le Chateau haunte (1897)   1
The Haunted Curiosity Shop (1901)   1
Hawking, Stephen   57
Hawkings, Karen   103
Hawkins, Joan   137
Haylett Bryan, Alice   11, 208
He Who Gets Slapped (1924)   78
Heller-Nicholas, Alexandra   196–201
Hellraiser (1987)   151
Hemdale Film Corporation   154
Hemmings, David   199
Hepple, Peter   42
Herts, Kenneth   27, 28
Herts-Lion Productions   27–9, 31

Herzlinger, Brian   85
Hickox, Douglas   151
Higgins, Paul   247
High Tension/Switchblade Romance/Haute Tension (2003)   207, 218
Hill, Mike   90
Hill, Walter   176
hillbillies   170–2, 180, 183, 208
Hilligoss, Candace   20, 23–8, 30
Hitchcock, Alfred   138
Hitler, Adolf   35
Hoberman, J.   156
Hoeveler, Diane Long   90, 101
Holden, Stephen   33
Hollywood   1, 22, 23, 27, 28, 40, 46, 47, 85, 111, 149, 153, 154, 159, 183, 188, 200, 201, 206, 209, 214, 217
Hollywood Reporter   110, 112
home video   38, 150, 154, 155, 157, 162
Hong Kong   1, 8
Hood, Robert   201
Hoogeveen, Carla   189
Hooper, Tobe   152, 170
Horeck, Tanya   215
Hornaday, Ann   113
The Horror of Party Beach (1964)   80
Horrorella   91
Houghton, Don   37, 52
Hounded (2022)   123
Hour of the Wolf/Vargtimmen (1968)   32
House of Hammer   5
Howerd, Frankie   41, 42
Howerton, Glenn   118
Howland, Olin   81
The Howling (1981)   200
Howling III: The Marsupials (1987)   11, 200–1
Hoyle, Brian   157–60
Hubler, Manfred   139
Hughes, Nicky   224
Humphries, Barry   191, 201
The Hunt (2020)   9, 109–21, 123
Hunt, Peter R.   38
Hunter, I. Q.   3, 4, 45, 47, 50, 51, 156, 217
Hurst Media   207
Hussey, Olivia   194
Huston, John   155
Hutchings, Peter   46–8

Huxley, David 6

I Am Legend (1954) 229
I Spit on Your Grave (1978) 176
Illinois 200
Imbalanced Equilibrium 240–4, 246–50, 252, 253
impressionism 134, 135, 141
India 1
Indonesia 1
Inn of the Damned (1975) 11, 189–92, 202
Insalaco, Amanda 92
Inside/À l'intérieur (2007) 11, 206–11, 215–19
Inside (2016) 209
Instagram 4
International Movie Database 215, 216, 219
Invaders from Mars (1954) 80
Invasion of the Saucer Men (1957) 72
Investigative Outsider 12, 240–54
The Invisible Man (2020) 111
Ireland, Dan 155, 157
Irreversible (2002) 218
isolation 90, 138, 173, 175, 224, 225, 228–31
IT (1986) 73
IT (1990) 79
IT (2017) 79
It Came from Outer Space (1953) 83
Italy 1

Jackson County Jail (1976) 10, 182–4
Jackson, Glenda 150
Jacobs, Nathalie 133
Jacopetti, Gualtiero 139
Jaeckin, Just 138
Jancovich, Mark 3, 83, 217
Janisse, Kier-La 7
Jansen, Peter W. 55
Janssens, Charles 140, 144
Japan 1, 83
Jeanne Dielman, 23 quai du Commerce, 1080 Bruxelles (1975) 133
Jenkins, Henry 83
Jethro Tull 42
J-Horror 1

Johns, Marion 201
Johnson, James 160
the Joker 79
Jones, Mark Lewis 247
Jones, Tommy Lee 183
Juno, Andrea 6
Jürgens, Anna-Sophie 78–9, 85, 86
Just Before Dawn (1981) 176

Kael, Pauline 66
Kafka, Franz 143
Kallitsis, Phevos 9
Karlen, John 137
Kasch, Andrew 209
Kath & Kim (2002–7) 191
Katzin, Lee H. 122
Keach, Stacey 191
Kellett, Bob 41
Kelley, Emmett 78
Kelley, Sheila 251
Kelling, George L. 96, 103
Kellner, Douglas 114
Kellogg, Ray 83
Kendall, Tina 215
Kermode, Mark 157
Kern, Leslie 90
Kershaw, S. P. 241
Kerwin, Harry 176
Khnopff, Fernand 136
Kidman, Nicole 193
Kilgore, Charles 176–7
Killer Klowns From Outer Space (1988) 8, 72–7, 79–86
Killer Klowns Wiki 85
Kine Weekly 40
King Kong (1933) 76, 84
King, Stephen 56, 59, 61, 64, 65, 73, 79
Kirkpatrick, Jason 118
Kiss the Blood Off My Hands (1948) 188
Klevberg, Lars 85
Klushantsev, Pavel 199
Knee, Adam 189
Knights Templar 35
Kolman, Allan 233
Kopec, Dak 224
Kościelski, Kamil 8, 69
Krupat, Edward 230
Kuberski, Philip 57

Kubrick Stanley 8, 55–9, 61, 64–9
Kuhn, Andrea 90, 91, 96, 100
Kümel, Harry 9–10, 131–2, 134–45
kung fu 8, 35, 49
Kurrus, Theodore 177

La Bozzetta, Angie 191
the labyrinth 56, 57, 60, 61, 63, 64, 67–9
Lacey, Bruce 150
The Lair of the White Worm (1988) 10, 149–51, 153–7
Lake Leman (Switzerland) 159
Lamond, John D. 189
Lampo, Hubert Leon 142, 143
Land of the Dead (2005) 226
Landis, John 154
Lang, Brett 121
Lang, Fritz 223
Lanza, Joseph 159
Lanzi, Emmanuel 210
Laputa 55
Last Night in Soho (2021) 12, 241, 243, 244, 250, 252–3
Last Year at Marienbad/L'Année dernière à Marienbad (1961) 131
Latham, Rob 89
Laugh, Clown, Laugh (1928) 78
Laughlin, Michael 189
Laugier, Pascal 11, 206–9
Lawrence (Kansas) 19, 21, 25–7, 29–31
Leach, Britt 182
LeBank, Ezra 77
Lee, Christopher 244
Lees, Loretta 100
The Legend of the 7 Golden Vampires (1974) 8, 35–8, 42–52
Lemmons, Kasi 93
Lennon, John 42
Leone, Damien 85
Leone, Sergio 191
Levison, Nat 191
Levitt, Stan 22, 30
Lewis, Herschell Gordon 169
Ley, John 194
Leyland Motors 44
Leys, Simon 135
Licassi, Peter 74
Lieberman, Jeff 176

Lindelof, Damon 117, 118, 121
Lisztomania (1975) 150, 162
Little Hell (Chicago) 92
Little Sicily (Chicago) 92
Liverpool 91, 100
Livid/Livide (2011) 209
Lloyd, Danny 56
LoBrutto, Vincent 64
London 41, 42, 225, 228, 250, 252
London College of Fashion 252
London Film Festival (1986) 155
Lord Charles 42
Lord, Natalie 224
Los Angeles 226
The Love Witch (2017) 162
Lugton, James 193
Luhrmann, Baz 191
Lynch, Lashana 242
Lysaght, Karen D. 96

Maccabe, Collin 90
McCann, Ben 208
McCarroll, Meredith 172, 175
McCollum, Victoria 111
McCrea, Joel 122
McDowell, Malcolm 227
Machado, Isabel 172
Mackay, Josie 190
MacKenzie, J. C. 120
McKenzie, Thomasin 252
Mackey, Mary 182, 183
McMahon, Conor 85
McNaughton, Eric 5
McQueen, Steve 81
Maddaus, Gene 121
Madigan, Amy 119
Madsen, Virginia 91, 228
magic realism 132, 142–3
The Magnificent Seven Deadly Sins (1971) 41
Magritte, Henri 133
Magritte, Rene 134
Mahler (1974) 150
The Making of Killer Klowns (2001) 79, 82, 83
The male gaze 21, 50, 51
Malpertuis (1943) 131
Malpertuis (1973) 9, 131, 132, 139–45

Man Bites Dog/C'est arrive pres de chez vous (1992)   133, 134
Mann, Craig Ian   9
Marchasson, Francois-Regis   210
Marschall, Susanne   67
Martens, Erik   140
martial arts   37, 38, 45, 49, 50
Martin, Adrian   196, 197
Martyrs (2008)   11, 206–9
Martyrs (2015)   209
masculinity   8, 35, 36, 46, 50–2, 172, 173, 175, 177, 183, 185
Masters, Kim   110
Masters of Horror (2005–7)   152
Matheson, Richard   229
Mathijs, Ernest   3, 4, 112, 131, 133–5, 137, 144, 145, 210, 212
The Mating Game (1976)   42
Maudlyne, Ihejirika   92, 103
Mauger, Ivan   42
Maurice (1987)   156
Maury, Julien   11, 206–9, 211
Means Coleman, Robin   90
The Medieval Babes   159
Meikle, Denis   37
Melbourne (Australia)   195
Melia, Matthew   10, 149, 153, 156, 158, 159
Méliès, Georges   1
Melville, Jean-Pierre   212
Mendik, Xavier   3, 4, 10, 112, 210, 212
Menzies, William Cameron   80
Merchant-Ivory   155, 156
Metropolis (1932)   223, 225
Metsers, Hugo   143
Mexico   1
Meyer, Brendan   250
Midnight (1982)   176
Midnight, the Stars and You (1934)   60
Miike, Takashi   152
Miller, Cynthia J.   8, 9, 80
Miller, Michael   10, 182
Milner, Bill   248
Milner, John   132, 136
Mimieux, Yvette   182
the minimal complete plot   240, 244
Mira (1972)   133

Miska, Brad   206–9, 215, 217
Mississippi   117
Mitchell, Don   96
Mitchell, Warren   41
Moine, Raphaëlle   188
Mojave Desert   122
Mondo Candido (1975)   139
The Money Programme   39–41
Monroe, Maika   250
Monsieur Hawarden (1969)   132, 134, 135, 141, 143
Monster Mag   5
the monstrous female   22, 47, 50
Montreal   232
Moody, Lynne   183
Moore, Joel David   250
Moore, Nora   177
Mora, Philippe   11, 197, 200
Moreau, David   208
Morin, Edgar   135, 139
The Mormon School of Dance (Salt Lake City)   26
Morricone, Ennio   139
Morris, John   190
Mosley, Philip   144
The Most Dangerous Game (1924)   122
The Most Dangerous Game (1932)   109, 110, 121, 122, 194
The Movie That Wouldn't Die (1990)   31
Moxey, John Llewellyn   10, 183, 184
Mulvey, Laura   21, 46, 50, 51
Murphy, Michael J.   159
Muschietti, Andy   79
Music for Strings, Percussion and Celesta (1951)   65
The Music Lovers (1971)   150
The Mutations (1974)   42, 45

national identity   188, 201, 202
National Review   113
Navarro, Meagan   209
Nelson, Barry   59
Nelson, John Allen   75
nemein   12, 240, 242, 244, 245, 247, 250–2
nemesis   241, 246, 248–51
neo-liberalism   114, 115, 118, 120
the Netherlands   43, 132

New French Extremism   213–16, 218, 219
New Orleans   110
New World Pictures   152, 153, 157
New York City   225, 228
The New York Dolls   42
The New York Times   113, 154
The New Yorker   32
New Zealand   200
Newman, Oscar   96
Next of Kin (1982)   189, 201
Ngai, Sianne   90
Ni Fhlainn, Sorcha   90
Nicholas, Paul   151
Nichols, Michael Beach   85
Nichols, Rachel   211
Nicholson, Jack   56, 61
Nickolai, Nate   111
Night of Fear (1973)   189, 198
Night of the Living Dead (1968)   84
Nightmare in Badham County (1976)   10, 183–4
Nightmares (1980)   189
No Time to Die (2021)   242
Noble, Nancy   182
Noe, Gaspar   213, 214, 218
Nolin, Michael   160
Nolte, John   113
Norway   38, 39, 41–3
Not Now Darling (1973)   45
Not Quite Hollywood: The Wild, Untold Story of Ozploitation! (2008)   188, 195, 196
Nullarbor Plain (Australia)   192
Nunn, James   11, 224, 234, 236

Obama, Barrack   115
O'Connell, Jack   236
Offscreen Film Festival (Brussels 2014)   156
the oil crisis of 1973   36
Olson, Chris/Christopher J.   21, 22, 83, 84
On Her Majesty's Secret Service (1969)   38
One Man and His Pig/Vase de Noces (1974)   133
One Million Years B.C. (1966)   40
Orpheus/Orphee (1950)   32

Orser, Leland   250
Orwell, George   119
Oslo   42
Ostend   131, 136–8
Otto, Barry   201
Ouimet, Danielle   137
The Oysterband   156
Ozon, Francois   213
Ozploitation   10, 11, 196, 197

Pabst, G. W.   138
Page, Grant   191
Palley, Thomas   115
Palmer, Tim   215
Palud, Xavier   208
Panayotakis, Costas   114, 115, 120
Pannozzi, John   75, 81
Panorama Entertainment   29
paracinema   83, 85, 155
Paradis, Alysson   210
Paris   228
Parkfilm   132
the patriarchy   21, 22, 36, 37, 46, 48, 49, 51, 52, 176, 177
Patrick (1978)   199–200
Peary, Danny   38
Peck, Jamie   115
Pedler, Martyn   197
Peirse, Alison   7
Pepe, Louis   10, 149, 160, 161
Perkins, Anthony   153
Petrie, Susan   233
Petrovitch, Michael   194
Philadelphia   183
Phillips, Kendall R.   110, 115, 121
Phillips, Leslie   41
Phillips, Wyatt D.   82
Photoplay Film Monthly   42
Pichel, Irving   109, 194
Pierce, Preston   180
Pierrot (clown)   77
Pilon, Daniel   140
Pinedo, Isabel   82
The Pink Fairies   42
Pirie, David   145
Pitman, Jack   41
Pizzagate   116
Plan 9 From Outer Space (1959)   84

Platts, Todd K.   111
Plaza, Paco   11, 211, 224, 229–32
Poe, Edgar Allan   150, 154, 158, 160
Poelvoorde, Benoît   133
Polanski, Roman   228
Poor Pretty Eddie (1975)   176
pornographic films   172, 213
Powell, Robert   150
Praz, Mario   136
The Preservation Man (1962)   150
Price, Vincent   151
Prosperi, Franco   139
Psycho (1960)   138
Punch   42
Punter, David   47

Quandt, James   213
queer representation   51, 172
Rabanne, Paco   138
Rabun County (US)   173, 175, 176

race   37, 47, 49–52, 90, 91, 101, 102, 104, 172, 176, 183, 184, 226–8, 230
Rackman, Steve   194
Rademakers, Fons   133
Radford, Benjamin   78
Rafferty, Terence   32
Raffin, Deborah   183
Rafter, Nicole Hahn   171
The Rainbow (1989)   153, 155
Rau, Andrea   137, 138
Raw/Grave (2016)   208
Ray, Jean   131, 132, 140, 141
Ray, Robert B.   135
Reagan, Ronald   114, 115
The Real McCoys (1957–63)   171
[*Rec*] (2007)   11, 211, 224, 229–32
Redden, Billy   173
Reddick, Lance   251
Reed, Robert   184
Reilly, Katie   109
Relph, Edward   232
Rentadick (1972)   41
Republicans   9, 109, 116, 117, 120, 121
Repulsion (1965)   228
Resnais, Alain   131
Reynolds, Burt   172
Rhys, Elen   247

Richardson, Michael   134, 137
Richardson, Natasha   154
Rigby, Jonathan   240
Rigg, Diana   252
Rituals (1977)   176
RKO Pictures   1
Roadgames (1981)   11, 188, 191–4, 198, 199
Robbery (1967)   38
Roberts, Emma   117
Robinson, Richard   176
The Rocky Horror Show (Oslo production, 1978)   42
Rollin, Jean   144
Rolling Stone   32
Romero, George A.   84, 226, 229
Ronfeldt, David   241, 249
Rops, Felicien   133, 136
Rose, Bernard   9, 89–92, 96, 100, 101, 103, 104, 228
Rose, Della   184
Rosemary's Baby (1968)   228
Rosmer, Milton   156
Ross, Gene   177
Rouche, Jean   212
Roussel, Nathalie   210
Rowley, Stephen   91
Royer, Carl   89
Royle, Nicholas   142
Rue Morgue   152
Ruiz-Tagle, Javier   92
The Running Man (1987)   122
the rural anti-idyll   169, 170, 174–7, 179–81, 183, 185
the rural body   171, 173–7, 179–81, 185
Russell, Elize   157
Russell, Ken   10, 149–63
Russia   200
Russo, John A.   176
Ryan, Mark David   196

Saidi, Aymen   210
Salome's Last Dance (1970)   153, 155
Salt Lake   20, 21, 24–6
Salt Lake City   20, 25, 26
Saltair (Utah)   19, 21, 24–6
Samuel, Joanne   201
Sandbrook, Dominic   36

Sanders, Paul   120
Sands, Julian   155
Santarcangeli, Paolo   68
'Sarkozy horror'   208
Sarkozy, Nicolas   208
Sarris, Andrew   134, 145
Satan/Sheitan (2006)   208
Savage, Vic   83
Savages (1974)   122
Scandinavia   37–9, 42, 45, 48, 49
scary city syndrome   89–91, 96, 100, 105
Schaefer, Eric   197, 199
Schaffstall, Katherine   110
Schneider, Steven J.   6, 89
Schoedsack, Ernest B.   84, 109, 194
Schwartzel, Erich   110, 112
Schwarz, Jeffrey   91, 92, 103
Schweitzer, Dahlia   229–31
Sconce, Jeffrey   83, 85, 217
Scott, A. O.   113, 118
Scott, Ridley   225
Scum of the Earth/Poor White Trash Part II (1974)   10, 176–81
Seattle Film Festival   155
second wave feminism   35, 46, 52
Second World War   35, 92, 224
The Secret of the Loch (1934)   156
Selbo, Julie   242, 243
Sellars, Peter   40
Sellin, Christine   22, 33
The Seventh Seal/Det sjunde inseglet (1957)   32
sex comedies   38–41, 45
The Sex Discrimination Act of 1975 (UK)   36
The Sex Life of the Belgians/La Vie sexuelle des Belges 1950-1978 (1994)   133
Sexton, Jamie   144, 145, 212
sexual assault   173–4, 178, 181–4, 234, 248, 252
sexual equality   22, 36, 37, 46
Seydoux, Lea   242
Seyrig, Delphine   131, 136, 138
Shaffer, Bill   7, 20, 31
Shaffer, James   31
Shaker, Tom   8, 9
Shakespeare, William   151, 206
Shaw Brothers studio   8, 37
Shaw, Run Run   37
Sheen, Michael   247
Shelley, Mary   150, 154
Shelton, James   12, 242
The Shining (1980)   8, 56–69
Shivers (1975)   11, 224, 232–4
Shoard, Catherine   242
Shropshire Star   45
Shudder   209, 210
Siegel, Michael   74
Siegel, Tatiana   110
Silva, Henry   199
Similar Equilibrium   240–4, 247, 249, 253
Simpson, M. J.   2
Sims, David   109
Sinden, Donald   41
Sinker, Mark   161
Sjostrom, Victor   78
Skinn, Dez   5
slasher films   72, 89, 90, 100, 195, 197, 198, 208, 209
Smith, Constance   231
Smith, Elbert   82
Smith, Kyle   113
Smith, Matt   252
Smith, Neil   96
Smith, Sheridan   235
Smithson, Alison   224
Smithson, Peter   224
Snapshot (1979)   195–6
Sneegas, Larry   30
Snyder, Suzanne   73
social class   77, 91, 93, 100–2, 104, 105, 113, 115, 117–19, 122, 171, 174, 175, 178, 224–6, 228, 231, 232, 234, 235, 237
Sofidoc   132
Solberg, Niels   38, 40, 42, 43
Sontag, Susan   137
Soren, David   132, 138
Sorokin, Pitirim   137
Sour Spirit   67
South America   27
South Korea   1
The Southbank Show   157
Southeast Asia   37
Southern Comfort (1981)   176

Soviet Union   227
Spain   1, 211, 229, 230
Spall, Timothy   155
spatial tension   11, 90, 91, 97, 101, 104, 223, 225–7, 229, 230, 232–4, 236, 237
Squires, John   110
St. George's Taverns £5, 000 Pub Entertainer of the Year Contest   42
Stafford, Anne   178
The Stage and Television Today   42
Stamp, Terence   252
Stark, Graham   41
Steele, Barbara   233
Steele, Jamie   133, 134
stereotypes   39, 116, 172, 175, 179, 180, 182, 185
Stevens, Dan   246, 250
Stevenson, Robert Louis   153
Stewart, Robin   44
Stieber, Zachary   113
Stitches (2012)   85
Stoker, Bram   43, 150, 151, 155
Stone, Philip   58
Strange Case of Dr. Jekyll & Mr. Hyde (1886)   153
Strictly Ballroom (1992)   191
Strock, Herbert L.   27
Strynckx, Peter   143
Suebsaeng, Asawin   113
the Suez Crisis   35
The Sunday Times   206
Suplee, Ethan   116
surrealism   134, 135, 138, 139, 141, 143, 144, 152, 156, 212
Surviving the Game (1994)   122
Swank, Hilary   116
Swift, Jonathan   55
Switzerland   159
the Symbolist movement/Symbolism   132, 136, 141, 142
Symphonie Fantastique: An Episode in the Life of an Artist (1971)   67
Szu, Shih   47

Tabourin, Jean-Baptiste   210
Tangerine Dream   200
Taylor-Joy, Anya   252

teen comedies   72
Teenage Zombies (1959)   80
Television Mail   42
The Tenant/Le locataire (1976)   228
Tenney, Del   23, 80
The Terminator (1984)   195
Terry, Don   92
Testro, Lucas   200
The Texas Chainsaw Massacre (1974)   170
textual poaching   83
Thatcher, Margaret   202
Theatre of Blood (1973)   151
Them/Ils (2006)   208
Theodore, Nik   115
There's a Girl in My Soup (1970)   40
Thi, Coralie Trinh   218
Thirst (1979)   189, 197, 199, 201
13 Demon Street (1959)   27
31 (2016)   85
Thomas, Betty   182
Thomas, Sarah   39
Thompson, David   143
Thompson, Kirsten Moana   90
Thompson, Kristin   85
Thompson, Ronnie   11, 224, 234, 236
Thompson, Terry W.   122
Thornton, Sigrid   195
Thrower, Stephen   5, 177
Tigon British Film Productions   1
Timber Wolf Resort   67
Time-Life Video library   154
Tinker, Tim   225
Todd, Tony   91, 228
Todorov, Tzvetan   240
Tohill, Cathal   6
Tombs, Pete   6, 7
Tommy (1975)   154, 161
Tonkiss, Fran   230
Toronto   152
Total Film   209
Toto the Hero/Toto le Héros (1991)   133
Tower Block (2012)   11, 224, 234–7
The Towering Inferno (1974)   223
Trapped Ashes (2006)   152, 158, 163
Trapped/Baker County, U.S.A. (1982)   176
Travers, Peter   32

Travis, Pete 223
Treadways, Harry 161
Treadways, Luke 161
Trenchard-Smith, Brian 11, 122, 188, 193–5
Trick or Treat Studios 85
Trimark Pictures 153
Trinder, Tommy 42
Tropiano, Stephen 80
Trouble Every Day (2001) 215
Trump, Donald 9, 109–13, 116, 117, 119, 120
Tryon, Chuck 112
Tucker, James 113
Tudor, Andrew 253
Turkel, Joe 58
Turkey 1
Turkey Shoot (1982) 11, 122, 194–5, 202
Turner, Kathleen 153
28 Days Later (2022) 229
Twiggy 159
Two Thousand Maniacs! (1964) 169
2001: A Space Odyssey (1968) 57, 64

United Artists 27
Universal Orlando 85
Universal Pictures 1, 110–13, 151
Universal Studios Hollywood 85
University of Colorado 31
Up Pompeii (1971) 41
Usai, Paolo Cherchi 67

Vale, Lawrence 104
Vale, V. 6
Valentino (1977) 152, 153
The Vampire Lovers (1970) 46, 48
Vampyr (1932) 135
van Ammelrooy, Willeke 143
van Dormael, Jaco 133
Van Eecke, Christophe 158, 159
Van Riper, A. Bowdoin 80
Vanity Fair 113
Variety 41, 42, 85, 111, 113, 156
Vartan, Sylvie 131
Verhoeven, Paul 155
Verlinden, Pieter 143
Vernon, John 75

Vestron Pictures 152–4
Vestron Video 154, 155, 157, 159
Vid-America 30
video 149, 154, 157, 158, 160, 163
video nasties 154
Vidler, Anthony 89
Vietnam war 179
Villa Diodati 151, 155, 158, 159
Virgin Vision 152–5, 157
Vivas, Miguel Ángel 211
Vogel, Ellen 135
Voight, Jon 173
Volk, Stephen 154, 155
von Sternberg, Josef 134, 138, 145
Voyage to the Planet of Prehistoric Women (1968) 199

Waddell, Calum 197, 198
Wakeman, Rick 151
Walker, Alexander 151
Walker, Johnny 153
Wallace, Tommy Lee 79
Wang, Han Chen 44
Ward, Roger 194
Warren, Jerry 80
Washington D.C. 116
The Washington Post 113
Wasser, Frederick 154
Watergate 171
Watson, R. T. 110
Watts, Jon 85
Webb, Andy 173
Weight, Richard 36
Weinstein, Harvey 207
Welch, Raquel 40
Welles, Orson 131, 140
Wells, Simon 244
the Wembley Festival of Music 42
werewolf 194, 200
West, Alexandra 213
West, Dean 119
Western genre 37, 189–91
Whannell, Leigh 111
Whisky Mountain (1977) 10, 180–1
the White House 121
white trash 10, 171, 176, 182
Whitehouse, Mary 154
Whittle, Peter 206, 207, 215, 217

Whore (1991)   153, 155
The Wicker Man (1973)   12, 151, 241, 243–9, 253, 254
Wilcox, Fred M.   83
Wild Strawberries/Smultronstallet (1957)   32
Williams, Tony [film director]   189
Williams, Tony [writer]   6
Williams, Vanessa   97
Williamson, J. W.   170, 172–5, 183
Wilson, James Q.   96, 103
Wincer, Simon   195, 200
Wingard, Adam   12, 241
Winthrop, Henry   137
The Wizard of Oz (1939)   76
the Women's Liberation Movement   36, 46
Woo, John   122
Wood, Ed   84
Wood, Robin   104
Woodcraft, Saffron   231

Woods, Harry M.   60
Woodward, Edward   244, 246
Worth, David   176
Wright, Edgar   12, 241
Wrinkles the Clown (2019)   85
Wuyts, Herman   141
Wyrick, Laura   90, 91, 100

Yates, Peter   38
Yeaworth Jr., Irvin S.   72
Young, Neil   208
Yuzna, Brian   152

Zahler, Craig   195
Zarchi, Meir   176
Zéno, Thierry   133
Zimmermann, Stefan   190
Zobel, Craig   9, 109, 121
Zombie, Rob   85
Zombieland (2009)   85
Zorbaugh, Harvey Warren   92